𝕮𝔥𝔢 𝔖𝔱𝔞𝔯-𝔏𝔢𝔡𝔤𝔢𝔯

Munchmobile

A SLICE OF JERSEY

YOUR ULTIMATE GUIDE TO PIZZA IN THE GARDEN STATE

BY
PETER GENOVESE

ACKNOWLEDGMENTS

Thanks, first of all, to our readers, those faithful followers of the Munchmobile who have sent in their restaurant recommendations and category suggestions and all those applications to ride the Big Dog over the years. You have followed us in print, on nj.com, on Facebook, on Twitter, and every year you astound us with your knowledge, spirit and enthusiasm.

Without you, the Munchmobile would never have gotten off the ground — or been as popular as it is today.

A big shout-out goes to members of the Pizza Patrol, whose dedication, drive and companionship made the eating of 1,000 slices in six months a fun, frantic, tiring but never tiresome effort.

That means Jeff Burnett, Joan Dwyer, Marty Schneider, Gina Bruno, Scott Wiener and Al Windrem, the last three staying until the end, which was no small accomplishment because I kept extending our goal — from 100 to 200 to 250 and finally 333 pizzerias.

All team members took copious notes, did their required "homework" assignments and ate with a zeal usually reserved for those on the competitive eating circuit. Good pizza, bad pizza, all that in-between pizza — they treated each slice with care and attention.

The Star-Ledger's Features Department is home to the Munchmobile and its driver, and the weekly Pizza Patrol reports, which led to this book, would not have been possible without the entire Features copy desk, especially Sarah Golin and Tracy Politowicz. They took every last-minute copy change with surpassingly good humor, grace and professionalism.

Mark Morrissey, who designs the summer Munchmobile pages, brought his artistic sense and style to the Pizza Patrol reports.

Thanks to our photo department, especially Tim Farrell, who joined us on several trips.

Fred Kaimann, numbers cruncher extraordinaire, saved me hours of work through his technical wizardry, and created our handy online map (at nj.com/munchmobile) with all the Pizza Patrol stops and winners.

Extra props go to Tracy Politowicz, who edited most of this book and spent an entire final weekend reading copy produced by the author and asking, more than once: "Don't you mean to say fluorescent, not flourescent?"

What can I say, I had flour on the brain.

Presiding over all matters Munch is Enrique Lavin, the features honcho who let us keep eating and eating, although I wish he somehow could have kept us away from all that so-so pizza.

FOREWORD

Long before we dressed the Munchmobile cartoon with a pizza slice on its roof to embark on what would become an epic Pizza Patrol, we knew there would be a book at the finish line.

We knew no other state newspaper would be crazy enough to undertake such a mission. (That said, no other newspaper that we know of is crazy enough to have a Munchmobile!)

"But, why bother with pizza?" many observers protested. Pizza is like – well, we all know the joke: Even when it's bad, it's still pretty good, they'd say.

We didn't want to settle on "pretty good."

Everyone has an opinion on what makes a good pizza pie. For me, it's the wood-burning, clay-oven baked Neapolitan-style squares made by Italian-Uruguayan immigrants at El Hornero in Quito, Ecuador, where I grew up. Nostalgia counts for something, but 2,800 miles is a little far to satisfy a pang. I can taste history at Santillo's Brick Oven Pizza in Elizabeth, where I first landed in Jersey after moving here from Wolfgang Puck's California.

Claiming what is a great pizza, especially in this pizza rich state that has more than some 3,000 pizzerias, will always be up for debate. At least now there'll be a point of reference provided by the guy who actually sampled pizza from some 350 establishments in Jersey.

There's a reason someone wrote on one of our newsroom whiteboards "Pete-zah." Call Genovese the Tsar of Pizza. He has the last word.

Say cheese!

Enrique Lavin

TABLE OF CONTENTS

INTRODUCTION

Pizza is the world's most popular food, a global favorite from Kinnelon to Katmandu.

Make that from South Brunswick to the South Pole. When asked by slashdot.org where they had eaten the best pizza in their lives, more people said Antarctica (1,262 votes) than either South America (797) or Asia (669). (What can you get as a topping down there — extra ice?)

Americans eat 100 acres of pizza a day, about 350 slices per second.

In the United States alone, pizza is a $36 billion business.

A quarter of Americans ages 18 to 24 eat pizza at least five times a month. A slice supplanted chicken nuggets as the favorite lunchtime food for American children years ago.

All of which made it clear there was a need for a comprehensive, exhaustive look at New Jersey pizza, and this book.

"A Slice of Jersey" is the first — and last — word on pizza in the Garden State. On one level, it is the story of The Star-Ledger's Pizza Patrol, our team of pizza fanatics who spent six months living, eating and breathing pizza.

We visited 333 places, trying three pizzas at each, then returned to our first stop and ate one more. One thousand slices in all.

Through the summer, fall and winter, we ate pizza, and took notes, and ate more pizza, and no doubt raised our cholesterol counts to alarming levels.

New Jersey, with some 3,000 pizzerias, is not quite the center of the pizza universe; New York City claims that title. But no other food evokes such passionate debate in the Garden State. The Pizza Patrol needs no reminder of that.

One Shore pizzeria owner, angry over our lukewarm review, said I needed "tongue surgery" because I had "difficulties tasting real Italian food."

A reader from Parsippany thought we should be "disbanded" because we were trying to "hurt" business owners and because it wasn't clear the reviews were opinions.

The positive comments far outnumbered the negative ones, though.

"The best aspect of your Pizza Patrol is your willingness to call a mediocre pie mediocre," wrote David Machlowitz. "Thank you for your candor."

We weren't trying to put anyone out of business; we were just trying to be honest.

We did visit more pizzerias in six months than many people hit in their lifetimes. We became knowledgeable about matters no sane person should claim: the grade of cheese, the type of oven, chunk vs. crumbled vs. pellet sausage, and so on.

Food is always a great conversation starter, especially in New Jersey, where I've long argued that the No. 1 hot topic is not politics or sports but food. We all know the best places to eat, and are only too willing to share — and debate — them.

Every place we visited is reviewed in these pages; I re-wrote all the capsules that appeared in the paper to make them more lively and personal without becoming too — sorry — cheesy.

To show how committed — or crazy — we were, we visited another 20 pizzerias just before this book went to press. We wanted to make sure the book's subtitle — "Your Ultimate Guide to Pizza in the Garden State" — lived up to its name.

In 'A Slice of Jersey', you'll find profiles of pizza-makers around the state; essays on the regional differences in pizza and the pizza industry in general; suggested pizza road trips; loads of best-of lists; the most comprehensive compilation of pizza websites, blogs and books you'll find anywhere; and much more — most of it material that has not previously appeared in the paper.

And at the end, a listing of every non-chain pizzeria in New Jersey, something you won't find anywhere else.

"A Slice of Jersey" is the only guide you'll ever need to the state's — and the world's — No. 1 food. It's handy and compact: It'll fit nicely in your car's glove compartment. Or your back pocket.

So, enjoy the book. If you have any comments, feel free to e-mail me at pgenovese@ starledger.com or call (973) 392-1765.

Hey, look, it's time for lunch. Think I'll grab a slice.

Peter Genovese
Newark, New Jersey

WHY WE LOVE PIZZA

What is it about pizza that inspires such craving the world over? That makes it the world's most popular food?

Is it its wonderful portability – you can take your slice anywhere, and even enjoy it while talking on your cell phone? Can't do that with a steak, or chicken Francaise, not even a burger.

Is it the affordability and instant gratification? A buck and a half will buy you a slice, and you can enjoy it right out of the oven.

Or maybe the combination of cheese, sauce, and dough is just impossible to resist.

In the following piece, I'll try to describe our love affair – more like unbridled passion – for pizza.

Greasy, garlicky, messy, runny, oily, chewy, cheesy, crunchy, filling and fattening.

Why do we love pizza so much, when on paper, or a plate, it sounds so unappetizing?

Is it because it's the ultimate fast food — a quick, hot meal that provides instant gratification?

Is it the simple, savory blend of tomatoes, cheese and crust?

Or is it tied to some Jersey-flavored Proustian memory of summer and the boardwalk?

You could argue that pizza is the state food; certainly no other food is as hotly debated. Quickest way to start an argument in the Garden State? Begin a sentence with, "My favorite pizzeria is . . ."

As a member of The Star-Ledger's Pizza Patrol, I was constantly reminded — oh, like every two minutes — of Rule No. 1 of Jersey Life: Say what you want about my politics, my family, my wardrobe, my car and my lifestyle, but don't you dare tell me your favorite pizzeria is better than mine.

"Really?" began a typical post on nj.com after our Best Pizza in New Jersey winners were announced. "You forgot . . ."

From Denville to Delhi, from Union Beach to Ulan Bator, pizza has won the hearts, minds and stomachs of consumers around the world like no other food. Americans alone eat 350 slices a second, putting 250 million pounds of pepperoni on their pizza every year.

Willis HRH sells pizza delivery insurance; it even has a "pizza department."

My most fervent wish: a worldwide pepperoni shortage. The world's most popular topping is the world's most boring topping. When was the last time you had great pepperoni?

Yeah, thought so.

The world's most popular food — American schoolchildren prefer a slice of pizza over chicken nuggets or anything else for lunch — can be found in practically every country.

I once ate at a Pizza Hut in Bangkok. I'm not proud of that, I'm just coming clean. The half-mushroom, half-sausage tasted exactly like the one back home.

Europe, according to Liz Barrett, editor-in-chief of PMQ Pizza Magazine, "is wild about pizza." Domino's has more outlets per capita in Iceland than in any other country.

The one country where the pizza business is "exploding," according to Barrett? India, "where Domino's and Pizza Hut are really going after each other to see who can open up the most locations."

Pizza shows no signs of slowing its gooey global march. You can get a slice at Pizza della Casa on Peace Avenue in Ulan Bator. Mama's Pizza in Fiji is said to do a credible pie.

Jeff Varasano, owner of a celebrated pizzeria in Atlanta, calls pizza "the most sensuous of foods."

I don't agree; I think pizza is the most utilitarian and blue-collar of foods.

Flour, yeast, cheese, sauce: It's simple to make.

Palm-sized, portable, foldable: You can take it, or place it, anywhere.

Hot, warm, cold: It can be enjoyed at any temperature.

Right out of the oven, later that day, two days later: Pizza's staying power is unparalleled.

Nuke it, throw it in the oven, toss it in a frying pan: It's as good as new.

Here's my favorite pizza story. One of our 2010 Munchers, Kristin Federico, has an Aunt Alice. Alice lives in Canarsie. Seems she was in the hospital last November for surgery.

"I told her I wanted to get her flowers," Federico recalled. "She said, 'Don't be ridiculous, get me a pizza.' "

Go ask Alice, I think she knows — about pizza's power to tempt, satisfy, even heal.

Greasy, garlicky, messy, runny, oily, chewy . . .

And totally irresistible.

THE PIZZA BIG PICTURE

Everyone knows pizza is big business — to the tune of $36 billion a year in the U.S. But what's the state of the pizza industry? What are the hot new trends? Liz Barrett, editor-in-chief of PMQ Pizza Magazine, provided this overview for "A Slice of Jersey."

Pizza has been a staple of the American diet for as long as we can remember. Whether your first memory involves sharing a pizza with your parents at the neighborhood pizzeria, smelling mom's homemade pizza baking in the oven, or grabbing a slice on your way home from school, pizza holds special memories for all of us.

Americans eat 100 acres of pizza every day — about 350 slices per second.

Today, the U.S. pizza industry is made up of 67,000 pizzerias, bringing in $36 billion per year and serving 350 slices per second. The four largest pizza chains — Pizza Hut, Domino's, Papa John's and Little Caesars — control about 31 percent of total industry sales, while independent pizzerias (considered below the top-ranking 50 in sales and unit counts) collectively hold the largest market share, representing close to 51 percent of industry sales.

Through good times and bad, pizza remains a popular option for both consumers and restaurateurs. Those pizzeria operators who noticed a decrease in sales due to the recent recession learned that increased marketing through social networking sites, promotional events and community service — not to mention the always-popular couponing — were effective ways to fight back against a strained economy.

Economic conditions also affected methods of distribution: Takeout numbers rose, delivery numbers fell and more consumers started dining in at their local pizzerias (dine-in figures grew from 19 percent in 2009 to 28 percent in 2010).

While pizza, in some form, has been around for thousands of years, the industry is still growing and innovating. With Pizza Hut, Papa John's and Domino's leading the way, online ordering has continued to grow by leaps and bounds over the past three years.

In 2008, a survey conducted by PMQ found that 13 percent of respondents used online ordering. Today, 21 percent have implemented the new technology. With online ordering, the door was opened to mobile marketing, barcode couponing and a full range of social networking via the internet. Even the mom-and-pop pizzerias you grew up with are open to these new technologies when they see how they've boosted business for others.

Pizzeria operators are also willing to adapt and change to better serve customers through greening efforts. Many in the industry are seeking out ways to reduce their store's impact on the environment by investing in recycled and reusable materials, purchasing locally sourced and organic ingredients, and reducing the amount of waste they produce.

Menu diversification has also become more prevalent as pizzeria operators expand their menus to include sandwiches, salads, appetizers, pasta, desserts and more. Those who operate a bar inside their pizzeria have also experienced new sales increases thanks to an ever-growing craft beer market.

Savvy restaurateurs recognize that most of the time, consumers aren't visiting a pizzeria alone, and the more people at the table that you can please — many times by simply using ingredients you already have on hand — the more chances you have of a return visit.

—Liz Barrett, editor-in-chief, PMQ Pizza Magazine

10 STYLES OF PIZZA

John Arena, the co-founder of Metro Pizza in Las Vegas, teaches the first university-level pizza course in the country, titled "History and Culture of Pizza," at the University of Nevada School of Hospitality. His restaurants have been awarded dozens of local and national awards, and Arena has made pizzas for three American presidents.

He has identified 10 regional styles of pizza. What's the difference between New York style and Old New York style pizza? Arena explains all in the following pages.

While Italians may rightfully claim to be the originators of the dish that we have come to know as pizza, there can be little doubt that the United States has developed the most diverse expressions of this culinary mainstay.

This is a result of many factors including cross-cultural influences, creativity and the vast array of ingredients and equipment available to ambitious American-based pizza chefs. Unlike classic French cuisine, the rustic Italian cooking arts that inspired American pizza are highly regionalized and resistant to rigid structure and rules. Students of the pizza-making craft have felt free to experiment and innovate so that in the United States we now have dozens of identifiable pizza-making styles often coexisting side by side.

Because my restaurants are located in Las Vegas, which has residents and visitors from all over the world, we feature several different types of pizza that are representative of diverse techniques and preferences. The ability of pizza to absorb and adapt to social, cultural and historical influences has allowed it to thrive in changing marketplaces and find a place on menus throughout the world.

Some chefs would claim that there are as many pizza styles as there are people who make them. However, in the United States the dominant popular forms can be identified by some basic key elements, including dough type, stretching and shaping method, sauce and spice profile, cooking methods and topping variations. In the past, most of the variations could only be found in their place of origin. In the modern era, all of the styles have adherents throughout the country.

NEW YORK STYLE (modern)

Classic thin-crust New York style pizza remains the most popular form in the United States. The basic dough will always use high gluten bromated flour, milled from wheat primarily grown in North Dakota and Minnesota.

Fresh yeast is used with long fermentation times employed to create flavor and texture. Olive oil is added for enhanced flavor and to prevent sauce penetration in the dough. This pizza is always hand-stretched to order with a minimum size of 16 inches in diameter and a pronounced rim.

Sauce is a smooth, thin tomato sauce made from sweet, vine-ripened California tomatoes that can be seasoned with oregano and occasionally thyme. High butterfat, low moisture shredded mozzarella cheese from Wisconsin is preferred, with an additional light sprinkle of imported Romano cheese added after the pizza is baked.

Typically, this pizza will be cooked directly on the stones of a gas-fired oven, with many pizzamakers claiming that the older stones are superior.

NEW HAVEN STYLE

Loosely based on the pizza of Naples. Local residents use a dialect-based pronunciation, always referring to this type as "ah-beetz."

The dough recipe for this pizza uses a medium protein all-purpose flour and a high percentage of water. This formulation results in loose dough that is hand-stretched on a marble table.

The dough is usually too soft to pick up and is simply flipped onto the pizza paddle before being slid into a coal-fired oven, which produces a crispy yet tender crust. Typically these pizzas are irregular in shape and distinctively charred.

Sauce is similar to New York style, but may include fresh garlic. Cheese can be a combination of low moisture mozzarella and New England cheddar, however these pizzas tend to be light on cheese.

New Haven is famous for the clam pizza, which uses only olive oil, garlic, fresh clams and oregano without any form of cheese.

> The largest pizza ever baked was 122 feet in diameter, made at the Norwood Hypermarket, Norwood, South Africa, in 1990. Ingredients included 9,900 pounds of flour.

SOUTHERN NEW JERSEY STYLE TOMATO PIE

On the surface, this pizza appears similar to the New York style, but there are several distinct differences.

Typically dough formulation will not include olive oil. While the hand-stretching method is the same as New York style, this pizza is topped with locally-produced shredded mozzarella before the sauce is applied. Sauce is smooth, but thicker than New York style sauce and is splashed on the pizza randomly, with Romano or domestic Parmesan cheese added on top.

The "cheese first" method produces a crisper crust with creamier melted cheese. Traditional toppings are limited to anchovies, or sliced sausage that is pre-cooked and then distributed on the pizza before baking.

PHILADELPHIA STYLE TOMATO PIE

While similar in name to the New Jersey pizza, this type is actually quite different. Dough is made from all-purpose flour, allowed to ferment and then stretched and placed in a square black steel pan that is coated with olive oil or baked directly on the stones of an oil-fired oven.

A light sprinkle of shredded mozzarella is generously covered by a chunky slow-simmered tomato sauce that contains yellow onion, fresh garlic and a large amount of extra virgin olive oil. The pizza is topped with grated Parmigiano Reggiano before baking.

CHICAGO STYLE THIN CRUST

This pizza is sometimes referred to as "Tavern Pizza." Dough is made from all-purpose flour with low water content and a high percentage of vegetable oil. Fast-acting dry yeast is preferred with short fermentation times.

Dough is never hand-stretched, but is instead rolled out in advance using a rolling pin or a mechanical dough sheeter in high volume restaurants. This method produces a flat tight crust with no raised edges.

Pizzas are topped with a tangy, thick tomato paste that has been heavily seasoned with oregano and granulated garlic. All toppings are placed under the shredded mozzarella cheese. Raw sausage that has been removed from the casing is the most common topping.

Pizzas are baked in a rotating or carousel deck oven at relatively low temperatures. This method produces a crackerlike crust. Pizza is cut in small squares before serving.

CHICAGO STYLE DEEP DISH

While many people consider this pizza to be a Chicago creation, it is actually a variation of the savory holiday pies first introduced to southern Italy by Albanian refugees in the 15th century.

The rich biscuit-like texture of the crust is achieved by using winter wheat flour from the Midwest mixed with a high percentage of shortening and sometimes aided by the inclu-

The first U.S. pizzeria opened in New York in 1905.

sion of cornmeal or semolina.

A small amount of beer may be included in the mix to create more complex flavors and aroma. Dough is pressed into heavy, high-sided, black steel pans that have been coated with oil, shortening or butter.

This pizza gives the appearance of having a thick crust because the dough has been shaped up the side of the pan, but it should not be confused with thick-crust pizza.

Dough is allowed to rest in the pans for 15 minutes or more and then is filled with layers of mozzarella, toppings, and a covering of smooth or crushed tomato sauce that is seasoned with oregano, domestic Parmesan and sprinkled with olive oil.

The most common toppings include fennel-flavored sausage, pepperoni and cooked spinach that has been seasoned with nutmeg. Pizzas are baked in deck or carousel ovens at 425 degrees for up to 45 minutes.

MOUNTAIN OR WESTERN STYLE

The climate and active lifestyle of these areas' residents have contributed to this distinct type of pizza. Dough is formed using warm water and fast-acting yeast. Often whey or milk will be added for mildly sweet dough or recipes will include sourdough starter.

Crust is medium to thick with a pronounced rolled edge. Pizza is topped with a relatively light amount of thick, tangy sauce that is seasoned with oregano, thyme, dry basil, marjoram and granulated garlic. Pizzas are covered with large amounts of part skim milk California mozzarella cheese, sometimes mixed with yellow cheddar.

Pepperoni is the most common topping. However, more exotic local ingredients may be added, including ground American bison meat.

Pizzas are baked on wire racks in conveyor ovens and are usually cooked lightly with no distinct charring or blistering. In colder climates this pizza will be served with a side order of honey for dipping the remaining crust at the completion of the meal.

CALIFORNIA STYLE (modern)

There has been pizza in California since the first Italian immigrants arrived in the 19th century, but until the 1980s, no unique style had developed.

In the last 25 years the influence and innovation of California-based chefs has revolutionized American cooking trends. Organic, locally grown ingredients combined with the fusion of Asian and classic European techniques have inspired a new "Golden Age" in pizza baking.

Typical dough formulas will use organic unbleached bread flour often combined with honey or sugar to produce a chewy, pliable crust. Pizzas are hand-stretched with a pronounced rim and do not exceed 12 inches in diameter.

Wood-fired ovens often using aromatic woods such as mesquite or hickory are preferred, but gas-fired open-flame brick ovens will be used when local ordinances prohibit the burning of wood. Toppings are selected in accordance with seasonal availability.

Noticeable Asian influence can be seen in the use of fresh, lightly cooked vegetables that retain beautiful color and texture. Great emphasis is placed on the balance of flavors and texture. A wide variety of locally produced artisan cheeses are employed in combination, including cow, sheep and goat's milk cheeses.

The two most recently resurrected forms are:

AUTHENTIC NEAPOLITAN STYLE

This type of pizza is gaining in popularity but is not without controversy. Many pizzamakers view the rules and criteria established by self-appointed organizations to be confining and created more with the intent of selling Italian products and equipment than with producing the best quality pizzas.

On the other hand, a properly made Neapolitan style pizza is truly delicious and an exercise in culinary simplicity and restraint. Dough consists of Italian flour combined with only water, sea salt and fresh yeast; no other ingredients are allowed.

Gentle mixing is followed by varying lengths of fermentation with longer times currently in favor. Dough is carefully hand-stretched to no more than 12 inches in diameter with a pronounced "cornicione" or edge that becomes well-blistered when baked.

Tomato sauce is thin and consists only of vine-ripened San Marzano tomatoes from Campania that have been passed through a food mill. Cheese must be fresh-sliced mozzarella from the area surrounding Naples but can be made from either cow or water buffalo curd.

Fresh basil is applied either under the cheese or after the pizza has baked. Pizza may be finished with a light sprinkle of sea salt, Parmigiano Reggiano and olive oil.

The pizza must be baked in a wood-fired oven using non-aromatic wood. The oven must be manufactured in Italy or assembled by Italian artisans from Italian materials.

In the past, this pizza was limited to four varieties, but in modern times, seasonal and regional toppings are common and it is not unusual for an Italian pizza-maker to have as many as 200 different combinations in his repertoire.

OLD NEW YORK STYLE PIZZA

Recently this type of pizza has been recognized as an emerging trend in the United States. It is often marketed as the original style of Italian-American pizza, although this claim is highly debatable.

Origins aside, what is certain is that this method can produce unique and delicious pizzas. Dough is made from American high gluten flour, water, salt and fresh yeast. Early Italian immigrants to the U.S. were amazed at the variety of flours available and developed recipes to take advantage of this abundance.

Pizzas are thin and hand-stretched with a small raised edge that becomes very charred and blistered from the intense heat of the oven. Sauce is made from crushed San Marzano toma-

> There is one pizzeria for every 4,000 Americans. In Italy, there is one pizzeria for every 1,400 Italians.

toes, and each pizza is individually seasoned with oregano and Romano cheese.

Pizzas are topped with thin slices of cow's milk mozzarella from New York state that is specially formulated with slightly lower moisture content than traditional mozzarella di buffalo or fiore di latte.

Raw vegetables are never placed on these pizzas; instead most toppings are pre-roasted in the coal ovens before being added to the pizzas. Hand-sliced pepperoni with a high fat content is prized for its tendency to char, cup and release flavorful oils on the pizza.

The baking time for coal-fired pizza can be as short as 90 to 120 seconds. Unlike modern New York pizza, this type is rarely sold by the slice and the pizzas never exceed 18 inches in diameter.

THE PIZZA PATROL

The item appeared innocuously enough in the paper in April 2009.

Three years ago, the S.W.A.T. Dog team visited nearly 100 hot dog joints around the state in an effort to name the state's best dogs.

This summer, we're putting together a top-secret Pizza Patrol to rate everyone's favorite food. We're looking for a half dozen pizza lovers with passion, knowledge and enthusiasm. We'll go out several evenings a week.

We might as well have said, "We'll give $10,000 to the first person who shows up at The Star-Ledger's offices in Newark." The responses came fast and furious.

"I'd like to be considered for your top-secret Pizza Patrol because I think my maturity — and good taste when it comes to pizza — would be make me a valuable member," said Joseph Leist of Hamilton. "If you're going to eat artery-clogging food, then it had better be good artery-clogging food."

Barbara Lantz Niro of Cranford said she would happily throw her husband "under the bus" for a solo chance on the Munchmobile, while Sean Tonner of Stewartsville sent a piece of cardboard with a clump of actual sauce on it.

Several applications were epic-length. Some, not so much. One read, in its entirety: "I am a pizza lover and I can eat it seven days a week."

"Can there be any doubt that pizza is nature's perfect food?" asked Jeff Burnett of Berkeley Heights. "What could possibly be more heavenly than the blend of crispy crust, robust tomato sauce and savory mozzarella cheese?"

Richard Raposa of Rockaway said he was prepared "to perform the ultimate sacrifice": give up his recliner and exercise. "I am ready, willing and able to complete the mission because you have juxtaposed two of the most beautiful words in the English language — 'free' and 'pizza.'"

Fifty percent of an average pizza's total food cost is from the cheese.

And then there was Anita Fischer O'Meara, a self-described "tall, thin German, Irish and French blonde" who said if she was selected, she would starve herself, "then eat like I am going to the electric chair."

It sure wasn't easy picking the Pizza Patrol.

But in the end, we selected six. There was Burnett, who said he would devote himself to "exposing those establishments which are clueless."

Joan Dwyer, a self-described "glorified nanny" from Elizabeth who said she had found her "calling in life."

Marty Schneider of Ridgewood, whose friends called him Mr. Food because he seemed to have a restaurant suggestion for every town on earth.

Al Windrem, who works for an exterminating company, told us he spent most of his spare time "thinking about or eating pizza."

Gina Bruno, an Edison schoolteacher and past Munchmobile participant.

Last but not least, Scott Wiener, who runs tours of New

York City's best pizzerias (scottspizzatours.com). Wiener would be our pizza go-to guy, much as John Fox was our ultimate hot dog source on the S.W.A.T. Dog team.

With the Munchmobile driver, who's eaten a few pizzas in his life, they made up what you could call the Mozzarella Magnificent Seven.

> Twenty-five percent of Americans ages 18 to 24 eat pizza at least five times a month.

From the beginning our mission was clear: Visit pizzerias all over New Jersey, sample three pizzas at each, and give our honest opinions. For the first time in the state's pizza history — in any state's history, we were told by industry observers — a team of tasters would visit and review hundreds of pizzerias in a short period of time.

We wouldn't take the easy way out: Pick 10, 20 or 25 pizzerias from reader suggestions, visit them and anoint them the best in the state.

Our journey was both a food odyssey and a road trip that never seemed to end. We hit big cities and small towns, major highways and back roads.

The scores of place names chronicled a Jersey most of us never see:

Carmel. Gloucester City. Clayton. Mount Freedom. Carneys Point. Seaville.

Our northernmost stop was Candy's on Route 206 in Montague, where a sign proclaimed it the first — and last — pizzeria in New Jersey. Our southernmost stops were several in Cape May, where we are still trying to find good pizza. At one point, we were within walking distance of the Delaware Memorial Bridge. Once, we paid a visit to a truck stop and tried on furry winter hats of undetermined animal origin.

The silly moments got us through the summer, fall and winter.

The Mozzarella Magnificent Seven dwindled to a Finicky Four. Burnett, Dwyer and Schneider would depart the group because obligations and well, life, got in the way.

Our mission sounded glamorous at first, but it turned out to be hard work. Weekends and holidays were sacrificed. Days were long. I got to know the Cheesequake, Monmouth and Forked River rest stops along the Garden State Parkway quite well, often needing to pull over to sleep on the long ride home.

We received thousands of e-mails suggesting where to go. Some, quite literally. One reader called for us to be "disbanded" because we "just move in on places and make a fast judgement" and because every article was "negative."

When I wrote that the pizza from a place called Romeo's tasted "like it needs a Juliet, or love from somebody," the owner shot back:

"Last time we checked, you were a reporter, not a comedian. Such comments aren't helpful because it gives the impression of having an agenda against us. Our customers are appalled about your comments that they feel your tongue needs surgery (because you have difficulties tasting real Italian food)."

But no one was harder on the Pizza Patrol than the Patrol itself; we were constantly heaping good-natured abuse on each other. No one, not even the Munchmobile's driver, was safe.

Bruno, who would end up being the team's only female member, would describe the experience as a "six-month dinner date."

Our original goal was 100 pizzerias. That was bumped to 150. Then 200.

Then 250. Then we decided to stop at 333 and re-visit our first pizzeria for one last slice, which, given that we had sampled three pizzas at each place, gave us exactly 1,000 slices. It took us six months.

Windrem remembers telling his wife, Barrett, then pregnant with their first child, that the Pizza Patrol would be done by September "at the latest."

When the pizza sampling continued into October, and November, and December, Windrem would describe it as "the Groundhog Day of pizza eating."

At 9:20 p.m. on Dec. 15, 2009, we walked into Il Forno in Secaucus, the 333rd pizzeria visited. Then we drove to Nutley and Michael's Pastaria, where we began in June, for our 1,000th slice.

What did we get out of this seemingly impossible journey? A sense of pride and accomplishment, for one. We had taken a state's food pulse like no one had done before. Could we have accomplished our mission by visiting, say, 100 pizzerias? I don't think so. We would have missed many worthy contenders, for sure.

If I was proud of anything, it was when the winners were announced and readers who may not have been following the series from day one started asking the same question. And that was: "Did you visit such-and-such place?" In nearly every case, we already had.

"Shocking — didn't even bother to go to South Jersey," one poster on nj.com, The Star-Ledger's website, complained.

Oh yes we did, many times over.

"From what I read," added someone named njpetey, "it sounds like the Pizza Patrol doesn't go west of I-287, since there are NO reviews of any Morris or Sussex County pizzas. Did you guys go that far west, or don't we exist?"

My response: "If you read the reviews, you would realize

we were all over Morris County — visited almost 30 places. That's a lot."

And then there was sadpunkin, who bristled when I said the plain at DeLucia's, our winner in that category, featured great "crunch."

> A slice of a Domino's hand-tossed large pizza contains 248 calories: 72 calories from fat, 40 calories from protein and 136 calories from carbohydrates.

"I don't get it — the best pizza goes crunch? If my pizza goes crunch, it's burnt!"

My response: "If your thin-crust or crispy plain doesn't go crunch, you're eating Play-Doh."

The online give-and-take was lively, to say the least; check out the chapter titled "Our Lovable Pizza Posters."

In "A Slice of Jersey," we'll share what we learned about pizza — the good, the bad and everything in between.

"Debating pizza is something I am now over-qualified to do, as is asking too many questions of my local pizza man," Bruno said of the experience.

Windrem had a different take on the six-month mozzarella mission.

"By the end," he said, "my baby didn't recognize me, my dog wouldn't play with me and my wife would complain that I smelled like sausage."

— Peter Genovese

PIZZA PATROL BY THE NUMBERS

Stops: 333
Slices: 1,000
Miles driven: 9,000
First stop: Michael's Pastaria, Nutley
Stop No. 100: Conte's, Princeton
Stop No. 200: Ciro's Pizza, Colonia
Stop No. 300: Enzo's, Hackettstown
Last stop: Il Forno Pizza Cafe, Secaucus
Fastest ordering time: 16 seconds, Di Mola's, Clinton
Best sign: "For better service, do not carry on conversations with the employees." (Donna's Pizza, Palisades Park)
Northernmost stop: Candy's, Montague
Southernmost stop: Louie's Pizza, Cape May

OUR LOVABLE PIZZA POSTERS

"The Star-Ledger in New Jersey has gone nuts this week, posting the results of a six-month-long pizza fact-finding mission throughout the Garden State."

That was the post from Adam Kuban on slice.seriouseats.com, the nation's leading pizza blog.

When we announced the winners of our Best Pizza in New Jersey competition, the online pizza world went nuts. Or so it seemed.

The first several posts were complimentary: "really thorough job," "love it!" and so on. Then the debate, dissension and diatribes began.

"Shocking — didn't even bother to go to South Jersey," complained one of the earliest posters, flyers08. "As a transplant from South Jerz to North Jerz, I've been to several on this list, while a few deserve it, there are pizzaries (sic) in SJ that would mop the floor with others."

Okay, someone standing up for South Jersey, great.

But as a South Jersey resident, I had to set the record straight:

"Did you read the weekly reports?? They've been running in the paper since July. We were all over South Jersey . . ."

Which we were.

"The sad part of this," motownfoodie weighed in, "is that while there are a few really good pizzas to be found in NJ, the vast majority is mediocre at best. Very sad!!!"

Then the fun began.

"Whoa! Wait a minute!" wrote a clearly incensed jerseagirl. "Isn't there something missing here?? Like HOBOKEN, the alledged (sic) home of the BEST pizza with the largest slices?? What happened?"

My response: "Ranked Hoboken among our best pizza towns, but none of the places in Hoboken — and we hit them

> Some of the more popular toppings around the world are pickled ginger, minced mutton and tofu (India); eel and squid (Japan); coconut (Costa Rica); green peas (Brazil); and mockba, a combination of sardines, tuna, mackerel, salmon and onions (Russia).

all — were as good as our winners. Biggest doesn't mean best slice."

Didn't hear back from jerseagirl. Too bad.

"No Sciortino's pizza in South Amboy?" inquired landofcanaan. "This place is an institution in Central Jersey and even survived being forced out of its original coal fired brick oven location. Talk about best sausage pie . . . you guys seriously missed the mark on that one!"

"It was good, but it didn't crack the top four," I replied.

"VJ's in Pompton Plains is the ultimate best," wrote someone with the curious tag of iooooooooooooooooo. "Worst would be Carnival Spot in Pompton Plains. Did you even bother sampling either one?"

"We were at VJ's — it's okay," was my reply. "It's the 'ultimate best' in where, Pompton Plains?"

I was starting to enjoy this.

"So, there's no good pizza in the upper nw 30% or more of

> Miley Cyrus likes to put ketchup on her pizza.

NJ?" glenrd wanted to know. "No Warren County, no Sussex County, no Passaic County, Morris County, hardly a touch in Bergen County? You guys need to get out of your rut more."

Busterballz rushed to our defense: "Sun Ray Pizza in Little Falls got an Award of Excellence for its sausage. Learn your geography, pal, that's PASSAIC COUNTY."

I couldn't resist piling it on. "No Passaic? What do you call Clifton and Paterson?"

It referred to two of our Award of Excellence winners, Bruno's and Patsy's.

Stringbean33 took offense — all-caps offense — to our giving Buona Pizza in Westfield an Award of Excellence in the plain pizza category.

"BUONA PIZZERIA IN WESTFIELD? ARE YOU GUYS KIDDING? WHEN I GO THERE I GET EVERYTHING BUT THAT PIZZA. DISGUSTING CHUNKY TOMATOS AND CHEAP GUMMY CHEESE. YUG!"

Voiceofreason spotted an error — "Buona is on Westfield Avenue in Clark" — then offered a correction.

"Oopsie, my bad, different Buona, doh!"

FromJohnnyPinNNJ: "This was a great series. Especially liked this week's daily articles on all things pizza culminating in today's awards. They should publish a book, or at least a guide."

Hmm, not a bad idea . . .

Things started to get colorful, literally.

"La Rustique," the aptly-named Devils Advocate said of the Jersey City pizzeria awarded best margherita, "is like Wonder bread covered in Velveeta and V-8 juice."

"Have you ever been there, or do you have something against the restaurant, Jersey City, or, for that matter, good pizza?" I asked.

"I live in Jersey City and that was the first place I tried," Devils Advocate replied. "I tried it more than once, too. I have noticed that people either love it or hate it. Jersey City is a miserable pizza town, unfortunately."

"Oh, man," moaned james1787, "Pete & Elda's on Rt 35 in Neptune didn't make it in there for one of the best thin crust? Perhaps it was not amongst the 333 visited places."

My reply: "We were there. One word: overrated. You can get much better pizza nearby."

The Hudson County online contingent seemed particularly bothered by our picks.

"Did you even go into Bayonne at all?" wondered djeveled.

> The Jonas Brothers have a song called "I Fell in Love With the Pizza Girl," which includes the lyrics:
> "Love showed up at my door yesterday
> It might sound cheesy but I wanted her to stay
> I fell in love with the pizza girl
> Now I eat pizza every day"

"La Fontana? Nino's? Joe's? Naples? No Hoboken pizza either? You need to bring me along next year!"

"You're kidding, right?" I replied. "We hit 10 places in Bayonne and a half dozen in Hoboken. Joe's was the last stop on our first Bayonne trip. Wished we hadn't stopped. Naples — don't get me started on that place. Bayonne pizza: big disappointment."

Then things got personal — between perezr8 and busterballz. When perezr8 recommended Roma Pizza in North Bergen, busterballz had this to say:

"Roma? Get outta here. You might as well be talking about the Sbarro at Newark Airport. You gotta bring the A game to this discussion, chief."

Perezr8 was not cowed:

"First, you obviously don't know what your talking about if your comparing it with Sbarro's. Roma is a independent place great sauce and fresh pies made on the regular so u dont get stiff slices that have been under a heat lamp. Second, Roma is not that that far fetched, considering that alot of people here mention Benny's in Hoboken as good pizza."

Busterballz's comeback: "Oh, excuse me, perezr8. Let me re-phrase: Roma tastes like freshly made Sbarro. Everyone keeps yapping about these sentimental neighborhood joints as if they stand a chance against the game changers like De Lorenzo's, Papa's, Star, etc. Please, man. Mattingly might be my all-time favorite Yankee, but that doesn't mean he's in the same class as Ruth and Gehrig. Get my drift?"

I was encouraged by the many comments from South Jersey readers.

Even the misinformed ones.

"Maybe South Jersey was ignored because they like the Flyers, not the Devils," gavin123 offered.

I could not let that one go.

"The leader of the Pizza Patrol is a Flyers fan. Your comeback, please."

There was no comeback.

There were pleas for Gabby's in Flemington and Verona Pizza and Rose's in Garfield and Park Tavern in Rutherford, among many others.

"I can't believe Lovey's in Hasbrouck Heights is not on this list!" ParkBench Willy wailed.

Impizza couldn't take it any more.

"All you people do is bitch. Did anyone send a e-mail? I did and they went. Can't hit everything. Did anyone try two or more on the list? I did 4 of 6. Who here tried DeLucia's? How do you know if you didn't try?WHA WHa u didn't do this you didn't do that."

Busterballz again:

"Very true. A bunch of angry, tastebud-deficent babies posting on here because their favorite pies got called for what they are: terrible. My favorite is De Lorenzo's in Trenton. Am I complaining because some place I never heard of won top honors in the plain slice division? Hell no! Instead, I'm heading over to DeLucia's first chance I get to find out what the hype is about. Then I'll be qualified to pass judgement. I suggest all the armchair critics zip it and do the same."

But no one was ready to "zip it," and that was good; I wanted the debate to go on forever.

"From what I read," wrote njpetey, "it sounds like the Pizza

David Smith II from Smith's Pizza Plus, Emporium, Pa., garnered the largest dough stretch at the 2009 American Pizza Championship. His winning number: 72.25 centimeters, or approximately 29 inches.

Patrol doesn't go west of I-287, since there are NO reviews of any Morris or Sussex County pizzas. Did you guys go that far west, or don't we exist?"

"If you read the reviews," I replied, "you would realize we were all over Morris County — visited almost 30 places. That's a lot."

Sadpunkin was bothered by my description of DeLucia's crunchy plain pizza.

"I don't get it — the best pizza goes crunch? If my pizza goes crunch — it's burnt!"

My response: "If your thin-crust or crispy plain doesn't go crunch, you're eating Play-Doh."

Another angry reader from South Jersey, this time mriotman: "Camden County? Gloucester County? Salem County? Cape May County? Cumberland County? Burlington County? Atlantic County? I'm not even a South Jersey native. But I didn't see any Pizza Patrol in any of these areas."

I shot back:

"You didn't see us in South Jersey? Must have been sleeping. Let me repeat: We hit every county multiple times. I live down the Shore, so you know we weren't going to ignore it. If you read the story, you would have seen that my favorite pizza all year was at Palermo's — Burlington County. There was a separate list of 10 best South Jersey pizzerias — apparently you missed that, too."

Coral chimed in: "So, there's no place south of Trenton that is worthy of a mention? Did you even drive south of Mercer County for your research?"

Grrr.

"If you read the story, you'll notice Palermo's in Bordentown won an Award of Excellence for margherita. And I voted it my favorite pizza of the year. Palermo's was also on my top-10-pizzerias-in-South-Jersey list. BTW, we hit all 21 counties — multiple times."

The debate went back and forth for hours. At 5:38 the next

The soldiers of Darius the Great (521-486 B.C.) baked bread flat upon their shields and then covered it with cheese and dates during long marches. Cato the Elder, in his history of Rome, described a "flat round of dough dressed with olive oil, herbs and honey baked on stones."

morning, Cmippolito sugggested several pizzerias in South Jersey. Zoie22 and I exchanged fond memories of Pizza Como in Clinton, where I once lived.

And then came the best exchange of the last 24 pizza hours, between hunter08 and the ubiquitous impizza. The blow-by-blow account:

hunter08: "Did you guys get a chance to stop @ Manville Pizza in Manville NJ? I've been going there for 40 years and still wait 20-30 minutes in a crowd 6 deep for one of their pies on Friday night. Classic pizza joint and the guys have the red and white striped shirts."

impizza: "Any good pizza you will wait 30-40 mins on a Fri. it's not a big thang.. manville pizza is under cooked. but based on the people who live in the ville would think manville pizza is great. where else would you go?"

hunter08: "Your kidding right? I drive from my home in Princeton, wait through Rt. 206 rush hour traffic pass upwards of 25 pizzerias just to get to this place. Not only that, Manville has 6 pizzerias within 1 mile not to mention the 15 in nearby Hillsborough. The fact that Manville Pizza has not only survived, but trounced the competition in its 42 years of existence is surely a testament to its great pizza."

impizza: "You have to be kidding me? I know people who live in Manville and would never eat that stuff. You are so

---

There are 67,554 pizza stores. Independents own 59 percent of pizzerias and control 51 percent of the sales, according to June 2008 - June 2009 figures from PMQ Pizza Magazine. Of the chains, Pizza Hut did 14.4 percent of the business; Domino's, 8.3 percent; Papa John's, 5.5 percent; and Little Caesar's, 2.9 percent.

---

close to Robbinsville why don't you go to Delorenzo's for the best pizza in the state? I know why. You need to get to Manville pizza so you can turn on the ovens and open the doors for lunch."

hunter08: "And I know people in Trenton that would never eat Delorenzos whats your point? Opinions are like impizzas.........is that how that goes? I was simply stating my experiences, no reason to get defensive."

impizza: "Hunter — just saying you like bad pizza. Go to DeLorenzo's and get a dam [sic] fine pie. I'm glad Manville pizza has been open for 42 years . . . I am. Do you have to strap a 2x4 to your back?"

I jumped in: "I think we should invite a bunch of you guys (and girls) for a live pizza debate. That would be lively!"

Then impizza: "I'm down like James Brown."

Hunter08's reply: "ohh its on now!!! You done brought the freak out of me!! btw whats with the 2x4 comment, I'm staring at my monitor for the past five minutes and can't for the life of me figure out what your getting at. please clarify. if its a personal thing feel free to treat me to a slice of Delorenzos. I will be glad to listen to you and try to help."

And so it went. Hunter08 and impizza dropped out, others joined in. Three months after the announcement of the winners, comments were still coming in, a testament to both pizza's popularity and food's status as Jersey's No. 1 hot topic.

When the winners were announced, Adam Kuban wrote this on slice.seriouseats.com:

"I've been bad about posting about this, though, because these folks have BLOWN MY PIZZA MIND with the sheer volume of their work. I have no idea where to begin."

For the entire online pizza debate, you can begin at nj.com/munchmobile. Feel free to chime in. This is one food fight that promises to go on for some time.

THE BEST PIZZA IN NEW JERSEY

For those who missed it, or want it in one handy place, this was the announcement of the winners in our Best Pizza in New Jersey competition.

Finally, the winners.

After six months, 1,000 slices and 9,000 miles on the Munchmobile, the Pizza Patrol sat down and picked New Jersey's best pizza.

It wasn't easy.

We sampled plenty of mediocre pizza during our three-season search in 2009, as the weekly reviews attest. We also enjoyed plenty of great pizza, which made the selection of winners difficult.

Our six overall winners span a range of looks and locales — from a tiny pizza parlor in Raritan Borough and a strip mall pizzeria in Lyndhurst to a no-bathroom, no credit-card legend in Trenton and a spacious sports bar/pizzeria in Orange.

Reactions from our winners ran from joy and jubilation to surprise and disbelief. Allie DeLucia, owner of DeLucia's Brick Oven Pizza in Raritan Borough, our plain pizza champion, kept repeating the same word — "Really?"

Yes, Allie, really.

"I'm a true believer that anything can be improved," said Charlie Wilson, owner of La Rustique Cafe in Jersey City, our pick for best margherita pizza in New Jersey.

It's hard to imagine our winners needing to improve. Our pizza mission was unprecedented — no one had visited hundreds of pizzerias in one state in such a short period. We hit 333 pizzerias in all — 11 percent of the estimated 3,000 pizzerias in New Jersey. And now it's time to rest — and let our winners enjoy the spotlight. Here are the winners, with three Award of Excellence winners, in alphabetical order, in each category.

BEST PLAIN

DeLucia's Brick Oven Pizza, 3 First Ave., Raritan Borough; (908) 725-1322. Maybe it's the cheese — part skim mozzarella, as opposed to the whole milk mozzarella used by many pizzerias. Maybe it's the 93-year-old oven. Or maybe it's the girls.

Apart from Allie DeLucia, his son, Christian, and Allie's brother, Buddy, it's an all-girl crew at DeLucia's. Cristina DeFalco and Carly Mobert were making the pizzas when we stopped by.

"We've always had just girls here," Allie DeLucia said. "I don't know why."

His grandfather, Constantino, opened DeLucia's in 1917 as a bakery. They started making pizza here in the 1930s. Allie, Christian and Buddy make the dough every day; none of that premade stuff for them.

"I was brought up that way," Allie said. "What the hell, do

the work."

DeLucia's plain pizza is all about the crunch — one bite, and you're hooked. A plain slice cannot rely on toppings or other form of coverup; it must stand on its own. The crust, sauce — and that crunch — make DeLucia's the best plain pizza in New Jersey.

Award of Excellence: Buona Pizza & Restaurant, 243 South Ave. east, Westfield; (908) 232-2066. Buona, open since 1977, looks like your average neighborhood pizzeria, but the pizza is anything but. We visited Buona's on our second trip, in early July; the memory of the plain slice lasted right through the summer.

> Mike Jensen, who operates a mobile pizza oven, bought the town of Nothing, Ariz., for $1.1 million in 2009. He opened the town's old minimart and started making pizzas in a portable wood-fired oven trailer that he built.

Award of Excellence: Papa's Tomato Pies, 804 Chambers St., Trenton; (609) 392-0359. The two De Lorenzo's in Trenton get all the attention, but this wood-paneled pizzeria has the history. Opened in 1912, Papa's is the second-oldest pizzeria in the country. The owner is Nick Azzaro, grandson of founder Joe Papa. Nick does a mustard pie (it's weirdly compelling), but stick to the plain; it's a doughy delight.

Award of Excellence: Spirito's, 714 Third Ave., Elizabeth; (908) 351-5414. This legendary Elizabeth restaurant is known for its ravioli — and pizza. The plain pizza, with its distinctive crackly crust, is a standout. Pizza Patrol member Al Windrem called it "awesome." The rest of us agreed.

BEST SAUSAGE

De Lorenzo's Tomato Pies, 530 Hudson St., Trenton; (609) 695-9534. They don't make them like this anymore. Wooden booths, tile floors, no bathrooms, no credit cards and a cop stationed outside at night.

De Lorenzo's is pizza old-school. Alexander "Chick" De Lorenzo opened the pizzeria in 1947; today, Gary Amico and his wife, Eileen, Chick's daughter, run De Lorenzo's. Gary makes the pizzas and Eileen works the formidable 1940s-vintage cash register. The secret to De Lorenzo's success?

"Good recipe, thin well-done pizza," Gary Amico replied.

If there was an overriding theme on the Pizza Patrol, it was the abundance of subpar sausage. De Lo's sausage pizza is superlative; the sausage is from City Beef in Trenton.

"All three of our children were raised in that high chair," said Susan Brooks of Hamilton, who eats at De Lorenzo's every Thursday with her sister, LuAnne Nutt. They always order a plain pizza with extra tomato sauce.

"Don't tell anyone about this place," Brooks pleaded.

Sorry, Susan. The word's already out.

Award of Excellence: Luna Restaurant, 429 Main St., Three Bridges; (908) 284-2321. Luna, tucked into a white house in this small village, did all three pizzas well. Pizza Patrol member Scott Wiener loved the plain's "perfect blend of crispy exterior and tender interior." But the sausage pizza is the standout.

Award of Excellence: Luigi's Famous Pizza, 3329 Doris Ave., Ocean Township (Monmouth County); (732) 531-7733. We visited a half dozen "Luigi's Famous" or "Famous Luigi's" — none related to each other. This Luigi's, sequestered on a street of warehouses, is the best. Windrem described the sausage pizza as a "grand slam." It was definitely the hit on our first Jersey Shore pizza run.

There are a dozen or more pizza-related "holidays," including National Pizza Month (October) and National Pizza Day (October) and National Sausage Pizza Day (mid-October) and National Cheese Pizza Day (September) and National Pizza with Everything On It Except Anchovies Day (November) and National Pizza Party Day (May) and, well, you get the idea.

Award of Excellence: Sun-Ray Pizza, 440 Main St., Little Falls; (973) 256-0724. Great pizza can be found on the other side of the railroad tracks. This pizzeria, alongside the train tracks in Little Falls, serves hefty rectangular chunks of sausage on its pies. You may find yourself pulling them off, one by one; they're that good.

BEST MARGHERITA

La Rustique Cafe, 611 Jersey Ave., Jersey City; (201) 222-6886. Charlie Wilson, owner of La Rustique, takes his pizza seriously. He tore down the restaurant walls to install his $25,000 three-ton stone hearth pizza oven. Wilson, who once owned a Rite Aid pharmacy in Jersey City, is a self-taught pizza-maker. "I got the burns to prove it," he said, laughing.

The most popular pizza at La Rustique is the margherita,

and for good reason. "San Marzano tomatoes, mozzarella, grated cheese, extra-virgin olive oil — that's it," he said. He prefers San Marzano over California tomatoes because they're sweeter and "heartier."

Wilson roasts his own vegetables, and makes his own mozzarella and meatballs. Gezim Drishti is the main pizza-maker.

One enduring Pizza Patrol memory: eating our pizzas outside La Rustique on a warm summer night. Team member Gina Bruno, who dispensed superlatives as if they cost her money, called the margherita "tremendous."

Award of Excellence: Antonio's Brick Oven Pizza, 453 Main St., Metuchen; (732) 603-0008. If there's one shortcoming to Jersey pizza, it's the lack of sauce. The deep-dish margherita at Antonio's is a tomatoey, crusty success. There may be bigger names on the Middlesex County pizza map, but no one does a margherita better than Antonio's.

Award of Excellence: Denino's Pizza Place, Aberdeen Townsquare, Route 34, Aberdeen; (732) 583-2150. Our major complaint with Denino's? That there is only one Jersey location of this Staten Island legend! The margherita is a marvel. "Fragrant — smells like a garden," said a wowed Wiener.

Award of Excellence: Palermo's Restaurant and Pizzeria, Glen Brook Shopping Center, 674 Route 206 south, Bordentown; (609) 298-6771. A sassy sauce and marvelous mutz add up to margherita magnificence at this plain-Jane pizzeria. The Munchmobile driver's favorite pizza of the year.

BEST SICILIAN

Mr. Bruno's Pizza & Restaurant, 439 Valley Brook Road, Lyndhurst; (201) 933-1588. Sicilian may have been the most closely contested category, and it came down to a battle of the Bruno's — one in Lyndhurst, one in Clifton. Mr. Bruno's boasted the best sauce of all our Sicilians; you can buy bottles of the stuff here.

"We make it the old-fashioned way — the jars are boiled with the sauce in it," said Anthony Livreri, who runs the pizzeria with his brother, Lenny.

"We use very good Italian peeled tomatoes, fresh garlic, fresh herbs," Livreri added. "It's not an overcooked sauce, and we don't go heavy on the spices."

When Wiener sampled a slice on a return visit, he was transported back to our initial visit in July.

"It's all coming back — a Sicilian that is light is a beautiful thing," he said.

Award of Excellence: Bruno's, Clifton Plaza, 1006 Route 46 west, Clifton; (973) 473-3339. Fun place; we loved our waitress, Michelle. A big, puffy crust and tons of tomatoey flavor equal one superb Sicilian.

Award of Excellence: Fratelli's Restaurant Pizzeria,

Union Square Mall, 500 Route 35, Middletown; (732) 747-4737. We love rules like the one at Fratelli's: You cannot order a brick-oven pizza to go. "It doesn't sit well in the box," a staffer explained. Joan Dwyer admired the "nice crunch" and "smooth flavor" of the Sicilian, cooked in the regular oven.

Award of Excellence: Pizza Masters Pizza & Restaurant, 532 Broadway, Bayonne; (201) 437-4802. We sampled plenty of average pizza in Bayonne; Cafe Bello and Pizza Masters stood out. Everything — sauce, cheese, crust — came together in Pizza Masters' Sicilian. Bruno called it a "cloud-nine pizza."

BEST THIN-CRUST

Star Tavern, 400 High St., Orange; (973) 675-3336. The secret to the great thin-crust pizzas at Star? It might be the round steel pans, the sides of which are cut out halfway around to allow quick removal of the pizza. The pies are taken from the pans and finished off directly on the oven surface; in all, pizzas take 12 to 15 minutes to cook in the 650-degree oven.

The Star opened in 1945; current owner Gary Vayianos took it over from his dad, Aristotelis, who bought the restaurant in 1980.

"Our recipe is simple," Vayianos said. "If I told you what was in it, you'd be surprised."

Of course, he didn't tell us; pizza-makers are notoriously reluctant to reveal secrets. The Star turns out pizza at a prodigious rate: 7,000 to 10,000 pizzas a month.

Something we didn't know: Vayianos and James Racioppi, owner of fabled Jimmy Buff's in West Orange and East Hanover, attended Newark Academy at the same time.

Award of Excellence: Miller's Tavern, 2 Beaver Ave., Annandale; (908) 735-4730. Roadhouse. Biker bar. Neighborhood hangout. Pizzeria. Call Miller's what you want; it makes for a great afternoon, or evening, out. Bruno admired the pizza's "distinct" flavor, while Windrem called it an "easygoing" pie. Like Miller's itself.

Award of Excellence: Nellie's Place, 9 Franklin Turnpike, Waldwick; (201) 652-8626. Kinchley's in Ramsey gets most of the accolades, but we judged Nellie's king of the Bergen thin-crust crowd.

Award of Excellence: Patsy's Tavern & Pizzeria, 72 Seventh Ave., Paterson; (973) 742-9596. If the Pizza Patrol ever held a reunion, Patsy's would be the place we'd pick. Great neighborhood bar; its pizza, with a crackery crust, is a saucy, greasy delight.

BEST SPECIALTY

La Sicilia Pizza & Ristorante, 155 Washington Ave., Belleville; (973) 751-5726. Giuseppe Ali has restaurant cred; he worked as a cook at renowned Casa Dante in Jersey City. So it should come as no surprise that La Sicilia, open just three years, has turned into a popular lunch and dinner spot.

Ali's most popular pizza, and our pick for the state's best specialty pizza, is the Palermo, a heavenly blend of fresh mozzarella, marinara, garlic and grated cheese. Your neighborhood pizzeria doesn't make a pizza like this, trust us.

"This is a very popular pizza in Sicily," Ali said of his native land. "It's like a Grandma (pizza) but the Grandma doesn't put the fresh mozzarella underneath (the sauce)."

Wiener admired its "total balance," while Bruno said she'd put the tart, tomatoey sauce "on anything."

Ali also offers sandwiches and entrees, but start with the pizza. And don't forget to take home some of his killer cannoli.

> Sign of the pizza apocalypse: Throw Dough (throwdough.com) is the official training dough of the U.S. Pizza Team.

Award of Excellence: De Lorenzo's Tomato Pies, 530 Hudson St., Trenton; (609) 695-9534. The only pizzeria to earn a second mention on our list. De Lorenzo's clam pizza may be better than its sausage.

· **Award of Excellence: Santillo's Brick Oven Pizza, 639 S. Broad St., Elizabeth; (908) 354-1887.** We were singing the praises of Santillo's well before bloggers and magazines "discovered" this takeout-only pizzeria. Al Santillo — he alone is worth the trip — makes a "1964 pie" with imported Romano and extra-virgin olive oil. 1964? It's great this or any other year.

Award of Excellence: Stan's Chitch's Pizzeria, 14 Columbus Place, Bound Brook; (732) 356-0899. Tile floors, high-backed green booths, striped wallpaper. It's That '70s pizza parlor! You've got to love a place where the table cheese and basil comes in Gerber baby food jars. The meatball pizza won honors here; Wiener called it "super good."

PIZZA TIMELINE

The history of pizza, at least in this country, almost begins in Trenton.

In 1910, Joe's Tomato Pies opened in Trenton's Italian-centric Chambersburg section, several years after the country's first pizzeria, Lombardi's, opened in New York City. In 1912, Papa's Tomato Pies opened, also in Chambersburg.

Papa's is still open, making it the second oldest pizzeria in the country, after Lombardi's.

For the most significant dates in pizza history, read on.

1830: The earliest known pizzeria, Antica Pizzeria Port'Alba, opens in Naples, Italy.

1905: Lombardi's on Spring Street in New York City is issued America's first mercantile license to bake pizza.

1910: Joe's Tomato Pies opens in Trenton's Chambersburg section.

1912: Papa's Tomato Pies opens, also in Chambersburg. Unlike Joe's, it is still open.

1924: Anthony "Totonno" Pero opens Totonno's Pizzeria in Coney Island.

1925: Frank Pepe opens Frank Pepe Pizzeria Napoletana in New Haven, Conn.

1926: Pizzeria Regina opens in Boston.

1929: John Sasso opens John's Pizzeria in Greenwich Village in New York.

1929: Marra's opens in Philadelphia.

1933: Patsy's opens in East Harlem, New York.

1934: Sciortino's begins business in Perth Amboy. It is now in South Amboy.

1934: The Reservoir Tavern opens in Parsippany.

1934: State Street Pizza (now Modern Apizza) opens in New Haven, Conn.

1957: Celentano Brothers releases the first supermarket frozen pizza.

1958: Frank and Don Carney, students at the University of Wichita (now Wichita State University) open Pizza Hut in a converted bar next to the family grocery store. Two years later, there were 25 Pizza Huts. By 1968, there were 310. By 1977, Pizza Hut was a billion-dollar-a-year company with 3,400 stores worldwide.

1959: The first Little Caesar's opens.

1962: Pep Simek, who with his brother ran a bar bordered by a cemetery in Medford, Wis., breaks his leg dancing and spends most of the winter tinkering with pizza recipes for bar patrons. Tombstone Pizza is born.

1967: The first Domino's franchise opens.

1984: The first Papa John's opens.

1995: Kraft, which had purchased Tombstone in 1986, unveils Di-
Giorno and its revolutionary "self-rising" crust.

— From various sources

PIZZA EXCERPTS

The weekly Pizza Patrol reports in the paper not only provided reviews of every place visited, but also glimpses into the always-demanding, never-glamorous job of pizza taster. We started in July, 2009.

WEEK 1

The Pizza Patrol's weighty mission this summer is to hit 100-plus pizzerias around New Jersey in an attempt to find the state's best pizza.

What better place to start than Nutley? Pizza is practically a religion there, and the town's annual pizza contest has been wracked by controversy.

No sooner had we sat down at one well-known Nutley pizzeria than the owner called, telling the Munchmobile's driver that he didn't appreciate the Big Dog's put-down of his pie in our own Nutley pizza showdown four years ago. Didn't we know how great his pizza is?

Pizza Patrol members — all hard-core pie lovers — will call it the way they see it this summer. We don't care who wins. We just want to find New Jersey's best pie: regular, thin-crust, Sicilian, whatever.

The average per-store annual sales for all pizzerias in the United States is $542,456.

WEEK 4

The Pizza Patrol cannot be stopped, or even slowed down! At the urging of the Munchmobile driver, who will undoubtedly need food therapy before the summer is over, the PP now hopes to visit not 100, but 150 pizzerias — or more — before its mission is complete.

You may be wondering how we choose pizzerias. Our not-so-esteemed leader closes his eyes, grabs a dart and . . . wait, that's not how we do it! We go out twice a week, visiting five pizzerias each time — based on readers' suggestions — then make occasional all-day weekend trips. Such as this week's 10-pizzeria prowl of Essex County.

WEEK 5

Calm down.

Many of the hundreds of e-mails sent to the Pizza Patrol's attention in the past month have started in a similar fashion.

"Are you guys kidding? You went to (fill in the blank) county and didn't hit (fill in the blank) pizzeria? What were you thinking?"

Calm down. We are not even halfway through our bold, daring, unprecedented mission (only because no one's been crazy enough to do it before). We are going to visit 150 pizzerias this summer — 50 more than originally planned.

We have many miles and much more pizza to go before

we rest, or collapse, in a cheesy heap. We will get to all your pizzerias. In the meantime, keep calling! You can recommend your favorite pizzeria anytime.

WEEK 6

Apparently, everyone on the Pizza Patrol wants to be a comedian.

"What's that?" asked PP member Marty Schneider, pointing to the pizza at Brothers in Red Bank.

"Cheese," Alex Windrem cracked.

PP member Joan Dwyer said the plain pie at Brothers had a "Yankee Doodle Dandy flavor," while Schneider took one bite of the pizza at Luke's in Wall and proclaimed, "It's a Lindsay Lohan pie — totally clueless."

Maybe the hard work (85 pizzerias visited as you read this) and stress are starting to have an effect on the team members. One thing is for certain: Our pizza net is ever-widening. This week's report deals with Monmouth and Warren counties. In the following weeks, we'll be all over the state. You can recommend your favorite pizzeria any time.

WEEK 7

The e-mails were encouraging, bordering on ecstatic. Our pizza excursion to Bayonne was a can't-miss proposition.

"An icon in town for 25 years," a reader said of the Big Apple Sports Palace.

"This place has been there since I was a kid in the '60s," added another reader, speaking of Pompei Pizza.

"The pizza is thin, and the sauce is excellent. Tastes the same after all these years."

A fan of Tony May's had this to say: "There is so much pizza in Bayonne, and I grew up there. But in 40 years of eating pizza, I've never had better than this."

There is so much pizza in Bayonne. So much mediocre pizza, if our one-night, eight-stop trip was any indication. But every pizza town deserves a second chance. If we missed your favorite pizzeria, let us know. Bayonne must be better than this. We hope, anyway.

WEEK 8

The Pizza Patrol never rests. By the time you read this, our saucy six will have visited 115-plus pizzerias in New Jersey. There are about 3,000 pizzerias in New Jersey, according to the National Association of Pizzeria Operators, publishers of Pizza Today magazine. While the Pizza Patrol cannot visit every pizzeria (we could if we visited four pizzerias every night for the next two years, though), the PP certainly won't miss any well-regarded ones.

WEEK 9

We'd like to report we've had nothing but top-notch pizza this summer. That would not be true. There's a lot of so-so pizza across the Garden State, as you can tell by our Pizza Patrol reports to date. We sure hope things improve.

By the time you read this, we will have visited 135 pizzerias around the state. The original goal: 100. The revised goal: 150. The newly revised goal: 200.

Forget about what this is doing to our collective cholesterol counts; we will not rest until we have done the Jersey pizza scene justice.

WEEK 12

Our all-day Pizza Patrol trips are not for the fidgety, finicky or fainthearted. Ever try up to 30 pizzas in one day? That's what we do on these all-day trips. It all adds up — on our waistlines, mostly.

Our latest excursion was a whirlwind tour of Middlesex County, from Woodbridge and Edison to East Brunswick, South Brunswick and Monroe. We ate pizza in a supermarket, in a pizzeria that had burned down the year before, in several downtowns and one parking lot late at night.

One of the stranger scenes of the summer: the Munchmobile driver placing a pizza on the sidewalk in front of a neon sign so he could shoot it in decent light. "What is that guy doing?" passers-by no doubt wondered.

What are we doing? We're eating pizza, and going through more paper plates this summer than most people do in a lifetime.

WEEK 13

There's no truth to the rumor that the Pizza Patrol will visit all 3,000 pizzerias in New Jersey. Not that we couldn't do it, of course, but you have to draw the line somewhere.

We're coming down the stretch in our search for New Jersey's best pizza. When you read this, we will have hit 175 pizzerias and the Munchmobile driver will be on a cross-country road trip, with pizza the last thing on his mind. But he's preparing himself for the final Pizza Patrol push.

"Ain't no stoppin' us now, we're on the move."

The Pizza Patrol visited its 200th pizzeria this week, and since we've come this far, we may as well go for 250.

WEEK 15

Pizza Patrol members have not come to blows since they started four months and 220 pizzerias ago.

It almost happened on a recent excursion in Jersey City. Make that a recent hike through Jersey City, as the Munchmobile driver, of the belief that finding a parking spot for the Big Dog would be a challenge, asked — ordered? — the crew to walk clear across town to John's on Sussex Street and back.

Blisters, and tempers, were raised.

The biggest surprise so far this year is not the shortage of good sausage or first-rate Sicilian but that the Munchmobile driver's lifeless body has not been found in a 55-gallon drum with the words "We've had enough!" scrawled in pizza sauce across his forehead.

The driver keeps pushing the Patrol members to visit more pizzerias, eat more cheese, and hit towns and counties they've never heard of, much less visited.

Their response: Bring it on, buster.

On a recent trip, we found ourselves at a truck stop in Carneys Point. Been there? Yeah, didn't think so.

Our excursions are typically all over the map, which is why our most recent outing — this is Trip No. 25, if you're keeping score at home — took in Passaic, Morris and Warren counties.

According to Domino's Pizza Tracker, which allows customers to track their pizza after they order online, Republicans spend more per order than Democrats, rely more on credit cards and tend to order two large pizzas at a time. Democrats rely more on delivery and like more variety with their orders, going for more side items.

WEEK 16

An unseasonably warm day, blue skies, brilliant sunshine and the prospect of spending most of the day at a gloriously quiet Jersey Shore.

Sounds like the makings of a great Pizza Patrol trip.

Uh, not quite.

The Munchmobile driver temporarily misplacing his notebook may have been the first omen. Or maybe it was the flock of seagulls, which hovered over us, malice in their beady little eyes, on the Ocean City boardwalk.

"What are you writing down?" the owner of Three Brothers from Italy asked as we awaited our pizzas at the Ocean City boardwalk stand.

It was that kind of day. The "World's Largest Pizza" made another appearance (three pizzerias have made the claim, so far), and so did some of the most inedible sausage on this or any other planet. When the sausage looks like hamster food, it's time to ask yourself some basic questions, like "Why are we eating this stuff?"

Because we have a job to do, and, by golly, we're going to finish it, murderous-looking seagulls or not.

"I hope this sausage doesn't spread out of South Jersey," team member Scott Wiener said at one point. "It's a plague."

The Pizza Patrol — down two members, one busy with a brand-new baby, the other using the lame excuse of work — did find quality pizza, even if it took several hundred twisty miles of driving to do so. Ocean City to Wildwood to Cape May to Vineland to Carmel — all in a day's work. Carmel? Isn't that in California? No, it's in Pizza Jersey. Step away from the sausage, it's time to get down to business.

When asked by Slashdot.org where they had eaten the best pizza in their lives, more people said Antarctica (1,262 votes) than either South America (797) or Asia (669).

WEEK 17

The Pizza Patrol has visited fluorescent-lit pizzerias, up-scale restaurants, neighborhood taverns, biker bars, one log cabin, one Pizza Palace (Sam's in Wildwood), pizzerias with king, queen and prince in their names, not to mention places called Stan's Chitch's, Jolly's, JoJo's, Candy's and Bunny's.

We hit a new high — or was it low? — on our latest trip, a journey down the Delaware from Trenton to Pennsville. No, we weren't actually on the Delaware — this Dog doesn't float — but instead followed the river to what we hoped was a minor cheese epiphany or two.

How we ended up late at night at a truck stop in Carneys Point, within walking distance of Delaware, the state, the Munchmobile driver is still not sure. Maybe by this point we just didn't care what or where we were eating. Maybe it was the girl at one pizzeria who didn't so much slide as toss paper plates across the counter at us.

Whatever the reason, it didn't explain why we were at the

truck stop — the Flying J Plaza, if you must know — trying on warm furry caps of unclear animal origin. Beaver? Raccoon? Sabertooth tiger? Who knows? The Munchmobile driver regrets not buying one; driving a van with a hot dog on the roof while wearing a muskrat atop one's head is a great way to get noticed.

WEEK 18

Rule No. 101 of Pizza Patrol: Chicken belongs in a sandwich or on a plate, not on pizza.

Rule No. 102 of Pizza Patrol: Pineapple or pineapple juice belongs on an ice cream sundae, or in a piña colada, not on pizza.

Rule No. 103 of Pizza Patrol: Pepperoni is the most popular and boring topping, and is pretty much the same all over the world, so it doesn't belong on pizza. At least not on our pizza.

Rule No. 104 of Pizza Patrol: Anyone who puts a hot dog on a pizza has issues for which professional help is surely available.

"Can you recommend another pie?" a Pizza Patrol member will ask after ordering our usual half plain/half sausage.

"Buffalo chicken; it's our most popular," is often the reply.

Rule No. 105 of Pizza Patrol: . . . Oh, never mind.

WEEK 19

The holiday season is upon us, which can mean only one thing.

Pizza.

What, you were expecting something about shopping tips, gift trends and mall parking lot strategy?

Think about it. The most precious commodity in the next month is time. There simply isn't enough of it to do all that needs to be done. It's important to keep fit as the stress — and credit card purchases — mount. You need extra reserves of energy and endurance to survive, and what better food than pizza? It's quick, cheap, filling, nutritious and you can eat a slice and talk on your cell at the same time while cruising the mall.

Mall pizza is pretty much chain pizza, and because this is a Munchmobile story, we're not going there, but there's plenty of good pizza near Jersey malls and shopping centers. Which brings us, somehow, to the latest Pizza Patrol report. By the time you read this, the Patrol will stop dreaming the impossible dream because that dream will have come true.

No, not finding a good Sicilian, but hitting 300 pizzerias, 200 more than the original goal. Think about that. The overwhelming majority of people will not visit even 25 different pizzerias in their lives. We're visiting 300-plus in five months. Staggering. Which describes both the number of places and the way we'll be walking when this is over.

Break out that shopping list, gas up the car, and don't forget Uncle Ernie — you didn't get anything for him last year. And think pizza. Hmm, maybe you can even give a half plain/half sausage as a gift. But not to the Munchmobile driver. He's had plenty enough since July, thank you.

WEEK 20

Cammarata's Pizza Pantry in Livingston looks like a barebones deli, but its Old World pizza (puffy crust, plum tomatoes, oregano) is a winner, and a great way to start this day.

"A very intelligent pizza; it's got everything in the right place," said Scott Wiener.

Intelligent pizza? Why not? The Old World pie is certainly smarter than the Munchmobile driver, who recently announced that the patrol's latest goal is 1,000 slices — 333 pizzerias (three slices at each) — plus a slice at one more. Which is why the Pizza Patrol needed to make hay (considering the toppings we've seen this year, it wouldn't surprise us if that ends up as one somewhere).

WEEK 21

The end is near. No, not the end of the world, something far more serious — the end of the Pizza Patrol's incredible journey. Five months, 300-plus pizzerias and enough cheese to single-handedly keep the dairy economies of Wisconsin and France afloat. Not to mention the absolute last word on New Jersey pizza.

WEEK 22

The Pizza Patrol has received its share of grief since July, mostly in the form of e-mails that begin, "How can you say such-and-such pizzeria is better than (insert legendary pizzeria name here)."

Well, for one, it's our opinion, and two, if you want to read nothing but rave reviews about your favorite pizzeria, there are

Americans eat about 250 million pounds of pepperoni on their pizza every year.

any number of websites and message boards for that.

Some of them may even include comments from people other than the owners' friends, family and employees.

WEEK 24

Pizza Patrol members are the kind of people who can eat pizza anytime, anywhere. In fact, in addition to the 1,000 slices each has consumed on Pizza Patrol duty so far, they have eaten pizza dozens of times on their own since July 7, when we started our weighty mission.

The Munchmobile driver? He knows how to draw the line. Not counting those 1,000 slices, he has eaten pizza exactly once since July 7. Is he an oddball? Or the most normal? You decide.

> The Vinz Wine Bar in Escondido, Calif., holds weekly Dog Nights for canine customers, selling 8-inch puppy pizzas with cheese, bacon or pepperoni.

WEEK 25

There have been plenty of amusing moments during the Pizza Patrol's dates in Doughland.

We've eaten pizza in parking lots, on sidewalks, in parks and truck stops, on boardwalks, in the back of the van and by the side of the road.

We've met wise-cracking pizzeria owners who should have their own pizza reality show, like Alfred Rossino of Alfred's Tomato Pies in Blackwood and Al Santillo of Santillo's Brick Oven Pizza in Elizabeth.

But for sheer comedic theater, it was difficult to top the day the Munchmobile driver lost his voice. Fighting some unknown, clearly life-threatening ailment, but fully aware of his responsibilities, he pressed on, scribbling notes to team member Al Windrem when it came time to ask/answer questions.

Pretty funny stuff, if you're of the mind that the Munchmobile driver already talks too much to begin with.

WEEK 26

No credit cards or checks accepted, a turquoise-and-beige color scheme and waitresses with serious Jersey attitude. The menu features "famous" white pizza, "famous" cheesecake and that perennial favorite, "three meatballs and fries."

Spaghetti cooked to order? That costs extra.

Vesuvio Restaurant and Pizzeria in Belmar may have been the most lovably eccentric pizza joint the Pizza Patrol has visited, and that's saying something.

"Every flavor was bold," Al Windrem said of the plain pizza at the venerable Shore hangout. "Even the waitress," Gina Bruno added.

FINAL WEEK

And on the 162nd day, the Pizza Patrol rested. After six months of sampling and rating pizza throughout the Garden State, the team polished off its last slice — No. 1,000 — at the place where it all started in July: Michael's Pastaria in Nutley.

Was the team sad to see it all end? Were tears shed? Uh, not quite; several wanted to keep going.

But the Munchmobile driver — he who kept upping the goal (from 100 pizzerias to 200 and beyond) had to pull the pizza plug at some point. And besides, the sports desk was getting too dependent on our late-night deliveries of leftover pizza.

PIZZA PROFILES

SCIORTINO'S HARBOR LIGHTS, SOUTH AMBOY

PETER GENOVESE

The faded photograph, circa 1950, shows a group of young men — hair combed back, shirts unbuttoned — and women in crisp white blouses gathered around their parents at a dining room table.

It's Sunday dinner for the Sciortino family: Paulo and Francis Sciortino, and their 15 children. Sunday was always for Mass and dinner at the family's original restaurant on New Brunswick Avenue in Perth Amboy.

The Sciortinos lived upstairs, and all the kids worked at one time or another in the restaurant or the adjoining butcher shop and bakery.

Of all the people in the photograph, only Lucy Sciortino is still alive.

"My Aunt Lucy," says Lou Seminski, owner of what is now Sciortino's Harbor Lights, in South Amboy.

The Sciortino name is in no danger of fading, like that photograph. Seminski gets kidded for his last name — along the lines of "what's a Polish guy doing running Sciortino's?" — but he is most certainly a Sciortino.

Paulo and Francis were his grandparents. Seminski's father married one of their daughters, Mary, who ran the restaurant, along with her sisters Lucy, Helen and Isabell, for many years.

Seminski took over Sciortino's in 1989, and his daughters, Sherri and Sandra, and son, Louis Jr., will likely take it over when he retires.

The present-day Sciortino's looks nothing like the Sciortino's that opened in Perth Amboy in the early 1930s, making it one of New Jersey's oldest pizzerias. At Sciortino's in Perth Amboy, there was a small dining room, a brick oven and a pool in the backyard. Sciortino's Harbor Lights, which seats

Monster Fly Trap, which sells its "earth-friendly" items to pizzerias and other restaurants, claims to have killed 18 billion flies over the years.

135, is more sports bar than pizzeria, but the main attraction, as ever, is the pizza, with its trademark sweet Sciortino's sauce.

"Olive oil, sugar, a little parsley, basil, stir it up," says Seminski, sitting at a table near the cash register. "Let it sit overnight, use it the next day."

If only it were that easy. The pizzas are cooked in a conventional pizza oven, not the brick oven used in Perth Amboy, which causes some old-timers to grumble that the "new"

Sciortino's, which opened in 2006, is not as good as the old one. Seminski smiles when he hears that; he's used the same ingredients for years.

"The oven's different, that's it," he says, shrugging.

In the 1920s, his grandfather emigrated from Sicily, where he had been a dentist, butcher, even a wrestler. Paulo Sciortino's brother-in-law, Tony Coffaro, owned a bakery in Perth Amboy; Sciortino took the business over and started making pizza.

"When they first started, it was called tomato pie," Seminski explains. "They didn't have paste (for a sauce). There was no mozzarella — that didn't come until the 1940s. They chopped up tomatoes, put them in jars, sealed them. They didn't have the distributors like we do today."

Customers swore the secret to Sciortino's pizza was the brick oven, and there was major anxiety when Sciortino's moved to South Amboy. Seminski knew he had to get it right, so he spent a year visiting trade shows and testing various ovens before he found a gas-fired brick oven that came close to the original coal-fired brick oven.

But pizzas in the new oven tended to come out soggier than those in the old brick oven, so Seminski tweaked and fiddled. Now pizzas are cooked longer, at a lower temperature -— 550 degrees instead of 675 degrees.

There was angst in 2003 when Perth Amboy announced plans for a public safety complex. Sciortino's and 19 other properties would have to move. The pizzeria landed just across the river, in South Amboy, taking over the former Harbor Lights restaurant.

Today, the Sciortino family name and tradition remain firmly in place. Seminski's son, Louis Jr., an attorney, takes care of any legal matters. Daughter Sherri is a manager, while another daughter, Sandra, works in the kitchen. Dad does the ordering, the hiring and making sure the sauce "tastes the same, and that all the ingredients are there."

For those who will always associate Sciortino's with Perth Amboy, there's good news. Seminski says he will open a pizzeria in Perth Amboy sometime this year.

What will it be called?

"Sciortino's Pizza," Seminski replies. "What else?"

KATE & AL'S PIZZA, COLUMBUS

PETER GENOVESE

Buying glassware and toys and T-shirts and furniture at a giant flea market is one thing.

But pizza? What is it, marked down for a quick sale?

The Columbus Farmers' Market on Route 206 in Burlington County — despite its name, it's a sprawling, seemingly endless flea market — is home to not one but two pizzerias, and they're both good.

Kate & Al's Pizza, situated along the highway, and Pete's Pizza, located in the market's back 40, actually come from the same pizza family.

Alexander Stefan and his wife, Kate, opened Kate & Al's in 1955. The stand had originally been opened by Pete Bernath, Kate Stefan's brother. Bernath, who already had a pizzeria in Roebling, just west of Columbus, then opened a pizzeria in another section of the market and called it Pete's Pizza.

Al Stefan's business license indicated he would offer pizza, soft drinks, coffee and cigars, although it is not clear whether cigars were ever sold. Working in a choice corner of the market, the Stefans made tomato pies, which is what regulars called them then and now.

"The sauce is on top of the cheese," explains Samantha Stefan, their granddaughter. "That's what makes it a tomato pie."

The business was "popular from the start," according to Alexis Russell, Samantha Stefan's sister. "It was so unique. Tomato pie, perfect the way it was — no pepperoni, no toppings."

To the first-timer, pizzas from Kate & Al's and Pete's may look and taste similar: Sicilian-like square pizzas, heavy on the tomato sauce. Don't you dare mention this to Russell or Stefan, who worked at Kate & Al's when they were young, and have eaten the pizza at both places.

"There's a huge difference," insists Russell, who, like her sister, lives in Florida. "Pete's is a little sweeter. They have round pizza; we've never done round pizza. And they've never done a breakfast pizza."

It's an interesting way to start the day — a pizza with sausage and scrambled eggs on top, cooked in the oven.

The sisters' father, Alexander E. Stefan, took over Kate & Al's in 1964, when their grandparents moved to Florida.

"That business was pretty good. It supported six kids for many years," Russell says.

In the mid-1970s, their dad moved to Florida and opened a second Kate & Al's, in St. Petersburg. The pizzeria lasted just five years. Russell thinks she knows why.

"The quality of the pizza was nowhere near what they achieved in Jersey," Russell says. "They swore it was the water."

Alvin Scully was the longtime manager of Kate & Al's. He would send "very detailed" weekly business reports to Alexander E. Stefan on "how many pizzas sold, how many wasted, and so on," according to Russell.

Stefan would have Scully FedEx a half-baked pizza to

Craving a slice in Ulan Bator? You can get one at Pizza della Casa on Peace Avenue.

Florida each week — not so much for quality control, but because his kids missed the pizza so much.

Stefan would send his daughters north in the summer to work at the pizzeria; they'd wait on customers, or fold pizza boxes.

Alexander E. Stefan died suddenly of kidney failure in 2005. His second wife, Gloria Stefan — the sisters' stepmother — is the current owner. Russell remains an officer in the business. Darlene Scully, Alvin Scully's ex-wife, is now the manager at Kate & Al's.

The key to a Kate & Al's pizza is not the dough but the sauce, according to Samantha Stefan. The recipe is her grandmother's. "Less than 10 people," she says, know the recipe.

The workers at Kate & Al's are busy from the time the pizzeria opens (8 a.m. on Thursdays, Saturdays and Sundays, 10 a.m. on Fridays).

Waits can be an hour or more for a whole pizza, 15 to 20 minutes for a slice. Only 14 pizzas, cooked in cast-iron pans, can be made at a time — six pies in one oven, eight in the other.

Baby food jars on the counter are filled with crushed red pepper, oregano, salt and pepper. The jars became so popular that customers started walking off with them, so Kate & Al's started selling the jars for a dollar each.

Each mound of dough is weighed before being placed in the pan. It must weigh 1 pound, 2 ounces.

"We're not fancy," Russell says. "There's no throwing the dough in the air."

The busiest days at Kate & Al's are Thursdays and Sundays. "Sundays during football season, oh my Lord," Russell says, laughing.

On an average day, Kate & Al's will sell 200 or more pizzas.

"The demand for this pizza," Stefan says, "is unbelievable."

PATSY'S TAVERN & PIZZERIA, PATERSON

PETER GENOVESE

The night the stripper showed up, Gary Barbarulo was working in the cramped kitchen at Patsy's Tavern & Pizzeria, which his grandfather, Pasquale, opened in 1931.

Of course, Barbarulo didn't know she was a stripper. The attractive, fur-coat-clad woman showed up at the backdoor and told Barbarulo she was the wife of regular Paulie Pagnozzi, and there to pick up the pizza they had ordered.

When Barbarulo came back with her pizza, the woman was standing before him, coat open, naked. One of Barbarulo's cooks dropped the plate of spaghetti he was holding. Pagnozzi, former owner of legendary hot dog stand Johnny & Hanges, and a practical joker, had hired the stripper — Barbarulo never did get her name — for the occasion.

But Barbarulo got the last laugh. The next time Pagnozzi stopped at Patsy's, Gary slipped a piece of rug under his pizza. Made for some tough chewing.

Patsy's, in Paterson's Riverside section, was a fixture in this overwhelmingly Italian neighborhood in the 1930s, '40s and '50s. The demographics have changed, but Patsy's hasn't.

The cozy bar in front contains seven stools and three chairs, and the men's room is tucked just inside the front entrance. The handsome back bar appeared in Woody Allen's movie "The Purple Rose of Cairo." The dining room includes four sturdy wooden booths down one side, six down the other, and a faded tile floor that comes in roughly four shades of brown. Three pairs of antlers are mounted on the far wall; Barbarulo and his brother, Steve, are not sure which type of animals they're from. Credit cards are not accepted, and prepare for at least an hour wait for pizza on weekends.

"The dining room looks the same, the decor is the same, the booths are original," Steve Barbarulo says, grinning. "We changed a couple of lights once. We thought about putting in new booths. People went nuts."

Their thin-crust pizza is among the state's best, and the most popular pie here is garbage. No, really. Patsy's garbage pie includes sausage, mushrooms, pepperoni, meatballs and garlic.

"I think our pizzas are pretty damn good," says Steve Barbarulo, 51. "There are some totally terrible pizzas out there."

Gary, 49, makes the pizza "99 percent of the time," according to his older brother. Steve cooks the dinners. Popular dishes include broccoli rabe and eggplant parm. The meatballs and sauce are their grandmother's recipe.

"The sauce is more seasoned than most; we call it Sunday gravy," Steve Barbarulo says.

He and his brother are the only ones who know the pizza dough recipe. It's a secret others have tried, unsuccessfully, to obtain. Ten years ago, they hired a cook who stayed just one week — but asked a lot of questions. Turns out he worked for a pizzeria in a nearby town. He wanted that recipe.

The brothers make the dough daily; whatever is left over they give to their customers, who use it to make bread.

Their father, Ralph Barbarulo, ran the business from 1957 until he died in 1975. Then their mom, Marilyn, took over. Every night, she would sit in the same seat at the bar, greeting customers as they walked into the dining room.

· "Sometimes there'd be a line of people four to five deep wanting to say hello to her," Gary Barbarulo said.

The restaurant/bar is a popular place for high school reunions and special events, and if you want to hang out with the old-timers, Friday night is the night.

"We have people come in religiously every Friday," Steve Barbarulo says. "Some call, 'Steve, I won't be there Friday, tell everybody not to worry.' "

Patsy's — the bar still gets calls around St. Patrick's Day wondering if it serves corned beef sandwiches — may look old-school, but it's not hopelessly mired in the past. The

According to PMQ Pizza Magazine figures for June 2008 - June 2009, there are 2,898 pizza stores in New Jersey, which ranks it eighth among states for total stores. California, with 6,482, has the most, followed by New York, with 5,535; Pennsylvania, 4,540; and Florida, 3,927. New Jersey also ranks eighth in stores per 10,000 people. No. 1 in that category: Massachusetts.

brothers intend to start developing corporate accounts. They have never advertised, but there is a Patsy's Facebook page.

Customers over the years have included Bud Abbott and Paterson native son Lou Costello, actor Danny Aiello and box-ing manager Lou Duva. One unlikely visitor: the thrash metal band Slayer.

"They were just passing through," Gary Barbarulo says.

Each brother started helping in the restaurant — filling salt and pepper shakers — after he turned 8 years old; after age 12, each was allowed to make pizzas. Their father's aunts always worked in the kitchen.

It's still family at Patsy's. Steve's wife, Jill, and Gary's wife, Carol, waitress there.

"We are what we are," Steve Barbarulo says. "We're not fancy, we're not gourmet. It's a nice, friendly family restaurant."

MARUCA'S TOMATO PIES, SEASIDE PARK

PETER GENOVESE

This is a story about pizza and the Seaside boardwalk, but it starts in Trenton, which could be called the birthplace of Jersey pizza.

That may rile North Jerseyans, who look down on all pizza south of, say, Elizabeth.

But consider this: The state's oldest — and nation's second oldest— pizzeria, Papa's Tomato Pies, opened in Trenton's Chambersburg section in 1910.

De Lorenzo's Tomato Pies and DeLorenzo's Pizza, both in Trenton, are among the top pizzerias in the state; I'd put the first De Lo's, on Hudson Street, No. 1 on my list.

Mack and Manco, one of the Shore's best-known pies, had its origins in Trenton, where Anthony and Lena Macaroni operated a pizzeria.

Lena Macaroni was the sister of Anthony "Jake" Maruca, who owned, with his brothers, Maruca's Tomato Pies on South Olden Avenue in Trenton.

Jake's brothers were named Pasquale, Joe and Dominick, but everyone knew them by their nicknames: Patsy, Slippery and Spike.

In 1950, the family opened a Maruca's Tomato Pies on the Seaside Heights boardwalk. Although that location closed almost a decade later, another two were opened, including Maruca's current location, on the Seaside Park boardwalk, in 1955.

There is more to the Trenton, and Mack, and Manco, and Maruca, family pizza trees, but to include all the branches, I'd need an entire book.

"Sixty years," Domenic Maruca says of the family pizzeria's anniversary this year, "is a long time to be in business."

According to "The Dictionary of Italian Food and Drink," the word "pizza" first surfaced around A.D. 1,000 as "picea" or "piza," most likely a reference to the way cooks had to yank the hot pie from the oven.

He and his twin brother, Joseph, sons of Anthony Maruca, run Maruca's Tomato Pies. Joe describes himself as "quiet, fiercely private," while Domenic, the more talkative one, uses the words "diplomatic, personable and accommodating" to describe himself.

Joe is decidedly the more no-nonsense of the two. "You

come in here, you better behave. There's no flex."

Joe runs the store, Domenic manages the property and heads up a sideline business, Domenic's New York Style Pizza at the nearby Beach Bar in Seaside Heights. The pizzas there are not Maruca's knockoffs; there is a pecorino

> Carryout accounts for 36 percent of all pizzeria orders, while delivery accounts for 31 percent.

Romano-topped Brooklyn-style pie, a five-cheese pizza and a broccoli rabe and sausage pie, none available at Maruca's.

At the latter, it's just pizza and soda — no zeppoles, no calzones, no sandwiches.

The two brothers literally grew up on the boardwalk; the family lived in an apartment above the Seaside Heights Maruca's, on the boardwalk at Dupont Avenue.

Domenic remembers not wanting to work at the pizzeria, not in the summer anyway, when there was so much for a kid to do. His dad made him a bet: The day the boardwalk "moved" was the day he could stop working.

Not 10 minutes later, a delivery truck backed into the boardwalk, and it shook; everyone in the store felt it. Domenic, ecstatic, ran out of the store and down the boardwalk, his dad chasing him. Domenic may have won the bet, but he was back working in the pizzeria that day.

Domenic calls the pizzeria "the only neighborhood place on the boardwalk. Family-run business, four generations."

There are longer-established boardwalk businesses, including Kohrs, Berkeley Sweet Shops and Seaside Steak House, but none have the family feel of Maruca's. One of the brothers is always in the store.

They have used the same cheese supplier since 1950, the same cannery for their tomatoes since 1955. You could call these guys old-fashioned. They didn't offer paper plates until 1980; before that, slices were served on napkins.

"We didn't even give out straws until 1987," Joseph says, laughing.

Times, and portion sizes, have changed. In 1950, a large pizza was 14 inches in diameter; now, it's 18. In 1950, a large soda was 12 ounces; now, it's 24.

The flagging economy has shuttered dozens of pizzerias nationwide in recent years, although total U.S. pizza sales dipped just 0.5 percent from June 2008 to June 2009.

How did Maruca's do? "2008 wasn't bad, 2009 wasn't bad," Joseph says. "From where we were two years (ago), it's busier. We're moving forward, getting stronger."

"We make a living," his brother explains. "People say, oh,

they're loaded, they're in the pizza business, they're making $50 million. Are we going to get rich here, move to Vegas, live happily ever after? No."

The brothers say they're not interested in winning any "best pizza" awards.

"You still have to come in here and work every day," Joseph says.

"There's no best pizza out there," Domenic adds. "We're humble. You put out a product you're proud of."

Their Roto-Flex rotating oven has been in operation since 1968. They are big fans of their Doughpro dough press. "This machine does dough better than any human being," Domenic says proudly. "It doesn't get high, it doesn't get drunk, it shows up for work every day."

Like the brothers. Both their parents have died; of the uncles, only Uncle Joe — Slippery — is still alive. Maruca's, celebrating its 60th anniversary, seems poised to celebrate many more.

"Professionally, what's left to accomplish?" Domenic asks.

"Nothing," says his brother, finishing the thought.

"If this was the last interview and we closed tomorrow," Domenic continues, "it's been a good ride."

PIZZA TOWN U.S.A. ELMWOOD PARK

PETER GENOVESE

The gay, brightly colored, attractive Pizza Town U.S.A. . . . has found a ready acceptance among the lovers of good Italian food specialties, and is doing a thriving business.

Since pizza has become so popular in the past few years, it is only natural that this excellent roadside spot should offer that famous snack which has replaced the frankfurter as America's most popular dish. Unfortunately pizza is sold on practically every corner in the country — most of it poor, much of it indifferent in quality . . .

That item appeared in the Paterson Morning Call newspaper on July 25, 1958. A pizzeria named Pizza Town U.S.A. had opened on Route 46 that April, and it wasn't long before cars were backed up on Route 46 waiting to enter the parking lot. Pizza had experienced a nationwide surge in the early 1950s, and everyone wanted to try the new kid on the block.

At Pizza Town U.S.A., a slice of pizza was 15 cents. Whole pizzas went for $1 and $1.50. Calzones were 35 cents, zeppoles six for a quarter.

The pizzeria, which had replaced a Brown Cow ice cream stand, was the creation of one Ray Tomo, a restless, hard-driving man who seemed to open businesses — he would eventually own 50 — as fast as he could think of them.

"Nobody thought we would last," says Tomo, sitting on his patio, glass of Italian white wine in his hand. "My wife's family, the local businesses, no one."

That included his baker, who brought him just three loaves of bread on the pizzeria's first day of operation. The baker figured business would be so slow that's all the bread Tomo would need.

Pizza Town U.S.A. was not adequately heated the first winter, one Tomo remembers only too well.

"It was so cold that first year that if you wiped the counter, ice would come off your fingers," Tomo, now 84, recalls.

His employees would even stuff newspapers down their shirts to keep warm.

But the pizzeria prospered, and eventually there were six Pizza Town U.S.A. locations, in Elmwood Park, Paramus, Pompton Plains, River Edge, Springfield and Staten Island. Pizza Town U.S.A. was built on five Tomo principles: consistency, cleanliness, quality, fair price and "being nice to people." Tomo, born in Harlem, New York, wanted to call his business Pizza City, but there already was a Pizza City on Long Island, so he settled for Pizza Town.

It may come as a surprise to the legions of Pizza Town U.S.A. fans that Tomo, whose daughter, Michelle, and son, Bruce, now run the business, has never made a pizza. Oh, he made the calzones and zeppoles and sandwiches, but never the pizza.

"I never made a pizza in my life," the square-jawed Tomo says. "I can tell you how to make pizza. I told her how to make pizza." He looks at his daughter, sitting opposite him on the patio.

Twenty-five years ago, Michelle Tomo told her dad she wanted to take over the business. At first, he said no. He didn't think she had his ambition, his drive.

"I'll do everything you say, I'll do whatever you want," she told him.

For 15 hours a day over two weeks, Michelle stood next to her dad as he explained the pizza business step by step. Today, Michelle runs Pizza Town U.S.A. with verve and a healthy dose of Jersey attitude.

Michelle, 52, and her twin sister, Lisa, are often behind the counter. To the first-timer, they can come across as no-nonsense, unfriendly, curt.

"They have been around forever, but I don't know how," read a post on yahoo.com. "They are a very rude family. Go in, get your pizza, and leave."

But online posts are more likely to be in this tone: "Any-

Three of the top 10 weeks of pizza consumption occur in January. More pizza is consumed during Super Bowl week than any other week of the year.

one who complains about the service: Funny, they've been around 50 years, I think they know what they are doing. Once you become a regular there, you get personal attention. I don't even have to order, I just walk in and they throw in my usual order. They are human beings who work there, so what if they don't kiss up to you and tell you how happy they are when you order a $1.50 slice of pizza.

I can't stress this enough: If you like pizza, go to Pizza Town!

If you like a college girl to kiss up to you and tell you your family is cute, go to Pizza Hut."

No would argue this: Michelle Tomo is on a first-name basis with her regulars, more than her dad ever was.

"I never got intimate with customers," Ray Tomo says. "I was friendly, but I didn't want to know about your wife, who was in the hospital, or your kids. I give you cleanliness, I give you a good product, I don't have to know you, you don't have to know me."

Good luck trying to convince Pizza Town U.S.A.'s founder that pizza today is better than pizza in the old days.

"You cannot compare the pizza now with the pizza of

years ago," he says. "No way. The ingredients were different, the tomatoes were fresher, the cheese was better."

He mourns the time when business deals could be done on a man's word. In 1958, Tomo, short on cash, asked his sign- maker if he could pay for the Uncle Sam sign in six months. Fine, the sign-maker said.

"You know what a handshake deal was back then," Tomo grumbles. "The handshake is gone. America is no longer a handshake country."

Much of his brassiness has rubbed off on Michelle, who works 12-hour shifts on Tuesdays, Thursdays, Fridays and Sundays. She claims, among other things, that Pizza Town U.S.A. was the first pizzeria in the state to offer slices, and the first to sell zeppoles. It became a running joke on the Pizza Patrol: What else would she claim among the pizzeria's innovations? Cheese? Running water?

But if Michelle is a charter member of the P.T. Barnum School of Pizza Hyperbole, there's little doubt who is the founder.

"We were the first (pizzeria) on 46," Ray Tomo proclaims. "The first to offer pizza on any highway."

Whatever the case, Pizza Town U.S.A. — call it neon-lit circus tent-turned pizzeria — is one of the state's most color-ful pizza hangouts. The fluorescent-lit interior, with picnic benches, may remind one of a 1950s drive-in movie snack bar. "This window for pizza," announces one sign, "this win-dow for submarines and drinks," reads another.

The family owns another pizzeria — the Pizza Shoppe in Ocean Grove, which sells 9-inch pies only, no slices.

Ray Tomo liked Ocean Grove so much, he bought the former Aurora Hotel and turned it into the family's summer retreat, 24 rooms and all.

He insists his daughter drop off a Pizza Town U.S.A. pie at his house every so often so he can check on the ingredi-ents and quality. Once, the pizza wasn't saucy enough; he later discovered his brother had switched from a 16-ounce sauce ladle to a 14-ounce ladle. Less sauce was getting on the pizza.

"Failure," Pizza Town U.S.A.'s founder says philosophi-cally, "will follow you quicker than success."

TONY'S BALTIMORE GRILL, ATLANTIC CITY

PETER GENOVESE

Wait. Tony's Baltimore Grill, the legendary Atlantic City restaurant/bar, never once had a grill? What's up with that, Cheryll Huffnagle?

"Honey," she says, sweetly, "it was people from Baltimore, don't look at me."

The 62-year-old Huffnagle is co-owner of Tony's, which has remained resolutely old-school over the years while a casino city started, grew and towered over it.

The Naugahyde booths in the spacious dining room are the original ones from the restaurant's opening day, on April 1, 1966. The familiar white stucco exterior, red awning and window trim, and large outdoor sign advertising "Tony's Baltimore Grill. Spaghetti. Pizza" are Atlantic City landmarks.

The wall jukeboxes (seven plays for a dollar) still work; the bar is open 24 hours, and the kitchen is open till 3 a.m. every day except Thanksgiving and Christmas, when Tony's Baltimore Grill is closed.

There are no burgers or steaks on the menu (remember, no grill), although you can get spaghetti, seafood, sandwiches and that not-so-classic dish, three meatballs and french fries.

And thin-crust pizza, which is the main reason you go to Tony's Baltimore Grill anyway. The most pizzas ever made in one day here: 789.

"Was it a special day?" I ask.

"Yeah," Huffnagle wisecracks, "we were busy."

Call Tony's a seaside Patsy's of Paterson: a neighborhood bar steeped in history and tradition, a stubbornly old-timey joint that nevertheless manages to attract and enchant a younger clientele.

"I'll give you the short history," says Huffnagle, beginning a conversation that lasts two-plus hours. "In the 1920s, people from Baltimore opened a place on Connecticut and Atlantic avenues, uptown, called the Baltimore Grill. Tiny place, sat maybe 30 people, had a little bar."

John Tarsitiano bought the bar/restaurant in the 1930s, then sold it to his brother, Tony, hence Tony's Baltimore Grill.

In the 1960s, urban renewal led to Tony's moving across the street. Then Ricky Rich, Cheryll's father, entered the picture. Rich, then owner of Ricky's Hialeah Club, became business partners with Tony Tarsitiano. In 1966, they opened Tony's Baltimore Grill in the former Paddy McGahn's Piano Bar, at the corner of Atlantic and Iowa avenues, where Tony's is today.

"We tore out walls here, tore out walls there," says Huffnagel, taking in the expansive dining room. "The paneling here is 44 years old. African rosewood, hugely expensive at the time."

Her father and Tony Tarsitiano have since died; Huffnagle and Janet Rich Esposito, her dad's third wife, own 50 percent of the business, while Michael Tarsitiano, Tony's only son, owns the other half.

There are five booths in the bar and 16 in the dining room. The tile floor is on its fifth incarnation, having gone from beige and brown to black and beige to three variations of black and red.

The prices have changed over the years, but not drastically. In the early 1970s, a draft beer cost 40 cents, spaghetti and meatballs, $2.70, a cheese pizza, $2.85, while a Scotch was $1.10 and "better Scotches," $1.35.

By 1985, draft beer cost 70 cents and a cheese pizza, $3.50. Today, a draft beer is $1.50 or more, and a cheese pizza is $8.60.

There are 65 employees, including longtime managers Fred Pugh and Dave Bowen. Huffnagle and Esposito manage the restaurant side, while Michael Tarsitiano runs the bar. It may look like an old man's bar, with wooden booths and coat racks, but it's a surprisingly well-stocked one; 30 kinds of bottled beer, from Bud to Sierra Nevada and Hoegaarden, are available.

The most popular pizzas are the plain and the special, with mushrooms and sausage. "You don't come here for a turkey club," Huffnagle says, even though there is one on the menu.

The most striking evidence of the pizza's popularity: the least amount of pizzas ever sold was 56 — in a snowstorm.

When it comes time to add an item to the menu, Huffnagle does the taste-testing. She tried 15 to 20 kinds of bacon before selecting one for the BLT. She sampled 28 kinds of chicken before finding one suitable for Tony's buffalo wings.

> Mike Massimino, one of five astronauts on the Atlantis space mission, on pizza, the one thing they couldn't eat, or make, in space: "It is impossible in space; we don't have it, and someone would get a Nobel Prize if they can figure out how to get pizza in space."

Not a fun job, especially when you hate chicken, as she does.

But she loves mystery novels, especially those involving serial killers, and takes her Kindle to the gym.

"I'm disgustingly honest," Tony's co-owner says. "What you see is what you get. I have no pretense. I try to be respectful to my elders."

There are legions of loyal fans, including a local judge who always orders "the same stinking thing" — Huffnagle says this affectionately — for lunch. The antipasto.

"He can tell you if there are three carrots short," she says, smiling.

You can take your pizza home in a pan if you don't want to subject it to a box. The deposits is $1.75 per pan; customers have been known to return 20 or more pans at a time to get their deposit back.

The pizza boxes are minimalist works of art — black lettering on white background, reminiscent of old-time newsreels.

The same suppliers have been used for years — sausage from Delaware Market in Ventnor, bread from A. Rando and Formica Brothers bakeries.

There may be major change on this old-school hangout's horizon: credit cards, an earthshaking move for a place that has never accepted them. But don't worry, Tony's fans, everything else will remain the same. As long as Huffnagle is around, anyway.

"I love coming in here," she says. "If I come in and it's a disaster in here, I still love coming in. I don't golf, I don't fish, what the heck else would I do?"

THE MUNCH PHOTO ALBUM

How could you possibly capture the nonstop doughy drama that was the Pizza Patrol?

You could, if you had photographers documenting their every bite.

Munchmobile photographer Tim Farrell joined us on two of the 51 trips. And then there was Pete Genovese, snapping away with his duct-taped point-and-shoot camera. You should be able to tell which are Tim's photos and which are Pete's in the following pages.

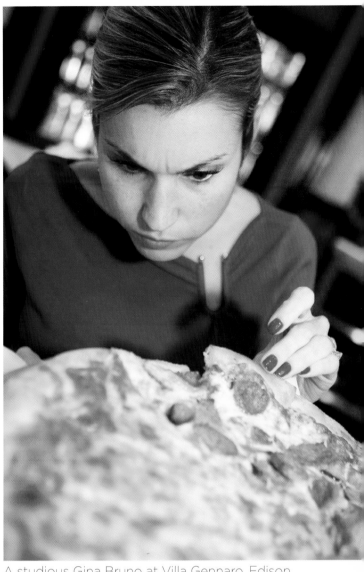

A studious Gina Bruno at Villa Gennaro, Edison

Best margherita pizza: La Rustique Cafe, Jersey City

Al Santillo, Santillo's Brick Oven Pizza, Elizabeth

Al Santillo, Santillo's Brick Oven Pizza, Elizabeth

Al Santillo, Santillo's Brick Oven Pizza, Elizabeth

Best pizza box: Pizza Time, Avenel

Best Sicilian: Mr. Bruno's, Lyndhurst

Deep-dish margherita, Antonio's, Metuchen

Cheesy slice, Three Brothers from Italy, Seaside Heights

Renee Teernstra, Larry and Joe's, Jersey City

Renee Teernstra, Larry and Joe's, Jersey City

Lou Yandoli, Grandma's Pizza truck, Jersey City

Stan's Chitch's sign, Bound Brook

The Big Dog, Bayonne

Scott Wiener, Benny Tudino's, Hoboken

Help yourself. Miller's Tavern, Annandale

Al Windrem chows down.

Scott Wiener takes measure of a pie.

3 Brothers from Italy, Ocean City

What a deal. Joe's Pizza & Pasta, Union

Donna's, Palisades Park

Antonino's, Blackwood

Gina Bruno, Seaside boardwalk

Marty Schneider outside Emma's Brick Oven, Cranford

Allie DeLucia, DeLucia's, Raritan Borough

Alfred Rossino, Alfred's Tomato Pie, Blackwood

Pizza Patrol, Seaside boardwalk

Charles Wilson and Gezim Drishti, La Rustique Cafe, Jersey City

Leftover pizza, Star-Ledger newsroom

Giuseppe Ali, La Sicilia, Belleville

Anthony Livreri, Mr. Bruno's, Lyndhurst

Straight to the point

Slice and a dog, Jersey City

Sign, DeLucia's, Raritan Borough

Gary Amico, De Lorenzo's, Hudson Street, Trenton

Pete Genovese, Carmine's Pizza Factory, Jersey City

Sam's Palace Pizza, Wildwood

Balsamo's, Lindenwold

Gina Bruno, Passariello's, Moorestown

OUR FAVORITE PIZZAS

You've read about the grand prize winners of our Best Pizza in New Jersey contest. So what were the favorite pizzas of each of our Pizza Patrol members? Our picks were all over the map, style-wise and geographically. Below, we pick our personal Top Ten and explain why.

GINA BRUNO

1. Sausage, **De Lorenzo's Tomato Pies**, Hudson Street, Trenton. The oversized free-formed crumbles of sausage were packed with intense flavor. The tart tomatoes partnered great with the meat, with just the right amount of seasonings.

2. Margherita, **La Rustique Cafe**, Jersey City. Each layer was dynamite. The crust had texture and crunch, the sauce was simple yet quite notable, and the cheese was fresh, soft and tremendously creamy.

3. Margherita, **Palermo's Ristorante Italiano & Pizzeria**, Bordentown. Pizza was admirable from every angle. The thin crust was distinct enough to notice, the tomato chunks popped with flavor with each bite, and, finally, the cheese was skillfully placed.

4. Palermo, **La Sicilia**, Belleville. The sauce was the highlight; well seasoned and distinct, it tasted as if it were simmered all day. Crust was crispy: the perfect platform for the sauce.

5. Plain, **Fratelli's Restaurant Pizzeria**, Middletown. The sauce was phenomenal; by itself, it could have been equally enjoyed. The brick oven cooked it well while adding a rustic and authentic flavor.

6. Meatball, **Pizzaland**, North Arlington. Meatballs were seasoned wonderfully and became incredibly crispy after cooking. The generous amount of cheese accentuated the meatball's flavor and made for a winning pair.

7. Deep-dish margherita, **Antonio's Brick Oven Pizza**, Metuchen. Another winner with a generous amount of quality sauce. The crust was fried-like and delivered flavor all in itself. Also excellent were the balance and distinctiveness of textures throughout.

8. Sicilian, **Joe's Pizza & Pasta**, Union. Fried-like, crispy and crunchy crust that underlied a moist and chewy dough. Burnt cheese that bubbled all over made for a great Sicilian slice.

9. Sliced tomato, **Miller's Tavern**, Annandale. The plain tomatoes were just sliced and laid on top of a decent thin crust pizza yet added such flavor. It was almost as if the tomato flavor seeped through the cheese and crust.

10. Grandma, **Forte Pizzeria & Ristorante**, Randolph. The pie was hand-crafted, simple and delicious. Fresh-from-the-garden taste: chunks of tomatoes, ripped-up basil pieces, cheese spread throughout, with just a drizzle of olive oil.

PETER GENOVESE

1. Margherita, **Palermo's Ristorante Italiano & Pizzeria**, Bordentown. At a pizzeria squeezed into a dreary stretch of Route 206 south in Bordentown, I found pizza nirvana. Crunchy crust, good sauce and excellent mozzarella added up to one perfect pizza. Life-changing experience? Maybe not. A pizza epiphany? Yes.

2. Deep-dish margherita, **Antonio's Brick Oven Pizza**, Metuchen. This came as a sidewalk flavor blast on a warm summer day. A model margherita, loaded with fresh tomatoey goodness.

3. Sausage, **De Lorenzo's Tomato Pies**, Hudson Street, Trenton. I could have easily picked the clam pizza here or at DeLorenzo's on

Hamilton Avenue. Great pizza, timeless surroundings, I should just move there and live in a row house down the street.

4. Marinara, **Luna Restaurant**, Three Bridges. This one came early on in our pizza journey, and the memory of that near-perfect combination of crisp and chew stayed with me all summer.

5. Sausage, **Luigi's Famous Pizza**, Ocean Township. Luigi's is sequestered in a neighborhood of warehouses and office buildings; you'll wonder if you have the right address. One bite of the sausage pie and you'll know you've arrived at pizza heaven.

6. Plain, **Romeo Pizzeria**, Orange. There were better pizzas and better sauces and so on. But none of the 1,000-plus crusts were more enjoyable than Romeo's crust; it's huge and puffy, like eating the thickest bread ever. I could put butter on it, I could put sauce on it, I could put anything on it.

7. White, **Mack and Manco**, Ocean City. Glistening with oily goodness, the white pie at this boardwalk legend achieves a simplicity and harmony many strive for, but few reach.

8. Margherita, **La Rustique Cafe**, Jersey City. I still remember biting into this pizza, standing on the sidewalk on a warm summer night. I knew then we had a winner in our best margherita category.

9. Roasted red peppers, mozzarella and tomatoes, **Rocco's Pizzeria**, Avenel. It's not on the menu, and doesn't really have a name, so ask for it. A specialty pizza that doesn't care to be fancy, just good.

10. Sicilian, **Mr. Bruno's**, Lyndhurst. It's all about the sauce here; it's made the old-fashioned way, with the bottles boiled in water. Makes nearly all other Sicilians around the state look lame.

SCOTT WIENER

1. Clam, **De Lorenzo's Tomato Pies**, Hudson Street, Trenton. I am blown away by this flavor explosion, so rough and rugged you may need to fasten your seat belt before eating.

2. Margherita, **Michael's Pizzeria & Restaurant**, West Caldwell. This is the blue collar margherita pizza, for those who feel too dainty when basil lands on their slice. Don't worry, the basil is surrounded by enough rich cheese and fruity olive oil to convert you to margherita-ism.

3. Sicilian, **Bruno's**, Clifton. I've never had a crust with this much personality. It's big and fluffy, not to mention delicious. This pizza is the answer to all your boring Sicilian pizza woes.

4. Margherita, **La Rustique Cafe**, Jersey City. Zesty pizza margherita is hard to find, but this one kicks you in the pants with its robust sauce and milky fresh mozzarella combo. It's both classic and unique at the same time, a real "best of both worlds" situation.

5. Palermo, **La Sicilia**, Belleville. You'll forget how much you like cheese when you taste this tomato-centric miracle. It's a celebration of garlic- and herb-infused sauce held in place by a thin square crust that commands respect with its simplicity.

6. Margherita, **Palermo's Ristorante Italiano & Pizzeria**, Bordentown. This margherita pizza is the perfect balance of fruity tomato,

sweet basil and milky mozzarella. All of the flavors combine with a touch of olive oil, almost letting you forget how light and airy the crust feels underneath all that elegance.

7. 1964 pizza, **Santillo's Brick Oven Pizza**, Elizabeth. This pie looks plain-Jane but packs a flavor punch with olive oil richness and creamy mozzarella cheese. The classic Santillo's crust lays a perfect foundation upon which this house of flavor is built.

8. Sicilian, **Mr. Bruno's**, Lyndhurst. I love the slightly tart tomato on top of a thin layer of mozzarella. This pie serves as a reminder that not all Sicilian pizza has to be thick squares of bread slathered with goopy cheese.

9. Plain, **Star Tavern**, Orange. For classic thin-crust (but not cracker) pizza, look no further than Star Tavern. It has both bite and tenderness at the same time, with a tight sauce-to-cheese ratio that makes you feel right at home.

10. Sausage, **Sun-Ray Pizza**, Little Falls. The sausage on this pizza is so gutsy, you'll find yourself picking it off your friend's slice. Do not resist.

AL WINDREM

1. Sausage, **De Lorenzo's Tomato Pies**, Hudson Street, Trenton. The chunky tomatoes, perfect sausage (out of casing) and perfect char from a gas oven make the tomato pies at this Trenton mainstay the best pizza I have ever put in my mouth.

2. Plain, **DeLucia's Brick Oven Pizza**, Raritan Borough. This is what pizza should taste like. It is cooked perfect every single time with a nice crisp crust.

3. Palermo, **La Sicilia**, Belleville. I feel that if this style of pizza was first brought to the United States, then pizza as we know it today would be different.

4. Plain, **Star Tavern**, Orange. Super-thin, greasy and cooked well. What else do I need to say?

5. 1964 pizza, **Santillo's Brick Oven Pizza**, Elizabeth. Imported Romano and extra-virgin olive oil — goodness, this pizza is great. Everyone must experience for themselves what a pizza from Santillo's is like.

6. Margherita, **La Rustique Cafe**, Jersey City. Quality is first and foremost at this Jersey City gem. San Marzano tomatoes, fresh "mozz" made on location. Quality equals taste.

7. Sausage, **Luna Restaurant**, Three Bridges. This place deserves to be in the conversation when talking about the best New Jersey has to offer.

8. **Grandma's Pizza truck**, Jersey City. Loved the style of pizza this truck produced. I still can't believe something that good came out of a truck!

9. Plain, **Spirito's**, Elizabeth. Things are just right at this Elizabeth hot spot. Pizza at Spirito's is not trying to show off, but it does.

10. Bruschetta, **Lovey's Pizza & Grill**, Morris Plains. At one point, I would have said this is not even pizza. The fresh-out-of-the-garden taste was tremendous, and helped change how I look at pizza today.

THE WORST PIZZA WE ATE

With the good, comes the bad. And the real bad. Here are the worst pizzas we had. The names of the pizzerias have been withheld to protect those guilty of seriously bad taste.

The crust was blackened, paper-thin and tasted like outdated flour. Its edges were dry, burnt and tasted like something that shouldn't be eaten — perhaps cardboard. On top was a sauce that was terribly acidic and needed seasoning. Cheese? Nothing even close was found. It had no stability, so when I tried to eat it, it turned to mush almost instantaneously.

PETER GENOVESE

It looked like something from a bad 1950s science-fiction movie, glowing a sickly yellow under the fluorescent lights. The crust tasted like a cheap pizza box, and the cheese had the consistency of Play-Doh. Call it the Blob, and it was far more menacing than anything Steve McQueen had to face.

SCOTT WIENER

If it looks like a paper plate covered with red finger paint, is it really a pizza? If it cracks like a shattered mirror when you cut it, is it really a pizza? If it falls apart when you try to pick it up, is it really a pizza? If the pasty, crimson surface-sludge makes you flash back to the time someone dared you to drink their lunchtime science project in the third grade, is it really a pizza? Apparently someone thinks so, but I'd rather pass.

AL WINDREM

For me, there is no question who had the worst pizza. First, picture a pizza in your head. Now completely forget what you think one looks like. A metal disk came out of a kitchen with what looked like tomato soup poured on it. Under the alleged tomato soup was a somewhat white, thin layer of an instant-foam type creation. Without a doubt, this was the worst thing I ate while I was on the Pizza Patrol, and maybe ever. And this is coming from a man who, prior to this experience, lived by the words, "Even bad pizza is good."

PETER GENOVESE'S BEST-OF LISTS

Peter Genovese's
Best-Of Lists

There were plenty of bests - and worsts - in our pizza year. You'll find my absolute favorite pizza in the chapter titled Our Favorite Pizzas. But what about such categories as best waitress, favorite pizza hangouts, best pizza towns, and strangest moment of our six-month adventure? All that and more can be found in the following pages.

Favorite crust: Romeo's, Orange

Best pizza cheese: Semolina, Millburn

Most memorable waitresses: Gina Chiafullo, Tony's Famous Tomato Pies, Long Branch; Michelle Ruvo, Bruno's, Clifton

Best pizza we ate in the van: Tie between Gia Nina's, Woodbury, and Cosimo's, Bloomfield

Most overrated pizza: Famous Ray's Pizza of New York, Verona: May be famous on the other side of the river, but not here.

Best sign: "For better service, do not carry on conversations with the employees." (Donna's Pizza, Palisades Park)

Best pizzeria name: Pizza And, Avenel

Most awkward pizzeria name: Brooklyn's Coal Burning Brick Oven Pizzeria (Hackensack)

Best lunch truck pizza: Grandma's, Jersey City (okay, it was the only lunch truck pizza we tried, but I can't imagine any truck doing it better).

Cutest pizzeria: Luna, Three Bridges

Most popular first name among pizzerias visited: Luigi's (four-way tie for second among Tony, Joe, Mario and Bruno)

Saltiest pizza in New Jersey: The Famous and Original King of Pizza, Cherry Hill

Cheesiest pizza: Three Brothers from Italy, Seaside Park

Biggest pizza in New Jersey: Benny Tudino's, Hoboken, at 30 inches in diameter

"World's" Largest Pizza: 3 Brothers from Italy, Ocean City, at 26 inches in diameter. How the world's largest pizza is smaller than New Jersey's largest pizza, I have no idea.

Best non-pizza item consumed on Pizza Patrol duty: Old-fashioned zeppoles, Nonna's, Florham Park; barbecue sauce, Old World Pizza, Princeton; pasta fagioli, Giovanni's Place, Butler; homemade meatballs, Tanolla's Pizza, Brielle.

Toughest way to get a free pizza: Buy 30 pizzas, get one free at Joe's Pizza & Pasta, Union, Union County

Best offer for big eaters: Eat one 26-inch pizza in one hour at 3 Brothers from Italy in Ocean City, get 10 free pizzas. Eat one pizza in 45 minutes, get 25 free. Eat one pizza in 15 minutes, get 100 free.

One town where there's no great pizza: Cape May

Most colorful characters: Alfred Rossino, Alfred's Tomato Pie, Blackwood; Al Santillo, Santillo's Brick Oven Pizza, Elizabeth

Strangest moment in our six-month pizza journey: When the guy behind the counter at Luigi's Famous Pizza in Hazlet removed the coupons from a menu before handing it over, saying they were for "customers." Guess we weren't.

Yes, I know Essex has the greatest concentration of pizzerias in New Jersey, and yes, I know people are passionate about Hoboken, Bayonne and other Hudson County pizza, and yes, I know all about pizza down the Shore — heck, I live there.

But the state's top pizza county is home to the state capital. In Mercer, you have the three DeLorenzo's — two in Trenton, one in Robbinsville — plus Papa's (only the second oldest pizzeria in the country) and such noteworthy pizzerias as Conte's in Princeton, Nomad in Hopewell and Mamma Rosa's in Hamilton.

1. **Mercer:** DeLo's, DeLo's, DeLo's — end of DeBate.
2. **Monmouth:** Pizza legends Federici's, Pete and Elda's, and Vic's, plus first-rate pizzerias such as Luigi's in Ocean, Denino's in Aberdeen, Luigi's in Lincroft; and Vesuvio in Belmar.
3. **Union:** N.J. Pizza Hall of Famers Santillo's and Spirito's head a distinguished list that also includes Nancy's Townehouse in Rahway, Joe's Pizza & Pasta in Union, Buona Pizza in Westfield, Mario's Tutto Bene in Union and Emma's Brick Oven in Cranford.
4. **Essex:** Best Pizza in New Jersey winners La Sicilia in Belleville and the Star Tavern in Orange, plus the Starlite in West Orange, Queen Margherita Trattoria in Nutley, Cosimo's in Bloomfield and Arturo's in Maplewood, among others.
5. **Passaic:** Neighborhood institutions Patsy's in Paterson and Mario's in Clifton, plus Bruno's in Clifton, Sun-Ray in Little Falls and Taste of Tuscany in Clifton.

TOP PIZZA TOWNS

1. **Trenton:** The two DeLorenzo's, and Papa's, for starters.
2. **Elizabeth:** Pizza heavyweights Santillo's and Spirito's, plus a host of lesser-known joints.
3. **Nutley:** In no other town is the competition, and war of words, fiercer.
4. **Hoboken:** Probably more pizzerias per square mile than any other town in New Jersey. Not saying they're any good, just that they're there.
5. **Clifton:** Bruno's and Mario's lead the list.
6. **Somerville:** Pizza Main Street, U.S.A.

These are not my favorite or best pizzerias; they're the pizzerias — or restaurants serving pizza — that are the most fun to hang out in.

Center Bar, Port Reading: Cozy neighborhood bar with jumbo pickled eggs and "chicken in a garden," whatever that is, on the menu. The BLT pizza may sound weird, but, actually, it's pretty good if you're in a tired-of-the-same-old pizza state of mind. You may drive right past the place the first time, like we did; there's no sign outside.

Chrone's Pizza, Mountainside: Small friendly neighborhood bar, the kind they just don't make anymore. We were there barely five minutes and people were telling us all about the good pizza and food places in the area — besides Chrone's, of course.

Larry & Joe's Pizza Restaurant, Jersey City: Lively pizza hole-in-the-wall popular with students from Dickinson High School, just down the street, plus downtown workers, sheriff's officers and others. And it delivers a good greasy slice.

Lido Restaurant, Hackensack: One of the more atmospheric pizzerias/restaurants in the state, with its padded booths, tile floors, white lights and a cranky old jukebox. Cash-only, too, just like the old times.

Log Cabin Inn, Columbia: Mounted antlers, funhouse-tilted floor, good pizza. Linda DeLuca, the pizza-maker, works in a room adjoining the restaurant. There's a counter inside, but if it's nice outside, take your pizza to the deck. The Delaware River is right across the street.

Miller's Tavern, Annandale: Confession: I've visited Miller's more times in the last two years than in the seven years I lived in Clinton, just down the road. Miller's is roadhouse, biker bar, pizzeria and juke joint all rolled into one. With one of the better thin-crusts in the state.

Pizza Town U.S.A., Elmwood Park: Fluorescent-lit roadside stand with an Uncle Sam-like character on the sign and red white and blue awning. Open since 1958, and the sisters who run it alone are worth the trip. The pizza is solid, nothing special, but a late-night visit to Pizza Town U.S.A. is an essential Jersey experience.

Stan's Chitch's Cafe, Bound Brook: Tile floors, high-backed chairs, striped wallpaper. It can only be Stan's Chitch's, the most color-fully-named pizzeria in Jersey. You've got to love a place where they use Gerber baby food jars for the salt and oregano. I wasn't as crazy about the meatball pizza as the others; the next great meatball pizza I eat will be the first great meatball pizza I eat.

Starting Point Bar & Grill, Bayonne: Ever wanted to see the Bayonne Bridge up close and personal? Park in front of the Starting Point; you can almost touch it. Love the classic rock albums on the wall — Cream, Iron Butterfly, Black Sabbath and many more. The pizza could be better, though.

Vesuvio Restaurant and Pizzeria, Belmar: No credit cards or checks accepted, a turquoise-and-beige color scheme and waitresses with serious Jersey attitude. Must be Vesuvio, the most lovably eccentric pizza joint we visited, and that's saying something. The menu features "famous" white pizza, "famous" cheesecake and that perennial favorite, "three meatballs and fries." Spaghetti cooked to order? That costs extra. The pizza? Pretty darn good.

BEST LINES OF OUR PIZZA SUMMER
(AND FALL AND WINTER)

"A newsroom pie" (Al Windrem, more than once).

"Come out cheese, wherever you are." (Gina Bruno, Natale's Italian Restaurant and Pizza, Clinton Township).

"The freakin' Munchmobile!" (Rosemarie Pendergast, outside Pizza Como, Clinton).

"What's that?" asked PP member Marty Schneider, pointing to the pizza at Brothers in Red Bank. "Cheese," Alex Windrem cracked.

"A snooze-fest" (Joan Dwyer, Luke's Pizza, Wall).

"Lovely and goopy" (Marty Schneider, Dicola's Pizza, Washington, Warren County).

"I could take a nap under this cheese blanket." (Scott Wiener, Pompei Pizza, Bayonne).

"It's Pies Off, not Pies On." (Joan Dwyer, Pies On, Toms River).

"It's like a Corvair — unsafe at any speed." (Al Windrem of the margherita pizza at Pizza King, Atlantic City).

"The dark cloud of garlic blocked out the tomato sun." (Scott Wiener, Mona Lisa Pizzeria Ristorante, Bayonne).

"Goopy and gooey and tasty" (Marty Schneider of the plain at DeLorenzo's, Hamilton Avenue, Trenton).

"I wouldn't call it a meatball but a spiced meat concoction." (Scott Wiener of the meatball pizza at Carmen's/Pete and Elda's, Neptune).

"A rockin' like Dokken pie" (Joan Dwyer of the margherita at A Mano, Ridgewood).

"You meet this Grandpa in an alley, you're going down." (Al Windrem of the peppery Grandpa pizza at Frank's Pizzeria & Restaurant, Newark).

"I better write an apology letter to my stomach." (Scott Wiener of the sausage pizza at Vincent's Pizzeria & Restaurant, Cliffside Park)

"Been there done that, got the photos back from Walgreens" (Marty Schneider of the Sicilian at Napoli, Jamesburg)

"We just pulled into Bland Central Station." (Scott Wiener of the Grandma at Krispy Pizza, Old Bridge)

"Has a nice jaunty relationship with the mouth" (Marty Schneider of the Sicilian at Papa Luigi Restaurant & Pizzeria, Carmel)

"I wonder what part of Italy this kitchen is from so I won't have to go there." (Gina Bruno at Italian Kitchen, Pennsville)

THE ONLY FUNNY LINES PETE GENOVESE WROTE ALL YEAR

"Papa may have been a rolling stone, but the one at Papa Vito Restaurant & Pizzeria (Rahway) needs help with his pizza-making."

"When the sausage looks like hamster food, it's time to ask yourself some basic questions, like 'Why are we eating this stuff?' " (after Week 16)

"The Munchmobile driver liked the shredded steak pie, but no one else did. The Munchmobile driver is used to this." (JoJo's Tavern, Hamilton)

"We were assured the meatballs at Capri Pizza (Kenilworth) are homemade. If so, they need to board up that house."

THE PIZZA DIRECTORY

ATLANTIC

Hammonton seems an unlikely pizza destination. New Jersey's blueberry capital is home to a dozen pizzerias, either in town or along the White Horse Pike (Route 30). The "tomato pie" — much more tomatoey than a standard pizza, and often square, like a Sicilian, is a Hammonton staple. A good one can be found at **BROTHER'S PIZZA** (80 S. White Horse Pike, Hammonton; 609-567-1080). The tomato pie boasts a fine, firm crust. The plain pizza, however, is seriously oily/greasy, and the sausage devoid of taste.

BRUNI'S PIZZERIA, (303 12th St., Hammonton; 609-561-5310). Pale green walls, American flag, no credit cards, a dozen tables inside, one outside. Bruni's, which opened in 1956, exudes small town, low-key tradition and timeliness. The plain pizza is good and tomatoey as per Hammonton tradition. Creamy cheese, but brittle crust. The "thick crust white," enlivened by garlic, came as a chewy surprise.

Chunky sausage is almost always a sign of a good sausage pie; that holds at **MARCELLO'S FAMILY RESTAURANT** (225 Bellevue Ave., Hammonton; 609-704-1901). You'll wish for more sauce on the plain, though. The tomato pie is nice and crusty. We hit this place late at night, and they delivered in the taste department.

MAURIZIO'S PIZZERIA & ITALIAN GRILLE, (4215 Black Horse Pike (Route 40), Hamilton; 609-645-0028). I practically jumped for joy when I spotted chunks of sausage, not the ubiquitous South Jersey pellet variety, on the pizza here. Hey, you take your pizza victories where you can get them. Nice sweet sauce on the plain, but the crust is soft and bland-tasting. Same story with the Grandma: good sauce, subpar crust.

The best thing you can say about **PIZZA KING** (2316 Atlantic Ave., Atlantic City; 609-340-8000) is that the wings are better than the pies. The plain and sausage pizzas are simply dreadful. The margherita is barely edible. I liked Pizza Patrol member Al Windrem's line — "It's like a Corvair — unsafe at any speed." Recommended only for those down to their last dollar or two after a night on the slot machines. And even if you were down to your last dollar, it would be better spent elsewhere.

And if you're in AC, there's only one pizza destination anyway, the amazing **TONY'S BALTIMORE GRILL** (2800 Atlantic Ave., Atlantic City; 609-345-5766). The eerily red-lit wooden-booth bar — call it "Twin Peaks" by the sea — is a reminder of a vanishing AC. When we tried to order a pizza for our party of seven, split between the bar and a booth, we were told that was not allowed. Not the ordering from the bar or booth, the splitting-of-party part, even though we were all next to each other. The plain pizza is a simple, no-nonsense delight, like the bar itself. The rest of the Patrol liked the meatball pizza; I didn't, finding the meatballs on a par with the ones you find in canned soup. The pizza boxes — with black-and-white lettering, like a 1940s newsreel — are among the most distinctive anywhere. One of my favorite pizza hangouts of the year.

VILLA FAZZOLARI/TERRAZZA PIZZERIA, (821 Harding Highway (Route 40), Buena Vista; 856-697-7107). Faux Italian villa-look restaurant out front, lively bar/patio area out back. This is where the locals spend their Sunday afternoon, if my visit was any indication. The plain pizza boasted a puffy, crispy crust, but sauce is at a minimum, and it's nothing special anyway. The bruschetta pizza is loaded with tomatoes — and even more cheese; the commendable crust can't save it.

BERGEN

One of Bergen County's most heralded, and upscale, pizza destinations, **A MANO** (24 Franklin Ave., Ridgewood; 201-493-2000), was founded with the purpose "of bringing authentic pizza Napoletana to the USA," according to the menu. The menu also includes antipasti, salads, pasta and calzones (high-end, indeed; the latter cost $13.99 and up). The wood-burning ovens are maintained at a "blistering" 1,000 degrees. The A mano pizza — with buffalo mozzarella, cherry tomatoes, prosciutto di parma, arugula and shaved grand cru cheese — is full of flavor, but difficult to handle. The margherita is simpler, and better. Queen Margherita in Nutley does a similar pizza; sample both and judge for yourself.

Pizza oven aficionados — we know you're out there — will undoubtedly know all the ins and outs of the Fish 75 rotating oven, the one used at **ANGELO'S PIZZERIA & RESTAURANT** (62 W. Pleasant Ave., Maywood; 201-843-5033). I get the rotating part, but why the word "fish" is attached to a pizza oven is beyond me. Good plain pizza, but could have used more sauce. The sausage could have used a flavor infusion. The bruschetta is worthy of your consideration, though. And if you're in tiny Maywood, be sure to stop at Seafood Gourmet, also on W. Pleasant Avenue, with good soups and seafood dishes.

ARLINGTON PIZZA (25 Schuyler Ave., North Arlington; 201-997-8373) came as a nice surprise. The lively lunchtime crowd should have tipped us off. The plain pizza is mondo-slippery but enjoyable. The sausage pizza is better than average, and I've had a lot of average, and worse, sausage pizza. The Sicilian pizza boasts a solid crust, but it tastes more like bread than pizza.

It was the story of our summer, and fall, and winter — the Pizza Patrol hitting dozens of pizzerias that did one pizza well and another not so well. Such is the case at **BELLA CAMPANIA** (456 Broadway, Hillsdale; 201-666-7700). The plain and sausage pies are decent. "Screaming for flavor" is how Pizza Patrol member Gina Bruno described the plain. But the margherita is a marvel. Scott Wiener praised its "fresh and sweet" flavor and "milky" mozzarella.

Award for most awkward pizzeria name in New Jersey? That goes to **BROOKLYN'S COAL BURNING BRICK OVEN PIZZERIA** (161 Hackensack Ave., Hackensack; 201-342-2727). The restaurant's history, recounted on the menu, somehow involves Mt. Vesuvius and a Roman emperor. We almost expected them to work the Renaissance, the nuclear arms race and global warming in there somehow. But the pizza stands out. The half plain/half sausage boasted a raised puffy crust — Wiener called it "lusciously tender." A pizza with peppers and red onions was saucy (thank you!) and satisfying. The sausage — skip it.

The owners of **BROTHERS** (Midland Park Shopping Center, 97 Godwin Ave., Midland Park; 201-444-4944) might want to bring in the sisters, if there are any, to make the pizza. The plain pizza is average and the sausage is subpar. The Sicilian is better, but that's not saying much. I received enthusiastic e-mails about Brothers; I don't understand why.

CAFFE CAPRI (119 Park Ave., East Rutherford; 201-460-1039) is a cute little restaurant at the end of Park Avenue. We did a New Jersey pizza tour with a half dozen pizza bloggers several years ago; this was one blogger's favorite place. The best thing about the margherita pizza is the peppery sausage. The pizza Parmigiana, a special with plum tomato, Parmigiana cheese, basil and eggplant, looked better than it tasted. Bland is the word.

CRICCO di PADRE (830 Kinderkamack Road, River Edge; 201-576-0101) received even more spirited e-mails than Brothers, but the evocative name merely added up to lackluster pizza. A half plain/sausage pizza screamed mediocrity. The St. Peter's pie, with clams, tomato, garlic and olive oil, was the single-A version of the Trenton DeLorenzo's Hall of Fame-worthy clam pie. One Pizza Patrol member likened it to "canned clams on a canned sauce."

Best sign in all the pizzerias we visited? Maybe the one at **DONNA'S PIZZA** (404 Broad Ave., Palisades Park; 201-944-2158). "For better service," it reads, "do not carry on conversations with the employees." How's that for some Jersey attitude? Ordering a pizza, apparently, does not amount to a conversation. The plain pizza is just that. Al Windrem, ever mock-metaphorical, said, "If this pie was in the city, it would be washing windows outside the Lincoln Tunnel." The formidable-looking but ordinary Sicilian features decent sauce but dubious-tasting cheese.

You should have seen the e-mails after our review of **KINCHLEY'S TAVERN** (586 N. Franklin Turnpike, Ramsey; 201-934-7777). This is probably Bergen's best-known pizzeria, and it's a fun, old-timey, cash-only pizza roadhouse. But you'll find better thin-crust elsewhere. The plain is just too cheesy. Sauce please! The sausage pizza, with a good grilled flavor, is better. Recommended: the fresh tomato pie.

Someone should rock the boat at **LA GONDOLA PIZZERIA** (1300 Route 17 north, Ramsey; 201-825-8990). The plain pizza is decent. The sausage pizza is, in a word, bad. The Grandma pie is somewhat better; one team member called it "spongy," another preferred "briny." On our visit, I wished I could have ducked into the restaurant, Greek City, next door, but this was the Pizza Patrol, not the Greek Patrol.

LIDO RESTAURANT (701 Main St., Hackensack; 201-487-8721) is one of the more atmospheric pizza joints in Jersey, with its padded booths, tile floors, white lights and a jukebox that may or may not work. Cash-only, too, just like the old times. The plain pizza is a cracker-crusted near delight; Scott Wiener described the sauce as "zippy" and the pie overall as "fun." He judged the meatballs on the meatball pie "great," but sorry, Scott, they weren't that good. Hey, I'm Italian, I know from meatballs. The sausage here needs work, too.

LODI PIZZA (Hamilton Avenue and Route 46, Lodi, 973-478-3306) makes for a great bleary-eyed late-night hangout, with a seriously greasy pie and the unavoidable photos of "The Sopranos" cast on the walls. Scott Wiener described the plain pizza as "dripping with person-ality," but it's more apt for the pizzeria, not the pizza. Just down the road is the unforgettable Pizza Town U.S.A. (see separate entry).

One bite of the Sicilian at **MR. BRUNO'S** (439 Valley Brook Ave., Lyndhurst; 201-933-1588) and you're in square-pizza heaven. It's all about the sauce here; it's so good they bottle it. The sauce is made the old-fashioned way; the sauce-filled jars are boiled in water. In our best-pizza-in-New Jersey Sicilian category, it came down to Mr. Bruno's and Bruno's, in Clifton. Give Mr. Bruno's the slight edge. Both pies are standouts. The half plain/half sausage at Mr. Bruno's is good, too.

NELLIE'S PLACE (9 Franklin Turnpike, Waldwick; 201-652-8626) is a cozy wood-paneled hangout, with a long bar in front and main dining room out back. Apparently one of Kinchley's cooks jumped ship to Nellie's years back. Whatever the case, Nellie's thin crust is better than Kinchley's. Several Pizza Patrol members loved the sausage; I didn't — too greasy. The margherita is a near mess; Scott Wiener criticized its "shoddy construction."

A fleeting glimpse on the opening credits of "The Sopranos" gave **PIZZALAND** (260 Belleville Pike, North Arlington; 201-998-9095) an international cult following. Tour buses often pull up in front of this brick-walled pizzeria. Those expecting fancy will be disappointed; it's a hole-in-the-wall with grungy charm. This place is known for its double-dough pizza; the DD meatball is double the grease, double the fun. On our first Pizza Patrol visit, they had run out of sausage; why wasn't Furio sent in to make sure it never happened again? The plain pizza is a nice greasy North Jersey pie. The sausage pizza is nowhere as good as the meatball pie. Greasy, inferior sausage.

Every time we stop at **PIZZA TOWN U.S.A.** (Route 46, Elmwood Park; 201-797-6172), the sisters who run the place lay claim to some inven-tion or other. Once, Michele Tomo told us Pizza Town was the first place to offer pizza by the slice in New Jersey. Another time, she told us

Pizza Town was the first to make zeppoles in the state! The next time, maybe she'll tell us they invented cheese. It's a roadside attraction; the pizza plays a secondary role. The tomato-cheese pizza is better than the regular plain. In any event, the sandwiches may be better than the pizza. And the sisters, oozing playful Jersey attitude, are a riot.

RENATO'S (36 S. Maple Ave., Ridgewood; 201-652-3554) makes a modest claim: "New Jersey's best pizza." That settles that! The sausage pizza is ordinary, but the plain features an abundance of tasty cheese. Pizza Patrol member Marty Schneider, who lives in Ridgewood, is a big fan of the Grandma pizza here, calling it a "Metropolitan Opera pie — it sings to me." But others were not so impressed with the drippy pie; good luck keeping the tomatoes moored.

At **ROSE'S PIZZA** (73 River Drive, Garfield; 973-773-9205) I ran into Joseph Pieroni, recently returned from duty in Iraq. "I was dreaming of this pizza," he said. I didn't have any dreams about the plain or sausage pizza, before or after, but the Sicilian shines. Nice crunch, and good balance of ingredients add up to one of the better Sicilians we had all year.

RUDY'S RISTORANTE (71 Closter Plaza, Closter; 201-768-8444) looks like your basic neighborhood pizzeria, and it delivers no more nor less in the pizza department. The plain pie is decent, if sauce-shy. The sausage needs to be sent back to the sausage assembly line. Best bet here: the margherita; we liked the high-quality tomatoes.

"Voted No. 1 pizza in town," reads the menu at **TURANO'S** (609 Stuyvesant Ave., Lyndhurst; 201-939-8055). Turano's may be the best pizzeria on Stuyvesant Avenue, but not the best in Lyndhurst; Mr. Bruno's holds that honor. The plain pizza features a nice crust, but otherwise it's nothing special. Better: the Grandma pizza. And there is a nice outside patio.

We hit a new sausage low at **VINCENT PIZZERIA & RESTAURANT** (535 Anderson Ave., Cliffside Park; 201-945-8625), sandwiched among Korean restaurants and markets in this Seoul-ful town. The one-liners came fast and furious here. "Man vs. food — food won," Al Windrem cracked. "I better write an apology letter to my stomach," Wiener added. The margherita pizza came off somewhat better.

BURLINGTON

BRANCO'S PIZZA FAMILY ITALIAN RESTAURANT, (428 Stokes Road, Medford; 609-654-4115). We got the lowdown on Leo's Yum-Yum here from the friendly owner. The sherbet-like ice cream is made in Medford. Just thought you should know. The plain pizza crust at Branco's reminds me of Bruno's Pizza Factory in South Plainfield, with the same distinctive pebbly crust. We've sampled every variety of sausage imaginable; the smooshed crumbly kind available here is instantly forgettable. The white pizza is more a green pepper pie, but the black olives, roasted red peppers and tomatoes make for an enjoyable, if oily, result.

KATE & AL'S PIZZA, (Store 101, Columbus Farmers' Market, 2919 Route 206 south, Columbus; 609-267-1147). Pizza in a flea market? You better believe it. Kate & Al's (see profile on page 66) has packed them in since 1955. Kate and Al were Kate and Alexander Stefan. The specialty is a square Sicilian-like pizza that is red-saucy to the max, with the sauce atop the cheese. Note: This is not your pizza-in-10-minutes neighborhood joint; it may take an hour or more for a whole pizza and 15 to 20 minutes just for a slice. Place your order (they'll write your name on a pizza box) and wander the immense flea market; the wait will be worth it.

I like pizza with attitude — a sauce or crust that dares to be different. The plain pie at **LA BELLA PIZZA** (Crossroads Shopping Center, 199 Route 541, Medford; 609-953-9148) may have the most attitude of any pizza in the state. It's all in the sauce, which is in-your-face tart/spicy. It practically knocked me off my feet at first bite. There's a sea of sauce and garlic, but somehow it works. This pizza is not for everyone, but it definitely worked for me.

The oven at **LUIGI'S PIZZA FRESCA** (1700 Columbus Road, Burlington; 609-239-8888) is a Lincoln Impinger. I have no idea what that means, but it sounds impressive. Judging by the plain pizza, they might want to upgrade to the Washington, or Jefferson, model oven, if there is one. "It's not delivery, it's Fresca," Gina Bruno said. Not a bad line, for early in the day. Creamy cheese on all the pies, though, and the Sicilian is a winner, albeit an undercooked one.

MANGIA BRICK OVEN PIZZA & GRILL (262 Dunns Mill Road, Bordentown; 609-298-7499) is smart and sleek — everything Palermo's (see next entry) is not, but don't hold that against it. The Grandma pizza here is one of the best anywhere, a heap of tomatoey, cheesy goodness, marred slightly by a brittle crust. Skip the too-cheesy plain pizza, unless you're of the belief that sauce has no place on a pie.

My personal pizza epiphany of our six-month-long search for Jersey's best pizza? The margherita pie at **PALERMO'S RISTORANTE ITALIANO & PIZZERIA** (674 Route 206 south, Bordentown; 609-298-6771). Crunchy crust, good sauce and marvelous mozzarella added up to one of the top five pizzas of any kind I sampled all year. The pizzeria is situated on a dreary stretch of Route 206, in a strip mall that could use some sprucing up. There are two other Palermo's stores, in Ewing and Roebling, but start at the original location, in Bordentown.

Keep repeating to yourself: There are three essential items to any pizza, there are three essential items to any . . . At **PASSARIELLO'S PIZZERIA & ITALIAN EATERY** (13 W. Main St., Moorestown; 856-840-0998) the sauce is nice and tangy, and the cheese good enough, but the crust . . . Wait, is that crust? It was basically cooked dough, with no flavor or personality. The pan pizza is similarly flawed. "A Sbarro's clone," one Pizza Patrol member observed, "but worse."

PETE'S PIZZA, (Store 611, Columbus Farmers' Market, 2919 Route 206 south, Columbus; 609-267-0166). Pete Bernath opened a pizzeria where Kate & Al's — Kate Stefan was his sister — now stands. Pete's is now located at the back of the flea market, next to my favorite hangout: the Amish market (good luck spending just a few minutes in there). Unlike Kate & Al's, Pete's calls its square pizza a Sicilian, and it's even more tomatoey than Kate & Al's, if that's possible. It's tough choosing between the two; grab a slice at each and crown your own flea market pizza winner.

RIVIERA RESTAURANT, (6 Stokes Road, Medford Lakes; 609-654-4300). You may have trouble pinpointing this pizzeria; all the surrounding street numbers were in the 700s. The plain pizza features a nice oregano coating, but the crust is too soft, pliant. Better-than-average sausage. The Sicilian is more thick bread than pizza; it's certainly no Kate & Al's, or Pete's.

"Best pizza in South Jersey," one Jersey-based magazine trumpeted about **TACCONELLI'S PIZZERIA** (450 S. Lenola Road, Maple Shade; 856-638-0338). What did they do, visit, like, three other places? The plain pizza is lame, and the sausage gritty. We were divided over the "Signature" pie, a white pie topped with cheese, garlic, spinach and chopped tomatoes. Scott Wiener liked it; Gina Bruno didn't approve of the "frozen spinach flavor." Hopefully, the Tacconelli's in Philadelphia, where the pizzeria started, is better than this one.

UPPER CRUST PIZZA, (Route 206 and Hawkins Road, Tabernacle; 609-268-8100). The town known as the Gateway to the Pines is not exactly the gateway to good pizza. The plain/sausage pizzas here are certainly not worth a trip from anywhere. The Bellagio pizza, with red peppers, prosciutto and mozzarella, promised much, but delivered little. "With all the ingredients, I thought I'd get more flavor," Gina Bruno observed.

CAMDEN

Alfred Rossino, owner of **ALFRED'S TOMATO PIE** (9 S. Black Horse Pike, Blackwood; 856-228-1234) is undoubtedly the only former motivational speaker/sales trainer current movie actor/pizzeria owner in New Jersey. Rossino — guy should have been on "The Sopranos" — is a nut. "They say I look like a mob guy; I don't know why they say that," he said, grinning. Funny guy, but serious about his pizza. He makes an excellent tomato pie, a DeLorenzo's-of-Trenton clone with distinctive sauce, charred crust and chunks of tasty sausage. The white pie is less successful; call it an oil-fest. He's not there every night, so you may want to call before you stop to make sure he is.

"Blackwood's Best" is the slogan at **ANTONINO'S PIZZA** (1034 Little Gloucester Road, Blackwood; 856-227-2900). Sorry, it's no contest; Alfred's Tomato Pie is better. The plain at Antonino's features a commendable crust, but the sausage pizza is average. The tomato pie boasts a robust tomato sauce, but the crust is a "total loser — chewy and gummy," as one team member put it.

BALSAMO'S PIZZA (791 Emerson Ave., Lindenwold; 856-784-1600) is "Home of the 24-inch Pizza," in case that ever comes in handy. The owner's an accomplished photographer; his pictures of Costa Rican flora and fauna adorn the walls. Alas, you'll remember the photos more than the pizza. The plain needs a sauce transfusion. Same goes for the Sicilian.

When is a Sicilian margherita not really either of those? When it's the Sicilian margherita at **BRUNO'S RESTAURANT & PIZZERIA** (509 Hopkins Road, Haddon Township; 856-428-9505). It's more like a Grandma, and it's good. Scott Wiener admired the "nice fruity sweet tomato" sauce. Four of the six team members called it the best pizza of our all-day South Jersey pizza excursion.

CACIA'S BAKERY, (1010 Black Horse Pike, Blackwood; 856-228-5986). Another cook-at-home pizza, similar to Croce's in Cherry Hill. But not as good. The crust is barely there, and the bland sauce needs a major upgrade. Good rolls, though. One of five Cacia's in South Jersey.

CAFE ANTONIO'S RISTORANTE & PIZZERIA, (827 Haddon Ave., Collingswood; 856-854-9400). Collingswood is an up-and-coming (if not already there) dining destination, and the tree-shaded center of town, dotted with restaurants and shops, makes for a great summer excursion. The plain pizza boasted a nice chewy crust, but it's not otherwise memorable. The tomato pie may be the reddest pizza ever; the sprinkles of basil barely have an effect on the crimson sea. In any event, the pizza, more puffy bread than anything, looked much better than it tasted.

CASA CAROLLO, (Route 73 and Baker Boulevard, Marlton; 856-797-1111). Intriguing Italian restaurant/sports bar combo, with more drink specials than a tiki bar in Cabo. The plain pizza makes for a decent, agreeably greasy slice. The margherita, though, is a winner, a bright, tomatoey surprise with a flaky crust. I'd put the sauce on my pasta anytime. Great bar pie? Right here.

CROCE'S, (811 Marlton Pike (Route 70), Cherry Hill; 856-795-6000). Old-school Italian deli, with imported pastas, olives and more. My pizza took all of four minutes; back in my car, I opened the box and discovered why: It's a cook-at-home pie. Popped in the oven six hours later, it still tasted fresh, with lots of fine, feisty tomatoey favor.

Many pizzerias live on their rep, not their ricotta. That seems to be the case at the **FAMOUS AND ORIGINAL KING OF PIZZA** (2300 Route

70, Cherry Hill; 856-665-4824). The place was packed; a line of cars stretched out the parking lot. Conclusion: South Jerseyans must love overly salty pizza; the pie here may kick up your blood pressure several notches. The sausage pizza? Call it infamous. And the white pizza is the mayor of Mediocre-ville. One taster said it had "personality issues," while another found it "too mushy."

Better "famous" than "famous and original" is the lesson we learned in Camden County. The **FAMOUS KING OF PIZZA** (Route 130 and Market Street, Gloucester City; 856-456-5110) is a low-rent-looking joint, but the pizza is better than the Cherry Hill King. It's not great or even especially noteworthy, just a decent going-down-the-highway slice. The white pie is greasy-good.

Just down the street from the Haddon Fire Company No. 1 — the second-oldest volunteer fire company in continuous existence in the U.S. — is **NICKY B'S** (23 South Haddon Ave., Haddonfield; 856-354-7600). Unfortunately, the pizza won't be making history any time soon. The plain pie is too chewy, the sausage decent, no more. The tomato-basil white pie turned out the best of the three, by default.

SAL'S PIZZAWORKS, (10 W. Main St., Marlton; 856-985-5111). Good lucking slipping in and out of the cramped parking lot. The bland, lazily-constructed pizza is not worth the effort anyway. More pellet sausage — yikes. The Sicilian is easily the best of the three, with a first-rate crust and good crunch. Well done.

VILLA BARONE, (753 Haddon Ave., Collingswood; 856-858-2999). Upscale Italian restaurant offers speciality pastas, eight kinds of chicken and veal dishes, and one appetizer I'll try if I return: the Mozzarella Tower. The plain pizza is good and saucy, but the crust needs work. The Capricciosa, with prosciutto, kalamata olives and fresh mushrooms, is just about perfect. Fresh, wholesome, tasty. Might have been the best mushrooms we encountered all year.

CAPE MAY

Much of the sausage we sampled in Cape May and Cumberland counties was pretty sorry. Why? They obviously used the same distributor. Jersey Sausage Pizza Rule No. 1: If your sausage is pellet-shaped, step away from the table immediately. Which we would have done at **BLUE MOON PIZZA** (301 Beach Ave., Cape May; 609-884-3033), but we had a job to do. The plain pizza is eminently forgettable. The Grandma Sicilian looked impressive, with its raised browned crust and swirls of cheese, but mark it down as another undercooked pie.

Grease is the word at **CARINI'S RISTORANTE & PIZZERIA** (9854 Pacific Ave., Wildwood Crest; 609-522-7304). The plain has little else going for it. Cardboard-like crust, and so-so sausage. The Sicilian is undercooked, undersauced and underwhelming. If you want a better

pizza, and pizza experience, visit Sam's Pizza Palace, on the Wildwood boardwalk.

DONATUCCI PIZZA (115 E. 17th Ave., North Wildwood; 609-729-6110) was once Santucci Square Pizza; owner Donna Leyland changed the name to reflect hers. Team member Gina Bruno likened the sauce to "Campbell's soup," but I liked it, a lot. It's not your usual straight-out-of-the-jar stuff. And the spicy, distinctive sausage takes no prisoners. The white pie seemed little more than baked cheese, though.

Let's make this as simple as possible: There's no good pizza in or around Cape May. We tried them all. The plain pie at **ITALIAN AFFAIR RESTAURANT & PIZZERIA** (3845 Bayshore Road, North Cape May; 609-884-0505) features creamy cheese, but that's it. The white pie got withering reviews. "Other than the crust, it's a catastrophe," according to Scott Wiener.

"The best pizza in town!" heralds the menu at **LOUIE'S PIZZA** (Gurney Street and Beach Avenue, Cape May; 609-884-0305). Seriously puffy crust on the plain — only Romeo's in Orange rivals it — but there is a vein of uncooked dough in the crust. Not good. More unappetizing pellet sausage. The margherita is cooked but pretty much tasteless. With what you'd spend on a pizza here, you can buy a half dozen hot dogs at nearby Hot Dog Tommy's, and leave much happier.

The only pizza in or around Cape May that aspires to something can be found at **LUCKY BONES BACKWATER GRILLE** (1200 Route 9, Lower Township; 609-884-2663). The restaurant, across the street from the ever-popular Lobster House, does creative personal-type pies, including the Skipjack, with arugula, prosciutto and mozzarella. The margherita teases with a tasty tart sauce, but the sausage is inferior. The Sofia pie, with shrimp, mozzarella, roasted garlic and olive oil, both disappointed and delighted. The shrimp tasted slightly off, but the rest of the ingredients worked.

MACK'S PIZZA, (3218 Boardwalk, Wildwood; 609-522-6166). Anthony and Lena Macaroni opened a pizzeria on Memorial Day weekend in 1953 on the Wildwood boardwalk; they sold exactly eight pizzas. Mack's is doing much better now, thank you. No Sicilian, no margherita pizzas here, although you can get a vegetable-topped "power pizza." The plain is thin-crusted and fairly standard, although I liked the tart, assertive sauce. More South Jersey pellet sausage: Skip it.

MACK & MANCO PIZZA (920 Boardwalk, Ocean City; 609-399-2548) is one of the heavy hitters on the Jersey pizza boardwalk scene, and the pizzeria, with three locations (one open year-round) on the Ocean City boardwalk, did not disappoint. The plain pie is oily/greasy-good, with nice creamy cheese. The sausage? No thanks. But the white pie, shimmering with olive oil, is a winner. Scott Wiener called it "awesome, simple, elegant." A slice at Mack & Manco is a quintessential part of any south Jersey Shore summer.

MAMA MIA'S RISTORANTE PIZZERIA, (2087 S. Shore Road, Seaville; 609-624-9322). Mama Mia's, situated next to a Hallmark store, produces one of the better plain slices Down the Shore. A sweetish sauce and hearty crust add up to pizza pleasure. "Better than half we ate all summer," Gina Bruno said. More than that, I think. The margherita is topped with scallions — that's different — but the bufalo mozzarella is clumpy, chewy.

More enthusiastic e-mails, more disappointment. One glance at the pellet-like sausage at **MARIO'S PIZZERIA & RESTAURANT** (1510 Bay Ave., Ocean City; 609-398-0490) was a foreshadowing of the mediocre meat ahead. Fortunately, the tomato-onion pizza is better. An intriguing combination, and it works.

"Celebrating half a century of excellence" is the slogan at **SAM'S PIZZA PALACE** (2600 Boardwalk, Wildwood; 609-522-6017). The boardwalk legend makes a good plain pie; it's oily/slippery, but there are signs of saucy life. Excellent crust. The sausage tasted like bland breakfast meat of some kind. The white pizza divided the crew. One team member likened it to "bad garlic pie," but I liked its peppery tone. Sam's is a good choice on the best boardwalk of all time.

Talk about incentive — or a sure-fire way to guarantee agita. If you eat a whole pie at **3 BROTHERS FROM ITALY PIZZA** (944 Boardwalk, Ocean City; 609-398-6767) in one hour, you win 10 free pizzas. If you eat one pie in 45 minutes, you win 25 pies. One pie in 15 minutes? One hundred free pies. This is the "world's largest pizza" — 26 inches in diameter — so have the Pepto ready. Hype and hoopla aside, the plain is a good pizza, on or off the boardwalk. And the sausage is better than Mack & Manco, just down the boards. Decent ricotta pie; it's no match for Mack and Manco's white.

I dug the pleasantly grungy outer dining room with Naugahyde booths and faded curtains at **TONY'S PIZZERIA & RESTAURANT** (Route 109, Lower Township; 609-884-2020). But you can't eat atmosphere. The plain pizza has a nice Italian breadlike crunch, but the sausage — of the pellet variety — is a big mistake. The meatballs on the homemade meatball pie tasted as if they were made in someone's backyard, not the house. Yuck.

About half the pizzerias in New Jersey seem to have been voted No. 1 in some poll or another at some point in their existence. "Voted No. 1 in all of South Jersey" is the pitch at **WALT'S ORIGINAL PRIMO PIZZA** (3 Shore Road, Somers Point; 609-927-4464). Whatever. We liked the plain — "greasy enough for the Shore, tasty enough for a second bite," according to Wiener. Avoid the sausage at all costs. I remember the Primo's on the Ocean City boardwalk being much better. Call Walt's No. 1 in Somers Point — maybe.

CUMBERLAND

BIG JOHN'S PIZZA, (90 Commerce St. east, Bridgeton; 856-455-3344). "What do you want, boss?" asks one of guys behind the counter of this high-ceilinged pizzeria, located next to Randy's, a store with bicycles, live bait and more. There's a strong, tart sauce on the plain pizza; it may not be to your taste, but it is to mine. Cast all dietary concerns to the wind and order a double thick pizza, a thick, chewy, cardiac-inducing delight. It reminded me of the pizza at Romeo Pizzeria in Orange. If the double thick at Big John's had double the sauce, it'd be a knockout.

CARMELO'S RISTORANTE, (31 E. Broad St., Bridgeton; 856-453-0023). There are a half-dozen pizzerias in the center of Bridgeton; Carmelo's is an acceptable choice — if you can't get into Big John's for some reason. The plain pizza features a soft, pillowy but bland crust. Skip the sausage: too greasy. The white is the way to go, with an agreeable garlicky/oily sheen.

The Pizza Patrol sampled pizza at truck stops, supermarkets, and service plazas, so it was only a matter of time before we encountered that all too common species known as shopping mall pizza. **LUCA'S PIZZA** (Cumberland Mall, 3849 S. Delsea Drive, Vineland; 856-327-2205) is across from the PayHalf store, if that helps. Loved the Venetian canal mural on the wall — is this Vegas or Vineland? The plain features a nice foundation/crunch, but that's about it. The sausage? Wish you hadn't asked. "There's a lot of talent here," patrol member Marty Schneider cracked. "They've somehow managed to have their sausage taste like fried chicken." Which, considering the general state of sausage in South Jersey, may not have been a bad thing. The Sicilian has an unhealthy-looking yellow sheen — maybe it was just the harsh lighting — and a lack of flavor.

The soft, puffy crust steals what little spotlight exists at **MANNY'S PIZZERIA & RESTAURANT** (426 N. High St., Millville; 856-327-5081). The Venetian, a white pie, is oily and totally forgettable. Manny's is not much to look at it; neither is the pizza.

MARTINO'S TRATTORIA & PIZZERIA (2614 E. Chestnut Ave., Vineland; 856-692-4448) is an attractive cafe-like space — dig the jungle of plants at the entrance — with a friendly staff. But the pizza needs work. The plain registers big on the blah scale. The cheese on the margherita pie is markedly better, but the crust seems dry.

Where in the world is Carmel? "You go one mile that way, you're in Vineland; you go one mile that way, you're in Bridgeton; you go one mile that way, you're in Rosenhayn," says Salvatore Saughelli, owner of **PAPA LUIGI RESTAURANT & PIZZERIA** (600 W. Sherman Ave., Carmel; 856-459-2100). The plain pizza is ordinary, but at least we didn't have to endure more pellet sausage, an unfortunate South Jersey specialty. The Sicilian is sauce-shy.

ESSEX

Belleville does right by pizza. Joey's Pizzeria (see page 124) makes an excellent Sicilian, La Sicilia won for best specialty pizza and **ALGIERI'S** (502 Union Ave., Belleville; 973-751-3577) serves a good and greasy plain slice. But the sausage is so-so. The margherita, with its sweet sauce and crisp crust, is nicely done.

We really wanted to like **ANGELO'S RESTAURANT & PIZZERIA** (303 Broad St., Bloomfield; 973-429-8505) because of the friendly staff. But our job was to rate pizza, not the people behind the counter, and Angelo's suffered. The plain pizza tasted like it was rushed out of the oven, and the sausage is weak. The margherita is forgettable. Too bad.

ARTURO'S OSTERIA PIZZERIA (180 Maplewood Ave., Maplewood; 973-378-5800) is one of the few pizzerias I'd also recommend for its food in general. Owner Dan Richter uses high-end ingredients in his pastas, and you can taste the difference. The plain pizza here features top-notch cheese, which made the choice of below-average sausage puzzling. But the margherita, with its fresh, tart tomatoes, is one of the best in the county.

Freddy Gianfrancesco is maybe the most talkative of the three brothers who own **BELL PAESE** (196 Franklin Ave., 973-667-8232). His plain pizza would not win any awards in Nutley, where they love to hand out pizza awards, but the bruschetta is the bomb. Tomatoes, onions, fresh garlic, basil and oregano make for a summery pizza that delivers year-round taste.

"Beware of the Attack Bunny" and "Home of the Upscale Pizza Crowd" are two signs on the window at **BUNNY'S RESTAURANT** (12-14 W. South Orange Ave., South Orange; 973-763-1377). We're not sure if "upscale" is supposed to define the pizza, or crowd. It's a colorful, lively hangout in one of my favorite towns, but the pizza should be better. One Pizza Patrol member likened the plain to "Italian grilled cheese." And the meatball pie is standard-issue.

We had a strange moment initially at **CAMMARATA'S PIZZA PANTRY** (126 S. Livingston Ave., Livingston; 973-994-0615). We placed the order, showed up 15 minutes later, when the boy behind the counter told us he hadn't started the pizza because he was too busy. Then he spent the next five minutes doing essentially nothing before starting to make our pizza. All was forgiven with one taste of the Old World pizza, a puffy-crust wonder with plum tomatoes and oregano. Fine, fennel-flecked sausage on the sausage pizza, too.

I'm picky about my pasta; my favorite is De Cecco, which you can find, along with good olives (my downfall), at **CAVALLO'S MARKET**

(173 Bloomfield Ave., Nutley; 973-667-1237). Wish the pizza were better, though. Scott Wiener called the plain pie "pretty sleepy," which seems like a wide-awake assessment. But the margherita is nicely done. "The grated cheese on top put it into pizza overdrive," Wiener said approvingly.

COSIMO'S TRATTORIA & AUTHENTIC BRICK OVEN PIZZA (194 Broad St., Bloomfield; 973-429-0558) turned into a memorable Munchmobile trip five years ago; I love their pastas, and the seafood salad. How's the pizza? First-rate. The margherita boasts a distinctive charred crust and smooth, delicate cheese. We ate the pizza in the Big Dog, and there were wows all around for the white pie. Comments included "beautiful" and "very elegant."

"The absolute best brick oven pizza in N.J.," began an e-mail about **DA VINCI'S** (223 Belleville Ave., Upper Montclair; 973-744-2300). A lot of our e-mails began this way; few lived up to the billing. Da Vinci's is no different. The plain pizza is so middle-of-the-road you'll never have to worry about crossing the white line. The margherita is less successful. One Pizza Patrol member described the sauce as a "snoozer," while another called it "a pathetic excuse for a margherita."

FAMOUS RAY'S PIZZA OF NEW YORK (10 Pompton Avé., Verona; 973-857-3434). "The Real One and Only!" trumpets the menu. Which means it's part of the Famous Ray's outposts in the city and not to be confused with the million other pizzerias with "Ray's" in their names. The plain pizza here is real average — unless you like a seriously greasy slice. "Looks like it's been on a roller coaster," Alex Windrem said. And it had enough cheese to single-handedly keep the American dairy industry afloat. The Grandma pizza, with tomato, basil, pesto, Parmesan, mozzarella and garlic, is bursting with tomatoes (good thing) but is mushy and undercooked (bad thing).

Boy, oh boy, do they take pizza in Nutley seriously. There's an annual pizza contest, which has been plagued with controversy; one year a winner was declared, then a recount taken, then another winner declared. The Munchmobile went into town, sampled every pizzeria, and named a third pizzeria (Queen Regina Margherita, now Queen Margherita Trattoria) best in Nutley. One of the better pizzerias from that trip was **FERRULLI'S PIZZA & HOMEMADE ITALIAN FOOD** (80 Centre St., Nutley; 973-667-7900). The plain pizza is solid but nothing special. Basic sausage pizza, and the Sicilian is overly bready.

We often ran into pizzerias that did one pizza really well, but failed with the others, which was always puzzling. The plain pizza at **FORTE PIZZERIA & RISTORANTE** (182 Bloomfield Ave., Caldwell; 973-403-9411) boasts an ordinary crust, and the sausage is of the familiar bland variety. But the Grandma pizza is loaded with tart tomatoes and patches of fine fresh mozzarella. There's another Forte in Randolph (see page 146).

"So this is the Munchmobile," a pie-carrying customer said on the way out at **FORTISSIMO OSTERIA/PIZZERIA** (484 Pleasant Valley Way, West Orange; 973-731-8095). Yeah, that's us, notebooks, point-and-shoot cameras and pizza cutter in hand. Nice surprise: all three pizzas are solid. One Pizza Patrol member admired the plain's "good cheese, good flavor, good sauce, good crust." Better-than-average sausage, too. The margherita featured a memorable sauce.

FRANK'S PIZZERIA & RESTAURANT (161 Bloomfield Ave., Newark; 973-482-8891) is one of those late-night hangouts more memorable for the atmosphere and clientele than the food. Dig the church confessional-like wall panels! The plain pizza has a nice crunch, but the cheese is average, and the sausage below-average. The red peppery Grandpa pie will get your attention any time of the day or night, despite a subpar sauce. "You meet this Grandpa in an alley, you're going down," Alex Windrem said.

Many of the pizzas we encountered on our travels were undercooked, which made me think of this spin on the Pink Floyd song: "Hey, pizza-makers, leave those pizzas alone!" The plain at **HOLLYWOOD RESTAURANT & PIZZERIA** (376 Fairfield Road, Fairfield; 973-808-0123) should, like scores of pizzas we encountered, have spent more time in the oven. The sausage needs an upgrade. The Grandma-like margherita is slippery but tasty. If they took it back to the pizza lab and did a little tinkering, it could be a standout.

If there's one thing that distinguishes much Jersey pizza, it's the dominance of cheese over sauce. We just don't get this; sauce generally costs less than cheese. The plain pie at **JOEY'S PIZZERIA & CATERING** (460 Joralemon St., Belleville; 973-751-8839) boasts a nice chewy crust, but where's the red stuff? But the Sicilian, with a commendable, slightly burnt crust, is excellent. There are exactly three tables here, so takeout is a good idea.

Call **LA PIZZA PIZZERIA & RESTAURANT** (Roseland Plaza, 178 Eagle Rock Ave., Roseland; 973-226-6268) La Pizza Average. "Strictly by the book," one team member observed. The Grandma pizza looked saucy but turned out meek and mild-mannered.

First-timers at **LA SICILIA** (155 Washington Ave., Belleville; 973-751-5726) see Giuseppe Ali's last name and assume he's Middle Eastern, wondering what he could know about pizza. Ali was born in Sicily, and his Palermo pizza, modeled after one popular in Sicily, is amazing. The pizza, with mozzarella, marinara, garlic and grated cheese, won top honors in the specialty pizza category in our Best Pizza in New Jersey competition. Ali's plain and sausage pies are good, and so is the rest of the food. Killer cannolis, too.

One reader told us that the pizza at **LA STRADA** (355 Millburn Ave., Millburn; 973-467-3420) had slipped under new ownership. Good tip. The plain pizza is underwhelming, and the sausage too salty. The

Sicilian divided our crew. Joanie Dwyer described it as "yummy for the tummy," but Gina Bruno labeled it "mediocre at best."

If we had a dollar for every pizzeria with "famous" in its name, we could buy out Pizza Hut and have money left over. The plain pizza at **MARIO'S FAMOUS PIZZERIA RESTAURANT** (1279 Broad St., Bloomfield; 973-338-4477) is greasy and salty. The owner objected to the word "greasy" in our review, and said it was a "fact" that his pizza isn't greasy. Whatever. There was no disagreement over this: the Sicilian is better. One crew member called it "hearty," another lauded the "nice" crust.

I was expecting big things at **MARIO'S PIZZERIA** (137 Delancey St., Newark; 973-466-3377), physically connected to Assaggini Di Roma, the best Italian restaurant in Newark. But the meatball pizza is a mistake, and the plain pie received "dried out" and "very dull" reviews. The sausage pizza is the best of the lot.

Our very first Pizza Patrol stop was **MICHAEL'S PASTARIA & RESTAURANT** (143 Franklin Ave; 973-661-5252). Co-owner Nick Conforti claims his great-grandfather opened the state's first pizzeria back in the 1920s in Newark. Maybe Nick and the sisters at Pizza Town U.S.A. in Elmwood Park should have a "famous firsts" throwdown! The plain pizza at Michael's seems light on the sauce, heavy on the cheese, but we loved the Grandma Irm's pizza, with marinara and mozzarella. Gina Bruno singled out the "nice chunks of tomatoes in the sauce" and the crust "folded up around the edges."

The plain pizza at **MICHAEL'S PIZZERIA & RESTAURANT** (669 Bloomfield Ave., West Caldwell; 973-226-8862) may have set a new benchmark — Wiener called it "the greasiest pie in New Jersey" — but the margherita, glistening with olive oil, is a marvel. Wiener named it one of his favorite pizzas of the year. "As awful as the plain is, this one is wonderful," he said.

PIE-ZON PIZZA CAFE (410 St. Cloud Ave., West Orange; 973-325-8008) is one of the newer kids on the pizza block. The plain pizza is "on the greasy side, but it's a good grease," Alex Windrem noted. Decent sausage. The margherita, fresh-tasting and well-balanced, is the way to go.

The margherita pizza at **PIZZETA ENOTECA** (62 W. Mt. Pleasant Ave., Livingston; 973-740-2385) is one of the better ones you'll find anywhere. The plain and sausage are nicely done. Gina Bruno, who is as picky as they get, described the sauce on the margherita as "right on." Marty Schneider called all three pizzas "well-crafted."

Two-minute pizzas are the rule in the super-hot ovens at **QUEEN MARGHERITA TRATTORIA** (246 Washington Ave., Nutley; 973-662-0007). We named this popular pizzeria/restaurant best pizza in Nutley in a Munchmobile special report in 2005. Our Pizza Patrol, five years later, was similarly effusive. "The tomatoes kicked butt," one team member said of the margherita pizza. "This pie is king," added another. The marinara pizza, with tomatoes, black olives, anchovies and garlic, is nowhere as memorable, though.

When colleagues ask me to name the best pizza in Newark, I tell them **QUEEN PIZZA** (114 Halsey St., Newark; 973-624-7322). Admittedly, there's not much competition, but Queen, with its gumball machines, yellow-red booths and funky tilted floor, does the job. Scott Wiener admired "the great proportions of cheese and sauce." The Sicilian, meanwhile, needs a sauce transfusion. One taster likened it to "shopping mall pizza," while another described it as "pizza from central casting."

When we stopped at **RALPH'S** (564 Franklin Ave., 973-235-1130), word got to the owner, who called and told me he wasn't happy with our review of Ralph's in our Munchmobile 2005 report and didn't we know how popular the pizzeria was? I've said it before and I'll say it again: you'll find better pizza in Nutley. The "famous thin-crust" doesn't deserve the tag, but it's a good pizza. The sausage is just not as good as Michael's. A specialty pizza with cheese, sauce and fresh basil features tasty enough cheese, but didn't have much else going for it.

This is not going to go down well with fans of the Reservoir Tavern in Parsippany, but I think **THE RESERVOIR RESTAURANT** (106 W. South Orange Ave., South Orange; 973-762-9795) is better. The South Orange Reservoir began in Newark on Ninth Street and 14th Avenue — where Jimmy Buff's was born. Excellent sausage pie here; the sausage comes from Angelo's Deli in West Orange. The plain pie is less distinguished. The double dough pizza is decent, but not especially distinctive.

You've got to love the ditzy charm at the **ROMAN GOURMET** (153 Maplewood Ave. Maplewood; 973-762-4288). A boom box hangs above the Slush Puppie machine. The menu offers a "bailout pizza," and a sign reads. "Mom's back from Italy. . . Homemade chicken soup. Pasta fagioli." The plain pizza, while short on sauce, makes for a quality slice. But the sausage is salty and greasy, the margherita runny.

Romeo, Romeo, wherefore art thou Romeo? In Orange, that's where, and he makes a damn good pizza. My vote for most distinctive if not outrageous crust in New Jersey, in fact, goes to the plain at **ROMEO PIZZERIA** (408 Central Ave., Orange; 973-674-8907). It's a puffed-up, eminently chewy crust of Himalayan proportions. The sausage should be better, though. The Sicilian is monster truck-sized, with a skyscraper crust. But it lacks flavor, or finesse.

On one all-day North Jersey run, we wondered if it was National Weak Crust Week, since we kept running into flimsy crusts like the one at **RUSSILLO RISTORANTE & PIZZERIA** (675 Bloomfield Ave., West Caldwell; 973-228-4100). And the sausage, like most of

Jersey pizza sausage, needs to be replaced. But we liked the fresh, feisty bruschetta.

RUTHIE'S BBQ & PIZZA (61½ Chestnut St., Montclair; 973-509-1134) is a popular hangout for Montclair High School students, and hipsters in general, with its blues music posters and informal jam sessions. The pizza is probably better than the barbecue — nice, fluffy crust on the plain, and a pleasant margherita.

Walk into **SANTINI'S** (355 Franklin Ave., 973-661-5205), and you feel like you stepped into the 1970s, with its mirrored walls, curved ceiling, low lighting and PacMan carpet. Decent plain slice, but the Sicilian is kind of sorry. "Gummy; it's going to sit in my stomach," one crew member moaned.

SEMOLINA (343 Millburn Ave., Millburn; 973-379-9101) is more high-end restaurant than pizzeria; the pizzas seem like an after-thought at the bottom of the menu, but they're well worth trying. "Outstanding" and "dynamite" were two words used for the plain. I thought the best cheese of the summer was here. Definitely not one of the best sausages, though. We liked the pomodoro, with cherry tomatoes, basil, pecorino and armigiana cheese. "Tasted like all the ingredients were picked from the garden that morning," Gina Bruno said admiringly.

The folks at **SOHO PIZZA & GRILL** (540 Valley Road, Upper Montclair; 973-744-8708) really should do something about their sausage; it's subpar, and that's being kind. "The meat product on the pie," one taster noted, "was at an all-time low." The Grandma pie is better, fortu-nately. Bruno found the sauce too "tomato-pasty," but Wiener called it a Grandma "you'd want to take to lunch."

The **STARLITE RESTAURANT** (993 Pleasant Valley Way, West Orange; 973-736-9440), open since 1961, has plenty of pizza history and tradition. The pizza divided our crew. One said the plain "tasted like a frozen pizza," another labeled it "different, zesty." The sausage is better than average. We all agreed the provolone-marinara pizza is a winner. "Yum to the sharpness and chubby tomatoes," according to Bruno.

STAR TAVERN (400 High St., Orange; 973-675-3336) is prob-ably North Jersey's best-known pizzeria. Two Jersey food legends are within walking distance of each other: Jimmy's Buff's is nearby. Interestingly, Star Tavern owner Gary Vayianos and James Racioppi, Jimmy Buff's owner, attended Newark Academy at the same time. I've called the Star the gold standard of Jersey thin-crust pies, and our Pizza Patrol visit confirmed it; we named it best thin-crust in the state. It's all about the crunch, and char; pizzas are cooked for about six minutes in steel pans cut out halfway around, and then finished off on the oven floor. The Sicilian tomato pizza, with a tangier sauce, is a letdown, though. One Patrol member thought it "out of place in a thin-crust stronghold."

I remember our visit to **3 GUYS PIZZERIA & RISTORANTE** (366 Franklin Ave., Belleville; 973-751-4602) quite well. We arrived just before a torrential downpour (the Big Dog did need a wash, though). Call the plain pizza here your basic neighborhood pie. "It's Joe average," Joanie Dwyer said. The Grandma pizza may have lacked charm, or finesse, but it's solid.

"Down Neck's No. 1 Pizza" proclaims the menu at **TONY'S PIZZERIA** (59 Pacific St., Newark; 973-344-0590). If you insist. The plain pizza is irreparably greasy, and the margherita turned out to be little more than a basil-topped grease pie. One team member said the two pizzas "taste exactly the same."

One of the more distinctive sauces in our travels came at **TRATTORIA BELLA GENTE** (644 Bloomfield Ave., Verona; 973-239-4416). It's nice and tart and tomatoey. But the sausage is merely okay. The margherita, with that tasty sauce, made up for it. It's the kind of place I'd want to go back and try the rest of the food.

One of the Pizza Patrol's livelier moments came on our visit to **VALLE PIZZA** (41 Freeman St., West Orange; 973-243-2400), when we met Munchmobile "groupies" at Dillon's several doors down. Probably should have gone into the bar; the dominant taste on Valle's plain pizza is greasy cheese, or cheesy grease. The sausage, with its smoky-burnt flavor, is better than average. Good luck finding appreciable sauce on the Sicilian.

There's plenty of pizza in South Orange. The trick is finding good pizza. **VILLAGE TRATTORIA** (21 South Orange Ave., South Orange Ave.; 973-762-2015) falls somewhere in the middle of the pack. Al Windrem called it "good lunch stop" pizza. The margherita is covered with a too-cheesy blanket, and is basil-dominated.

VILLA VICTORIA (11 Park St., Montclair; 973-746-4426) is a cute little place, but you can't eat cute. One team member called the plain pizza "flimsy," another called it "bland." But the Greek pizza, with tomatoes, feta, sautéed red onions, black olives and mozzarella, came as a nice late-night surprise.

There's nothing fancy about **ZUCHETTE'S PIZZERIA** (71 Walnut St., Montclair; 973-744-4333), but this restaurant serves a nice, tomatoey, plain pie. The sausage pie is well above average. The Sicilian got mixed reviews; one taster liked the "tangy" sauce, another thought it undercooked. The owner takes pride in his cooking; one of these days I'll go back and try the pastas.

GLOUCESTER

Every college town boasts a ton of pizzerias — what would an all-nighter be without them? **CICONTE'S ITALIA PIZZA** (321 Mullica Hill Road, Glassboro; 856-881-4412), near Rowan University, formerly

Glassboro State College, rises above the pack. The plain pizza, peppery and greasy, won't let you down. The sausage is so-so, but the Sicilian is a solid B.

Some of our best pizzas were sampled in the front — and back — seats of the van. That was the case at **GIA NINA PIZZA AND ITALIAN RESTAURANT** (312 S. Evergreen Ave., Woodbury; 856-845-6500). The plain pizza boasts good sauce and cheese and an okay crust. The sausage is pretty good, for South Jersey. The tomato pie, loaded with sauce and grated cheese, is excellent. Another place I want to revisit to try the rest of the menu.

MOZZARELLA GRILL, (415 Egg Harbor Road, Sewell; 856-589-1000). Tucked at the end of a mini-mall several doors down from Fat Jack's BBQ, the Mozzarella Grill offers mozzarella sticks, chicken fingers and an appealing range of pasta and meat dishes. The margherita pizza is a disappointment — bland. The plain pizza has more character, with a pleasing, slightly burnt foundation. And the sausage boasts a nice peppery kick.

Never heard of Clayton? Well, it is home to Movie Man Video and Tan and **SICILIA PIZZERIA & SUB SHACK** (558 S. Delsea Drive, Clayton; 856-881-9566). Sicilia's plain pizza is a pleasant little pizza, even if the crust seems undernourished and undeveloped. The white, meanwhile, is no match for, say, its counterpart at Mack and Manco in Ocean City.

TOSCANA PIZZERIA & GRILL (Mullica Hill Plaza, 127 Bridgeton Pike, Mullica Hill; 856-478-2288) delivers — in the taste department. Scott Wiener admired the crust's "great woody flavor," but a pizza like this deserves better sausage. The Toscana pie — with prosciutto, mozzarella, sliced tomatoes, goat cheese, artichokes and baby greens — is first-rate. Mullica Hill itself, known for its antiques and craft shops, is worth a visit.

HUDSON

"Rated No. 1 in New Jersey," screams a sign at the one and only **BENNY TUDINO'S** (622 Washington St., Hoboken; 201-792-4132). This pizza joint, with its scruffy charm and cast of late-night characters, deserves its own reality show. Benny's also claims the biggest pizza — 30 inches in diameter — in New Jersey. The slices are humongous. The plain pie, against all odds, succeeds. Other team members liked the sausage, but I thought it greasy and ordinary. And the tomatoes on the margherita pie looked past their expiration date.

The ultimate pizzeria/tiki/sports bar in New Jersey? I'd vote for **BIG APPLE SPORTS PALACE** (412-414 Broadway; Bayonne, 201-858-1075). Mini-TV screens at the tables in the pizzeria portion, lively bar in front, tiki bar out back. Decent bar pie, and tasty sausage, but the margherita was described as a "disaster — the sauce tasted like it was jarred."

Bayonne, Bayonne — where did you go wrong? Our first trip to the city was a major disappointment; our worst slice of the 1,000 sampled in our six-month mission came here. Our second trip: much better, mostly because of **CAFE BELLO RISTORANTE** (1044 Avenue C, Bayonne; 201-437-7538). All three slices excelled. Great blend of mozzarella and ricotta on the white pizza with prosciutto, and the half-plain/half-sausage margherita is marvelous. Bello is bellissimo.

"It's a real Carmine," the girl at the counter said of the owner at **CARMINE'S PIZZA FACTORY AND CATERING** (102-104 Brunswick St., Jersey City; 201-386-8777). Good to know! This no-frills pizzeria is popular with students at James J. Ferris High School, across the street. But the plain and sausage pizzas need to go back to school. The margherita, saucy and sassy, boasts a nice chewy crust. I liked it a lot.

Hoboken didn't fare much better than Bayonne. There are several legendary names — John's, Grimaldi's (see separate entries) — but overall you'll do better in, say, Jersey City. **FILIPPO'S ON FIRST** (267 First St., Hoboken; 201-659-3333) didn't impress with any of its pizzas. The plain is too salty, and the crust lackluster. One taster described the sausage as "waxy." Do yourself a favor and skip the margherita.

"I walk the streets" was Frank Scalcione's motto when he ran for city council in Jersey City this year. And serve the pizza; Scalcione is the owner of **FRANK'S FAMOUS PIZZERIA** (415½ Monmouth St., Jersey City; 201-798-1173). The pie may not be a winner, but it's a viable candidate, with its nice crispy crust. Salty sausage, though. And the white pie is bland.

Food trucks have found a home in downtown Jersey City. The Taco Truck is highly recommended if you're in a Mexican mood. For pizza, visit **GRANDMA'S PIZZA** (along Hudson Street near Harborside Financial Center, Jersey City; 973-941-2372). "Once in a while, you've got to shake up your life," says owner Lou Yandoli, a former commercial video editor. He uses basically the same recipe used at Krispy Pizza in Old Bridge, but his Grandma pie, with an in-your-face tomato sauce, is superior to Krispy's. One of the three or four best pizzas in Hudson County can be found at a truck.

GRIMALDI'S (133 Clinton St., Hoboken; 201-792-0800) is one of two New York City pizza icons on the Jersey side of the Hudson, with John's. Grimaldi's fared better in our evaluation. Scott Wiener singled out the "really smooth" mozzarella, although Gina Bruno judged the crust "lackluster." The sausage is so-so; no disagreement there. The meatball pie is one of the better ones we sampled.

Pizzeria No. 333 turned out to be **IL FORNO PIZZA CAFE** (1536 Paterson Plank Road, Secaucus; 201-864-6576). Nothing remarkable going on here. Al Windrem singled out the "enjoyable" sauce, but Wiener called the plain "an average Joe." The sauce on the margherita tasted flat, lifeless.

JOE'S PIZZERIA & RESTAURANT (956 Broadway; Bayonne, 201-437-6677) was the last stop on our first Bayonne excursion; surely we would find good pizza at the end of the night? Uh, no. The sauce was described as "standard-issue Ragu," the plain pizza "on par with the rest of Bayonne."

JOHN'S (87 Sussex St., Jersey City; 201-433-4411). Judging by our visit, this New York pizza landmark should have stayed in New York. We made note of the "substandard" crust and "yucky" sausage, and called the white pie "Bland Central." Either a legend in their own mind, or something was lost in the translation from one side of the river to the other.

LARRY & JOE'S PIZZA RESTAURANT (533 Newark Ave., Jersey City; 201-656-4435) is a bustling little hole-in-the-wall, with a lunchtime crowd of high school students, sheriff's officers, and others. The plain pizza is good and greasy. Skip the meatball pizza; we're still looking for that one great meatball pie. But Larry & Joe's is my kind of pizza joint.

Call our visit to **LA RUSTIQUE CAFE** (611 Jersey Ave., Jersey City; 201-222-6886) a Mozzarella Moment. It's a cozy, comfy place, but you've seen its kind before. But you haven't seen this kind of pizza. The margherita pie, with homemade mozzarella, San Marzano tomato sauce, imported Parmesan, olive oil and fresh basil, is a stunner, boasting a distinctive tart sauce and browned crust. Gina Bruno, who dispenses superlatives as if they cost her money, called it "tremendous." The rest of us agreed with her, for once, naming the margherita the best in New Jersey. The Sicilian is a monster, puffed up like a titanic sauce/cheese turnover. You may not like it, or may run away from it in fear, but it dares to be different.

The plain pizza at **MONA LISA PIZZERIA RISTORANTE** (165 Broadway; 201-858-1812) is strangely devoid of sauce. Maybe not so strange, considering our Quixote-like search for sauce throughout New Jersey. The margherita has potential, but it's overwhelmed by garlic. "The dark cloud of garlic blocked out the tomato sun," Wiener noted.

"The taste Bayonne loves since 1950" is the motto at **NAPLES PIZ-ZERIA & RESTAURANT** (191 Broadway; Bayonne, 201-437-8879). If so, Bayonne is in trouble. The plain/sausage pizza is undercooked; one team member called it "dreadful." The "red pie" — all sauce — is somehow worse. Naples is an atmospheric haunt, with its high-backed booths, but the pizza seems stuck in a time we'd rather not visit.

We ate in pizzerias, we ate in the van, we ate in parking lots. At **NAPOLI'S** (1118 Washington St., Hoboken; 201-216-0900), we ate on the sidewalk. Why? The pizzeria had just closed; what else were we supposed to do? The pizza here is a good indoor — or outdoor — pie. One taster called it "pizazz-y, nice and milky," while another admired the crust's "beautiful consistency and texture." The sausage needs to be retired, but the clam pie is a treat.

NINO'S RISTORANTE & PIZZERIA (442 Bergen St., Harrison; 973-484-5770) makes a good plain pizza, but it's all about the Sicilian here. It's saucy and cheesy and definitely in the upper tier of Sicilians around the state. Al Windrem was a partial dissenter, arguing the crust "didn't stand up to the rest of the pie." Nino's Sicilian is not as good as Mr. Bruno's in Lyndhurst or Bruno's in Clifton, but it's not far behind.

Add **PAESANO'S PIZZERIA** (108 Kennedy Blvd., Bayonne; 201-437-3200) to the list of boring Bayonne pizza. "Thin and watery" and "so ordinary it invites no comparisons" were two comments. The Sicilian, nearly flavorless, needs a complete makeover.

We practically jumped for joy at **PIZZA MASTERS PIZZA & RESTAU-RANT** (532 Broadway; Bayonne, 201-437-4802). The plain/sausage was judged an "enjoyable sloppy mess," but the Sicilian is slammin.' Sauce, cheese, crust - everything worked in happy harmony. We discovered later in the summer that the owner of Bello's also owns Pizza Masters. Glad someone in Bayonne knows what they're doing.

The Sicilian at **POMPEI PIZZA** (480 Broadway; Bayonne, 201-437-5408) is so cheesy Scott Wiener mused that he could "take a nap under this cheese blanket." Other than that, it's ordinary. The plain pizza is no better. "This slice is flying coach," Alex Windrem noted. The sausage pizza, meanwhile, doesn't even get off the ground.

If you see a vacant table at **PRINCE OF PIZZA** (763 Bergen Ave., Jersey City; 201-434-9453), grab it. The plain pizza at this hole-in-the wall near Journal Square boasts minimal sauce and a threadbare crust, never a good combination. "This must be the no-bake recipe I've heard about," Wiener cracked. The Sicilian, though, came as a surprise. Oozing saucy goodness, it boasts a nice chewy crust. A better-than-average Sicilian, in an unlikely place.

One of my favorite pizza hangouts is the **STARTING POINT BAR & GRILL** (2 Avenue A, Bayonne; 201-243-0092). Nestled in the shadow of the Bayonne Bridge, this neighborhood bar is decorated with albums from Black Sabbath, Cream, Iron Butterfly and others. The pizza, alas, is off-key. The crust is a Chimney Rock Inn-like cracker crust, but it's instantly forgettable. The meatball pizza is only slightly better.

Dino Maggiore proudly showed off his Veroforno pizza ovens at **TONY MAY'S PIZZA AND GRILL** (53-55 Kennedy Blvd., 201-471-7351). I don't think he should be too proud of his pizza. The cheese tasted a bit off, although Scott Wiener was wowed by the crust, which he called "the most consistently cooked one I've ever seen." The margherita seemed middling.

Best lasagna in New Jersey? I'd vote for the one at **TRATTORIA LA SORRENTINA** (7831 Bergenline Ave., North Bergen; 201-869-8100). How's the pizza? The sauce and cheese make for a winning combo,

but the crust let the plain pizza down. Good sausage. The Sorrentina pizza, with prosciutto and arugula, split our jury.

HUNTERDON

Flemington is a busy little pizza center, with a dozen pizzerias scattered in and around the borough. Probably the best is **ANGELO'S CUCINA** (164 Route 31, Raritan Township; 908-788-3889). The plain pizza is not worth the drive around the Flemington Circle, but the sausage is fennel-feisty, and the margherita, from the brick oven, is a winner.

CAFE GALLERIA (18 S. Main St., Lambertville; 609-397-2400), cozy and intimate, was packed when we arrived, so we took our pizza and ate outside, despite the chill. The half plain/half sausage is ordinary, but the cheese-less tomato pie, with big chunks of tomato, is some kind of wonderful. It may have been my favorite slice in all of Hunterdon County.

CATANZARETI'S PIZZA & ITALIAN RESTAURANT (Village Square Shopping Center, 299 N. Main St., Lambertville; 609-397-2992) offers a boardwalk-worthy grease slice with a flimsy foundation. The margherita is somewhat better.

Another yin-and-yang pizza experience came at **DiMOLA'S PIZZA & RESTAURANT** (1541 Route 31, Clinton; 908-638-5612). The plain and sausage pizzas are screamingly ordinary. "The box (taste) without the box," one taster said. But the Sicilian is a soft, eminently chewy surprise. DiMola's won our award for quickest ordering time: 16 seconds. You won't believe how long some of our ordering took, much of it because the counter person was indecisive when we asked them to recommend a specialty pizza. And when they did, it was often buffalo or barbecue chicken. Uh, no thanks.

Frank's is one of the more popular pizzeria names in Jersey, right up there with Luigi's and Brothers (Sisters are seriously under-represented; we didn't find one pizzeria with Sister or Sisters in its name). **FRANK'S PIZZA & PASTA** (268 Route 202, Raritan Township; 908-788-3739) turns out a decent plain slice. The marinara pizza boasts chunks of tomatoes, but it came out under-cooked.

Strip-mall pizzerias are a Jersey staple; one of the better ones is **GIOVANNI'S PIZZA & PASTA** (Bishops Plaza, Route 22 east, Whitehouse Station; 908-534-4410). The plain pizza is an honest slice; the sausage pie features plenty of sausage but little flavor. The old-fashioned tomato pie is slippery and garlic-heavy, but we liked the crispy crust.

GIUSEPPE'S RISTORANTE (40 Bridge St., Lambertville; 609-397-1500) is a handsome little cafe/restaurant, but the pizza is not much to look at. There's little in the way of sauce on the plain pizza, and Scott

Wiener found the cheese "rubbery." The Nonna, a thin-crust Sicilian, fared better, despite its canned-tasting sauce.

The plain pie at **LENNY'S PIZZA AND PASTA** (8 Reading Road, Raritan Township; 908-237-0002) tasted as if it were made in an Easy-Bake Oven. "A flavor roadblock" is how Wiener described the crust. But the Brooklyn, a square thin crust, is a crusty contender.

LUNA RESTAURANT (429 Main St., Three Bridges; 908-284-2321) is located in a trim white house in the center of this village, just off Route 202. We fell in love instantly with the pizza. The half plain/half sausage is a perfect blend of crispy and chewy. The sausage is so good we gave Luna an Award of Excellence in our Best Pizza in New Jersey competition. The marinara pizza, with chopped Italian tomatoes, fresh garlic, oregano and olive oil, is nearly as good.

MILLER'S TAVERN (2 Beaver Ave., Annandale; 908-735-4730) is a fun combination of roadhouse/biker bar/pizzeria, with jukebox and pool table. It's always a challenge backing the Big Dog out of the small lot, which fronts a Route 78 exit ramp. The plain/sausage pizza here is commendable; Gina Bruno singled out its "distinct" flavor. The half tomato/half mushroom pizza received raves all around. "Awesome," said one judge. "It rocks!" added another.

"Well-constructed" doesn't mean "tastes well" in the world of pizza. The plain pizza at **NATALE'S ITALIAN RESTAURANT AND PIZZA** (Route 31 and Payne Road, Clinton Township; 908-735-4455) doesn't drip or run when you tilt it, but it also doesn't have much flavor. The bruschetta pie, while under-cooked, is tasty. Al Windrem called it a "newsroom pie." Funny; that's where most of the leftover pizza ended up each night.

Two out of three, Meatloaf once sang, ain't bad. The cheese and sauce on the plain pie at **NICOLA PIZZERIA** (Franklin and Bridge streets, Lambertville; 609-397-0212) are the right stuff. The crust — not so much. One team member called it "wimpy." Undistinguished sausage. The jury was divided on the margherita. Wiener called it "tasty," while Bruno judged the sauce "low quality."

I practically lived on the pizza at **PIZZA COMO** (5 Old Highway 22, Clinton; 908-735-9250) when I resided in Central Jersey's most picturesque town. It was located in the former Laneco Plaza, above town; it's now on the town's main drag. It's still good pizza, even if not everyone agreed. Bruno found it "gummy." Whatever. The Paradiso pie, with plum tomatoes, bacon, mushrooms, olives and mozzarella, is an unqualified hit.

TOMMY D'S PIZZA & PASTA (547 Rt. 22 east, Whitehouse Station; 908-534-5976) is new, and not surprisingly needs work. The plain pizza is the definition of bland. The margherita features a nice tomatoey sauce, but it's too sloppy/runny.

Over-cheesed and under-cooked seemed to be our lot on the Pizza Patrol. Yet another example of the latter came at **YORDANA'S RIS-TORANTE** (67 Church St., Flemington; 908-782-2276). The margherita is slippery-oily, but we liked the sauce.

MERCER

Often the plain pizza outdid a more complicated specialty pizza. That proved the case at **ANTIMO'S ITALIAN KITCHEN** (52 E. Broad St., Hopewell; 609-466-3333), where the plain pizza is a winning combination of crust and cheese. The sausage is fatty, but still above average. The Grandma-like Brooklyn pizza boasts organic plum tomatoes, but they aren't enough to rescue this by-the-numbers pie.

Just as the grease trucks are a rite of passage for any self-respecting Rutgers student or New Brunswick resident, so is **CONTE'S** (339 Witherspoon St., Princeton; 609-921-8041) for the average Princeton student or townie. Confession: We violated Rule No. 1 of Fight Club, er, Pizza Patrol, and ordered a half plain/half pepperoni on a regular's advice. The pepperoni here is not the usual world's most popular pizza topping. Yours truly, profoundly anti-pepperoni, found himself picking it off, piece by piece. The sausage, though, should be better; call it county college, not Ivy League, sausage.

Say "Trenton" and "pizza" to most people, and the reply is DeLorenzo's. The question is, which one? **DeLORENZO'S** (1007 Hamilton Ave., Trenton; 609-393-2952) is bigger than its Hudson Street counterpart. The pizza here is saucier than Hudson Street. Is it better? That's for you to decide. There's little if any difference in the quality of sausage; it's excellent both places. The fresh rosemary and roasted red peppers pizza is highly recommended for those who want to stray off the plain pizza path. This De Lorenzo's is bigger than the Hudson Street location and easier to get into, which matters in the summer.

De LORENZO'S TOMATO PIES (2350 Route 33, Robbinsville; 609-341-8480) is the sister stop of the fabled Hudson Street, Trenton location. The two could not be more dissimilar; Robbinsville is spacious, tony-looking, while Hudson Street looks like a 1940s movie set. The trademark clam tomato pie at both places is wonderful. "The fat lady is singing — this is great," said an awe-struck Al Windrem. With Hudson Street, one of the top half-dozen sausage pizzas of the year. All the pizzas boast nicely charred crusts.

Tile floors, pale green plates, no credit cards, no bathroom and a cop stationed out on the sidewalk. Must be **De LORENZO'S TOMATO PIES** (530 Hudson St., Trenton; 609-695-9534). Open just Thursdays through Sundays, and there's almost always a wait. But it is so worth it. The sausage pizza received top honors in our Best Pizza in New Jersey competition. The clam pizza is just about perfect. Comments included "tremendous," "awesome" and "tastes like heaven." Yeah, it's that good. Funny moment: Last time we were there, the cop grumbled good-naturedly because we had taken his usual parking spot out front. We offered it back, but he didn't want it.

I'd hate to be the owner of the pizzeria visited immediately after DeLo's, but **GENNARO'S PIZZERIA** (4613 Nottingham Way, Hamilton; 609-587-4992) acquitted itself well. Quality tomatoes and a fine, full-bodied flavor distinguished the plain pizza. The Brooklyn pie, a thin crust with fresh mozzarella, basil, olive oil and grated Parmigiana, received high marks from our picky patrol. In the same strip mall is an outpost of Primo's, which I consider the best sub Down the Shore.

"Friendship and macaroni are best when warm," reads a sign at **IANO'S ROSTICCERIA** (86 Nassau St., Princeton; 609-924-5515). Can't argue with that; cold macaroni never did anything for me. Nice creamy mozzarella on the plain pizza, and tasty, but fatty, sausage. The margherita pizza is oregano-heavy to the point where you don't taste much else.

Call **JOJO'S TAVERN** (2677 Nottingham Way, Mercerville; 609-586-2678) a Mercer County version of Strawberry's in Woodbridge, minus the latter's bright lights. The bar was packed, so we took our pizza outside on the little deck. The sauce is tangy and assertive, but the crust doesn't seem up to the task. Quality sausage. I liked the shredded steak pie, but no one else did. I got used to this real quick.

The Commodores were singing "Brick House" when we stopped at **MAMMA ROSA'S RESTAURANT** (572 Klockner Road, Hamilton; 609-588-5454), which was appropriate because Mamma's is a brick house-turned-restaurant. If you're into fresh-tasting, tomatoey pizzas, you'll love Mamma's. They use good sausage; it's Hatfield brand, from a Trenton supplier. The Sicilian is quite good.

NOMAD PIZZA CO. (10 E. Broad St., Hopewell; 609-466-6623) may have been the most attractive restaurant space we encountered, with brick floors, a long communal table and outdoor patio and garden. The bright blue oven provides eye candy. The margherita di bufala pizza contained serious ingredients — San Marzano tomatoes, buffalo mozzarella, aged Parmesan, organic basil, organic olive oil, sea salt — but suffered from slippage, and the too-soft, pliant crust came across as undercooked. The sausage, though, features a nice spicy kick. We liked the arugula with prosciutto pizza more.

It was dreary and raining when we arrived at **NONNO SAL'S** (Concord Square Shopping Center, 1905 Route 33, Hamilton Square; 609-890-7474), and the plain pizza, with slightly off-putting cheese, didn't improve our mood. But the No. 11 pie — Nonno Sal's Pizza Special, a Grandma or thin-crust square pizza with mozzarella, basil, crushed tomatoes and olive oil — is a treat. "Tastes like it came right out of the garden," Al Windrem said.

OLD WORLD PIZZA (242½ Nassau St., Princeton; 609-924-9321) is an unprepossessing little joint, but it turns out good product. Quality cheese, a nice sweet sauce and a fine crust add up to a model plain pizza. Scott Wiener admired the crust's "great bake." Gina Bruno found the dough on the white pie "a little dry," but Old World and Iano's, across from the Princeton University campus, are better than anything we found by the Rutgers campus in New Brunswick. Old World's hot barbecue sauce is a must-try. I wanted to run right out and buy a rack of ribs and spread it all over.

A sign at **PAPA'S TOMATO PIES** (804 Chambers St., Trenton; 609-392-0359) describes it as "the second oldest tomato pie restaurant" in the country. Only Lombardi's in New York City, which opened in 1905, seven years before Papa's, predates it. Papa's, named after founder Joe Papa, is a lively, intimate wood-paneled hangout. Nick Azzarro, Papa's grandson, can be found working the crowd like a nightclub entertainer. The plain pizza is a straightforward delight; we gave it an Award of Excellence in our Best Pizza in New Jersey contest. Decent sausage pizza — should be better. The white ricotta pizza is sloppy but enjoyable. One pie here you won't find anywhere else: a mustard pie, with mustard and tomato sauce. Weirdly compelling.

Worst slice of the 1,000 sampled? My vote goes to the Sicilian at **PIZZA STAR** (Princeton Shopping Center, 301 N. Harrison St., Princeton; 609-921-7422). It glowed a sickly yellow under the fluorescent lighting and bore an eerie resemblance to spongy French toast. "We use 100 percent real cheese," the pizza box trumpets. It's 100 percent bad cheese. The crust is no better. "Like chewing on an eraser," Wiener wailed. The best things here are the wall mosaics by artist Victoria Bell.

Hopefully, students at the Lawrenceville School are smart enough to realize that **VARSITY PIZZA & SUBS** (1296 Lawrenceville Road, Lawrenceville; 609-882-4100) will never make the dean's list. It didn't help that Varsity was the last stop on a trip that included Papa's and DeLo's. "I felt like I woke from this beautiful pizza dream to see this nightmare," Wiener said. Bruno described the plain pizza as "painful." The Brooklyn Sicilian had even less going for it, with its "Pillsbury dough crust and canned tomatoes," according to Joan Dwyer.

MIDDLESEX

ALFONSO'S FAMILY TRATTORIA & WOOD BURNING PIZZERIA

(647 Route 18, East Brunswick; 732-257-7111) sounded promising, but failed to deliver. The sausage needs an upgrade — but we've said this at scores of pizzerias. The crust seems too chewy, and the margherita is lackluster.

One of the newer kids on the pizza block is **ANGEL'S** (5 Joyce Kilmer Ave., New Brunswick; 732-545-0129), which advertises "the best cheesesteak in N.J." Well, it's better than the pizza. The plain is not cooked through, and it shows no evidence of pizza mastery, or mechanics. The cheesesteak pizza — not a stuffed pie, the ingredients are on top — is an upgrade, and as a late-night snack better than anything you'll find at the Rutgers grease trucks, not far away.

The plain pizza at **ANTONIO'S BRICK OVEN PIZZA** (453 Main St., Metuchen; 732-603-0008) boasts a nice burn around the edges, but the sauce is ordinary. The deep-dish margherita, however, is a tomatoey, crusty success. I called it "a top 20, maybe top 10" pizza at the time, and in the end the team agreed, giving Antonio's an Award of Excellence in our Best Pizza in New Jersey margherita category.

Can't say we found any really good pizza anywhere on Route 18. **BROTHERS PIZZA & RESTAURANT** (1020 Route 18, East Brunswick; 732-254-7171) uses decent cheese, but there isn't much else going on. One team member said the sauce on the margherita "tastes totally canned."

"Trust the crust" is the byword at **BRUNO'S PIZZA FACTORY** (1713 Park Ave., South Plainfield; 908-769-8016). You'll either love or hate the crispy crust and the pebbly foundation. The latter may throw you at first, but I liked it, and Bruno's spare, fluorescent-lit charm. Good sausage pizza, but subpar Sicilian. Quirky little pizza dive.

The plain-sausage pizza at **CAFE GALLO** (1153 Inman Ave., Edison; 908-756-5752) is the doughy definition of average. The Grandma pie fared better, although there was dissension. One team member described it as "close to perfect," another said it represented "a sauce party I wouldn't attend."

Tiny Jamesburg is home to a half-dozen pizzerias on either side of the railroad tracks. The plain pizza at **CAFE NAPOLI** (200 Buckelew Ave., Jamesburg; 732-521-2100) features a nice crunch but would benefit from more sauce. The Sicilian is screamingly ordinary. "Been there, done that, got the photos back from Walgreens," Marty Schneider wittily noted.

You might drive right past the **CENTER BAR** (46 Marion St., Port Reading section of Woodbridge; 732-969-2390), as we did. Sequestered in a residential neighborhood, it's a cozy hangout with jumbo pickled eggs and "chicken in a garden," whatever that is, on the menu. The plain pizza didn't make much of an impression, and the sausage tasted more like a meatball, but we loved the house specialty, the BLT pizza. "It could have gone wrong in all different areas, but it didn't," Gina Bruno said. The bacon lover in me wished it had more of my favorite pork product in it.

CIRO'S PIZZA (140 Lake Ave., Colonia; 732-388-5556) is one of those longtime neighborhood pizzerias with dependable, and thoroughly average, pies. The sauce is so weak it may need propping up. Go with the Sicilian; one judge liked the "fruity" sauce, another called it "nice and sweet."

Sometimes you can just look at a pizza and judge that it's going nowhere. That was our experience at **EDISON PIZZA & ITALIAN RESTAURANT** (2303 Woodbridge Ave., Edison; 732-985-1733). The Sicilian boasts a nice light crust but is unfortunately light on flavor. Good pasta dishes here, though.

We practically celebrated when we found saucy pizzas like the plain at **FERRARO'S RESTAURANT & PIZZERIA** (1067 Inman Ave., Edison; 908-561-7373). It's a snap-crackly thin-crust delight, with a pleasant sweet sauce. The sausage and Sicilian pizzas, alas, are losers.

You're back in the land of bland at **GIUSEPPE'S BRICK OVEN PIZZE-RIA & RESTAURANT** (24 Summerfield Blvd., Dayton; 732-274-8808). The plain pizza cries out for seasoning, spice, something. The sausage tastes like something, but it's not sausage. The verdict on the upside-down Brooklyn: nice try, not-so-nice pizza. "Maybe they should have turned it right-side up," Bruno said sarcastically.

"A taste of Brooklyn in Jamesburg" is the slogan at **JAMESBURG PIZZA** (27C E. Railroad Ave., Jamesburg; 732-521-1414). The sauce on the plain pizza is better than most. The margherita pie came as a nice sweet surprise. Jamesburg as a pizza destination? You bet. And Mendoker's Bakery is across the street if you want to pick up a dozen doughnuts or a cheesecake for dessert.

A banner at **KRISPY PIZZA** (2323 Route 516, Old Bridge; 732-679-9600) proclaims Krispy's Brooklyn location as the winner of the "2005 Battle of the Boroughs." Fine, but that doesn't mean it'll play on this side of the river. The plain pizza is just that. Crispy? Not this crust. The sausage shavings are greasy. The Grandma is an improvement, but she's showing her age, or lack of class. "We just pulled into Bland Central Station," Scott Wiener cracked.

I'm not sure what's famous at **LA ROSA FAMOUS PIZZERIA & ITAL-IAN RESTAURANT** (335 Lake Ave., Metuchen; 732-549-6505). It's sure not the sausage, which is close to awful. "Not my mom's sauce," Bruno said. "Not anybody's mom's sauce," Wiener added. Two words for the Sicilian — skip it. Our advice: Go to nearby Antonio's, on Main Street.

The plain pizza at **LA VILLA RESTAURANT & PIZZERIA** (355 Applegarth Road, Monroe; 609-655-3338) is a step or two up from frozen. The sausage pizza has close to zero flavor. The Grandma pizza, though, is a winner. One judge admired its "rich taste," another called it "simplicity at its best."

What a surprise — a pizzeria named after a Luigi! The sauce at **LUIGI'S RISTORANTE & PIZZERIA** (93 Smith St., Perth Amboy; 732-826-5900) tastes like it came right off the assembly line. The plain doesn't hold together well, the cheese and sauce slip-sliding away. The bruschetta, though, is another matter, with the red onions providing pop.

Thanks to **MARIA'S PIZZERIA & RESTAURANT** (671 Harris Ave., Middlesex; 732-748-1122) for staying open; we arrived near closing time. But no thanks for the pizza, which Al Windrem described as "watery and tasteless." The margherita is not much better. They have may rushed things, but we certainly didn't ask them to.

Call **MENLO PIZZA & SUBS** (170 Lafayette Ave., Edison; 732-548-0660) a saucy survivor. The pizzeria, within walking distance of Menlo Park Mall, has been in business since 1972. The plain pizza is slippery, greasy and ordinary. Same old sausage. We learned early on in our mission not to get excited by the words "homemade meatballs." The ones here make no impression.

PANICO'S BRICK OVEN PIZZA BAR & GRILL (94 Church St., New Brunswick; 732-545-6161) is part of Panico's, a mainstay of the New Brunswick restaurant scene. The bar/grill is an attractive space; now they should do something about the pizza. It's cooked well, but that's the best we could say about it. The sausage reminds us of much of our South Jersey sausage, and you don't want to go there. The Sicilian tastes like tasteless bread, if that's possible.

The natural question at **PIZZA AND** (1636 St. Georges Ave., Avenel; 732-382-1100) is, Pizza And what? Well, pasta, subs and wings, among other things. You can walk right into the Pathmark from the front door (or is it the back?) and do your food shopping. The plain pizza is no Rocco's (entry below). We may have done better picking one up in the frozen food section. But the sausage is mildly zesty, and the Sicilian features a nice crunch and pillowy crust.

PIZZA TIME (1076 St. Georges Ave., Avenel; 732-636-5195) doesn't look like much, inside or outside, but pizza appearances can be deceiving. The plain slice is among the two or three best in the county. The Sicilian could have been a contender — if it wasn't undercooked. Pizza Time gets my award for best N.J. pizza box, a full-color view of the Ponte Vecchio in Florence. An added treat: Colonia Dairy Maid is right across the street. Pizza and ice cream — there's no need to live on anything else.

PJ'S GRILL & PIZZA (166 Easton Ave., New Brunswick; 732-249-1800) offers variations of the sandwiches at the Rutgers grease trucks, if you're so inclined. The best thing about PJ's plain pie is the agreeably greasy cheese. The crust, meanwhile, needs an overhaul. Pellet-like sausage, and that's never a good thing. The PJ's Pizza — mozzarella, basil, tomatoes, olive oil, pesto — is a mistake. Friendly staff, unfriendly pizza.

ROCCO'S PIZZERIA (57 Avenel St., Avenel; 732-750-5800) looks like your typical neighborhood pizzeria, until you step inside and notice the espresso machine (great espresso here), or some of the atypical pies issuing from the oven. There's one with roasted red peppers, mozzarella and tomatoes. Ask for it; it's not on the menu. It made my list

of top 10 specialty pizzas of the entire year. The plain pizza is heavy on the sauce (good thing) and cheese (not so good thing). Better-than-average sausage pie.

Call **ROME PIZZA** (334 North Ave., Dunellen; 732-968-1394) a pizza diner, with its counter and stools. The plain pizza tasted like every other forgettable plain pizza. The sausage needs work, and so does the Sicilian, with a sauce "that tastes like Ragu." Rome wasn't built in a day; this Rome may need a few days to straighten itself out.

The plain pizza at **SANTINO'S ITALIAN RESTAURANT & PIZZERIA** (499 Ernston Road, Sayreville; 732-721-3163) is an average cheesy-greasy pie, but the sausage pie is better than most. But the Grandma pie should be thrown out of the Santino family. The sauce tastes borderline sour, and the texture is gummy.

I remember Sciortino's in Perth Amboy, with its brick oven and impossibly small parking lot. Sciortino's is now on the other side of the river as **SCIORTINO'S HARBOR LIGHTS** (132 S. Broadway, South Amboy; 732-721-8788). It's as good, and distinctive, as ever. The sweet sauce is not for everyone, but we liked it. One team member described the plain as "a thing of beauty." The sausage pie should be better, though. The meatball pie is decent. Sciortino's is a must-stop for any pizza lover; you be the judge of the sauce.

You'll never accuse N.J. pizzeria owners of modesty; **STEFANO'S WOODBURNING PIZZA & RISTORANTE** (1297 Centennial Ave., Piscataway; 732-562-9696) claims "the best wood-burning pizza in New Jersey." But here's one pizzeria that backs up its big talk. The plain pizza is a delight, with a chewy crust. Good-quality sausage. The Genovese — I am not making this up! — is a first-rate combo of prosciutto, mozzarella, oregano and olive oil. Definitely one of the better specialty pies around.

The plain pizza at **STELTON PIZZA** (1315 Stelton Road, Piscataway; 732-985-2626) is not worth the trip from anywhere; the cheese tasted third-rate. The sausage had a boardwalk-stand flavor, but that kind of pizza is better appreciated on the boardwalk. The Sicilian is better, though still middle of the road. Wiener did admire its "well-baked" nature.

We may have received more e-mails for **STRAWBERRY'S PUB & PIZZA** (110 Amboy Ave., Woodbridge; 732-634-3131) than any other pizzeria in New Jersey. The bar was packed when we visited, so we put our pies on the Official Pizza Patrol Pans — you know what a cardboard box does to pie! — and took them outside, where we broke out the Official Pizza Patrol Folding Table. Team members singled out "the balance of seasoning" and "bold sauce" on the plain pizza. Tasty sausage. We couldn't make up our minds about the clam casino pie. Marty Schneider found the smell of the green peppers off-putting, and Bruno said the clams "tasted like a bad trip to the boardwalk," but Al

Windrem and Wiener liked the pie. I was somewhere in the middle, if that's possible.

Boy, did I hear it from one reader after our review of **TONY'S PIZZA & RESTAURANT** (716 Oak Tree Road, South Plainfield; 908-754-1181). She had been going to Tony's for years, and felt we couldn't have been more wrong. But the plain pizza seemed a bit soupy, and thoroughly unremarkable. The Sicilian is somewhat better; one crew member praised its "delicious" cheese, although another found "a bit of a burnt flavor."

The soundtrack at **VILLA GENNARO ITALIAN RESTAURANT** (75 Route 27, Edison; 732-549-8554) went from Placido Domingo to "Grazing in the Grass" to Badfinger. I could only think: "I'm so dizzy, my head is spinning . . . " The plain came across "kind of gummy," with an "unappealing" crust. But we liked the margherita for its "right combination of sauce and cheese."

MONMOUTH

If a pizzeria or restaurant was crowded, we simply took our pizza outside and ate it in the parking lot, as we did at **BROTHERS** (2 Morford Place, Red Bank; 732-530-3356). The sauce-shy plain pizza could have been a contender; Al Windrem's description — "warning track power" — was appropriate. The plum tomato-spinach-ricotta pie is markedly better.

CARMEN'S/PETE & ELDA'S (Route 35, Neptune City; 732-774-6010) is probably the Jersey Shore's best-known pizzeria. But like Vic's in Bradley Beach, another pizza legend, it left the Pizza Patrol underwhelmed. One team member tasted "too much flour," another likened the crust to "cardboard." The meatball pizza is an improvement. "The meatball spices things up," Al Windrem said. I remember the pizza here tasting much better when I lived in nearby Manasquan.

COAL FIRED BRICK OVEN (624 Brinley Ave., Bradley Beach; 732-869-9770), with its attractive, café-like space, aspires to rise above the pizza pack. But they need to pay attention to the pizza, not the decor. The plain is in need of sauce. Good luck finding sausage on the sausage pie, but it does boast a nice spicy kick. The pesto pizza? "Dry chewy crust — needs to take a dip in the ocean," said an unimpressed Scott Wiener.

D'ARCY'S TAVERN (310 Main St., Bradley Beach; 732-774-9688) is a lively neighborhood bar. The pizza? Probably best appreciated with a beer. "Tastes like grilled cheese," Gina Bruno said. "Wish it tasted like grilled cheese," Windrem added. Unfortunate, past-shelf-life tomatoes on the margherita. Great sign in window of army surplus store next door: No Vomiting in Doorway.

DENINO'S PIZZA PLACE (Aberdeen Townsquare, Route 34, Aberdeen; 732-583-2150) is the sole Jersey outpost of the Staten Island pizza legend. Judging by the three pizzas we sampled, they should consider opening more here. The plain features "great bite and flavor." The sausage is not on the same lofty level as De Lorenzo's on Hudson Street, but it's not far behind. The margherita is close to magnificent. "Fragrant — smells like a garden," according to Wiener. We gave Denino's an Award of Excellence in the Best Pizza in New Jersey margherita category.

What N.J. pizza lover doesn't know **FEDERICI'S FAMILY RESTAU-RANT** (14 E. Main St., Freehold Borough; 732-462-1312). Frank Federici and his wife, Ester, bought the present restaurant in 1921; the pizza recipe has remained the same since 1946. Neat touch: You can get your takeout pizza in a bag, which keeps the pizza fresher and crunchier. The plain pizza seemed sauce-shy, but we admired the "great cracker crust." Wiener gave the meatball pie a "good" rating, but I thought it adequate, at best.

FEDERICI'S SOUTH RESTAURANT (6469 Route 9, Howell; 732-364-8220), owned by Dave Federici's sister and brother-in-law, seems a few notches down from the original Federici's. The flavor seems to have gone way south. We made note of the "limp" crust and "fatty" sausage. The meatball pizza is nicely seasoned, but is burdened by the same insubstantial crust.

Best pizza in Bradley Beach? It's not at the legendary Vic's but at **FERRARO'S FAMOUS TOMATO PIES** (400 Main St., Bradley Beach; 732-775-1117). The half plain/half sausage has little going for it except good sausage. But the tomato pie, with San Marzano tomatoes, is a dazzler. Bruno called it "an all-around great pie," and the rest of us agreed.

Frank Federici, brother of Dave Federici of Federici's, owns **FRANKIE FED'S PIZZA & PASTA HOUSE** (831 Route 33 east, Freehold Township; 732-294-1333). The crust here seems crispier, more well-done than Federici's. Frankie Fed's Pizza, with eggplant, sliced tomatoes, prosciutto and tri-colored peppers, is a winner. Wiener singled out the "rich-tasting eggplant," while Bruno liked the "nice and crunchy peppers." Overall, I liked Frankie Fed's more than Federici's.

We like rules like the one at **FRATELLI'S RESTAURANT PIZZERIA** (500 Route 35, Middletown; 732-747-4737). You cannot order a brick oven pie as takeout — it doesn't sit well in the box. The brick oven half plain/half sausage rocked our world. One team member called it "dynamite," another "outrageous." We liked the Sicilian so much we gave it an Award of Excellence in that category.

The cheese on the plain pizza at **FREDDIE'S RESTAURANT & PIZZERIA** (563 Broadway, Long Branch; 732-222-0931) tasted a bit off.

But we liked the sausage pie, despite the flimsy crust. The margherita, while garlic-heavy, delivered.

Looking for a "sissy" pie? You can get it at **LUIGI'S FAMOUS PIZZA** (477 Middle Road, Hazlet; 732-787-4669). It's short for Sicilian. The plain pizza is oregano-lively, and recommended. Skip the sausage; it tastes past its expiration date. Bland Grandma pizza. The strangest moment of our pizza season came here. The guy behind the counter removed the coupons from a menu before handing it over, saying they were for "customers." Uh, what were we?

We must have hit at least 50 pizzerias claiming to be famous for something or other. **LUIGI'S FAMOUS PIZZA** (3329 Doris Ave., Ocean; 732-531-7733) lives up to the name. The plain pizza is flavor-packed, and the sausage pizza received one of three Awards of Excellence in the sausage category. Nice Sicilian, but overshadowed by the plain and sausage pizzas. Luigi's is just north of the Asbury Circle; look for the Staples across the highway.

Maybe it's something about the Luigi's name. **LUIGI'S FAMOUS PIZZA & RISTORANTE** (650 Newman Springs Road, Lincroft; 732-842-2122) is known for its squarish plain and sausage pies. They're both excellent, with distinctive crusts and fresh-tasting sauce. The Sicilian, though, should stay in the kitchen. Luigi's is just off Parkway exit 109 in case you want to pick one up on the way home or back from the beach. Highly recommended.

The verdict on **LUKE'S PIZZA** (2601 E. Hurley Pond Road, Wall; 732-280-9255), across the street from Wall High School: great location, boring pizza. Joan Dwyer called it a "snoozefest." Bruno seemed the only admirer, describing it as "very basic" but "enjoyable." The Grandma is garlic-y, but otherwise forgettable.

There are a million variations of Ray's Pizza in the New York metro area, or so it seems. Add one more to the list: **RAY'S REAL PIZZA** (3429 Route 35 north, Hazlet; 732-203-1600). There's apparently a "Little Ray" and "Big Ray" working here. We liked the plain pizza, suitably greasy. But the sausage is a mistake, and there is only a trace of sauce on the Sicilian.

When I wrote that the plain pizza at **ROMEO'S** (325 Route 36 north, Port Monmouth; 732-787-1110) tasted like it needs a Juliet, or love from somebody, the owner replied that I should be a reporter, not a comedian, and that his customers had suggested I needed "tongue surgery," whatever that is. But none of us were much taken by this Romeo. One team member described the plain as having "no flavor." Another couldn't "detect a pulse" in the Grandma pizza.

Across the street from Federici's is **STEFANO'S PIZZERIA & RES-TAURANT** (35 E. Main St., Freehold Borough; 732-462-5656). The Pizza Patrol couldn't agree on anything here. Bruno called the sauce "off-tasting" and the sausage "tough to chew," but I liked the crunchy crust. Marty Schneider described the Grandma pizza as "great," and Wiener called it "completely worthy of a stop," but I thought the sauce tasted canned, familiar. Well, Pizza Patrol is a democracy.

You can't always get what you want, especially when it comes to pizza. The plain pie at **TANOLLA'S PIZZA** (713 Riverview Drive, Brielle; 732-528-5544) features spry seasoning but a weak crust. Decent sausage. The Grandma pizza is a well-behaved Grandma, but it's no match for its counterpart at Grandma's Pizza truck in Jersey City. Love the homemade meatballs here. They should give the sausage the same attention.

Is **TONY'S FAMOUS TOMATO PIES** (228 Morris Ave., Long Branch; 732-222-3535) the best pizza in Long Branch? "There is no competition," bartender Gina Chiafullo bragged. She may have more character than the pizza. We liked the plain and sausage, both significantly better than your average bar pie. The margherita? Not so much. There's a train stop right behind the restaurant, if that matters.

VESUVIO RESTAURANT AND PIZZERIA (705 Tenth Ave., Belmar; 732-681-5556) is a trip. It was old-school before the term was invented — waitresses with Jersey attitude, famous this-or-that on the menu, a dining room that scarcely seems to have changed since the 1940s. Spaghetti cooked to order? That'll cost you extra. The plain pizza features a pleasant burnt top. Bruno singled out the "beautiful" sausage. The white pizza, with mushrooms, is first-rate. One-of-a-kind place, one-of-a-kind pizza. It may be my favorite Shore pizzeria north of LBI.

VIC'S ITALIAN RESTAURANT (60 Main St., Bradley Beach; 732-774-8225) is one of the Shore's most popular pizzerias, but most of the Pizza Patrol wondered why. "Tastes like the pizza at every place you (visit) that's been around 50 years," Windrem said. Joan Dwyer, who grew up on Vic's, not surprisingly described the plain as "delicious." In the summer, the place is packed, so what do we know?

MORRIS

ANNA MARIE'S PIZZERIA & TRATTORIA (321 Route 15 north, Wharton; 973-328-6966) is in the Busy Lady Shopping Plaza. How about some equal time for the guys? We need a Busy Man Shopping Plaza! The plain pizza here tastes as if someone were busy doing something else while making it. Promising-looking chunks of sausage, but a downer taste-wise.

Check out the cute "History of Pizza" display at **AVELLINO'S PIZZA & GRILLE** (445 Ridgedale Ave., East Hanover; 973-887-2821). It's like one of those science projects we all did as kids, except that it's devoted to pizza. The plain pizza is nice and cheesy, even if the crust is a bit too chewy. The margherita is nicely seasoned and the cheese creamy, but the sauce tastes dried out.

You get one chance with the Pizza Patrol; our reports were based on one visit — any more, and we'd be eating pizza well into our old age! I did an Eat With Pete review on **CAMBIOTTI'S TOMATO PIE CAFE** (102 Shippenport Road, Landing; 973-770-1020) several years ago, and raved about its pizza. I wasn't as wowed during our Pizza Patrol visit, although I still liked it. One team member thought the crust on the plain "average," although another admired the "greasiness." The Four Seasons pie, with mushrooms, olives, artichokes and prosciutto, features a tangy sauce, sleeping under the pillow of toppings.

We received many e-mails about **CARMINE'S PIZZERIA RESTAU-RANT** (75-77 Main St., Netcong; 973-347-2404), but this neighborhood fixture did nothing to separate itself from the pizza pack. "Typical grease pie" and "just the same as everybody else" were two comments. A mozzarella/basil/tomato pie came off on the watery side.

A deli that doubles as a pizzeria is not usually a good sign. That proved the case at **CASELLA'S PIZZERIA & FINE ITALIAN DELI** (139 Route 10 east, Succasunna; 973-341-3110). Scott Wiener singled out the crust's "nice crunch," but added he was "not in a rush to go back." Marty Schneider, less forgiving, called it "a step up from frozen." The Sicilian featured spotty cheese/sauce distribution.

The **COLUMBIA INN** (29 Route 202, Montville; 973-263-1300) is more stylish than its rambling exterior would lead one to believe. The spacious bar is a good place to watch a baseball or football game, or you can head to one of the tables in the casual-cool dining room. The plain pizza is a thin-crust akin to Federici's, but the crackery crust seems to hold up better here. Nearly tasteless sausage, though. We liked the margherita; good flavor and diced tomato action.

There's plenty of pizza in Florham Park. Nonna's (see separate entry) makes a first-rate sausage pizza. **FLORHAM PARK PIZZERIA & RESTAURANT** (187 Columbia Turnpike, Florham Park; 973-966-1062) does a decent Grandma, with nice chunks of tomato. The plain pizza is average, with a doughy, indistinct crust. Verdict on the sausage: big pieces, little flavor.

You can trust the Forte name. Both the Forte in Caldwell and **FORTE PIZZERIA & RISTORANTE** (486 Route 10 West, Randolph; 973-328-4300) turn out solid pizzas. The plain at the latter is a nice, straightforward pie. The Grandma pie, though, is the standout, with big chunks of fresh tomatoes. Joan Dwyer said it made her tongue "sing."

Sometimes, you just know you're going to get a good pie. Maybe it was just the appearance of the friendly older couple at **GIOVANNI'S PLACE** (Birchwell Shopping Center, 1295 Route 23 South, Butler; 973-838-5510) that raised our hopes. We loved the cheese on the half plain/half sausage. The tired-tasting crust needs work, though. The Sicilian drew raves all around; Al Windrem called it "a kick-butt Sicilian." If you're not in a pizza mood, try the soups; they're pretty good.

GIULETTA & ROMEO PIZZERIA (7 Ronald Drive, East Hanover; 973-599-0550) is a vest-pocket pizzeria; we ate our pizzas outside, on the Pizza Patrol's Official Folding Pizza Table. The plain pizza is greasy — nothing wrong with that — but undistinguished. So-so sausage, for what seems like the millionth time. And their Grandma would not be welcomed into our family. "Tough crust, lacks spring or air," Scott Wiener said.

"The Pizza You Can't Refuse" is the motto at the **GODFATHER PIZZERIA** (200 Route 10 west, East Hanover; 973-887-4830). Well, the plain is one pizza you can refuse, and you don't have to worry about Luca Brasi showing up at your door. The Grandma fared somewhat better. Windrem singled out the "good crisp," while Wiener said "they followed the instructions" for this by-the-numbers pie.

Anything called the **GREAT AMERICAN PIZZA & GRILL** (276 E. Main St., Denville; 973-625-2223) better live up to its name. This strip-mall pizzeria doesn't. A team member took one bite and couldn't eat anymore. The Sicilian is slightly better; Joan Dwyer admired its "nice crunch."

ITALIAN VILLAGE PIZZA (300 Main St., Madison; 973-822-3344) had trouble reaching "average" status. The sauce and cheese need work. The sausage pie is okay. The margherita? No better. One taster made note of the "dried-up basil," another the "undercooked dough."

Screen door, tiny parking lot out back, and pizza with a difference. That's **LOVEY'S PIZZA & GRILL** (91 W. Hanover Ave., Morris Plains; 973-455-0677). The plain boasts a distinctive raised crust; Windrem said it was "cooked to perfection." The sausage pie is not rave-worthy, but it's a step in the right direction. The bruschetta pie was one of the top two or three bruschettas we tried all year.

M&S PIZZA (333 Route 46, Dover; 973-361-3756) is not to be confused with M&S II, just down the road. The plain pizza features a decent sauce, but the sausage, fished from a plastic container, should have stayed there. The Sicilian boasts a worthy crust, a not-so-worthy everything else.

I remember three things about **NONNA'S** (176 Columbia Turnpike, Florham Park; 973-410-0030). The rolling-pin-wielding Grandmas on the menu, the pretzel-like old-fashioned zeppoles, and the sausage pizzas, definitely one of the better ones we sampled. But the Grandpa pie — thicker than the more familiar Grandma pie — tasted bland. Grandma should straighten this Grandpa out.

Another Luigi's, and this one no match for the ones in Ocean Township or Lincroft. The plain pizza at **ORIGINAL LUIGI'S** (275 Route 10 east, Roxbury; 973-584-0181) is a bit doughy and borderline undercooked. Go with the Sicilian; one judge called it a "workingman's pizza."

Step back in pizza time at **PIZZA PALACE** (1169 Sussex Turnpike, Randolph; 973-895-3344), with its tile floors and fluorescent lighting. Ordinary, familiar-tasting cheese, but the sausage is greasy-good. The margherita pizza is an agreeable blend of cheese, garlic and tomatoes.

Odd moment at **POMODORO** (125 Morris St., Morristown; 973-538-6000). When I pointed out the "Voted No. 1 pizza in Morristown by The Star-Ledger" sign in the window, and told the manager that it was extremely unlikely the paper had said so, the manager conceded it may have been another paper's award. The plain pizza is oregano-heavy, but the crust is good and chewy. The margherita looks pretty but tastes ordinary.

The **RESERVOIR TAVERN** (90 Parsippany Blvd., Parsippany; 973-334-5708) is one of North Jersey's most famous, and atmospheric, restaurants/hangouts. Dig the deer heads and golf clubs on the wall. Order your pizza at the bar, or wait for a table. Al Windrem judged the plain pizza "perfectly cooked, nice and airy," but Gina Bruno described the sausage as "embarrassing." The bland margarita pie reminded Bruno of "cheese bread." The Reservoir in South Orange — no relation to the one in Parsippany — does a better sausage pizza.

Sauce was in short supply on our pizzas from beginning to end. We found another cheese-laden pizza at **RIDGEDALE PIZZA** (86 Ridgedale Ave., Cedar Knolls; 973-267-6262). Comments on the plain pizza ranged from "wimpy" to "pizza-flavored" chewing gum. The cheese succeeds somewhat in the ricotta/mozzarella/fresh tomatoes pizza.

If **ROMANELLI'S PIZZA & ITALIAN EATERY** (42 Lincoln Place, Madison; 973-377-9515) is the best pizza in Madison, as we were told, Madison is in trouble. Scott Wiener described the plain as "totally Domino's." Pellet-like sausage, and you know how we feel about that, but at least it's spicy. The old-fashioned bruschetta pie came as a nice surprise. "Fresh tomatoes, lightly seasoned, very nice," according to Wiener.

Long Valley has character and charm; it hasn't rubbed off on the plain pizza at **SALERNO'S RESTAURANT & PIZZERIA** (Route 24 and Old Farmers Road, Long Valley; 908-876-1283). The cheese tasted gummy, and the crust is nearly nonexistent. The sausage teeters on tastelessness. The Sicilian is a small step in the right direction. One team member judged it "fine," another called it "really dense."

Alex Magyar, former owner of the late, lamented Gabby and Vinny's Brick Oven in Point Pleasant Beach, has landed at **SPLASH SEAFOOD & PASTA** (1 Fairmount Road, Long Valley; 908-876-9307). No boring

bar pies here. The plain pizza is loaded with flavor, although one taster found it salty. The margherita pizza boasts a fine fruity sauce. Magyar knows what he's doing; we hope the owners of Splash will allow him to make pies closer in style to those at his Shore pizzeria.

We didn't find any standout pizza in Morristown. The plain pizza at **SUVIO'S PIZZA RISTORANTE** (83 Washington St., Morristown; 973-538-1660) is a failure in the flavor department. The Sicilian is nice and saucy, albeit somewhat greasy. "Impressive sauce, but that was the extent of the enjoyment," Gino Bruno said.

There's a comfortable outdoor patio at **THAT'S AMORE** (99 Bloomfield Ave., Denville; 973-586-8856). But the pizzas need work. Scott Wiener said he "couldn't pick the sausage out of a lineup," which didn't sound like a good thing. The margherita looked better than it tasted.

There's something to be said for your basic greasy Jersey slice. You can find it at **V & J PIZZA** (Plains Plaza Shopping Center, Route 23 north, Pompton Plains; 973-839-9757). That doesn't mean we're giving it high marks, though. "The kind of pizza you'd expect to find in a strip mall," one team member said. Good luck finding the sauce on the Sicilian; the global sauce shortage strikes again. Decent crust, though.

OCEAN

Judging by all the plaques and certificates we saw on pizzeria walls, a thousand or so "best of" awards must be handed out in New Jersey every year. The owner at **FRANCESCO'S** (297 Route 72 west, Manahawkin; 609-597-0040) was quick to point out all the accolades he had won. The plain pizza featured a "nice airiness" and "the tomatoes tasted like they were picked today." The sausage, alas, is subpar. Grandma pies shouldn't be this greasy.

GENARO'S OLD WORLD BRICK OVEN PIZZA & CALZONE (66 Brick Blvd., Brick; 732-255-1955), almost hidden in a shopping center in Brick, is one of the new kids on the pizza block. Bruno admired the "creamy" and "really delicate" nature of the Neapolitan supreme, with mozzarella di bufala. I just wished it had more sauce. The sausage is nice and spicy. Good cheese on the Sicilian, but the pie is doughy and undercooked.

"We've been Boss of the Sauce three years running," owner John Cataldo at **JOHNNY G'S ITALIAN RESTAURANT** (1812 Hooper Ave., Toms River; 732-255-8900) said of a local pizza contest. It is a bold, but not necessarily award-winning, sauce, and the best thing here. The plain and sausage pizzas are average. Joan Dwyer labeled the Florentine pizza a "full personality" pie.

The two best boardwalk pizzerias are Mack and Manco (see separate entry in Cape May County) and **MARUCA'S TOMATO PIES** (1927 Promenade, Seaside Park; 732-793-0707). This is Jersey Shore pizza done simply and done right. One Patrol member called it "too good for the boardwalk," another described it as a "home run." The margherita drew raves all around for its "excellent" crust and "top-notch execution."

The plain pizza at **PANZONE'S PIZZA** (22nd and Boulevard, Surf City; 609-494-1114) seemed as if it had taken off the summer and fall. "Really lame" sausage, according to Gina Bruno. The Sicilian, with its bready bottom, is the best bet here. This location of Panzone's is open year-round, so it has something going for it.

Opera music on the sound system couldn't save the pizza at **PIES ON** (1500 Route 37 east, Toms River; 732-270-4444). "It's Pies Off, not Pies On," Joan Dwyer cracked. The margherita pizza is better but still needs work. "An entropic pie," said Marty Schneider, dipping into his doughy dictionary. "It all fell apart."

The plain at **PJ's PIZZA & GRILL** (151 Van Zile Road, Brick; 732-840-3012) is your standard-issue Jersey Shore grease pie. Al Windrem, the biggest admirer, called it "extra salty but packed with flavor." Sausage is below average, though. The margherita got a wow from Scott Wiener, who singled out the "fruity chunks of tomato" and "fresh mutz."

Call **RAY'S NEW YORK PIZZA & RESTAURANT** (545 Mill Creek Road, Manahawkin; 609-597-5050), just off Route 72, a pizza roadhouse, with its white-shingled exterior. The bland sausage let down the overall pizza, but Windrem said Ray's would nevertheless "smash" the legendary Famous Ray's in Verona, the city and elsewhere. Dwyer called the Grandma pie "sassy." Bruno described the sauce and cheese as "awesome" but found the crust lacking. If you're on the "mainland," no need to schlep all the way to LBI for pizza; meander over to Manahawkin.

One of the more memorable Munchmobile trips of all time was a 2002 Down the Shore run that included trying to eat the cheesesteak-stuffed pizza at **SLICE OF HEAVEN** (610 N. Bay Ave., Beach Haven; 609-492-7437) on the beach in a gale-force wind. That pizza, loaded with peppers and onions and featuring a nice browned top, is still worth the trip in any weather. "Good for a tailgate," Bruno observed. "Good for bodybuilders," Wiener added.

Good luck finding a bigger pizza than the behemoths at **THREE BROTHERS FROM ITALY** (1901 Promenade, Seaside Park; 732-830-4188). Put them in the Guinness Book of World Pizza Records. Big doesn't mean better, especially when it comes to the boardwalk. The sausage is, in a word, awful. But the plain won't do you wrong. The Sicilian is one of the eight wonders of the New Jersey Pizza World — it's amazingly almost all cheese. "This pizza should be on the back of a milk carton — missing sauce," Windrem noted.

Highlight of our visit to **TWO BROTHERS II ITALIAN RESTAURANT & PIZZERIA** (Bennetts Mills Plaza, 2275 W. County Line Road, Jackson;

732-905-3003)? The water tank on the counter. Drop a coin into the tiny slot, win a free pizza. One guy has done it 16 times. Hey, we found amusement where we could get it. The half plain/half sausage is so-so. Decent sauce on the Sicilian, but good luck finding it.

PASSAIC

You think it's tough finding parking in Hoboken? Try downtown Paterson day or night. Scott Wiener ran in and picked up our pizzas at **BROADWAY PIZZA** (56 Broadway, Paterson; 973-279-3996) as I held a more or less legal parking spot nearby. It wasn't worth the effort. The crust on the plain pizza is lackluster, and the sausage is subpar — and that's being kind. The Sicilian, with little sauce and runny cheese, looked as if it had been in an accident.

What is it with guys named Bruno and Sicilian pizza? We picked Mr. Bruno's in Lyndhurst as New Jersey's best Sicilian. **BRUNO'S** (1006 Route 46 west, Clifton; 973-473-3339) is close behind. A big puffy crust and tons of tomatoey flavor equal near nirvana. It's a rough-hewn, rustic Sicilian compared with its more polished counterpart at Mr. Bruno's. The plain pizza at Bruno's, though, is a disappointment; hard to believe it came from the same oven. Our favorite waitress of the year: Michelle at Bruno's.

More of the same-old, same-old at **CIAO BELLA PIZZA & RESTAU-RANT** (57 Route 23 south, Wayne; 973-785-0930). Gina Bruno found the plain pizza a "crunchy surprise, but overall not a traffic stopper." The sausage is bland personified. Call Grandma, or at least the pizza named after her, eccentric. It's doughy and overloaded with basil besides.

Talk about Temptation Corner. Right across the street from **DOMI-NICK'S PIZZERIA** (304 Union Blvd., Totowa; 973-942-4141) is Pappy's, a hot dog landmark. We ran into too cheesy pizzas all year, and the troubling trend continued at Dominick's. "Not bad, but they forgot to put sauce on it," Bruno said. The Grandma is nice and saucy; we made note of the "fine fresh flavors" and its "pizazz."

MARIO'S RESTAURANT & PIZZERIA (710 Van Houten Ave., Clifton; 973-777-1559) is a neighborhood legend; a family celebrating Grandma's 80th birthday arrived just as the Big Dog did. The plain pizza, like Mario's itself, is straightforward, unpretentious and thoroughly enjoyable. The sausage, unfortunately, is thoroughly bland. Other team members liked the meatball pie, but I thought the meat had a mushy, mealy taste.

Good plain pizza, but not much else, at **PASQUALE'S PIZZERIA & RISTORANTE** (46 Route 23 north, Little Falls; 973-256-8246). There was praise for the plain's "great flavor" and "admirable amount of sauce, but Scott Wiener labeled it "pretty greasy and average." Add another undercooked Sicilian to the too long list.

They don't make pizzerias, or bars, like **PATSY'S TAVERN & PIZZE-RIA** (72 7th Ave., Paterson; 973-742-9596) any more. High stools in the front bar; Christmas tree-like lights in the main dining room. "We don't advertise at all," co-owner Steve Barbarulo said in the kitchen. "It's all word of mouth." His grandfather, Pasquale, started Patsy's in 1931. The plain, with its crackery crust, is a saucy, greasy delight. The meatball pie at Patsy's is better than its counterparts at Stan's Chitch's in Bound Brook and Tony's Baltimore Grill in Atlantic City, but I don't think anyone else agreed.

"Voted No. 1 pizza in the tri-county area," proclaims **PIZZA 1** (1185 Ringwood Ave., Wanaque; 973-835-1600). I'm assuming they mean Passaic, Bergen and Rockland, and I want to see the ballots. The plain pizza is just that, and the sausage is of the pellet variety, and please don't make me go there. The Grandma pizza — not on the menu, you must ask for it — featured a commendable cheese/sauce mix, but the crust is lightweight.

Dig the mural of the black-masked Pulcinella cooking a pizza over Mount Vesuvius at **SCOTTO'S PIZZERIA & RESTAURANT** (58 Main Ave., Clifton; 973-667-5697). They might want to consider using a volcano, instead of an oven, to cook the pizza. We found it "real greasy, real salty." The sausage is subpar. The margherita looked pretty, "but the sauce is straight from the supermarket," according to Bruno. "The fresh 'mutz' is swimming in the sauce," Windrem noted.

We gave out plenty of awards; someone should give us one for enduring so much bad sausage. Fortunately, there are pizzerias like **SUN-RAY PIZZA** (440 Main St., Little Falls; 973-256-0724) that care about quality. Sun-Ray, located alongside the railroad tracks, uses hefty chunks of tasty sausage. The Sicilian, though, is less successful. "Fell off the flavor train one stop — maybe two — before," said Bruno, using an apt metaphor. We did give Sun-Ray one of three Awards of Excellence in the Best Pizza in New Jersey sausage category.

TASTE OF TUSCANY RESTAURANT & PIZZERIA (Styertowne Shopping Center, Clifton; 973-916-0700) is not easy to find, but you will be rewarded. We praised the "tasty" and "perfectly balanced" plain pizza, and the "nice melange of flavors" on the Grandma pizza.

SALEM

The van, and the pizza, went south at **GIOVANNI ITALIAN STYLE PIZZA** (1 North Virginia Ave., Penns Grove; 856-351-0700). The plain pizza? You might want to go to the supermarket. The Sicilian, according to one reluctant sampler, "tasted like stale bread."

"Best cheesesteak on the planet," Bruce Willis (a graduate of Penns Grove High School) reportedly said of **ITALIAN KITCHEN** (339 North Hook Road, Pennsville; 856-678-2098). Maybe, but Bruce should try the pizza. Windrem called it "a new low in cheese pie." The white pizza tastes like the kind of pizza you'd get at a convenience store, which Italian Kitchen mostly is. "I wonder what part of Italy this kitchen is from so I won't have to go there," Bruno joked.

PAPA LUIGI PIZZA & RISTORANTE, (39 N. Main St., Woodstown; 856-769-4455). Every other pizzeria in New Jersey, or so it seems, has a "Best Pizza in ——" plaque or certificate on its wall. Papa Luigi's, named best pizza in Salem County in various contests, actually may deserve the honor. The plain pizza is a decent doughy slice; the best part is the crunchy crust. The Sicilian, more of a squarish Grandma, is less successful, with an oily/buttery crust.

We expected to hit new pizza lows at **PEPPERONI'S THE SUPER SLICE** (Flying J Plaza, 329 Slapes Corner Road, Carneys Point; 856-351-1804). It is, after all, located at a truck stop. But the pizza isn't half bad. "Not the worst we had tonight," Wiener said encouragingly. Maybe the eating experience would be improved if you wore one of the gift shop's beaver caps on your head.

SOMERSET

There's a lot of dough — money-wise and pizza-wise — in Somerset County, with Somerville the center of the action. In fact, I named it one of the top pizza towns in the state. **ALFONSO'S FAMILY TRATTORIA & GOURMET PIZZA** (99-101 W. Main St., Somerville; 908-526-0616) is fancier, but not necessarily finer, than the no-frills Central Pizzeria, down the street. Neither the cheese nor sausage is worthy of attention. More does not equal better when it comes to pizza. Case in point: the Monte Carlo pizza, with plum tomatoes, fresh basil, olive oil, fresh mozzarella, roasted red peppers, sun-dried tomatoes and Parmesan. One Pizza Patrol member described it as a "chaos pie," another called the mozzarella "plastic-y."

John Bottino, the owner of **CAFE GIARDINO PIZZA PASTA CAFE** (125 Washington Valley Road, Warren; 732-560-9635) is the former owner of the Big Apple in Bayonne, which accounts for the Bayonne mural on the wall and "Bayonne-style" pizza on the menu. Nicely cooked plain slice, and the sausage is tasty. The margherita seemed a bit runny, but we liked the tart tomatoes and firm crust.

CALABRIA MIA PIZZERIA & GELATERIA (83 W. Main St., Somerville; 908-429-7747) tries to separate itself from the pizzeria pack with its gelato counter, but the pizza brings it down to earth. The crisp-crust plain and sausage are average. One taster described the quattro stagione pie, with artichokes, prosciutto, mushrooms and black olives, as "a mess," while another found it "soggy, watery, but with some flavor."

CARLO'S PIZZA & PASTA (572a Union Ave., Bridgewater; 732-469-9200) delivered a "runny" plain slice, by team consensus, although one judge labeled the plain "a very good integration of sauce, cheese and crust." The primavera pie fared better. We liked its fresh taste, although it was garlic-heavy.

There are fancier pizzerias than **CENTRAL PIZZERIA** (126 W. Main St., Somerville; 908-722-8272), but good luck trying to find a better plain pizza. "Quite lovely," Scott Wiener said. "The cheese is rich without being heavy." So-so sausage pie, though. The Sicilian is a hefty high-rise, but on the undercooked side and would benefit from more sauce. Central Pizzeria is my choice in Somerville, which could qualify as Pizza Central.

CHIMNEY ROCK INN (800 N. Thompson Ave., Bridgewater; 732-469-4600), like Kinchley's in Ramsey and Sun Tavern in Roselle Park, seems to be living on its rep. The cracker crust is not strong enough to defend itself. The plain pizza, according to Al Windrem, "is suited for softball games and pitchers of beer." The margherita delivered in the flavor and cheese departments, despite the crust. Chimney Rock, with another location in Gillette, is a popular gathering spot, but if you're going there for just pizza, look elsewhere.

On each trip we took as part of the Pizza Patrol, at least one pizzeria separated itself from the doughy pack. On one excursion early in the summer, that place was **DeLUCIA'S** (3 First Ave., Raritan Borough; 908-725-1322). A 93-year-old oven and a no-frills dining room add up to plain pizza perfection; we named DeLucia's best plain pizza in New Jersey. The plain is all about the crunch — one bite, and you're hooked. A plain slice cannot rely on toppings or other form of coverup; it must stand on its own, and DeLucia's stands at the head of the class.

Nothing special going on at **DOMINICK'S** (404 W. Union Ave., Bound Brook; 732-356-5533) except for an exceedingly cheesy, runny plain pizza. The Sicilian is better; one team member liked the "zing" in the sauce.

You can tell the good cheese from the cheap cheese. The former rules at **DOMINICK'S PIZZA SHOPPE** (307 Routes 202/206, Somerset Shopping Center, Bridgewater; 908-526-0330), just off the Somerville Circle. But the crust is a bit on the limp side, and the sausage should be sent to the minor leagues, where it belongs. We really liked the tomatoey Trenton pie, with its "fresh," "bright" taste.

JOE'S FAMILY PIZZERIA & RESTAURANT (856 Route 206, Hillsborough; 908-874-6661) may be single-handedly keeping the oregano industry afloat; they sure do love it on their pizzas. The plain pizza is covered with the stuff, but no amount of covering up will help this pizza. The sausage tastes right out of the box, or can. The Sicilian is doughy to the max; call it Sicilian bread.

It wasn't always easy coming up with a consensus on our trips. Take our visit to **LA PIZZERIA** (318 Routes 202 and 206, Pluckemin; 908-781-5525). Al Windrem described the half-plain/half-sausage as "a little greasy, but tasty," while Joan Dwyer called it "a nothing-to-write-home-about pizza." Windrem loved the sauce on the Napolitan, with tomatoes, mozzarella, garlic and basil, but Marty Schneider called the crust "terrible."

MANVILLE PIZZA & RESTAURANT (31 S. Main St., Manville; 908-526-1194) is a cute, screen-doored pizzeria, and the plain pizza is a slice above. "A professional pie," one judge said. The Sicilian is mondo-doughy. Not a good thing. One taster called it "bready," another said it had "too much air."

PAISANO'S PIZZERIA & RESTAURANT (Watchung Square Mall, 1511 Route 22, Watchung; 908-755-1944) packs them in, but the plain and sausage pies are ordinary. Try instead the "Jimmy" pizza, named after an employee, an extra-thin pie with extra cheese.

There was a shortage of good sausage from day one of the Pizza Patrol. One of the better sausage pizzas came at **PANATIERI'S PIZZA & PASTA** (1910 Washington Valley Road, Martinsville; 732-469-2996). The plain pizza earned "zesty" and "good coverage of sauce and cheese" remarks. One team member called the Grandma pie "medio-cre." Another said the "flaky dough" and the tomatoes "come together for me."

If it wasn't good sausage that was in short supply, it was sauce. Often, both, as at **PORTOBELLO PIZZERIA & RESTAURANT** (Hillsborough Promenade, 315 Route 206, Hillsborough; 908-904-4111). The plain pizza needed a sauce transfusion, and the cheese seemed "waxy" tasting. Skip the bruschetta Sicilian.

And then when we found sauce, it was the kind better left in the jar, or garbage. That was the case at **RODOLFO'S PIZZERIA & RES-TAURANT** (1325 Route 206, Montgomery; 609-924-1813), with its ketchupy-tasting sauce. The Sicilian is a mistake — off-putting sauce and cheese.

Gina Bruno had a good line about the plain pizza at **RUSSO'S PIZZA SHOPPE & RESTAURANT** (713B E. Main St., Finderne; 732-469-0625). "Good if you're allergic to tomatoes," she said. The Sicilian is saucy — and way too bready.

Finally, sauce! The plain pizza at **SAL'S GOURMET PIZZERIA & RES-TAURANT** (220 Triangle Road, Hillsborough; 908-369-6944) didn't stand out, but the Grandma-like Brooklyn boasts a nice tart tomato sauce. All the crusts seemed bland and unsubstantial. But Sal the owner is a character.

Tile floors, high-backed green booths, striped wallpaper — it's "That '70s Pizza Parlor!" It can only be **STAN'S CHITCH'S CAFE** (14 Columbus Place, Bound Brook; 732-356-0899), which probably hasn't changed in 50 years. The staff was a little frosty at first, but they

warmed up. The plain pizza was described as "gritty" and a "great bar pie that needs a beer." The group loved the meatball pie; one called it "super good." I didn't think it was anything special, though. There wasn't one meatball pizza all year I fell in love with.

The plain pizza at **TUSCANY BISTRO** (Routes 202/206 and Washington Valley Road, Pluckemin; 908-658-3388) screamed powdered garlic. Maybe you'll hear it scream, too. "I can feel the heartburn coming," Bruno wailed. The margherita pizza, while oregano-heavy, boasted some of the best mozzarella we've had all year.

Weak plain pizza, good specialty pizza again, this time at **VENETO RESTAURANT** (554-556 Allen Road, Basking Ridge; 908-901-0111). The sauce tasted "over-seasoned" and "canned." But the margherita pizza, with its distinctive starred edges, may be the year's most stylish pie. Nice creamy cheese.

SUSSEX

A sign outside **CANDY'S PIZZA RESTAURANT** (Route 206, Montague; 973-293-8441) calls it the first — and last — pizzeria in New Jersey. Pennsylvania — and New York — are just minutes away. This is a funky time-warp place, with surprisingly good pizza. We liked the "delightfully textured crust" and "good sauce, good crust, good cheese" on the plain pizza. The sausage, though, tasted more like undercooked bacon, and the bland Sicilian is a "snoozer."

Apart from Strawberry's in Woodbridge, no pizzeria received more e-mails than **CASA MIA PIZZA PASTARIA** (20 White Deer Plaza, Sparta; 973-729-6606). Not sure what the fuss is, though. The plain pizza is just plain undercooked, and there's nothing special about the ingredients. Scott Wiener described the sausage as "state fair sausage," which sounds about right. A pizza with pesto and tomatoes fared somewhat better. Lake Mohawk offers plenty of attractions; good pizza is not one of them.

CESCO'S PIZZA (538 Route 94 south, Fredon; 973-383-2840) is a pleasant roadside bar-pizzeria. Emphasis on the bar. The plain/sausage pizza needs work. One judge wondered if there had been "cutbacks in the sauce department." The Caprese, with chopped tomatoes, fresh mozzarella, olive oil and basil, sounded great and tasted okay. "A flood came through and washed the flavor away," Gina Bruno observed.

The plain/sausage pizza at **DOMINICK'S PIZZERIA** (19 E. Clinton St., Newton; 973-383-9330) is grease-packed, if you're so inclined. But the crust is dull and ordinary. We liked "the sweet basil action" and "tangy" sauce on the Grandma pizza, but the crust is a letdown.

Lots of history at the **LOCKWOOD TAVERN** (77 Route 206, Byram; 973-347-0077), which once housed the local post office. Dig the heavy beams and brick walls. But the plain pizza has little history, or

flavor. If you have a serious calcium deficiency, head here; the pan pizza probably boasted more cheese than any pizza we had all year. "Wonder what happens if you ask for more cheese?" one team member cracked.

Driving through the town of Sussex late one night, we ran into a Munchmobile fan delighted to see the Big Dog at last. "There is no good pizza in Sussex County," she lamented. After a visit to **LORENZO'S PIZZERIA AND RESTAURANT** (67 Main St., Sussex; 973-875-5055), we would have agreed. The plain pizza tasted like supermarket pie, with "bubblegum crust." The Sicilian featured good cheese, but the rest of the pizza should have been sent to bed.

Right after Lorenzo's, we hit **NEWTON PIZZA & RESTAURANT** (47 Sparta Ave., Newton; 973-383-6525). Scott Wiener called the plain "totally average" and the Sicilian "totally uncooked." At that point, it was totally time to get home.

UNION

"Best pizza in New Jersey," proclaims the new, stylish **BROOKLYN PIZZA** (482 Race St., Rahway; 732-499-0049). Maybe it should start with trying to be the best pizza in Rahway. The crust should return to crust school, and the cheese tasted low-grade. The white pizza is instantly forgettable.

"A man is incomplete until he's married — then he's finished," reads a sign at **BRUNO'S PIZZERIA** (500 Morris Ave., Elizabeth; 908-351-3113). The plain pizza here is a Joe's-of-Union-clone, with an agreeable, slightly burnt top, but it's short on flavor. The sausage pizza is better. If the Sicilian had more sauce, it would be a contender.

BUONA PIZZA (243 South Ave. east, Westfield; 908-232-2066) looks like your basic fluorescent-lit, strip-mall pizzeria. The all-white pizza received a convoluted but accurate "unexpectedly not bad" review from one judge. But we loved the plain/sausage pizza for its "perfect blend of sauce and cheese." The plain was so good we gave it one of three Awards of Excellence in the plain pizza category.

Fun, friendly staff at **CAFE GROSSI** (301 Springfield Ave., Berkeley Heights; 908-665-8555), but they should take their pizza more seriously. The plain pizza is "undercooked and overcheesed," although the sausage pizza is better. The Zodiac pizza — essentially a margherita — is wan and watery and "in need of a drought."

We were assured the meatballs at **CAPRI PIZZA** (524 Boulevard, Kenilworth; 908-276-7494) are homemade. If they are, they need to board up that house. To one team member, the sausage tasted like "Swanson's Salisbury steak." I think that's being kind. The plain pizza is the way to go; we liked the "most enjoyable" crust.

CHRONE'S PIZZA (906 Mountain Ave., Mountainside; 908-233-9922) is a lively neighborhood bar; patrons were quick to share stories and restaurant tips. The plain pizza is saucier than most; Al Windrem called it a "pleasant surprise." Subpar sausage, though. The meatball pizza is above average. I'd go back for a beer first, a pizza second.

CIOFFI'S OF SPRINGFIELD (762 Mountain Ave., Springfield; 973-467-5468) is an attractive, well-stocked deli, but the pizza needs beefing up. One team member called the plain "full-bodied, solid," — he was the only one who liked it. The sausage — skip it. The pan pizza is seriously thick; Scott Wiener liked the "contrast between the bottom and middle," but Gina Bruno thought the bottom "dry."

We've seen more than our share of strip-mall pizza, but **CLEMENTE'S PIZZERIA & CAFE ITALIANO** (430 Springfield Ave., Berkeley Heights; 908-665-7867) separates itself from the pizza pack. The plain pizza is suitably greasy, and the sausage better than average. The Grandma pizza, nice and tomatoey, is instantly likeable. It may be the best Grandma in Union County.

If you can make a decent specialty pizza, it seems a plain would be no problem, right? Not so at **COPPOLA RISTORANTE & PIZZERIA** (590 Central Ave., New Providence; 908-665-0266). Good luck finding the sauce on the too-cheesy plain pizza, and the sausage seemed salty. Wiener and Bruno were fans of the Grandma, but I thought it was one Grandma showing its age, or lack of skill.

A street fair and a perfect summer evening made a table at **EMMA'S BRICK OVEN** (101 N. Union Ave., Cranford; 908-497-1211) impossible, so we took our pizzas outside. We admired the "balanced, sweet" sauce on the plain, but the Emma Pie, with buffalo mozzarella, tomatoes, provolone, fresh garlic and basil pesto sauce, is one of those pizzas that sounds good on the menu but fall short in taste.

Nice tangy sauce on the plain pizza at **FRESCO PIZZA & PASTA** (1210 Raritan Road, Cranford; 908-276-0407). But more so-so sausage; enough already! The margherita pie was an instant hit with the group, with its "fresh-tasting" cheese and "nice division of labor; each ingredient carried its own weight." The non-pizza menu sounded intriguing; I'd like to go back and try the pastas and specialty sandwiches.

The plain pizza at **GENNARO'S** (1100 South Ave., Westfield; 908-654-7472) "gets lost in the sea of average pizza," one team member noted. Best bet in Westfield: Buona Pizza (see separate entry).

The plain pizza at **GLENDALE PIZZERIA & RISTORANTE** (1367 Stuyvesant Ave., Union; 908-964-6266) is forgettable. The sausage, according to Wiener, tasted maple-syrupy, like breakfast sausage at your local supermarket. Go with the Grandma pie, tart and sassy. "I'd party with this Grandma," Al Windrem said.

With a name like **GOOMBAS PIZZA** (1424 Morris Ave., Union; 908-688-7500), you're not expecting great pizza, but we liked the plain pizza, and the sausage even more. "Bada-bing," said Bruno, resorting to "Sopranos"-speak. But somebody should put a contract out on the boring, bland margherita.

The staff was unresponsive on our first visit to **JOE'S PIZZA & PASTA** (2062 Springfield Ave., Union; 908-964-3157). On our second visit, we met Joe Fiore, son of owner Frank Fiore, who couldn't have been nicer. His cooked-in-a-pan pizzas are distinctive; you won't confuse them for another pizzeria's. The Sicilian is a near all-star, thoroughly cooked and thoroughly enjoyable. Ask Joe to tell you about the Springfield Avenue pizza wars, when there were two pizzerias at each end of what is now Joe's parking lot. We got a kick out of the special offer here: Buy 30 pizzas, get one free. Wow!

At **JOEY'S ITALIAN KITCHEN** (2704 Morris Ave., Union; 908-964-7655), we asked co-owner Debbie Swerdloff the strangest thing she's ever seen on a pizza. "American cheese," she replied. Hey, Debbie, we saw much stranger in our travels, like onion rings and hot dogs. The plain/sausage pizza is okay. But the Roma pizza, with prosciutto, artichokes, plum tomatoes and fresh mozzarella, is a keeper. Joey's was the last stop of Munchmobile 2009, when we tried various pastas, all quite good. Highly recommended.

Dig the crazy stone walls at **JOLLY'S PIZZERIA & RESTAURANT** (271 Morris Ave., Springfield; 973-376-0392). The decor would not win any awards, but the pizza is worth a trip. We called the plain pizza "comfort food — cheesy and greasy." The Sicilian, while undercooked (story of our summer, fall and winter), is more distinctive, at least crust-wise. Bruno likened it to pizza bread, "but it blends well together."

The buildup — e-mails from readers, a chat with the owner while waiting for our pizza — was considerable at **LA FAMIGLIA SORRENTO** (631 Central Ave., Westfield; 908-232-2642), but the pizza came as a letdown. We didn't like the "gummy" crust and "pasty" sauce. More average, bland sausage. The Sicilian is soft, bready and boring.

LARCHMONT PIZZA (2726 Morris Ave., Union; 908-964-9550) is a dependable, no-surprise neighborhood pizzeria. The plain is decent, the sausage, less so, but the pan pizza featured a tasty little red sauce.

MARIO'S TUTTO BENE (495 Chestnut Ave., Union; 908-687-3250) is a handsome restaurant/bar with surprisingly good pizza. We liked the "zippy" sauce on the plain, and the sausage is one we wished we had on, oh, 200 sausage pizzas this year. The meatball and onion pizza is called three different things on the menus here, but we call it excellent.

NANCY'S TOWNEHOUSE (1453 Main St., Rahway; 732-388-8100), a cozy subterranean bar/restaurant in new-look Rahway, is all about the thin crust. And it's one of the better ones. We marveled at its "attitude" and

"very chewy thin crust." Raves for the "stellar" sausage on the namesake pizza. The tomato/ricotta/garlic/mozzarella pie, a special, boasts a distinctive crackly/airy crust, but one team member thought it too garlicky.

Papa may have been a rolling stone, but the one at **PAPA VITO RESTAURANT & PIZZERIA** (1008 St. Georges Ave., Rahway; 732-499-9119) needs help with his pizza-making. The plain is just okay, while Wiener ranked the sausage in the "bottom five" all summer. The tomato/basil pie is somewhat better. The best slice here — lasagna — was the one Wiener won by getting a lucky ball in the gumball machine. Such is life on the Pizza Patrol.

PIZZA HOUSE/PIZZA CHEF (123 N. Union Ave., Cranford; 908-276-0939) is two pizzerias in one. The best we could figure is that pizza from the Pizza Chef side of the menu is thicker, and is available with whole wheat dough. The plain/sausage pizza seemed ordinary. The Ciao Bella, with basil, tomato and garlic, is bland and forgettable. But it's a cool little pizzeria, because of or in spite of its divided personality.

PIZZA VILLA (550 North Ave., Union; 908-289-3684) serves up what one team member called "good dorm-room pizza." But not one you'd necessarily want to bring to your house. The sausage pie is ordinary to the max, and the Sicilian is soft and bland-tasting. Windrem called it "a cheesy two-by-four."

We hit bottom, or something close to it, at **POMPEII PIZZERIA & RESTAURANT** (72 Westfield Ave., Clark; 732-381-6240). The plain pizza tasted like hot melted cheese, and the sausage had an odd sweetish taste, "almost like candy." The margherita pizza looked forlorn and tasted worse, with a seriously runny sauce.

REGGIO PIZZERIA (895 Magie Ave., Union; 908-354-9466) is one of the funkier pizza joints in the state, with tile floors, diner stools, a TV in the corner, and a fireplace. Here's a first: a Big Mac pizza, with "special sauce." The plain is slippery, but worthy of your time and effort. Inferior sausage. The Grandma pizza looked promising, but clumpy ricotta and subpar sauce doomed it. I remember this place well; with no voice on this particular trip, I was forced to scribble on a napkin when I wanted to say something. Pretty funny.

There's no place quite like **SANTILLO'S BRICK OVEN PIZZA** (639 S. Broad St., Elizabeth; 908-354-1887). Walk down the driveway, open the screen door and place your order. If you want to eat there, bring your own table and set it up in the driveway, because it's takeout only. Or take it to one of several "approved" bars in the neighborhood. Al Santillo, the owner, is a character; no one makes pizza like he does — or so he says. His half plain/half sausage boasts a standout crust, although several team members were not impressed. The 1964 pie, with imported Romano and extra virgin olive oil, is more praiseworthy. We liked the "great bake" and "aggressive" crust. We gave Santillo's an Award of Excellence in the specialty pizza category.

There are not too many places where they'll let you walk through the kitchen if you come in through the wrong door, but we did that at the legendary **SPIRITO'S** (714 Third Ave., Elizabeth; 908-351-5414). Our waitress was wonderful, but the bartender gave new definition to the word grumpy. The plain pizza, with a distinctive crackly crust, brought instant gratification. One taster called it "awesome," another settled for "savory." The sausage should be better, though. The meatball pie? Better than most, but still nowhere near meatball nirvana. Spirito's received an Award of Excellence in our plain pizza category.

We all agreed the pizzas at **SUMMIT BRICK OVEN** (21 Union Place, Summit; 908-598-0045) are well-constructed, whatever that's worth. Marty Schneider described the margherita pizza as "top-notch," but the rest of us disagreed, calling it "solid" and "decent."

What can we say about the "world famous" **SUN TAVERN** (600 W. Westfield Ave., Roselle Park; 908-241-0190) that hasn't been said before? How about this: You can get better pizza at a half-dozen or more places nearby. Gina Bruno liked the plain's "burnt cheese" flavor, but Wiener disapproved of the "really weak crust." The Old World pizza, essentially a white pie, is a small step up. I'd put the Sun slightly above Chimney Rock Tavern and Pete & Elda's, but that's not saying much.

The plain pizza at **TWO TONY'S PIZZERIA** (628 N. Stiles St., Linden; 908-925-1977) is a honest, blue-collar pie, like the town Two Tony's calls home. The sausage is mildly flavored, but otherwise unremarkable. The Sicilian is overly cheesy, but nevertheless tasty. One taster called it "really nice and light, with a great crisp," another labeled it a "three-star Sicilian."

Sal Passalacqua opened **UPPERCRUST PIZZA** (468 Springfield Ave., Berkeley Heights; 908-464-8585) next to his restaurant, Dimaio's, which hosted our Best Mozzarella in New Jersey contest finals several years ago. The plain pizza boasts a good airy crust, but comes up short in the sauce and cheese categories. But the focaccia pizza, with tomato, basil and grated cheese, is first-rate. "If more pizzerias did this crust, we'd be happier campers," Wiener mused. Or eaters.

The half-plain/half sausage pizza at **VILLAGE TRATTORIA** (103-105 Summit Ave., Summit; 908-608-1441) is a "good middle-of-the-road pie" and "would feed the masses well," although the sauce "tastes a little canned," according to our evaluation. The advertised Grandma pizza is much closer to a margherita. Joan Dwyer admired its garlic flavor, but Wiener came closer to the consensus, labeling it "bland."

WARREN

It's a matter of "if only" at **DICOLA'S PIZZA** (50 Route 31 north, Washington; 908-689-0250). As in, if only the sauce were better; everything else worked. The half-plain/sausage pie features the right amount of grease; one judge called it "lovely and goopy."

"Roller rink pizza" was Scott Wiener's succinct description of the pizza at **DOMINICK'S PIZZA** (128 Route 94, Blairstown; 908-362-6460). And the Sicilian seemed to be little more than bread with sauce.

The haphazardly placed cheese on the Sicilian at **ENZO'S PIZZERIA RESTAURANT** (903 High St., Hackettstown; 908-850-0010) looks as if it's spread from way above. Decent plain pizza, but below-average sausage.

On to the fun, funky **LOG CABIN INN** (47 Route 46, Columbia; 908-496-4291). Linda DeLuca works in a room adjoining the cozy roadhouse, with its deer heads and tilted floors. The plain pizza is a good, hearty pie. The sausage — DeLuca goes through 80 pounds on the weekend — consists of big, fat, tasty chunks. A whole wheat pizza with half mushrooms came as a nice, "wholesome" surprise. The Log Cabin made my list of Top Five Pizza Hangouts in New Jersey.

The decor at **MAMA'S/CAFE BACI** (260 Mountain Ave., Hackettstown; 908-852-2820) is better than the dough. The crust needs work. "I'm chewing but I'm not tasting," Wiener observed. The Della Nonna pie, with artichokes and sun-dried tomatoes, sounded better than it tasted.

Sometimes you wonder what the kitchen is thinking. That's the case at **MEDITERRANEAN BISTRO** (301 W. Washington Ave., Route 57, Washington; 908-689-5107). The arugula-scallops-strawberries pie sounds intriguing, but the result is a mess, and the crust is second-rate at best. The half-plain/half-sausage fared somewhat better, but it should lose the chunks of garlic.

The trick at **NICOLOSI'S PIZZA** (755 Route 22 west, Phillipsburg; 908-859-0759) is finding the place; it's tucked at the end of a row of what look like professional offices. They make a quality pie, but it's not especially memorable. "A go-to pizza, but not stellar because of the soggy bottom," Wiener said of the half plain/half-sausage. The Sicilian is "all-around good," and the sausage better than average.

NJ PIZZA HALL OF FAME

Forget the Baseball Hall of Fame and the Rock and Roll Hall of Fame, not to mention the National Jousting Hall of Fame, the United States Croquet Hall of Fame and the World Kiting Hall of Fame.

New Jersey, almost the pizza center of the world (New York holds the honor, but we're close enough), needs a Pizza Hall of Fame to celebrate the achievements of the 3,000 or so pizzerias that call the Garden State home.

As we draw up plans for the construction of the New Jersey Pizza Hall of Fame and Museum (to be built from industrial-grade mozzarella and pizza sauce, of course), we will take this opportunity to announce the 10 inductees in our inaugural Hall of Fame class.

These are not necessarily the best pizzerias in the state; they are pizzerias with history, tradition and character. You won't find any pizzerias or restaurants fewer than, say, 10 years old on this list; you have to pay your dues to get into the Pizza Hall of Fame!

We'll induct several more pizzerias to the New Jersey Pizza Hall of Fame in 2011. Have a nomination? Send it to pgenovese@starledger.com.

Without any further ado, the envelope, please . . .

Carmen's/Pete & Elda's Pizzeria, Neptune City

Probably the Shore's best-known pizzeria, Pete & Elda's has been packing them in for 50 years. Good luck finding a space in the spacious parking lot on a summer weekend. The pizza is a snap-crackly thin crust, available in small, large, extra large, super, small super and extra large super versions. Eat an extra large by yourself, get a T-shirt proclaiming yourself a member of Pete & Elda's Whole Pie Eater's Club. And don't you dare talk on your cell phone in the dining room; it's prohibited.

De Lorenzo's Tomato Pies, Trenton

There are actually three pizzerias with the family name, De Lorenzo's on Hudson Street in Trenton and on Route 33 in Robbinsville, and DeLorenzo's — notice the lack of space between the letters — on Hamilton Avenue in Trenton. The Hudson Street location is the Hall of Fame inductee. Alexander "Chick" De Lorenzo opened the pizzeria in 1947; Gary Amico and his wife, Eileen, Chick's daughter, run De Lorenzo's today. Wooden booths, tile floors, no credits cards and no bathroom — all part of De Lo's charm. They make the best sausage pizza in the state, maybe the best pizza, period.

Federici's Family Italian Restaurant, Freehold Borough

What becomes a pizza legend most? Consistency. Federici's has used the same pizza recipe since 1946; Frank Federici and his wife, Ester, bought the present restaurant, part of the Walcott Hotel, in 1921. They and their children lived in two of the hotel's four modest upstairs rooms. In 1950, what was then Frank's Bar became Federici's Restaurant. The pizza is a thin-crust wonder; one Pizza Patrol member admired its "great cracker crust." Federici's is the only pizzeria we ran across that offers takeout pizza in a specially made bag; it keeps the pizza crunchier and fresher.

Mack and Manco, Ocean City

Trenton pizza-makers Anthony Mack and Vincent Manco opened their first boardwalk pizzeria in Ocean City in 1956. Other locations, in Ocean City, Wildwood and Atlantic City, followed. The third generation of the Mack and Manco families run the three current stores, all on the Ocean City boardwalk. The Ninth and Boardwalk store in Ocean City is open year-round; it's an open-air, white-walled, unpretentious place. The white pizza, shimmering with olive oil, ended up on my list of 10 favorite pizzas of the year. A slice at Mack and Manco is a must in any Jersey Shore summer.

Mario's Restaurant & Pizzeria, Clifton

Mario Barilari opened his resturant in 1945, making Mario's "the longest running family restaurant in the city," according to one account. About 1,300 pies are made here every week.

Dining room to the left, bar to the right, with waitresses who have worked here for 20 years or more. That the restaurant has no website should not surprise anyone. The thin-crust pizza is honest and straightforward. Like Mario's itself.

Pizza Town U.S.A., Elmwood Park

In 1958, when Pizza Town U.S.A. opened, slices were 15 cents and whole pizzas $1 and $1.50. "A special pie called calzone, which resembles an apple turnover, is prepared in snack size for 35 cents," according to a story in the Paterson Morning Call newspaper. Ray Tomo opened Pizza Town; his daughter, Michelle, now runs it. But she must drop off pizzas every so often at dad's house so he can make sure the pies are up to snuff. The neon-lit circus tent-like pizzeria, with its Uncle Sam sign, is one of Jersey's true roadside attractions.

Reservoir Tavern, Parsippany

Nicola Bevacqua opened the Reservoir Tavern, named for the Jersey City Reservoir, across the street, in 1936. It's one of the state's most famous, and atmospheric, restaurants, with golf clubs and mounted deer heads on the wall, a bustling bar and waiting area. There are chicken, veal, seafood and other dishes on the menu, but a trip to the Reservoir without pizza "is nearly sacrilegious," according to the restaurant's website. It's a saucy pie, with an airy crust. Most people believe the restaurant is in Boonton; the restaurant's own website lists a Boonton address. But it's in Parsippany.

Santillo's Brick Oven Pizza, Elizabeth

Walk down the driveway, open the screen door, give your order at the counter. If you want to eat your pizza right away, you'll have to do it in the driveway, in your car, or in one of Santillo's "approved" eating spots, including a nearby bar. Al Santillo's grandfather, Louie, opened a pizzeria on Fourth Avenue and South Seventh Street in Elizabeth in 1918. Santillo's father, Alfred, opened the current location in 1957. The sandy-haired Santillo alone is worth a visit. He offers pizzas popular in different eras, like the 1964 pie, with imported Romano and extra virgin olive oil. "This," a grinning Santillo says, behind the counter, "is where magic happens."

Star Tavern, Orange

The Star opened in 1945 in Orange — the City of Orange Township, if you want to be technical about it. Gary Vayianos took the restaurant over from his dad, Aristotelis, who bought it in 1980. The walls have been spruced up, and security cameras scan every inch of the parking lot, but the thin-crust pizza is cooked the same way: in round steel pans whose sides are cut halfway around so the pizza can be removed quickly. The pizzas come flying out of here; the Star turns out 7,000 to 10,000 pies a month. The pizzas are saucy more than cheesy, slightly charred and pretty close to perfect. The Star is the gold standard in Jersey thin-crust.

Tony's Baltimore Grill, Atlantic City

Red-lit, wooden-boothed bar that never closes, in the city that almost never sleeps. Menu items like a celery and olive salad, and a meatballs and french fries platter. Draft beers? Just $1.25. The pizza is thin-crust only: no Sicilian, no margherita, no buffalo or barbecue chicken. Tony's is no-nonsense, which doesn't mean it lacks character. The waitresses, who have heard and seen it all, may seem frosty at first, but don't worry; they, and you, will warm up. The kitchen's open until 3 a.m. every day. The pizza boxes look right out of a 1940s newsreel, with black lettering on a white background. Classic, like Tony's.

THE PIZZA WEB

The Pizza Web

Americans eat 350 slices of pizza every second.

A quick Google search may have you convinced that 350 pizza blogs and websites are created every second.

The number is expanding faster than the internet, or so it seems.

Passion 4 Pizza, Pizza Maniac, Pizza Goon and Angry Pizza; 31 Days of Pizza and Year of the Pizza; Me, Myself and Pie, Ethical Pizza and I Dream of Pizza; the inevitable WikiPizza and the more helpful Encyclopizza.

And don't forget Morta di Fame, which means dying of hunger, in case your Italian is rusty.

In the following pages, you'll find the ultimate guide to the Pizza Net — notable pizza blogs, sites and online resources from here to Tokyo. Yes, Tokyo. The Japanese love pizza, even if it doesn't look like anything you'll find in the U.S. Octopus pie, anyone?

WEBZINES

Pizzatoday.com: The website of Pizza Today, the official publication of the National Association of Pizzeria Operators.

PMQ.com: The website for PMQ Pizza Magazine, "The Pizza Industry's Business Resource." Runs Pizza TV and Pizza Radio.

GENERAL SITES

Cheesereporter.com: Breaking news from the world of cheese. You can't make this stuff up.

Encyclopizza: Visit correllconcepts.com/Encyclopizza/_home_encyclopizza.htm.

Passion-4-Pizza.com: A story of "a beautiful Italian-American girl from Long Island" who met "a nice Jewish boy from Brooklyn" and fell in love. And more.

Pizza.com: DDC, a domain development company, paid $2.6 million for the name in 2008 and hopes to turn it into the leading online pizza resource.

Pizza-making Forum: Everything you ever wanted to know about making pie at pizzamaking.com/forum.

Pizza Marketplace: Bulletin board for the latest pizza business news at pizzamarketplace.com.

Pizzaovens.com: In case you ever wanted to buy a new or used Henny Penny or Lincoln Impinger.

Pizzatherapy.com: Not really therapeutic, but a wide-ranging pizza resource.

Scott's Pizza Tours: Take a tour of legendary New York City pizzerias with the Pizza Patrol's Scott Wiener. Visit scottspizzatours.com.

Tipthepizzaguy.com: Tips on tipping from "a group of former drivers from different stores who feel shortchanged by the number of customers who did not tip."

United States Pizza Team: There really is one. Follow their exploits at uspizzateam.com.

Virtual Pizza Parlor: Build your own pizza, and learn whether it's good for you at people.bu.edu/salge/pizza/pizza/build_pizza.html.

The Web's First Japanese Pizza Page: The menu at a Japanese pizzeria named Pizza Studio. The Seafood Special includes shrimp, squid, octopus, clam, scallops and crab legs. Yum. Visit chachich.com/mdchachi/jpizza.html.

WorstPizza.com: A sample entry: "A more fitting name would have been cheese bread. Or bad cheese bread. Or 'don't order this.'" Actually, there are plenty of positive reviews, too.

PIZZA BLOGS

Angry Pizza: "Undercover pizza detectives" scour New York City for the best pizza. If you don't agree with them, "you can shut your pie hole." Visit angrypizzany.blogspot.com.

Best Pizza in Hong Kong: There's more pizza there than you might think. Visit bestpizzainhongkong.blogspot.com.

Chicagopizzaclub.com: "The Internet's #1 Source for Pizza Reviews

and News from the Pizza Capital of the World." If you say so.

Deliverage: The life of a Portland, Ore., pizza delivery man. His "conversation" with one customer's parrot is a riot. Visit deliverage.blogspot.com.

Diary of a Pizza Girl: You think pizza delivery is a glamorous job? "I hate teenage girls," PG says after being shortchanged by three of them. "I'm glad I never was one." Visit apizzagirl.blogspot.com.

Ethical Pizza: The latest on vegan baking, breads and pizza at ethicalpizza.com.

I Dream of Pizza: "Some people collect snow globes," says Jason Feirman, its founder. "Whenever I travel, I stop and try the pizza." Visit idreamofpizza.com.

Jeff Varasano's NY Pizza Recipe: "Pizza is the most sensuous of foods," says Varasano, owner of a celebrated Atlanta pizzeria. Visit varasanos.com/pizzarecipe.htm.

LAPizza: Founder says he will visit a different pizza joint in the Los Angeles area at least five days a week until he finds the "perfect" slice. Visit losangelespizza.blogspot.com.

Liza and Gary's DC Pizza Blog: "Self-proclaimed pizza experts'" search for the best pizza in Washington, D.C. Visit dcpizzablog.blogspot.com.

Me, Myself and Pie: One of the newer pizza blogs, from Brooks Jones, who is making a feature documentary on pizza. Visit pizzacommander.blogspot.com.

Minnesota Punch Pizza Blog: "John and John," owners of Punch Pizza in Minneapolis, blog about all things pizza, and not just in the Twin Cities, at minnesotapizzablog.com.

Morta di Fame: "My name is Jen," says its founder. "I'm half crazy and like to cook." What more do you need to know? Visit mortadifame.blogspot.com.

New York Pizza Finder: Interesting — not a guide to pizza in New York but to New York-style pizza around the country at newyorkpizzafinder.com.

Pizza and Coffee: Just what it sounds like. Visit pizzaandcoffee.com.

Pizzablogger: The latest pie talk in "Baltimore, Maryland and beyond" at pizzablogger.org.

The Pizza Files: "One man's quest for one man's favorite pizza" in St. Louis, Mo., at pizzafiles.com.

Pizza Goon: Owner of a pizzeria in Athens, Ohio, discourses on pizza in general at pizzagoon.com.

Pizzalicious!: "This is a blog about the food I love most," says Lauren, its founder. Visit pizzaliciousblog.blogspot.com.

Pizza Maniac: One man's journey to create "the perfect pizza." Visit pizzamaniac.com.

Pizza Ottawa: You never know when you'll find yourself there, craving a slice. Visit blindstare.com/pizza.

Pizza Rules!: Designer/skateboarder/musician and Brooklyn resident Nick Sherman searches for good pie. Every April, he eats nothing but pizza — or so he says. Visit pizzarules.com.

Pizzuh: A guide to the pizza joints and mobile trucks in Austin, Texas. Will come in handy during South by Southwest, the annual

music, media and film festival in Austin. Visit pizzuh.com.

Of Sex and Pizza: "Diary of a single, almost 30-year-old, queer, college graduated, pizza delivery girl and phone sex operator." Any questions? Visit sexandpizza.wordpress.com.

Slice: "America's Favorite Pizza Weblog" is by turns fun, serious, informative, geeky and borderline-obsessive about the world's favorite food. Visit slice.seriouseats.com.

Slice Harvester: New York-centric pizzeria reviews at sliceharvester.blogspot.com.

31 Days Of Pizza: Sean Taylor eats at least a slice a day every October. Funny. Visit 31daysofpizza.blogspot.com.

Turn on Your Lights!: Dispatches from the dark side of the pizza delivery world. "I was to deliver one small cheese pizza with jalepeños to an address in a very questionable part of town . . ." Visit thesecretdiaryofthepizzguy.blogspot.com.

World Pizza Champions: Watch pizza-makers stretch dough while standing on their hands! Watch them set pizzas afire! Visit worldpizzachampions.com.

Year of the Pizza: Seth Mazlow chronicles his year of free pizza, which he earned by winning a contest at Austin's Homeslice Pizza, at yearofthepizza.com.

PIZZA ROAD TRIPS

Pizza Road Trips

Okay, you're tired of reading about pizza, and you want to go out and try some. Where do you begin, especially with nearly 3,000 Jersey pizzerias to choose from?

Pizza Boy to the rescue. Not to be confused with Mighty Munch. Whatever happened to him, anyway?

Just as I did in "Jersey Eats" with casual eateries, I'll map out suggested itineraries. The trips will contain a mix of legendary and lesser-known pizzerias — all essential stops for a pizza lover like you.

In case you're wondering, the reviews below are not duplicates of those in the capsules section, but expanded versions to show why they should be on every must-visit list.

They're all recommended for one reason or another; sometimes it's for more than the pizza. I've grouped the road trips into counties, with suggested starting points. Feel free to create your own Jersey pizza itinerary; in fact, if you have a good one, send it to me at pgenovese@starledger.com.

FIRST — AND LAST — PIZZA IN NEW JERSEY

Start in Morristown and promptly leave; we didn't find any worthy pizza in the county seat. Head over, instead, to **NONNA'S** (176 Columbia Turnpike, Florham Park; 973-410-0030). We tried the sausage pizza early in our Pizza Patrol journey, and it remained one of the better ones right until the end six months later. Do yourself a favor and try the old-fashioned zeppoles; bet you can't eat just one.

Then take the Columbia Turnpike (Route 510) toward **LOVEY'S** (91 W. Hanover Ave., Morris Plains; 973-455-0677). Love the screen door, the local flavor (moms and soccer- or baseball-uniformed kids) and the plain pizza, with its distinctive raised crust. And they make a first-rate bruschetta pizza.

Follow Route 202 north to the revered **RESERVOIR TAVERN** (90 Parsippany Blvd., Parsippany; 973-334-5708). First off, it's in Parsippany, not Boonton, where countless clueless bloggers and food writers have put it. It is one of North Jersey's most famous, and atmospheric, restaurants/hangouts. Maybe it's the deer heads and golf clubs on the wall, or the location, right by the Jersey City-owned reservoir. No, that's not a misprint. Anyway, the Reservoir has legions of admirers. The plain pizza is good, but the sausage and margherita pizzas both need work. The Reservoir in South Orange — no relation to this one — does a better sausage pizza.

Stay on Route 202 for the short ride to the **COLUMBIA INN** (29 Route 202, Montville; 973-263-1300). The restaurant is more stylish than its rambling exterior would lead one to believe. There's history inside those brick walls; built in the 1870s, the building once served as Montville's town hall. The spacious bar is a good place to watch a baseball or football game, or you can head to a table in the casual-cool dining room. The plain pizza is a thin-crust akin to Federici's, but the cracker-y crust seems to hold up better here. We didn't like the sausage, but the margherita pizza featured good flavor and diced tomato action.

Take Route 287 north to Route 23 north and **GIOVANNI'S PLACE** (Birchwell Shopping Center, 1295 Route 23 south, Butler; 973-838-5510). You know when you get a good vibe about a place? There was something about the friendly elderly couple here that promised "good food ahead," and we were not disappointed. We loved the cheese — although not the crust — on the half plain//half sausage, but the Sicilian is excellent. And don't forget to try the homemade soups. Good pasta fagioli.

Time to head west, young pizza man — and woman. Follow Route 287 south to Route 80 west and take exit 28, bearing right onto Shippenport Road to **CAMBIOTTI'S TOMATO PIE CAFE** (102 Shippenport Road, Landing; 973-770-1020). Cambiotti's was the subject of both Eat With Pete and Munchmobile reviews in The Star-Ledger, and did well both times. The Pizza Patrol was definitely underwhelmed, with comments like "average" crust and an overall "greasiness." But I like it, and it sure beats most of the pizza in Morris County.

Back on Route 80 west to the next exit — 27 — following signs for Route 183 and then Route 206 to the **LOCKWOOD TAVERN** (77 Route 206, Byram; 973-347-0077). Lots of history amid the brick walls and wooden beams; the tavern was built in the early 1800s, when the road from Elizabeth to Newton was called the Union Turnpike. The building once housed the local post office; now it's a cozy bar/restaurant with maybe the cheesiest pizza in New Jersey. Have a calcium deficiency? Order a pan pizza here and you'll be cured.

Route 206 in Sussex County is a nice stretch of road all the way to the Pennsylvania border; it's nothing like Route 206 in Somerset and Mercer counties. Follow it to **CANDY'S PIZZA RESTAURANT** (Route 206, Montague; 973-293-8441). Look for the sign advertising it as the first — and last — pizzeria in New Jersey. If you end up on the toll bridge leading into Pennsylvania, you've gone too far. The plain pizza here was a late-night wonder, with what one team member called a "delightfully textured" crust. Skip the Sicilian, though.

Take Routes 206/521 south, then follow 521 as it splits to the right in Culvers Inlet. It's one of the state's more scenic roads, skipping through Middleville and Stillwater (check out the general stores in each). Turn right onto Route 94 west in Blairstown and follow it down to Route 46 and the **LOG CABIN INN** (47 Route 46, Columbia; 908-496-4291). It's my favorite roadhouse in New Jersey, with deer heads on the wall and tilted floors. Serves good pizza, too, in the adjoining room. Say hi to Linda DeLuca, the pizza-maker. In nice weather, take your pizza outside to the deck. Not far away: the legendary Hot Dog Johnny's, in Buttzville.

HIGH-END PIES AND PIZZA DIVES
(PASSAIC, BERGEN AND HUDSON COUNTIES)

Begin this field trip with Michelle Ruvo. She's the flip, funny waitress at **BRUNO'S** (1006 Route 46 west, Clifton; 973-473-3339). My favorite waitress of the pizza year, in fact. When it came time to pick the best Sicilian pizza in New Jersey, it came down to Bruno's and Mr. Bruno's in Lyndhurst, and it wasn't easy. We gave an oh-so-slight edge to the latter, but Bruno's Sicilian is super, with a big puffy crust and tons of tomatoey flavor. It's a rough-edged, rustic Sicilian compared to its more polished counterpart at Mr. Bruno's.

From Route 46, take Van Houten Avenue to the venerable **MARIO'S RESTAURANT & PIZZERIA** (710 Van Houten Ave., Clifton; 973-777-1559). Mario's reminds me of Vic's in Bradley

Beach — a neighborhood fixture/legend with a bar and dining room. It's the kind of place you take Grandma to celebrate her 80th birthday; someone was doing just that when we arrived. The plain pizza, like Mario's itself, is straightforward, unpretentious and enjoyable. And it's better than Vic's.

Follow Van Houten back to Route 46 west, exit at Browertown Road and follow it down to Main Street and **SUN-RAY PIZZA** (440 Main St., Little Falls; 973-256-0724). It's located alongside the railroad tracks, but don't let that throw you. It serves one of the state's best sausage pizzas, with hefty chunks of tasty sausage. Sun-Ray received one of three Awards of Excellence in the Best Pizza in New Jersey sausage category.

Take Main Street to Union Boulevard to **DOMINICK'S PIZZERIA** (304 Union Blvd., Totowa; 973-942-4141). The too-cheesy plain pizza is underwhelming, but we liked the saucy, sassy Grandma pizza. Get your cholesterol raised in two easy steps; across the street is Pappy's, know for its chili dogs.

It's kind of twisty to our next stop, but your navigation skills will be rewarded. Follow Union Boulevard east and north to West Broadway and turn right, following it through Paterson, where you turn left onto Madison to Seventh Avenue and **PATSY'S TAVERN & PIZZERIA** (72 7th Ave., Paterson; 973-742-9596). High stools in the front bar; Christmas tree-like lights in the main dining room. They don't make them like Patsy's anymore. Pasquale Barbarulo opened the bar in 1931. His grandsons, Steve and Gary, are now the owners. We ran into a bunch of guys who meet here, sans wives, once a month. The plain pizza, with its cracker-y crust, is a saucy, greasy delight. The meatball pie here is better than those at Stan's Chitch's in Bound Brook and Tony's Baltimore Grill in Atlantic City.

Patsy's is a tough act to beat, and only one pizzeria within 25 miles can do it — **Pizza Town U.S.A.** (Route 46, Elmwood Park; 201-797-6172). Follow Madison Avenue south, make a left onto Broadway, a right onto River Road and then River Drive to Route 46 east. Where do you begin with this red-white-and-blue-awninged roadside legend? How about the sisters who run the joint? Every time we visit, they claim to have been the first in New Jersey to offer something: first pizza by slice, first zeppoles. What's next, running water? The pizza is good and greasy, but it won't win any pizza awards. The tomato-cheese pizza is better than the regular plain. The sandwiches are probably better than the pizzas. But Pizza Town U.S.A. is a late-night must-stop on any Jersey pizza itinerary.

You can walk to the Parkway from Pizza Town U.S.A. Follow it north to Route 17 north to Ramsey and **KINCHLEY'S TAVERN** (586 N. Franklin Turnpike, Ramsey; 201-934-7777). Now, I liked Nellie's Place in Waldwick more, but Kinchley's is Bergen's best-known pizzeria, a fun, old-time, cash-only pizza roadhouse. It's like Pete and Elda's in Neptune — you gotta go at least once see what all the hype is about. But you'll find better thin-crust elsewhere. The plain pizza at Kinchley's is just too cheesy. Sauce please! The sausage pizza, with a good grilled flavor, is better. I liked the fresh tomato pie most.

Follow Route 17 south to Sheridan Avenue, which becomes North Maple Avenue and runs into Ridgewood, where you'll find one of Bergen County's most heralded, and upscale, pizza destinations. **A MANO** (24 Franklin Ave., Ridgewood; 201-493-2000), was founded with the purpose of bringing "authentic" pizza Napoletana to the U.S.A. The wood-burning ovens are maintained at 1,000 degrees, so that pizza comes out fast. The A mano pizza — with buffalo mozzarella, cherry tomatoes, prosciutto di parma, arugula and shaved grand cru cheese — is flavor-packed, if difficult to handle. The margherita is simpler, and better.

Then you'll want to take Linwood Avenue east to Pascack Road (Route 63) north and make a right onto Hillsdale Avenue to **BELLA CAMPANIA** (456 Broadway, Hillsdale; 201-666-7700). There's nothing special about the plain or sausage pizzas, but the margherita is first-rate, with a fresh, sweet taste and excellent mozzarella. Definitely one of the better ones we had all year.

Hackensack may not come immediately to mind as a pizza destination, but we found two memorable pizzerias in the county seat.

I love **LIDO RESTAURANT** (701 Main St., Hackensack; 201-487-8721), with its padded booths, tile floors, white lights and a jukebox that may or may not work. I fiddled with it, the waitress fiddled with it, but apparently it was taking the night off. Lido is cash-only, like the old times it conjures. The plain pizza is a cracker-crusted near-delight. The meatball and sausage pizzas, not so much.

Try saying **BROOKLYN'S COAL BURNING BRICK OVEN PIZZERIA** (161 Hackensack Ave., Hackensack; 201-342-2727) five times fast. Awkward name, but agile pizza. Wait, can pizza be agile? It's different here, anyway. The half plain/half sausage boasted a raised puffy crust, and the pizza with peppers and red onions is saucy (thank you!) and satisfying.

Follow Route 17 south through Hasbrouck Heights, Wood-Ridge and Rutherford to **MR. BRUNO'S** (439 Valley Brook Ave., Lyndhurst; 201-933-1588). Best Sicilian pizza in New Jersey? Right here. The sauce, made the old-fashioned way — the sauce-filled jars are boiled in water — is superior. Call Mr. Bruno's and Bruno's in Clifton No. 1 and No. 1A for the state's best Sicilian.

What better way to end the Bergen County portion of this road trip than a stop at fabled **PIZZALAND** (260 Belleville Pike, North Arlington; 201-998-9095). Never been there? You've probably seen it, on the opening credits of "The Sopranos." Call it a pizza dive, a hole-in-the-wall with late-night charm. Known for its double-dough pizza, which is double the grease, double the fun — and calories. The plain pizza is a good-and-greasy North Jersey pie. Best bet: the meatball pizza.

Then it's right down the Belleville Pike (Route 7) past truck yards, warehouses, generating plants, swamps and other quintessential Jersey scenery into Jersey City. Sorry, Hoboken, Jersey City has better pizza. Start on the waterfront, at **GRANDMA'S PIZZA** truck (along Hudson Street near Harborside Financial Center, Jersey City; 973-941-2372). Owner Lou Yandoli makes a terrific Grandma pizza, with a tart tomato sauce. Pizza out of a lunch truck? Why not?

Another must-visit in Jersey's second largest city is **LA RUSTIQUE CAFE** (611 Jersey Ave., Jersey City; 201-222-6886), which we judged the state's best margherita pizza. Say hello to Charlie Wilson, the owner. The Sicilian, with a seriously puffed-up crust, is a chewy delight. More than just pizza here; the menu features chicken, veal and seafood dishes.

Then cruise down Kennedy Boulevard into Bayonne and a double pizza dip. First, **PIZZA MASTERS PIZZA & RESTAURANT** (532 Broadway; 201-437-4802), with its first-rate Sicilian pizza. PM looks like your basic neighborhood pizzeria, so we were as surprised as anyone when that pizza landed on our table.

For a more refined dining experience, visit **CAFE BELLO RISTORANTE** (1044 Avenue C, Bayonne; 201-437-7538). You can eat at the bar, and pizzas are cooked in a brick oven around the corner from it. It was tough picking a favorite pizza here; a half plain/half sausage margherita is a good start.

THE CENTER OF THE JERSEY PIZZA UNIVERSE
(ESSEX AND UNION COUNTIES)

The question "Where's the best pizza in Newark?" is a difficult one to answer because, well, there isn't any great pizza in the state's largest city. But you won't be let down at **QUEEN PIZZA** (114 Halsey St., Newark; 973-624-7322). It's not much to look at, with its gumball machines, yellow-red booths and tilted floor. But the plain pizza came as a nice surprise; we just didn't expect a place this faded-funky to make good pie. Skip the Sicilian, though.

You want to try either end of the pizza spectrum? Head down Springfield Avenue to Maplewood. Stop first at **ARTURO'S OSTERIA PIZZERIA** (180 Maplewood Ave., Maplewood; 973-378-5800), one of the few pizzerias with really good food besides. Wild mushroom ravioli, pasta with wild boar ragu — you get the idea. The margherita pizza, with fresh mozzarella, tomato sauce and basil leaves, and nicely charred around the edges, is one of the county's three or four best. The sausage could be better, though.

Then walk up Maplewood Avenue to the **ROMAN GOURMET** (153 Maplewood Ave., Maplewood; 973-762-4288) and its ditzy charm. A boombox hangs above the Slush Puppie machine, and a sign reads, "Mom's back from Italy. . . Home-made chicken soup." Nothing fancy about the place, or the pizza. Stick to the plain instead of the salty sausage or runny margherita.

Hop back in your car, follow Valley Street and then Scot-land Road to Central Avenue and **ROMEO PIZZERIA** (408 Cen-tral Ave., Orange; 973-674-8907). There are better pizzas, and crusts, out there, but Romeo's, to me, boasts the most distinc-tive crust in New Jersey, a puffed-up, eminently chewy crust. I could eat it, without sauce or cheese, all day; it's that addictive.

You go from one crust extreme to the other from Romeo's to **STAR TAVERN** (400 High St., Orange; 973-675-3336). "The most famous pizza and pizzeria in New Jersey" is a stretch; I'll call it North Jersey's best-known pizzeria, and the gold stan-dard in thin crusts. Pizzas are cooked for six minutes in steel pans, then finished off on the oven floor. The pizza always tastes the same; there's something to be said for consistency.

Star is at the corner of High and Washington. From the parking lot, turn right on Washington, which becomes Dodd Street, which leads you into Bloomfield and **COSIMO'S TRATTORIA & AUTHENTIC BRICK OVEN PIZZA** (194 Broad St., Bloomfield; 973-429-0558). The restaurant is known for good Italian food (love the seafood salad). But don't forget the pizza. Recommendation: the margherita, with its charred crust and smooth, tasty cheese.

You'd expect Belleville, with its Italian population, to be a pizza haven. The two best are owned by guys named Joe. **JOEY'S PIZZERIA & CATERING** (460 Joralemon St., Belleville; 973-751-8839) may make the county's best Sicilian, with a sturdy, slightly burnt crust. Think takeout; there are just three tables.

Giuseppe (Joe) Ali gets good-natured grief for his Middle Eastern-sounding last name — what could he know about pizza? But the native Sicilian knows it well; the Palermo pizza at **LA SICILIA** (155 Washington Ave., Belleville; 973-751-5726) was judged the best in the specialty pizza category in our Best Pizza in New Jersey competition. Mozzarella, marinara, garlic and grated cheese combine for one killer pie. Don't forget to take home some of Joe's cannolis.

If I didn't mention one pizzeria in Nutley, there'd probably be picketing and protests; that's how seriously they take their pizza here. The best is **QUEEN MARGHERITA TRATTORIA** (246 Washington Ave., Nutley; 973-662-0007). The pizzas come out fast from the super-hot oven — in two minutes — but they're never rushed. The margherita, as befits the restaurant's name, is a must.

Then take one of the best food roads in New Jersey — Bloomfield Avenue — to Caldwell and **FORTE PIZZERIA & RISTORANTE** (182 Bloomfield Ave., Caldwell; 973-403-9411). Make a date with Grandma here; the Grandma pizza is loaded with fresh, tart tomatoes and good mutz. There's another Forte, with an equally fine Grandma, in Randolph.

Elizabeth, the Union County seat, is also its pizza capital. And no other town in the state besides Trenton boasts a double dose of doughy legends like Santillo's and Spirito's. **SANTILLO'S BRICK OVEN PIZZA** (639 S. Broad St., Elizabeth; 908-354-1887) is run by the inimitable Al Santillo, who is a floor show all his own. "No one makes pizza like this," he growls. Okay, Al, whatever you say. But the pizza at his takeout-only shop is superior. The 1964 pie, with imported Romano and extra virgin olive oil, won an Award of Excellence in the specialty pizza category in our Best Pizza in New Jersey competition.

Miss the front door? You can always walk in through the kitchen at **SPIRITO'S** (714 Third Ave., Elizabeth; 908-351-5414). You go to Spirito's for two things: the ravioli and the pizza. Want butter with your bread? You'd better bring it. One customer complained the restaurant, which opened in 1933, "is in desperate need of a new look," but I couldn't disagree more. There's a place for old school. Order a crackly-crusted plain pizza and a beer, and you won't care if the place was built in 1233.

Our next two stops are in Union and named after guys named Joe. **JOE'S PIZZA & PASTA** (2062 Springfield Ave., Union; 908-964-3157) looks more like a diner than a pizzeria, with its green padded booths, but the cooked-in-a-pan pizzas are one-of-a-kind. If you shudder at charred crusts, look elsewhere, but they give the pizzas here character and flavor. Buy 30 pizzas, get one free. What a deal.

Joseph and Debbie Swerdloff run **JOEY'S ITALIAN KITCHEN** (2704 Morris Ave., Union; 908-964-7655). The Roma pizza, with prosciutto, artichokes, plum tomatoes and fresh mozzarella, is nicely done, but make sure you order one or more of the pastas, such as the linguine with white clam sauce or the angel hair with garlic and oil. This isn't a fancy place, but the food is excellent.

Time to head west on Route 28 to Westfield and **BUONA PIZZA** (243 South Ave. east, Westfield; 908-232-2066) You can't tell a book, or pizzeria, by its cover, or storefront. The fluorescent-lit Buona is plain-Jane, but the pizza is anything but. The plain won an Award of Excellence in our Best Pizza in New Jersey plain pizza category.

Then dip down into Rahway by way of Central Avenue and Westfield Avenue for one of the state's thin-crust legends. **NANCY'S TOWNEHOUSE** (1453 Main St., Rahway; 732-388-8100) may seem out of place in suddenly stylish Rahway, but the pizza has not changed, even if the skyline has. It's all about the crust here — crackly, airy, eminently chewable.

Then find your way over to Route 78 and the Interstate Pizza Corridor. Okay, it doesn't actually exist, but I like the sound of it. There's no shortage of pizzerias in Summit, New

Providence and beyond, but Berkeley Heights boasts two good ones. The first is **CLEMENTE'S PIZZERIA & CAFE ITALIANO** (430 Springfield Ave., Berkeley Heights; 908-665-7867), which proves that Jersey strip mall pizza doesn't have to be boring. Best bet here: the Grandma pizza, good and tomatoey. Probably the county's most likeable Grandma.

In the past five years, many restaurant owners have added pizzerias next door. One of the better ones is **UPPERCRUST PIZZA** (468 Springfield Ave., Berkeley Heights; 908-464-8585). Sal Passalacqua opened it next to Dimaio's, which he owns. Recommended: the focaccia pizza, with tomato, basil and grated cheese.

LOOKING FOR ROCCO, ANTONIO AND A CHICKEN IN THE GARDEN
(SOMERSET, MIDDLESEX AND HUNTERDON COUNTIES)

I picked Somerville as one of New Jersey's top pizza towns, so let's start our Central Jersey road trip on Main Street of the Somerset County seat.

CENTRAL PIZZERIA (126 W. Main St., Somerville; 908-722-8272) would not win any design awards, but its plain slice is the best, most honest in town. Open since 1955, Central is a no-frills pizzeria/restaurant, although there is a handsome little bar in back. There are more-heralded pizza places in town; I'll take Central.

Take Main Street (Route 28) to the Somerville Circle and Route 202 south to First Avenue and **DELUCIA'S** (3 First Ave., Raritan Borough; 908- 725-1322). With its screen door, a warm illuminated glow inside, a dozen tables and booths, kitchen off to the side, DeLucia's is a real slice of Pizza Americana. It opened in 1917 as a bakery, and started making pizza in the 1930s. It has a crispy, crunchy pie, and the best plain pizza in New Jersey, according to DeLucia's.

Follow Route 28 east, back through Somerville, to one of the dozen pizza must-stops in New Jersey. That would be the one-and-only **STAN'S CHITCH'S CAFE** (14 Columbus Place, Bound Brook; 732-356-0899). They don't make them like this anymore; the place reminds me of someone's den. You can sit in the front bar area, or the dining room out back. Table cheese and basil come in Gerber's baby food jars. Stan's Chitch's — best pizzeria name in New Jersey — won an Award of Excellence for specialty pizza (meatball) in our Best Pizza in New Jersey competition.

At **STEFANO'S WOODBURNING PIZZA & RISTORANTE** (1297 Centennial Ave., Piscataway; 732-562-9696), ask for the Genovese. No, really. The combination of prosciutto, mozzarella, oregano and olive oil make for one of those rare "designer" pizzas that actually taste better than they look. Stefano's claims "the best wood-burning pizza in New Jersey," which is a bit much, but the pizza here is markedly better than the strip mall norm.

BRUNO'S PIZZA FACTORY (1713 Park Ave., South Plainfield; 908-769-8016) doesn't look attractive from the inside or outside. Fluorescent lighting and 1950s school cafeteria-like tables do not make for high expectations. But you've got to "trust the crust," as the neon sign says. It's a crispy crust, with a pebbly foundation, unlike any other pizza out there.

Then it's time for some Brainy Borough pizza. Metuchen received its nickname for all the smart, celebrated people who once lived there; the Brainy Boro post office still stands. Main Street is one of the state's most diverse and rewarding dining destinations, and the best pizzeria in town is **ANTONIO'S BRICK OVEN PIZZA** (453 Main St., Metuchen; 732-603-0008). For those tired of overly-cheesy pizza, try the deep-dish margherita here; it's tomatoey to the max, and terrific.

Strawberry's gets all the pizza publicity in Woodbridge, but I'd rather hang out in the **CENTER BAR** (46 Marion St., Port Reading; 732-969-2390). The plain and sausage are nothing special, but the BLT pizza, which tastes exactly like it sounds, is recommended. The cozy neighborhood bar also offers "chicken in a garden," whatever that is. Not a basket, a garden.

Sometimes you have to know the inside pizza story. There's a pizza with mozzarella, roasted red peppers and tomatoes at **ROCCO'S PIZZERIA** (57 Avenel St., Avenel; 732-750-5800). It doesn't have a name, and it's not on the menu, but it was one of my 10 or 15 favorite pizzas all year. A neighborhood pizzeria with excellent espresso? That's Rocco's.

Talk about temptation. **PIZZA TIME** (1076 St. Georges Ave., Avenel, 732-636-5195) is right across Route 35 from the Colonia Dairy Maid, one of the state's roadside ice cream legends. The plain pizza at Pizza Time may be the county's best. Good Sicilian, too, even if it was slightly undercooked.

Take Route 35 south through downtown Woodbridge, across the Victory Bridge to **SCIORTINO'S HARBOR LIGHTS** (132 S. Broadway, South Amboy; 732-721-8788). The legendary Sciortino's in Perth Amboy shut down in 2003, re-opening at the former Harbor Lights restaurant in South Amboy the following year. Sciortino's sauce is one of the state's most recognizable — sweet and sassy. And this just in: Sciortino's will open a pizzeria in Perth Amboy sometime this year, according to owner Lou Seminski.

I heard from quite a few readers that there was no good pizza in Hunterdon County. Well, here are four, housed in a variety of settings and towns. Start in Lambertville, worth a day trip on its own. **CAFE GALLERIA** (18 S. Main St., Lambertville; 609-397-2400) is a small, intimate restaurant with a wide-ranging menu (everything from ginger couscous and tofu eggplant to a T-bone cooked in a brick oven). The oven is the source for the pizza, and the cheese-less tomato pie is excellent.

Follow Route 202 north to Three Bridges (part of Read-

ington) and **LUNA RESTAURANT** (429 Main St., Three Bridges; 908-284-2321), located in a red-trimmed white house. Soup, calzone, paninis and salads are also on the menu, but pizza is the star attraction. All three pizzas sampled were first-rate; the sausage pizza won an Award of Excellence in our Best Pizza in New Jersey competition.

Then make your way over to Route 31 and take it north to Clinton and two very different pizza experiences. I'm partial to **PIZZA COMO** (5 Old Highway 22, Clinton; 908-735-9250) because I had a pizza from there once a week when I lived in town. Pizza Como, then in the Laneco Plaza above Clinton, is now in the center of town, and the pizza's still good. Recommended: the plum tomato-topped Paradiso pizza.

Then hop over to neighboring Annandale and **MILLER'S TAVERN** (2 Beaver Ave., Annandale; 908-735-4730), which might be the state's most fun pizza hangout. It's a neighborhood bar/biker hangout/pizzeria/roadhouse rolled into one. Put some quarters in the jukebox and order a thin-crust pizza, one of the best anywhere.

DE LO, DE LO — DELICIOUS

(MERCER COUNTY)

Trenton heads the list of top pizza towns in New Jersey, and it has nothing to do with yours truly being a native son. When you have pizza legend DeLorenzo's (locations on Hudson Street and Hamilton Avenue, with the Hudson Street DeLo's being named top sausage pizza in our Best Pizza in New Jersey competition), and Papa's, only the second oldest pizzeria in the country, for starters, it's hard making a case for another town.

I've heard any number of people call **DE LORENZO'S TO-MATO PIES** (530 Hudson St., Trenton; 609-695-9534) inferior. I'm not sure what they're eating, or what they're comparing it to. There simply isn't a better sausage pizza in the state than DeLo's. And the wondrous clam pie was in the running for best specialty pizza in our Best Pizza in New Jersey competition. The Hudson Street location — no bathrooms, '50s decor, plastic glasses, no credit cards — is an essential stop on any Jersey pizza lover's itinerary.

DELORENZO'S (1007 Hamilton Ave., Trenton; 609-393-2952) is the bigger of the two DeLo's, which doesn't mean it's any easier to get into on a Friday or Saturday night. You're either a fan of one or the other DeLo's; pizzas at the Hamilton Avenue location are saucier. But we really couldn't taste much difference in the sausage and clam pies between one DeLo's and the other.

Take Hamilton Avenue to Klockner Road and **MAMMA ROSA'S RESTAURANT** (572 Klockner Road, Hamilton; 609-588-5454). Look for the brick house; the owners live upstairs. If you're searching for tomatoey pizzas — I know we were, all summer and fall — you'll love the pizzas here. The Sicilian is the one of the better ones sampled in our six-month pizza road trip.

You'll probably find many former Princeton University students who spent more time at **CONTE'S** (339 Witherspoon St., Princeton; 609-921-8041) than the library by the time they graduated. This venerable bar may remind you of a German beer hall, minus the dirndl-clad waitresses. Pepperoni is the most popular — and most boring — topping on Earth. If more pepperoni were like Conte's, I'd eat more of the stuff.

Then it's an easy, scenic ride on Route 518 to picturesque Hopewell and **NOMAD PIZZA CO.** (10 E. Broad St., Hopewell; 609-466-6623), with its bright blue potbellied oven. Nomad bears no resemblance to your neighborhood pizzeria, with its long communal table and outdoor patio and garden. There are only two things on the menu: pizza and salads. Quality ingredients — San Marzano tomatoes, shiitake mushrooms, fresh organic basil, imported mozzarella di bufala — are used. Recommended: the arugula with prosciutto pizza.

FLEA MARKET PIZZA
AND OTHER SOUTH JERSEY FINDS
(BURLINGTON AND CAMDEN COUNTIES)

Wait a minute, you're thinking, pizza in a flea market? I'm not going there.

Well, go there. The first thing you should know about the sprawling Columbus Farmers' Market (2919 Route 206 south, Columbus, Burlington County) is that this place can be impossibly crowded on Thursdays and weekends. It is much more flea market than farmers' market, with inside shops and outside stands jammed with collectibles, craft items, appliances, shoes, clothes and just plain stuff.

The second thing you should know is that the outside stands are closed on Friday, which is the best time to visit the two indoor pizzerias. **KATE & AL'S PIZZA** (609-267-1147), which opened in 1955, is the more popular of the two. A whole pizza can take an hour or more to receive; you might wait 15 to 20 minutes just for a slice. But the wait is worth it, for a pizza — somewhere between a regular crust and a Sicilian — that boasts a nice tomatoey flavor.

PETE'S PIZZA (609-267-0166) is located just outside my favorite part of the entire flea market — the Amish market, brimming with cakes, cookies, pastries, bread, even barbecue. The pizzeria, with its diner-like wraparound counter, opened in 1948. "What's better, the round pizza or the Sicilian?" I asked the waitress. "The Sicilian," she said without hesitation. I made quick work of a slice back in my car — and resisted the temptation to eat another. It's that good.

My favorite pizza of the 350 sampled in our six-month

Pizza Patrol mission? The margherita at **PALERMO'S RIS-TORANTE ITALIANO & PIZZERIA** (674 Route 206 south, Bordentown; 609-298-6771). The crunchy crust, fresh-tasting sauce and excellent mozzarella made for pizza perfection. Don't be dissuaded by its location on a less-than-scintillating stretch of Route 206; Palermo's produces great pizza.

Must be something in the water in Bordentown. **MANGIA BRICK OVEN PIZZA & GRILL** (262 Dunns Mill Road, Bordentown; 609-298-7499), just off Route 130, makes a very good Grandma pizza, full of tomatoey, cheesy goodness. Wish some of that sauce had migrated over to the way-too-cheesy plain pizza.

Take either Route 295 or Route 206 south to Route 70 east or west to Medford and **LA BELLA PIZZA** (Crossroads Shopping Center, 199 Route 541, Medford; 609-953-9148). Call La Bella La Bold One; the sauce was the strongest/spiciest of all those I sampled. My first thought was that they had accidentally thrown on fra diavolo instead of pizza sauce. You'll either love it or hate it; I liked it its tomatoey, garlicy brashness.

Then it's Route 70 west to Route 130 south to Collingswood, which has blossomed into a prime dining destination in recent years. The best pizza in town is **VILLA BARONE** (753 Haddon Ave., Collingswood; 856-858-2999). The plain pizza makes for a nice slice; the winner here is the Caprisio pizza, with fresh, tasty mushrooms and kalamata olives.

The Famous and Original King of Pizza, in Cherry Hill, has legions of fans. The **FAMOUS KING OF PIZZA** (Route 130 and Market Street, Gloucester City; 856-456-5110) has far fewer fans, but it's better. It's a honest, no-nonsense slice, like this stretch of highway. Recommended: the white pizza.

OLD SCHOOL DOWN THE SHORE
(MONMOUTH AND OCEAN COUNTIES)

You're going to need a couple of days to complete my Down the Shore pizza swing, unless you do it in hit-and-run, Pizza Patrol fashion. The stops are arranged from north to south.

You'll get off to a great start at **DENINO'S PIZZA PLACE** (Aberdeen Townsquare, Route 34, Aberdeen; 732-583-2150). The Staten Island pizza legend has opened in New Jersey, and we're all the better for it.

I don't care what you order, as long as it's a margherita pizza; we gave it an Award of Excellence in our Best Pizza in New Jersey competition.

There are dozens of pizzerias named Luigi's in New Jersey; two are on this list. The first is **LUIGI'S FAMOUS PIZZA & RISTORANTE** (650 Newman Springs Road, Lincroft; 732-842-2122). Squarish regular pizzas are the attraction here; the first-rate crust and sauce separate them from the pack.

Follow Route 520 to Route 35 north into Red Bank and

then to **FRATELLI'S RESTAURANT PIZZERIA** (500 Route 35, Middletown; 732-747-4737). Proof it takes its product seriously here: the brick oven pizza is not available for takeout — it'll deteriorate in the box. Both the half plain/half sausage and Sicilian pizzas are top-notch.

The other Luigi's is **LUIGI'S FAMOUS PIZZA** (3329 Doris Ave., Ocean; 732-531-7733), just off the Asbury Circle. It's practically hidden in a neighborhood of office buildings and warehouses. Tiny place, but the pizza packs a big punch. The sausage pizza earned an Award of Excellence in our Best Pizza in New Jersey competition.

No pizza road trip through Monmouth County is complete without a stop in Freehold. And that means Federici's. **FEDERICI'S FAMILY RESTAURANT** (14 E. Main St., Freehold Borough; 732-462-1312) is the original, opened in 1921. It's thin crust done right, with a distinctive cracker-y crust. Neat touch: You can get takeout pizza in a special bag. A box is no friend to good pizza!

Of the three Federici-related pizzerias (Federici's South is in Howell), my favorite is **FRANKIE FED'S PIZZA & PASTA HOUSE** (831 Route 33 east, Freehold Township; 732-294-1333). The thin crust here seemed slightly crispier and tastier. And I do mean slightly; you can't go wrong at either Federici's in Freehold or Frankie Fed's.

I'm not a big fan of **CARMINE'S/PETE & ELDA'S** (Route 35, Neptune City; 732-774-6010), but you can't ignore the Jersey Shore's best-known pizzeria. The packed parking lot during the summer attests to its popularity. I do like one thing about Carmine's/Pete & Elda's: the no-cell-phones-in-the-dining room rule.

VIC'S ITALIAN RESTAURANT (60 Main St., Bradley Beach; 732-774-8225) is another Jersey Shore legend that leaves me cold, but like Pete & Elda's, it's a must-visit on history and tradition if nothing else.

For the best pizza in Bradley Beach, visit **FERRARO'S FAMOUS TOMATO PIES** (400 Main St., Bradley Beach; 732-775-1117). Famous according to whom, I don't know, but the tomato pie, with San Marzano tomatoes, is a treat.

A short ride down Route 71 is Belmar and **VESUVIO RESTAURANT AND PIZZERIA** (705 Tenth Ave., Belmar; 732-681-5556). This is my favorite Jersey Shore pizza hangout; the pie's good, too. Call it a Jersey Shore DeLorenzo's: no credit cards, decor and furnishings from another time and place. But, unlike DeLo's on Hudson Street, it has a bathroom. Recommended: the white pizza with mushrooms.

Route 71 to Route 35 to Route 70 will take you to **GENARO'S OLD WORLD BRICK OVEN PIZZA & CALZONE** (66 Brick Blvd., Brick; 732-255-1955). This pizzeria, located in a corner of a longish strip mall, is not easy to find, but your patience, and navigation skills, will be rewarded. The Neapolitan supreme pizza, with mozzarella di bufala, is supremely creamy, although you may wish for more sauce.

There's plenty of pizza on the Seaside boardwalk, including "the world's largest" at the Sawmill Cafe. The best, though, is at **MARUCA'S TOMATO PIES** (1927 Promenade, Seaside Park; 732-793-0707), celebrating its 60th anniversary this year. Try a plain, or margherita, pizza, then sample the competition; you'll taste the difference.

Long Beach Island didn't have any pizza worth bragging about; the best in the area is on the mainland, in Manahawkin. **RAY'S NEW YORK PIZZA & RESTAURANT** (545 Mill Creek Road, Manahawkin; 609-597-5050) is not related to Famous Ray's, or any other Ray's, in New York City, but it can stand on its own. The Grandma pizza is nice and sassy.

SOUTH OF THE PIZZA BORDER
(GLOUCESTER, CUMBERLAND, SALEM, ATLANTIC AND CAPE MAY COUNTIES)

It pains me to say this, because I live down there, but the pizza in South Jersey — apart from the Shore — is just not as good as the pizza in North Jersey. Then again, there are a million more pizzerias in North than South Jersey, so they do have the numbers on their side.

But there are pockets of good pizza below Camden/Cherry Hill. Woodbury, for distance. The Gloucester County town, near Thorofare and National Park (but you knew that) is just off Route 295. And it's home to **GIA NINA PIZZA AND ITALIAN RESTAURANT** (312 S. Evergreen Ave., Woodbury; 856-845-6500). The tomato pie is a South Jersey specialty, and Gia Nina does one of the better ones in South Jersey.

Mullica Hill, a short ride away down Route 45, makes for a pleasant day or overnight trip, with its antique and crafts shops. For the best pizza in the area, visit **TOSCANA PIZZERIA & GRILL** (Mullica Hill Plaza, 127 Bridgeton Pike, Mullica Hill; 856-478-2288). The pies are served on wooden flat-boards. Nice touch. It's not just cosmetic, either. The trademark Toscana pizza, with prosciutto, goat cheese, artichokes and baby greens, is a winner. Sure, you can get an ordinary cheese or sausage pizza, but try the specialty pies.

It's another short ride down Route 45 to Woodstown. "Voted best pizza in Salem County" proclaims a sign at **PAPA LUIGI'S PIZZA & RISTORANTE** (39 N. Main St., Woodstown; 856-769-4455). For once, it may not be an exaggeration. The plain pizza is good and doughy, with a pleasant snap to the crust. Nearby attraction: Cowtown, New Jersey's only professional rodeo! It's held on summer weekends.

Route 40 east to Route 77 south takes you to Bridgeton, the Cumberland County seat. There are a half dozen pizzerias in the center of town; the best one is **BIG JOHN'S PIZZA** (90 Commerce St. east, Bridgeton; 856-455-3344). The 10 Commandments on a poster in the window, a TV in the corner, and no margherita or Sicilian pizzas in sight. Big John's doesn't fool around. The double dough pie is the way to go; it's thick, chewy and impossible to resist.

In Bridgeton, take Route 49 east through farm and fields to Tuckahoe and then Route 50 east to the Parkway. Time to hit my favorite spot on the Jersey Shore: Wildwood! Great boardwalk, impossibly wide beach — and some good pizza. **MACK'S** (3218 Boardwalk, Wildwood; 609-522-6166) is a boardwalk legend. It's not related to Mack and Mancos (see below), as many people think; Anthony and Lena Macaroni ran restaurants in Trenton and Seaside before opening their Wildwood store in 1953. Mack's serves a good plain slice, with a tart sauce.

A short stroll away is **SAM'S PIZZA PALACE** (26th and Boardwalk, Wildwood; 609-522-6017). Sam's bears zero re-semblance to a palace — call it a high-ceilinged pizza cafete-ria — but the storefront, opened by Sam Spera in 1957, has acquired near-cult status. The plain pizza might be the best of its kind on any Jersey Shore boardwalk; I especially love the crunchy crust.

I like a pizza, and pizza sauce, with attitude. Hey, this is Jersey, after all! The tart sauce and spicy sausage at **DONATUCCI PIZZA** (115 E. 17th Ave., North Wildwood; 609-729-6110) turned other team members off, but I really liked both. Do-natucci is a spinoff of the Santucci Square pizza mini-chain, which started in Philadelphia.

Jump back on the Parkway and head north to Ocean City. No summer on the Jersey Shore is complete without a stop at **MACK & MANCO PIZZA** in Ocean City. The Ninth and Board-walk location (609-399-2548) is open year-round; there are two other stores on the boardwalk. Anthony Mack and Vin-cent Manco, both from Trenton, opened their first pizzeria in Ocean City in 1956. The white pizza, glistening with olive oil, may have been my favorite white pizza of the entire pizza year.

Just down the boards is **3 BROTHERS FROM ITALY PIZZA** (944 Boardwalk, Ocean City; 609-398-6767). Big eaters, you may have met your match. Eat one of their whole pizzas in one hour, you win 10 free pizzas. The catch: The pizza is 26 inches in diameter. That's big. Believe it or not, it's a good pie, and the sausage is better than Mack and Manco.

You've got to love a bar that's open 24 hours, with a kitch-en that stays open until 3 a.m. every day. **TONY'S BALTIMORE GRILL** (2800 Atlantic Ave., Atlantic City; 609-345-5766), with its red shutters and welcoming neon sign, is a reminder of a vanishing Atlantic City. One popular platter: three meatballs, french fries and vegetable. The plain pizza is honest and no-nonsense, like Tony's itself.

The last stop on our whirlwind pizza tour is in the state's blueberry capital. There's some good pizza, especially tomato pie, in Hammonton (from Atlantic City, take the White Horse

Pike — Route 30). And it really is a tomato pie - square, like a Sicilian, and much more tomatoey than your average pizza. My favorite in Hammonton can be found at **BROTHER'S PIZZA** (80 S. White Horse Pike, Hammonton; 609-567-1080). Good crust and plenty of sauce add up to a tasty tomato pie.

BEST PIZZERIAS, BY COUNTY

Here are my picks for the best pizzerias in each county, with the house specialty or recommended pizza in parenthesis.

ATLANTIC

Brother's Pizza, Hammonton (tomato pie)
Tony's Baltimore Grill, Atlantic City (plain or meatball)

BERGEN

Bella Campania, Hillsdale (margherita)
Brooklyn's Coal Burning Brick Oven Pizzeria, Hackensack
  (pizza with peppers and red onions)
Mr. Bruno's, Lyndhurst (Sicilian)

BURLINGTON

Kate & Al's Pizza (square) and Pete's Pizza (Sicilian),
  Columbus Farmers' Market, Columbus
La Bella Pizza, Medford (plain or sausage)
Palermo's Ristorante Italiano & Pizzeria, Bordentown (margherita)

CAMDEN

Alfred's Tomato Pie, Blackwood (tomato pie)
Villa Barone, Collingswood (Capricciosa)

CAPE MAY

Donatucci Pizza, North Wildwood (plain or sausage)
Mack and Manco, Ocean City (white pizza)
Mama Mia's Ristorante Pizzeria, Seaville (plain)

CUMBERLAND

Big John's Pizza, Bridgeton (double thick)

ESSEX

Cosimo's Trattoria & Authentic Brick Oven Pizza, Bloomfield
  (white pizza)
La Sicilia, Belleville (Palermo)
Queen Margherita Trattoria, Nutley (margherita)
Semolina, Millburn (pomodoro)
Star Tavern, Orange (thin-crust)

GLOUCESTER

Gia Nina Pizza and Italian Restaurant, Woodbury (tomato pie)

HUDSON

Cafe Bello, Bayonne (white pizza with prosciutto)
Grandma's Pizza truck, Jersey City (Grandma)
La Rustique Cafe, Jersey City (margherita)

HUNTERDON

Caffe Galleria, Lambertville (tomato pie)
Luna Restaurant, Three Bridges (marinara or sausage)

MERCER

De Lorenzo's Tomato Pies, Hudson Street, Trenton (sausage or clam)
DeLorenzo's Pizza, Hamilton Avenue, Trenton (plain or clam)
Mamma Rosa's Restaurant, Hamilton Township (Sicilian)
Papa's Tomato Pies, Trenton (plain)

MIDDLESEX

Antonio's Brick Oven Pizza, Metuchen (deep-dish margherita)
Pizza Time, Avenel (plain)
Sciortino's Harbor Lights, South Amboy (plain)

MONMOUTH

Denino's Pizza Place, Aberdeen Township (margherita)
Fratelli's Restaurant Pizzeria, Middletown (Sicilian)
Luigi's Famous Pizza, Ocean Township (sausage)
Vesuvio Restaurant and Pizzeria, Belmar
    (white pizza with mushrooms)

MORRIS

Forte Pizzeria & Ristorante, Randolph (Grandma)
Giovanni's Place, Butler (Sicilian)
Lovey's Pizza & Grill, Morris Plains (bruschetta)
Nonna's, Florham Park (sausage)

OCEAN

Maruca's Tomato Pies, Seaside Park (margherita)
Ray's New York Pizza & Restaurant, Manahawkin (Grandma)

PASSAIC

Bruno's, Clifton (Sicilian)
Patsy's Tavern & Pizzeria, Paterson (plain or meatball)
Sun-Ray Pizza, Little Falls (sausage)

SALEM

Papa Luigi Pizza & Ristorante, Woodstown (plain)

SOMERSET

Central Pizzeria, Somerville (plain)
DeLucia's Brick Oven Pizza, Raritan (plain)

SUSSEX

Candy's Pizza Restaurant, Montague (plain)

UNION

Joe's Pizza & Pasta, Union (Sicilian)
Nancy's Townehouse, Rahway (plain or sausage)
Santillo's Brick Oven Pizza, Elizabeth (1964 pizza)
Spirito's, Elizabeth (plain)

WARREN

Log Cabin Inn, Columbia (sausage)
Nicolosi's, Phillipsburg (plain)

BEST U.S. PIZZA

Best U.S. Pizza

So what are the best pizzerias in the country? Here are four disparate lists. As you can see, New Jersey pizzerias didn't fare so well.

From "Everybody Loves Pizza" by Penny Pollack and Jeff Ruby (Emmis Books, 2005):

1. Una Pizza Napoletana, New York City
2. De Lorenzo's Tomato Pies, Trenton
3. Pizzeria Bianco, Phoenix, Ariz.
4. Pizano's, Chicago
5. Punch Neapolitan Pizza, St. Paul, Minn..
6. Wells Brothers Italian Restaurant, Racine, Wis.
7. Sally's Apizza, New Haven, Conn.
8. The Cheese Board Pizza Collective, Berkeley, Calif.
9. Frank Pepe Pizzeria Napoletana, New Haven, Conn.
10. Metro Pizza, Las Vegas, Nev.

Alan Richman, the wine and food correspondent for GQ magazine, traveled 20,000 miles across the United States in four months, visiting 109 pizzerias, sampling 386 pies. None of his 25 top U.S. pizzas is from New Jersey. At one point, he visited Philadelphia. then "journeyed to as distant a land as Trenton, New Jersey." (Uh, you can get there under an hour). He didn't find anything he liked in Trenton. His top 10 American pizzas:

1. Mortadella pie, Great Lake, Chicago
2. Plain pie, Lucali, Brooklyn
3. Panna pie, Pizzeria Delfina, San Francisco
4. Margherita with prosciutto, Pizzeria Bianco, Phoenix
5. Spinach and mushroom pizza, Bob & Timmy's, Providence, R.I.
6. White pie with potato, Sally's Apizza, New Haven, Ct.
7. Tomato pie, The Grandma, Los Angeles
8. Margherita, Co., New York City
9. White pie, Tacconelli's, Philadelphia
10. Margherita with pepperoni, Totonno's, Brooklyn

Heather Shouse, senior food and drink correspondent for Time Out Chicago, compiled this Best Pizza in America list for Playboy magazine:

Al Forno, Providence, R.I.
Coal Fire, Chicago
Di Fara, New York City
Ken's Artisan Pizza, Portland, Ore.
Modern Apizza, New Haven, Conn.
Pizzaiolo, Oakland, Calif.
Pizzeria Bianco, Phoenix
Pizzeria Mozza, Los Angeles
Serious Pie, Seattle
Tacconelli's, Philadelphia

Slice, which bills itself as "America's Favorite Pizza Weblog," assembled, for Every Day with Rachael Ray magazine, a March Madness-inspired bracket of 64 pizzerias across the country. Two Jersey pizzerias (De Lorenzo's in Trenton and Grimaldi's in Hoboken) made the list — and were promptly eliminated in the first round.

The final eight contestants were Pizzeria Mozza, Los Angeles; Apizza Scholls in Portland, Ore; Pizzeria Bianco in Phoenix; Varasano's Pizzeria in Atlanta; Motorino in New York City; Sally's Apizza in New Haven, Conn.; Burt's Place in Morton Grove, Ill. and Great Lake in Chicago. In the finals, Pizzeria Bianco ousted Motorino.

THE PIZZA PAGES

This is one list you won't find anywhere else. It's a list of every non-chain pizzeria or pizza restaurant in New Jersey. How good is that? Hey, "A Slice of Jersey" is the ultimate guide to pizza in New Jersey, so we're giving you nothing less than the ultimate Jersey pizza directory.

Since the Munchmobile has always celebrated independently-owned, Mom and Pop businesses, this list does not include chains such as Pizza Hut and Domino's. The information was current as of press time; if there's a pizzeria we missed, let us know. E-mail pgenovese@starledger.com or call the Munchmobile Hotline at (973) 392-1765.

This list is copyrighted. It may not be reproduced or used in any way without express written consent of The Star-Ledger.

100 Market Pizza, 25 Mountainview Blvd., Basking Ridge; (908) 647-0033.

2 Brothers Pizzeria, 350 Broad St., Newark; (973) 497-7700.

3 Boys From Italy Pizzeria, 415 Monmouth St., Jersey City; (201)795-5427.

3 Brothers From Italy, 1515 Boardwalk, Atlantic City; (609) 347-3131.

3 Brothers From Italy, 1603 Ocean Ave., Belmar; (732) 280-5900.

3 Brothers Pizza II, 2222 Boardwalk, Wildwood; (609) 729-4441.

3 Brothers Pizza Restaurant, 42 Wrightstown-Cookstown Rd., Cookstown; (609) 758-7200.

7th Star Pizza, 342 Garden St., Hoboken; (201) 653-7204.

A & LP Italian Food Center, 101 E 15th Ave., North Wildwood; (609) 522-3576.

A & S Pizza, 1302 Englishtown Rd., Old Bridge; (732) 251-0067.

A & S Pizza, 940 Easton Ave., Somerset; (732) 828-8981.

A & S Pizza & Restaurant, 475 Hurffville Crosskeys Rd. #4, Sewell; (856) 582-0220.

A & S Pizzeria LLC, 445 Union Ave., Paterson; (973) 553-1501.

A C Pizza Palace, 3206 Arctic Ave., Atlantic City; (609) 348-0626.

A C Pizza Palace II, 1413 Arctic Ave., Atlantic City; (609) 345-3333.

A C Popa Pizza, 1333 Pacific Ave., Atlantic City; (609) 344-6500.

A G Pizza & Restaurant, 220 Spring St., Newton; (973) 579-1480.

A G Pizza & Restaurant, 55 State Route 15, Lafayette; (973) 383-4414.

A J's Pizza Cafe, 550 N. Midland Ave., Saddle Brook; (201) 794-1477.

A Little Bite of Italy, 1419 Long Beach Blvd., Surf City; (609) 361-0506.

A Mano, 24 Franklin Ave., Ridgewood,; (201) 493-2000.

A Pizza, 550 N. Midland Ave; Saddle Brook; (201) 703-1100.

A Pizza Town, 205 N. Wood Ave., Linden; (908) 925-9803.

A'Veneto Pizza Restaurant, 27 Greenbrook Rd., North Plainfield; (908)753-5700.

A1 Pizza, 446 Ridge Rd. #A, Lyndhurst; (201) 531-0066.

Abbiamos Pizzeria Restaurant, 1003 Black Horse Pike, Hammonton; (609) 561-2839.

Abbie's Pizzeria, 137 Main St., Bloomingdale; (973) 838-2780.

Abruzzi Pizza & Cafe, 1556 N. Olden Ave. Ext., Ewing; (609) 278-4000.

Aby's Restaurant & Pizza, 141 Main St., Matawan; (732) 583-9119.

Adelphia Pizza, 416 Sicklerville Rd., Williamstown; (856) 875-6760.

Adelphia Pizza Llc, 188 Orlando Dr., Sicklerville; (856) 875-6760.

Agostinos Pizza, 221 Spring St., Newton; (973) 579-1480.

Al & Tucky's Pizza, 3 S. Wood Ave., Linden; (908) 862-0050.

Al Capone's Pizza & Restaurant, 602 Mantoloking Rd., Brick; (732) 920-7777.

Al Jon's Pizza & Sub Shop, 64 Princeton-Hightstown Rd., Princeton Junction; (609) 799-4915.

Al Pomodoro, 8 1st Ave., Paterson; (973) 742-0702.

Al's Pizza, 401 Prospect Ave., West Orange; (973) 669-1977.

Al's Pizza Works, 1231 Route 166, Toms River; (732) 286-7070.

Aladdin's Pizza, 1143 Main St., Paterson; (973) 247-9922.

Alba Pizza, 18 Broadway, Browns Mills, (609) 893-6808.

Albivi Brick Oven, 866 Perrineville Rd., Perrineville; (732) 446-8211.

Aldo Gourmet LLC, 234 Rock Rd., Glen Rock; (201) 251-1199.

Alex's Pizzeria & Steak House, 543 E. Landis Ave., Vineland; (856) 692-6991.

Alfonso's 202, 484 Route 202, Flemington; (908) 237-2700.

Alfonso's Family Trattoria, 99 W. Main St., Somerville; (908) 526-0616.

Alfonso's Pizzeria, 437 Park Ave., Scotch Plains; (908) 322-4808.

Alfonso's Pizzeria & Restaurant, 647 Route 18, East Brunswick; (732) 257-7111.

Alfonso's Pizzeria & Restaurant, 411 Route 206, Hillsborough; (908) 359-2727.

Alfred's Tomato Pie, 9 S. Black Horse Pike, Blackwood; (856) 228-1234.

Alfredo's Italian Restaurant, 1403 Route 47, Rio Grande; (609) 886-8116.

Alfredo's Restaurant, 1760 Easton Ave., Somerset; (732) 469-4422.

Alfredo's, 55 Washington Ave., Carteret; (732) 969-5001.

Algieri's Pizza, 502 Union Ave., Belleville; (973) 751-3577.

Aljon's Pizza & Sub Shop, 660 Plainsboro Rd., Plainsboro; (609) 275-1117.

All Natural Award-Winning Pizza, 1136 Asbury Ave., Ocean City; (609) 391-2212.

Alla Yodicci's Pizzeria, 990 Cedarbridge Ave., Brick; (732) 920-9293.

Allegro Pizzeria & Restaurant, 220 Triangle Road, Hillsborough; (908) 369-6944.

Allendale Pizza, 83 W. Allendale Ave., Allendale; (201) 995-1100.

Almadenton's Pizza & Restaurant, 190 Munsonhurst Rd., Franklin; (973) 209-1007.

Alpha Pizza & Sub Shop., 1408 3rd Ave., Alpha; (908) 454-4612.

Amalfi Pizzeria, 711 State Route 17, Carlstadt; (201) 935-0003.

Amato's Mama Mia's Pizza, 449 E. Broadway; Salem; (856) 935-6262.

Amato's Pizza & Restaurant, 600 Jacksonville Road, Burlington; (609) 387-9698.

American Deli & Pizza Inc., 1803 Bayshore Road, Villas; (609) 889-9300.

American Pie, 714 Route 18, East Brunswick; (732) 238-2096.

Ametis Gourmet Pizza, 166 Newark-Pompton Turnpike, Pequannock; (973) 696-4900.

Amici Pasta & Pizza, 225 DeMott Lane, Somerset; (732) 828-6545.

Amici's, 90 Park Ave., Madison; (973) 360-9100.

Amore's Pizza, 2042 W. County Line Road., Jackson; (732) 370-3368.

Ana Gees Pizzeria, 349 Broadway, Long Branch; (732) 571-2879.

Anacapri Pizzeria, 218 N. Wood Ave., Linden; (908) 486-7483.

Anajulia's Pizza, 34 S. Livingston Ave., Livingston; (973) 533-1537.

Anajulia's Pizza, 498 Inman Ave., Colonia; (732) 340-1600.

Anchor Inn Inc., 215 Florence Ave., Union Beach; (732) 264-0970.

Andi's Pizza, 71 W. Browning Rd., Bellmawr; (856) 931-2499.

Andiamo Restaurant, 23 Hardenburgh Ave., Haworth; (201) 384-1551.

Andre's Pizza Palace, 1312 W Brigantine Ave., Brigantine; (609) 266-1124.

Angel's, 5 Joyce Kilmer Ave., New Brunswick; (732) 545-0129.

Angela's Pizza & Restaurant, 1326 State Route 36, Hazlet; (732) 739-6232.

Angelina's Pizzeria, 53 Linden St., Hackensack; (201) 488-7477.

Angelina's Restaurant & Pizza, 168 Newman Springs Road East, Red Bank; (732) 530-0211.

Angelo Brick Oven Pizza Cafe, 806 Route 9, Freehold; (732) 683-0400.

Angelo Vincent's Pizza, 671 Palisade Ave., Cliffside Park; (201) 840-7880.

Angelo's, 164 Route 31, Flemington; (908) 788-3889.

Angelo's I, 1328 Boardwalk, Ocean City; (609) 398-1799.

Angelo's II Pizzeria & Restaurant, 435 Amwell Road, Hillsborough; (908) 359-2526.

Angelo's Italian Kitchen, 246 Market St., Elmwood Park; (201) 791-4578.

Angelo's Pizza, 245 Fries Mill Road, Turnersville; (856) 374-1600.

Angelo's Pizza, 878 Union Mill Road, Mt. Laurel; (856) 778-7222.

Angelo's Pizza, 123 W. Merchant St., Audubon; (856) 546-3020.

Angelo's Pizza, 627 N. Broad St., Woodbury; (856) 845-3450.

Angelo's Pizza, 56 S. Washington Ave., Bergenfield; (201) 385-5011.

Angelo's Pizza, 401 Bridgeboro St., Riverside; (856) 461-6515.

Angelo's Pizza, 115 Queen Anne Road, Bogota; (201) 489-8602.

Angelo's Pizza & Restaurant, 80 Main St., Sayreville; (732) 651-6155.

Angelo's Pizza & Sub Shop, 321 Broad St., Matawan; (732) 583-5880.

Angelo's Pizza Co., 301 E. Black Horse Pike, Williamstown; (609) 561-4010.

Angelo's Pizza Co., 200 Larchmont Blvd., Mount Laurel; (856) 231-8777.

Angelo's Pizzaaafe, 756 Route 46, Parsippany; (973) 335-4450.

Angelo's Pizzeria, 62 W. Pleasant Ave., Maywood; (201) 843-5033.

Angelo's Pizzeria, 72 Market St., Clifton; (973) 777-5599.

Angelo's Pizzeria & Restaurant, 4101 Landis Ave., Sea Isle City: (609) 263-1900.

Angelo's Pizzeria & Restaurant, 11 Anderson Ave., Fairview; (201) 945-3308.

Angelo's Restaurant, 303 Broad St., Bloomfield; (973) 429-8505.

Angelos II, 706 Boardwalk, Ocean City; (609) 399-8865.

Angelotti's Pizza & Trattoria, 4018 Route 9, Morganville; (732) 591-2100.

Anna Maria Pizzeria, 3668 Kennedy Blvd., Jersey City; (201) 459-9300.

Anna Marie's Pizza & Restaurant, 321 Route 15 north, Wharton; (973) 328-6966.

Anna's Pizza, 1226 Bergenline Ave., Union City[; (201) 325-9022.

Anna's Pizza & Pasta, 110 S. Black Horse Pike, Williamstown; (856)875-1926.

Annabel Pizza, 70 E. Main St., Sussex; (973) 875-1886.

Annabella's Pizza, 311 Smith Rd., Parsippany; (973) 887-3040.

Anthony Franco's Pizza, 489 S. Livingston Ave., Livingston; (973) 535-1998.

Anthony Franco's Pizzeria, 556 Route 17, Paramus; (201) 447-3999.

Anthony Franco's Ristorante, 1516 Route 23, Butler; (973) 492-1700.

Anthony Francos Pizza, 128 E. Main St., Ramsey; (201) 236-8000.

Anthony Francos Pizza, 8 Troy Lane, Lincoln Park; (973) 696-0708.

Anthony's & Mario's Family, 547 High Mountain Road, North Haledon; (973) 423-9201.

Anthony's Italian Restaurant, 6 Jacobstown Road, New Egypt; (609) 758-7158.

Anthony's Pizza, 65 Church St., Keansburg; (732) 787-2950.

Anthony's Pizza, 2510 Belmar Blvd., Belmar; (732) 681-7211.

Anthony's Pizza, 259 Fish Pond Road, Sewell; (856) 589-4422.

Anthony's Pizza, 316 Black Horse Pike, Glendora; (856) 939-0042.

Anthony's Pizza & Pasta, 47 S. Park Place, Morristown; (973) 285-5464.

Anthony's Pizza Palace, 2769 S. Broad St., Trenton; (609) 888-3936.

Anthony's Pizzeria, 51 W. Main St., Rockaway; (973) 627-1397.

Anthony's Pizzeria, 1011 Trenton Ave., Point Pleasant; (732) 701-1505.

Anthony's Pizzeria & Grill, 403 Route 9, Lanoka Harbor; (609) 242-2844.

Anthony's Restaurant-Pizzeria, 857 Mill Creek Road, Manahawkin; (609) 597-1156.

Antica Trattoria Pizza-Restaurant, 253 High St. east, Glassboro; (856) 863-0044.

Antimo's Italian Kitchen, 52 E. Broad St., Hopewell; (609) 466-3333.

Antonia's Brick Oven Cafe, 7 W, Front St., Keyport; (732) 888-0808.

Antonino's, 1034 Little Gloucester Road, Blackwood; (856) 227-2900.

Antonino's Pizza, 224 W. Merchant St., Audubon; (856) 547-7911.

Antoninos Jo Jo's Restaurant, 2405 New Road, Northfield; (609) 646-7565.

Antoninos Pizzeria, 1930 Route 88, Brick; (732) 836-1600.

Antonio's Brick Oven Pizza, 280 Route 9, Morganville; (732) 617-1600.

Antonio's Brick Oven Pizza, 453 Main St., Metuchen; (732) 603-0008.

Antonio's Italian Restaurant, 2008 Route 37 east, Toms River; (732) 929-2300.

Antonio's Pizza, 621 S. Main St., Williamstown; (856) 740-0400.

Antonio's Pizza, 12-76 River Road, Fair Lawn; (201) 703-5577.

Antonio's Pizza, 183 Smith St., Perth Amboy; (732) 442-3311.

Antonio's Pizza & Pasta, 2233 Route 9, Howell; (732) 462-0089.

Antonio's Restaurant & Pizza, 337 Applegarth Road, Monroe; (609) 395-9195.

Antonio's Restaurant & Pizza, 6900 Park Ave., Guttenberg; (201) 868-3500.

Apollo Pizza, 283 Egg Harbor Road, Sewell; (856) 218-0788.

Aposto Pizzeria, 76 Raritan Ave., Highland Park; (732) 745-9011.

Arlington Pizza, 25 Schuyler Ave., North Arlington; (201) 997-8373.

Armando's Restaurant, 144 Main St., Fort Lee; (201) 461-4220.

Arminio's Italian Corner, 236 Main St., Chatham; (973) 635-6953.

Arnieri's Pizzeria; 201 Middleton St., Riverside; (856) 764-1883.

Arturo's Brick Oven Pizza Co., 223 Bellevue Ave., Montclair; (973) 744-1029.

Arturo's Wood Fired Pizzeria, 180 Maplewood Ave., Maplewood; (973) 378-5800.

Atlantic City Boardwalk Pizza, 1245 Boardwalk, Atlantic City; (609) 345-2800.

Attilio Pizzeria, 67 Monmouth Road, Oakhurst; (732) 222-5655.

Attilio's Pizza, 4057 Asbury Ave., Tinton Falls; (732) 922-6760.

Attilio's Pizza, 5851 Route 42, Blackwood; (856) 228-5905.

Attilio's Pizza & Restaurant, 35 Broad St., Freehold; (732) 409-0590.

Attilio's Pizza & Restaurant, 561 Route 1, Edison; (732) 985-3111.

Attilio's Pizza & Subs, 8 Cliffwood Ave., Matawan; (732) 583-1433.

Attilio's Pizzeria Italian Restaurant, 941 Route 166, Toms River; (732) 240-1331.

Attilio's Restaurant & Pizza, 444 Ocean Blvd., Long Branch; (732) 870-2445.

Attilio's Restaurant & Pizza, 4345 Route 9, Freehold; (732) 462-2303.

Attilio's Restaurant & Pizzeria, 608 Newman Springs Road, Lincroft; (732) 842-7221.

Attilio's Route 9, 1091 River Ave., Lakewood; (732) 363-3533.

Augie's McBride Avenue Pizzeria, 478 McBride Ave., Paterson; (973) 684-9900.

Augustino's Restaurant, 1104 Washington St., Hoboken; (201) 420-0104.

Authentic Pizza & Pasta, 55 Mill St., Newton; (973) 383-2727.

Avalon Pizza, 2108 Dune Dr., Avalon; (609) 967-4688.

Avalon Pizza & Restaurant, 2813 Boardwalk, Avalon; (609) 967-7400.

Avellino Pizza & Cafe, 445 Ridgedale Ave., East Hanover; (973) 887-2821.

Baco's Pizzeria, 358 Mounts Corner Dr., Freehold; (732) 462-0990.

Bacoli Pizza, 174 New Hampshire Ave., Lakewood; (732) 886-7054.

Bagel Cafe & Pizza, 4364 Route 130, Willingboro; (609) 880-9797.

Baggios Restaurant & Pizzeria, 210 Main St., Fort Lee; (201) 585-7979.

Baldwin Pizzeria, 142 Baldwin Road, Parsippany; (973) 335-7731.

Balsamo's Pizza & Sandwiches, 791 S. Emerson Ave., Lindenwold; (856) 784-1600.

Bambino Pizza, 53 Grove St., Passaic; (973) 767-2670.

Bambino's Pizzeria, 1271 Route 22, Lebanon; (908) 236-9009.

Bani's Pizza Ristorante, 79 Union Blvd., Totowa; (973) 904-0544.

Bari Pizzeria, 2601 Bergenline Ave., Union City; (201) 865-1010.

Barone's Pizzeria & Trattoria, 222 Dutch Neck Road, Hightstown; (609) 426-1118.

Barone's Tuscan Grill Restaurant, 280 Young Ave., Moorestown; (856) 234-7900.

Basil T's Brewery & Italian Grill, 183 Riverside Ave., Red Bank; (732) 842-5990.

Basile Pizzeria, 265 Valley Blvd., Wood-Ridge; (201) 939-3399.

Basilicos Ristorante-Pizzeria, 27 43rd St., Sea Isle City; (609) 263-1010.

Bassett Pizza, 7 Bassett Hwy., Dover; (973) 366-3256.

Bay Avenue Trattoria, 122 Bay Ave., Highlands; (732) 872-9800.

Bayshore Pizza, 2515 Route 9, Ocean View; (609) 624-1717.

Bazzarelli Pizzeria & Restaurant, 117 Moonachie Road, Moonachie; (201) 641-4010.

Bedminister Pizza, 2480 Lamington Road, Bedminster; (908) 781-9391.

Bel Paese Pizza, 166 Halsey Road, Parsippany, (973) 515-9102.

Bell Paese Pizza, 196 Franklin Ave., Nutley; (973) 320-5567.

Bella Bettina Pizzeria, 833 3rd Ave., Alpha; (908) 859-3600.

Bella Capri Pizzeria & Italian Restaurant, 778 Lacey Road, Forked River; (609) 693-8721.

Bella Casa Pizza Cafe, 437 Ringwood Ave., Pompton Lakes; (973) 835-4706.

Bella Campania, 456 Broadway, Hillsdale; (201) 666-7700.

Bella Italia Pizza, 2111 Bergenline Ave., Union City; (201) 758-8822.

Bella La Pizza & Restaurant, 337 Route 18, East Brunswick; (732) 254-6665.

Bella Mia Pizzeria, 1219 Route 22, Phillipsburg; (908) 859-2255.

Bella Napoli, 441 Millstone Road, Millstone Township; (609) 259-2888.

Bella Napoli Pizzeria & Restaurant, 480 Route 33, Millstone Township; (732) 446-1500.

Bella Napoli Restaurant & Pizzeria, 265 S. New Prospect Road, Jackson; (732) 363-4110.

Bella Notte Italian Restaurant, 63 E. Main St., Little Falls; (973) 812-8939.

Bella Pizza, 333 N. Black Horse Pike, Williamstown; (856) 875-2555.

Bella Pizza, 401 Hackensack St., Carlstadt; (201) 933-9422.

Bella Pizza, 440 Main Road, Towaco; (973) 299-9177.

Bella Pizza, 5 Broad St., Elizabeth; (908) 352-8888.

Bella Pizza & Pasta, 340 S. Branch Road, Hillsborough; (908) 369-5554.

Bella Pizza Cafe, 100 Brown St., Delran; (856) 461-1480.

Bella Pizzeria, 500 Jersey Ave., Jersey City; (201) 435-7500.

Bella Re's Pizza, 49 Kearny Ave., Kearny; (201) 997-9770.

Bella Roma Pizzeria, 66 Main St., S Bound Brook; (732) 469-6448.

Bella Sicilia Pizza, 80 Main St., Hackensack; (201) 342-1414.

Bella Vita Cafe, 3585 Route 9, Freehold; (732) 866-8484.

Bella Vita Italian Restaurant, 17-61 River Road, Fair Lawn; (201) 791-2224.

Bella Vita Pizzeria, 809 W. Atlantic Ave., Laurel Springs; (856) 435-1600.

Bella's Pizziera & Sub Shop, 804 Ocean Ave., Belmar; (732) 280-2241.

Belladonna, 216 Central Ave., Hackensack; (201) 880-8340.

Bellariva Pizzeria & Restaurant, 1260 Springfield Ave., New Providence; (908) 665-0033.

Bellini's Restaurant-Pizzeria, 505 Avenel St., Avenel; (732) 750-1935.

Bellisima Pizza Inc, 547 W. Westfield Ave., Roselle Park; (908) 245-9003.

Bellisimos Pizza, 2103 Branch Pike, Cinnaminson; (856) 829-0036.

Bellissimo Pizza, 1258 Yardville Allentown Road, Allentown; (609) 259-5400.

Belmora Pizzeria, 400 Minnisink Road, Totowa; (973) 256-6230.

Benny Tudino's Pizzeria, 622 Washington St., Hoboken; (201) 792-4132.

Bensi, 11 River Road, North Arlington; (201) 246-0100.

Bensi of Denville Inc, 3056 Route 10, Denville; (973) 989-1023.

Bensi of Hillsdale, 387 Washington Ave., Hillsdale; (201) 722-8881.

Bensi Restaurant, 300 South Ave., Garwood; (908) 789-3061.

Bergen Point Pizza, 35 W. 1st St., Bayonne; (201) 443-8088.

Bergenfield Pizzeria & Restaurant, 344 S. Washington Ave., Bergenfield; (201) 385-2050.

Best Pizza, 520 Broadway, Newark; (973) 268-1180.

Biagio's Pasta & Pizza, 23-14 Fair Lawn Ave., Fair Lawn; (201) 791-5777.

Biba Pizza, 870 Broad St., Bloomfield; (973) 429-2299.

Big Apple Lounge & Restaurant, 414 Broadway, Bayonne; (201) 858-1075.

Big Apple Pizza, 700 Boulevard, Kenilworth; (908) 245-1666.

Big Jim's Pizzeria, 1 W. Haledon Ave., Haledon; (973) 942-9500.

Big Jim's Pizzeria, 279 Main St., New Milford; (201) 262-4600.

Big John's Pizza, 90 E. Commerce St., Bridgeton; (856) 455-3344.

Big John's Pizza II, 825 S. Delsea Drive, Vineland; (856) 691-3344.

Big John's Pizza Queen, 1383 S. Main Road, Vineland; (856) 205-0012.

Big John's Steaks Pizza & Deli, 1800 Marlton Pike E., Cherry Hill; (856) 424-1186.

Big Mouth's, 15 W. Hudson Ave., Englewood; (201) 871-0600.

Big Nick's Pizza, 72 Davis Ave., Kearny; (201) 998-8185.

Big Red Tomato, 1205 Anderson Ave., Fort Lee; (201) 224-6500.

Bill's Corner Deli, 2912 Park Blvd., Wildwood; (609) 729-4599.

Billa, 52 Speedwell Ave., Morristown; (973) 267-8020.

Bim's Pizzeria, 618 E. Main St., Millville; (856) 825-3558.

Bistro Street Pizza Co, 3600 E. Landis Ave., Vineland; (856) 691-5552.

Blue Flame Pizzeria, 601 New York Ave., Union City; (201) 866-4343.

Blue Moon Pizza, 301 Beach Drive, North Cape May; (609) 884-1170.

Boardwalk Grill & Pizzeria, 309 Fries Mill Road, Sewell; (856) 256-2000.

Boardwalk Grille & Pizzeria, 41 S. White Horse Pike, Stratford; (856) 784-9000.

Bob's Grill, 1368 Boardwalk, Ocean City; (609) 399-3438.

Bonetti's Pizza, 167 Texas Road, Old Bridge; (732) 656-1220.

Boston Pizza & Subs, 71 Pine St., Montclair; (973) 746-8700.

Boston Style Pizza, 450 Marlton Pike E., Cherry Hill; (856) 428-2900.

Boston's Pizza, 3548 Route 66, Neptune; (732) 922-0050.

Boston's Pizza, 1356 Fischer Blvd., Toms River; (732) 608-0104.

Botany Village Pizzeria, 266 Parker Ave., Clifton; (973) 546-4163.

Boy's Pizza, 341 Crows Mill Road, Fords; (732) 738-8222.

Branco's Pizza, 428 Stokes Road, Medford; (609) 654-4115.

Branda's Italian Grill, 1 Mount Olive Road, Budd Lake; (973) 448-0300.

Bravo Pizza & Pasta, 179 W. Broadway, Salem; (856) 339-0049.

Bravo Restaurant & Pizzeria, 1000 Bergenline Ave., Union City; (201) 863-5322.

Brazilian Pizza, 97 Wilson Ave., Newark; (973) 817-9400.

Brick House Pizza, 488 Mount Hope Road, Wharton; (973) 983-9393.

Brick Oven at Morristown, 90 South St., Morristown; (973) 984-7700.

Brick Oven of Florham Park, 162 Columbia Turnpike, Florham Park; (973) 822-0800.

Brick Oven Westfield, 117 Quimby St., Westfield; (908) 317-9500.

Bricks Pizza, 12 Ramapo Mountain Drive, Wanaque; (201) 891-5800.

Brighton Pizza & Pasta, 148 Brighton Ave., Long Branch; (732) 222-2600.

Broadway Pizza, 246 Livingston St., Northvale; (201) 767-4030.

Broadway Pizza, 605 Broadway, Long Branch; (732) 870-2311.

Broadway Pizzaria, 199 Oakwood Ave., Bogota; (201) 767-4030.

Broadway Pizzeria & Restaurant, 56 Broadway, Paterson; (973) 279-3996.

Broadway Pizzeria-Restaurant, 700 Broadway, Westwood; (201) 666-7222.

Brooklyn's Brick Oven Pizzeria, 15 Oak St., Ridgewood; (201) 493-7600.

Brooklyn's Brick Oven Pizzeria, 161 Hackensack Ave., Hackensack; (201) 342-2727.

Brooklyn's Brick Oven Pizzeria, 443 River Road, Edgewater; (201) 945-9096.

Brookyn Pizza, 482 Race St., Rahway; (732) 499-0049.

Brother Bruno's Pizza, 140 Hamburg Turnpike, Wayne; (973) 790-3321.

Brother's Pizza, 871 Highway 33, Trenton; (609) 586-2707.

Brother's Pizza, 868 Broadway, West Long Branch; (732) 571-7800.

Brother's Pizza, 9 Willow Way, Burlington; (609) 386-8999.

Brother's Pizza, 1105 Route 130 S., Cinnaminson; (856) 829-6474.

Brother's Pizza, 3860 Bayshore Road, North Cape May; (609) 884-2524.

Brother's Pizza, 80 S. White Horse Pike, Hammonton; (609) 567-1080.

Brother's Pizza II Cape May, 102 Sunset Blvd., Cape May; (609) 884-9299.

Brother's Pizza On Whitehorse, 1068 White Horse Ave., Trenton; (609) 585-3829.

Brother's Pizzeria, 948 Alexander Road, Princeton Junction; (609) 275-5575.

Brother's A & C Pizza, 343 21st Ave., Paterson; (973) 569-9900.

Brothers Pizza, 1020 Route 18, East Brunswick; (732) 254-7171.

Brothers Pizza & Pasta, 411 Mercer St., Hightstown; (609) 443-3411.

Brothers Pizza & Restaurant, 4500 Bordentown Ave., Sayreville; (732) 651-9888.

Brothers Pizzeria & Heros, 97 Godwin Ave., Midland Park; (201) 444-4944.

Brothers Pizzeria & Restaurant, 343 Passaic St., Passaic; (973) 471-6619.

Brothers' Pizza & Restaurant, 2 Morford Pl, Red Bank; (732) 530-3356.

Bruni's Pizzeria, 303 12th St., Hammonton; (609) 561-5310.

Bruno's Pizza, 93 Main St., Farmingdale; (732) 576-2043.

Bruno's Pizza & Restaurant, 1006 Route 46, Clifton; (973) 473-3339.

Bruno's Pizza Factory, 1713 Park Ave., South Plainfield; (908) 769-8016.

Bruno's Pizzeria, 500 Morris Ave., Elizabeth; (908) 354-3533.

Bruno's Pizzeria, 1023 Springfield Ave., Irvington; (973) 371-9093.

Bruno's Pizzeria, 1 Cape May Ave., Dorothy; (609) 476-4739.

Bruno's Restaurant & Pizza, 509 Hopkins Road, Haddonfield; (856) 428-9505.

Bruno's Sub Shop & Pizza, 167 W. Sylvania Ave., Neptune City; (732) 988-3399.

Brunswick Pizza, 1 Georges Road, New Brunswick; (732) 246-4640.

Brunswick Pizza & Grill, 2750 Route 27, North Brunswick; (732) 297-3388.

Brunswick Pizza Grill, 260b Commercial Ave., New Brunswick; (732) 246-4648.

Buena Vista, 2 Ashwood Ave., Summit; (908) 918-0600.

Bunny's Restaurant, 12-14 W. South Orange Ave., South Orange; (973) 763-1377.

Buon Appetito, 1374 Centennial Ave., Piscataway; (732) 465-1020.

Buon Appetito Pizzeria Restaurant, 2 Boonton Ave., Butler; (973) 838-3655.

Buona Pizza, 19 Olcott Square, Bernardsville; (908) 766-1993.

Buona Pizza Inc, 1300 Westfield Ave., Rahway; (732) 499-0400.

Buona Pizza Inc, 243 South Ave. E., Westfield; (908) 232-2066.

Burkaina Chicken & Pizza, 1446 N. Broad St., Hillside; (973) 391-1900.

Buzzy's Pizza, 134 E. Park Ave., Merchantville; (856) 622-2222.

Byram Pizza, 17 Route 206, Stanhope; (973) 347-6697.

C J's Fast Pizza, 531 Route 202, Raritan; (908) 253-0737.

C J's Pizza Box, 18 Redneck Ave., Little Ferry; (201) 440-6007.

C-View Inn, 1380 Washington St., Cape May; (609) 884-4712.

Cabrinas Pizzeria, 307 Bloomfield Ave., Nutley; (973) 667-4414.

Cacia's Bakery, 1010 S. Black Horse Pike, Blackwood; (856) 228-5986.

Cafe Amici, 393 Davidsons Mill Road, Jamesburg; (732) 521-9511.

Cafe Antonio's, 827 Haddon Ave., Collingswood; (856) 854-9400.

Cafe Antonio's Restaurant, 102 Flock Road, Trenton; (609) 587-8010.

Cafe Bello, 1044 Avenue C. Bayonne; (201) 437-7538.

Cafe Colore, 4095 Route 1, Monmouth Junction; (732) 355-0410.

Cafe Domenico Pizza Restaurant, 2797 Route 1, Lawrenceville; (609) 434-0266.

Cafe Figaro Pizza, 403 King George Road # 107, Basking Ridge; (908) 903-0880.

Cafe Galleria, 18 S. Main St., Lambertville; (609) 397-2400.

Cafe Gallo, 1153 Inman Ave., Edison; (908) 756-4745.

Cafe Giardino, 125 Washington Valley Road, Warren; (732) 560-9635.

Cafe Grossi, 301 Springfield Ave., Berkeley Heights; (908) 665-8555.

Cafe L'Amore, 455 Ramapo Valley Road, Oakland; (201) 337-5558.

Cafe Napoli, 200 Buckelew Ave., Jamesburg; (732) 521-2100.

Cafe Villa, 465 Main St., Chatham; (973) 635-0880.

Caffe Capri, 119 Park Ave., East Rutherford; (201) 460-1039.

Caffe Piazza, 649 Route 206, Hillsborough; (908) 359-9494.

Calabrese Pizzeria & Restaurant, 132 Franklin St., Bloomfield; (973) 748-0390.

Calabria Mia Pizzeria & Gelateria, 83 W. Main St., Somerville; (908) 429-7747.

Calabria Pizza Italian Grill, 615 New Jersey Ave., Absecon; (609) 641-0080.

Calabria Pizzeria, 1333 Saint Georges Ave., Colonia; (732) 499-9002.

Calabria Pizzeria Restaurant, 588 S. Livingston Ave., Livingston; (973) 992-8496.

Calandra's Pizzeria & Restaurant, 80 Bay Ave., Bloomfield; (973) 743-1888.

California Grill & Pizza, 13308 Long Beach Blvd., Long Beach Twp; (609) 492-1200.

Cambiotti's Tomato Pie Cafe, 102 Shippenport Road, Landing; (973) 770-1020.

Camillo's Restaurant & Pizza, 31 Macarthur Ave., Sayreville; (732) 390-4444.

Cammarata's Pizza Pantry, 126 S. Livingston Ave., Livingston; (973) 994-0615.

Cammerino's Pizza, 5 Meadowlark Drive, Glenwood; (973) 827-8887.

Campanellos Deli Pizzaria, 51 County Ave., Secaucus; (201) 974-1200.

Candela Restaurant & Pizzeria, 22 Lawn Park Ave., Lawrenceville; (609) 882-9119.

Candella II Pizzeria, 4120 Quakerbridge Road, Lawrenceville; (609) 799-8800.

Candy's Pizza Restaurant, Route 206, Montague; (973) 293-8441.

Cape May Pizza, 302 Washington St., Cape May; (609) 898-7779.

Capital Pizza, 615 White Horse Pike, Haddon Township; (856) 858-7800.

Capone's Gourmet Pizza & Pasta, 17 Washington St., Toms River; (732) 473-1777.

Capri Pizza, 528 Atlantic City Blvd., Beachwood; (732) 244-4750.

Capri Pizza, 524 Boulevard, Kenilworth; (908) 276-7494.

Capri Pizza, 659 Cross Keys Road, Sicklerville; (856) 629-9964.

Capri Pizzeria & Restaurant, 510 Bloomfield Ave., Verona; (973) 239-2660.

Capri Restaurant & Pizza, 6725 Black Horse Pike, Egg Harbor Twp; (609) 646-2831.

Capricci Pizzeria & Restaurant, 512 New Friendship Road, Howell; (732) 905-4080.

Capriccio Pizza, 485 Georges Road, Dayton; (732) 329-8640.

Capuano Italian Ristorante, 2025 Old Trenton Road, Princeton Junction; (609) 426-0020.

Capuano Italian Ristorante, 217 Clarksville Road, Princeton Junction; (609) 897-0091.

Carini's Ristorante & Pizzeria, 9854 Pacific Ave., Wildwood Crest; (609) 522-7304.

Carlo's Gourmet Pizza & Pasta, 351 Route 34, Matawan; (732) 583-8000.

Carlo's Gourmet Pizza & Pasta, 356 Route 9, Englishtown; (732) 972-1480.

Carlo's Gourmet Pizza & Pasta, 326 Route 9, Englishtown; (732) 536-6070.

Carlo's Pizza, 665 Bennetts Mills Road, Jackson; (732) 928-5555.

Carlo's Pizza, 605 E. Chestnut Ave., Vineland; (856) 696-0002.

Carlo's Pizza, 246 Lincoln Blvd., Middlesex; (732) 469-6621.

Carlo's Pizza & Pasta, 572A Union Ave., Bridgewater; (732) 469-9200.

Carlo's Pizza Ctr, 815 Roosevelt Ave., Carteret; (732) 541-8700.

Carlucci's Italian Grill, 335 Princeton Hightstown Road, Princeton Junction; (609) 936-0900.

Carmelo's Ristorante, 31 E. Broad St., Bridgeton; (856) 453-0023.

Carmen's Pizza-Italian Restaurant, 933 Port Reading Ave., Port Reading; (732) 541-5400.

Carmenucci Pizzeria & Italian, 849 W. Bay Ave., Barnegat; (609) 607-0073.

Carmine's Pizza Factory, 102 Brunswick St., Jersey City; (201) 386-6717.

Carmine's Pizzeria, 400 Amsterdam Ave., Roselle; (908) 241-5406.

Carmine's Pizzeria, 900 W. Brigantine Ave., Brigantine; (609) 266-5400.

Carmine's Pizzeria & Restaurant, 77 Main St., Netcong; (973) 347-2404.

Carnival Spot Pizza, 612 Newark-Pompton Turnpike, Pompton Plains; (973) 835-2600.

Carollo's, 6505 S. Crescent Blvd., Pennsauken; (856) 662-8590.

Carollo's Family Restaurant, 1 N. Black Horse Pike, Mount Ephraim; (856) 931-1600.

Carollo's Family Restaurant, 200 Route 73 N., Marlton; (856) 797-1111.

Carosello's Pizza & Pasta, 835 E. Clements Bridge Road, Runnemede; (856) 939-5277.

Carretino Restaurant, 340 S. Branch Road, Hillsborough; (908) 369-3663.

Casa Carollo, 200 Route 73 N., Marlton; (856) 797-1111.

Casa D Pizza, 2321 Route 22 W., Union; (908) 624-0555.

Casa Mia Pizza Pastaria, 20 White Deer Plaza, Sparta; (973) 729-6606.

Casa Mia Pizzeria Ristorante, 384 Totowa Road, Totowa; (973) 942-4000.

Casa Turano Pizzeria & Restaurant, 660 Passaic Ave., Nutley; (973) 667-7333.

Casa Turano Pizzeria & Restaurant, 455 Broad St., Bloomfield; (973) 748-6834.

Casablanca Pizza & Deli, 1624 Atlantic Ave., Atlantic City; (609) 348-4500.

Casamari, 710 Sunset Road, Burlington; (609) 387-7333.

Casanova Pizzeria & Restaurant, 103 E. Front St., Plainfield; (908) 561-2319.

Casella's Pizzeria & Fine Italian Deli, 139 Route 10 E., Succasunna; (973) 341-3110.

Casino Pizza & Restaurant II, 3205 Atlantic Ave., Atlantic City; (609) 572-1134.

Cassie's Pizzeria, 18 S. Dean St., Englewood; (201) 541-6760.

Castalia Trattoria, 997 McBride Ave., Woodland Park; (973) 785-8880.

Castillo's Pizzeria-Restaurant, 1200 S. Clinton Ave., Trenton; (609) 393-1616.

Catanzareti Pizza & Italian, 299 S. Main St., Lambertville; (609) 397-2992.

Cavallo's Market, 173 Bloomfield Ave., Nutley; (973) 667-1237.

Cbio Pizza Cafe, 287 Route 35, Red Bank; (732) 219-8800.

Cecilia's Pizzeria, 299 Jackson Road, Atco; (856) 767-3235.

Cedar Grill & Pizza, 295 Bloomfield Ave., Caldwell; (973) 403-7787.

Cenceno's Pizzeria-Restaurant, 108 Smith St., Perth Amboy; (732) 324-8488.

Center Bar & Pizzeria, 46 Marion St., Port Reading; (732) 969-2390.

Central Pizzeria & Restaurant, 126 W. Main St., Somerville; (908) 722-8272.

Century Pizza, 711 Bergen Ave., Jersey City; (201) 434-7100.

Cervone's Pizzeria, 85 Main St., Farmingdale; (732) 938-5700.

Cervones Pizzeria, 2063 Route 88, Brick; (732) 892-4220.

Cesco's Pizza, 538 Route 94 S., Newton; (973) 383-2840.

Charlie's Pizza, 860 Fischer Blvd., Toms River; (732) 288-9010.

Charlie's Pizza & Pub, 1354 Mountainview Drive, Toms River; (732) 657-8663.

Charlie's Pizzeria, 850 Paterson Ave., East Rutherford; (973) 471-4092.

Charlie's Pizzeria & Pub, 1980 Route 37, Manchester; (732) 657-8663.

Charlies Famous Pizza, 112 Lincoln Ave., Hawthorne; (973) 310-3511.

Charlies Pizza, 1000 Highway 70, Lakewood; (732) 370-3580.

Chelsea Pizza & Italian Grill, 2416 Atlantic Ave., Atlantic City; (609) 344-3838.

Chelsea Pizza & Subs, 738 Black Horse Pike, Pleasantville; (609) 383-9494.

Chelsea Pizza II, 1735 Atlantic Ave., Atlantic City; (609) 344-4141.

Cherry Hill Pizza, 110 Barclay Shopping Ctr, Cherry Hill; (856) 216-5311.

Chesterfield Inn, 633 Jacobstown Chesterfield Road, Chesterfield; (609) 298-1917.

Chevallaro's Pizza, 701 Park Ave., Riverton; (856) 786-4949.

Chez Pizzeria & Restaurant, 32 Broadway, Passaic; (973) 778-0869.

Chiafullos Navesink Pizza, 1010 Route 36, Atlantic Highlands; (732) 291-9040.

Chicago Pizzeria & Sub, 371 Monroe St., Passaic; (973) 777-9881.

Chicken Hut & Pizza, 772 Springfield Ave., Irvington; (973) 374-2888.

Chimney Rock Inn, 800 N Thompson Ave., Bridgewater; (732) 469-4600.

Chimney Rock Inn, 342 Valley Road, Gillette; (908) 580-1100.

Chris' Corner, 117 W. 2nd St., Bayonne; (201) 436-8181.

Chris' Pizzeria, 200 Park Ave., Rutherford; (201) 933-3315.

Chris' Pizzeria, 404 Valley Brook Ave., Lyndhurst; (201) 935-8448.

Chriss Pizzeria, 564 Van Houten Ave., Clifton; (973) 773-7646.

Christos Mini Mart & Pizzeria, 301 8th St., Jersey City; (201) 659-4045.

Chrone's Pizza, 896 Mountain Ave., Mountainside; (908) 233-9922.

Chuckles Pizza & Pasta Restaurant, 160 Lawrenceville-Pennington Road, Lawrenceville; (609) 895-6660.

Ciao Bella Pizzeria, 775 Hamburg Turnpike, Wayne; (973) 628-7939.

Ciccio Pizza, 134 Maple Ave., South Plainfield; (908) 753-4060.

Cici's Pizza, 85 State Rt 17, East Rutherford; (201) 438-8200.

Cici's Pizza, 818 Haddonfield Road, Cherry Hill; (856) 910-2424.

Cicilia Pizzeria, 95 Market St., Paterson; (973) 684-0652.

Ciconte's Italia Pizzeria, 915 W. Route 70, Marlton; (856) 983-4949.

Ciconte's Italia Pizzeria, 490 Crown Point Road, West Deptford; (856) 853-4919.

Ciconte's Italian Pizzeria, 321 Mullica Hill Road, Glassboro; (856) 881-4412.

Cifelli's Seven Day Special, 700 Chews Landing Road, Lindenwold; (856) 435-8799.

Cioffi's, 762 Mountain Ave., Springfield; (973) 467-5468.

Cioffi's Restaurant & Pizzeria, 929 Stuyvesant Ave., Union; (908) 964-3300.

Circle Pizza, PO Box 350, Avalon; (609) 967-7566.

Circle Pizza, 550 Broad Ave., Ridgefield; (201) 941-0650.

Ciro Pizza, 140 Lake Ave., Colonia; (732) 388-5556.

Citta Del Mare Restaurant, 3400 Atlantic Brigantine Blvd., Brigantine; (609) 266-2808.

Clemente's Pizzeria and Cafe Italiano, 430 Springfield Ave., Berkeley Heights; (908) 665-7867.

Clementia's Pizza, 216 Hergesell Ave., Maywood; (201) 820-1476.

Clifton Village Pizza, 1380 Clifton Ave., Clifton; (973) 458-0505.

Coal Fired Brick Oven, 600 Main St., Bradley Beach; (732) 869-1111.

Coffaro's Pizza, 58 Obert St., South River; (732) 257-1133.

Colandrea's Pizza & Restaurant, 800 Radio Road, Little Egg Harbor; 609) 296-1173.

Colella's Pizza, 1180 Willowbrook Mall, Wayne; (973) 785-0675.

Coliseum Pizzeria, 435 Cedar Lane, Teaneck; (201) 287-1470.

Colleen's Kitchen, 132 S. Pine Ave., South Amboy; (732) 525-9262.

Colombo's Pizzeria, 204 Main St., Lincoln Park; (973) 694-8330.

Colonia Pizza, 325 Inman Ave., Colonia; (732) 381-5150.

Columbia Inn, 29 Main Road, Montville; (973) 263-1300.

Columbus International Pizza, 8 S. Warren St., Trenton; (609) 393-5707.

Comet Pizzeria Inc, 1288 N. Broad St., Hillside; (908) 353-1400.

Con Sapore Pizzeria, 1504 Main St., Belmar; (732) 681-8686.

Conte's Bar, 339 Witherspoon St., Princeton; (609) 921-8041.

Coppola Pizzeria, 1222 Chews Landing Road, Clementon; (856) 784-3777.

Coppola Ristorante & Pizzeria, 590 Central Ave., New Providence; (908) 665-0266.

Corrados Restaurant Pizzeria, 611 Sicklerville Road, Sicklerville; (856) 629-7799.

Corsi's Pizza, 153 Newtons Corner Road, Howell; (732) 840-0044.

Cortina's Pizzeria, 134 Broadway, Hillsdale; (201) 666-1558.

Cosimo's, 194 Broad St., Bloomfield; (973) 429-0558.

Cosimo's Pizza, 1 Castle Blvd., Atlantic City; (609) 340-0070.

Cosimo's Pizza, 3710 Route 9, Freehold; (732) 863-4773.

Cosimo's Pizza, 118 E. Broad St., Westfield; (908) 654-8787.

Cosimo's Uno Pizzeria, 25-07 Broadway, Fair Lawn; (201) 796-8800.

Cosimos Pizza, 520 Atlantic Ave., Atlantic City; (609) 340-0070.

Cosmo Bella Pizza, 135 Newark-Pompton Turnpike, Pequannock; (973) 694-0321.

Cosmos Pizza Restaurant, 2 Madison Ave., Mt Holly; (609) 518-9159.

Costa's Pizzeria Restaurant, 120 Chestnut St., Roselle Park; (908) 245-2611.

Costello Pizzeria Llc, 615 E. Moss Mill Road, Galloway; (609) 652-0378.

Court House Pizza & Sandwich, 205 S. Main St., Cape May Court House, (609) 465-5930.

Cousin Mario's Pizzeria, 5401 Harding Hwy., Mays Landing; (609) 625-2523.

Cousin's Pizza, 187 Rivervale Road, River Vale; (201) 666-3100.

Cousins Pizza, 450 Livingston St., Norwood; (201) 767-4300.

Cousins Pizza & Restaurant, 543 Bloomfield Ave., Bloomfield; (973) 680-8200.

Cove II, 1231 9th Ave., Neptune; (732) 775-6111.

Covello's Pizza & Italian, 308 S. Broad St., Trenton; (609) 393-9358.

Cranbury Pizza, 63 N. Main St., Cranbury; (609) 409-9930.

Crazy Cow Steak & Pizza Co, 996 Woodlane Road, Beverly; (609) 835-9600.

Crazy Mikes Pizza, 1816 Route 35, South Amboy; (732) 316-9000.

Crecco's Cafe, 655 Westwood Ave., River Vale; (201) 664-7200.

Cresskill Pizza, 38 Union Ave., Cresskill; (201) 871-3795.

Cricco Di Padre, 830 Kinderkamack Road, River Edge; (201) 576-0101.

Crispy Crust Pizza, 44 W. Palisade Ave., Englewood; (201) 567-9502.

Croce's, 811 Marlton Pike, Cherry Hill; (856) 795-6000.

Crust & Crumble Pizzeria, 658 Cookman Ave., Asbury Park; (732) 776-7767.

Crystal's Corner Deli, 1031 Centerton Road, Elmer; (856) 358-1255.

Cucina Bella, 25 Broad St., Freehold; (732) 409-0590.

Cugino's Pizza, 2151 Lemoine Ave., Fort Lee; (201) 947-0947.

Curioni's Pizza, 80 Liberty St., Lodi; (973) 473-7934.

Cuzzins Pizza, 1787 Hooper Ave., Toms River; (732) 255-3000.

Czar's Pizzeria Grotto, 312 Howard Blvd., Mt Arlington; (973) 810-2380.

D & E's Pizza & Grill, 1916 Boulevard, Seaside Park; (732) 830-3700.

D & T Pizza Restaurant, 1600 Perrineville Road, Monroe Township; (609) 655-8642.

D A Villagio Pizza & Grille, 3018 Union Ave., Pennsauken; (856) 661-0909.

D Amario Pizzeria, 25 Park Ave., Rutherford; (201) 935-5817.

D'Arcy's Tavern, 310 Main St., Bradley Beach; (732) 774-9688.

D Martinon Italian American Pizza, 148 Market St., Passaic; (973) 272-7927.

D' Rica's Pizzeria, 106 W. Jersey St., Elizabeth; (908) 355-4150.

D'Ambrosio Pizzeria Restaurant, 2973 Marne Highway, Mount Laurel; (856) 778-9545.

D'Italia, 600 Delsea Drive N., Glassboro; (856) 582-4421.

D'Italia Pizzeria, 1500 Saint Georges Ave., Avenel; (732) 574-1120.

D'Rica's Pizzeria, 106 W. Jersey St., Elizabeth; (908) 355-4006.

Da Vinci's Pizza, 223 Bellevue Ave., Montclair; (973) 744-2300.

Danny's Pizza, 47 Main St., Bloomingdale; (973) 838-6700.

Danny's Pizza & Subs, 24 Ayers Lane, Little Silver; (732) 842-5505.

Danny's Pizza Pizzazz, 1288 Delsea Drive, Franklinville; (856) 694-4422.

Dannys Pizza Pizzazz, 484 S. Brewster Road, Vineland; (856) 692-1737.

Dannys Pizzeria, 714 Haddon Ave., Camden; (856) 963-8484.

Dante's Pizza & Restaurant, 214 Main St., Ridgefield Park; (201) 229-9770.

Dante's Pizzeria & Ristorante, 260 N. County Line Road, Jackson; (732) 942-9913.

Dante's Place Restaurant-Pizza, 373 Broad Ave., Leonia; (201) 592-9071.

Dantes Pizza & Restaurant, 408 Haledon Ave., Haledon; (973) 956-0855.

Dany's Pizza, 24 S. Kentucky Ave., Atlantic City; (609) 340-8500.

Dario Pizza Pasta Panini, 1358 Hooper Ave., Toms River; (732) 286-1554.

Davinci Pizza, 483 Woodlane Road, Westampton; (609) 871-2500.

De Fusco's Award Winning Pizza, 1248 Boardwalk, Ocean City; (609) 391-2212.

De La Rosa Restaurant-Pizzaria, 542 Cross Keys Road, Sicklerville; (856) 875-3444.

De Lorenzo's Pizza, 3100 Quakerbridge Road, Trenton; (609) 588-5630.

DeLorenzo's Pizza, 1007 Hamilton Ave., Trenton; (609) 393-2952.

De Lorenzo's Tomato Pies, 435 Hudson St., Trenton; (609) 695-9534.

De Lorenzo's Tomato Pies, 2350 Highway 33, Robbinsville; (609) 341-8480.

De Marco's Pizzeria Restaurant, 1926 Union Valley Road, Hewitt; (973) 728-1344.

De Palma Pizzeria & Ristorante, 1814 New York Ave., Union City; (201) 864-8877.

Delfino's Pizzeria, 500 Jefferson St., Hoboken; (201) 792-7457.

Deli & Pizza Shop Too, 1131 Cooper St., Beverly; (609) 877-6662.

Delio's Pizza & Hero Shop, 120 N. Broadway, South Amboy; (732) 721-9440.

Delizia Pizza, 613 Ridge Road # 1, Monmouth Jct; (732) 329-2277.

Delizia Pizza, 145 King St., Dover; (973) 366-3535.

Delizia Pizza Kitchen, 308 Wootton St., Boonton; (973) 334-3511.

Delli Santi's Pizzeria II, 244 Route 46, Fairfield; (973) 808-9876.

Delliturri's Tuscany Grill, 2014 Route31, Glen Gardner; (908) 638-0012.

DeLucia's Brick Oven Pizza, 3 First Ave., Raritan Borough; (908) 725-1322.

Delvetto's Restaurant, 3701 Route 33, Neptune; (732) 922-3775.

Denapoli's Pizza, 674 Broadway, Bayonne; (201) 823-3500.

Denino's Pizza Place, 1077 Route 34, Matawan; (732) 583-2150.

Denville Pizzeria & Restaurant, 20 Diamond Spring Road, Denville; (973) 625-4321.

Desi's Brick Oven Pizza, 424 Route 206, Hillsborough; (908) 281-5558.

Devine Pizza, 634 Arena Drive, Trenton; (609) 888-4005.

Devito's Pizza IV, 124 Tremont St., Trenton; (609) 393-2155.

Di Lisi's Pizza, 2503 Marne Highway, Hainesport; (609) 267-6001.

Di Maio Brothers Pizzeria, 105 Main St., Hackettstown; (908) 852-6369.

Di Maio Pizza & Restaurant, 468 Springfield Ave., Berkeley Heights; (908) 464-8585.

Di Mola's Pizza & Restaurant, 1060 Route 22, North Plainfield; (908) 754-1881.

Di Napoli Pizza, 205 S. White Horse Pike, Stratford; (856) 782-3770.

Di Roma Pizza, 2310 Atlantic Ave., Atlantic City; (609) 344-1116.

Di Stefano's Deli, 325 Wilson Road, Turnersville; (856) 227-6952.

Di Vincenzo's Pizza, 1101 Cinnaminson Ave., Cinnaminson; (856) 786-3777.

Di Vincenzo's Pizza & Restaurant, 120 Delsea Drive N., Glassboro; (856) 307-1777.

Dickie Dee's Pizza, 380 Bloomfield Ave., Newark; (973) 483-9396.

Dicola's Pizza, 50 Route 31 N., Washington; (908) 689-0250.

Diletto's Pizza, 182 W. Passaic St., Rochelle Park; (201) 843-5464.

Dilisi Pizzeria, 419 S. Delsea Drive, Vineland; (856) 696-0477.

Dilisi's Pizza, 11 Tomlinson Mill Road, Medford; (856) 596-0068.

DiMola's Pizza & Restaurant, 1541 Route 31, Clinton; (908) 638-5612.

Dino's Deli & Subs, 402 Zion Road, Egg Harbor Township; (609) 927-9842.

Dino's Pizza, 100 Route 46, Budd Lake; (973) 347-7100.

Dino's Pizza, 128 Watchung Ave., Montclair; (973) 783-7115.

Dino's Pizza & Restaurant, 1001 Fischer Blvd., Toms River; (732) 270-4411.

Dino's Sub & Pizza Shop, 8016 Ventnor Ave., Margate City; (609) 822-6602.

Dinos Coal Fired Pizza, 183 Old Tappan Road, Old Tappan; (201) 297-7443.

Divinia Ristorante, 461 Bloomfield Ave., Caldwell; (973) 228-5228.

Dolce Italia, 210 New Jersey Ave., Wildwood; (609) 522-6228.

Domenico's Pizza Place, 13 Upper Mountain Ave., Rockaway; (973) 627-9100.

Domenico's Trattoria, 1 1/2 Crosswicks St., Bordentown; (609) 298-6800.

Dominator Pizza, 2191 Spruce St., Trenton; (609) 406-9555.

Dominican Pizza, 422 Market St., Paterson; (973) 881-1113.

Dominic's Pizza, 1961 Route 1, Lawrenceville; (609) 695-5577.

Dominic's Pizza, 99 Route 73, Voorhees; (856) 768-0500.

Dominic's Pizza, 605 E. County Line Road, Lakewood; (732) 367-1115.

Dominic's Pizza Steaks & Subs, 5101 Route 42, Turnersville; (856) 232-0177.

Dominic's Pizzeria, 2461 Route 33, Neptune; (732) 922-1333.

Dominick's Pizza, 31 Lackawanna Ave., Gladstone; (908) 234-2480.

Dominick's Pizza, 304 Union Blvd., Totowa; (973) 942-4141.

Dominick's Pizza Inc, 1768 S. Lincoln Ave., Vineland; (856) 691-5511.

Dominick's Pizza Shop, 307 Route 202/206, Bridgewater; (908) 526-0330.

Dominick's Pizza Shoppe, 404 W. Union Ave., Bound Brook; (732) 356-5533.

Dominick's Pizza Shoppes, 44 Old Highway 22, Clinton; (908) 735-4412.

Dominick's Pizza Shoppes, 1125 Liberty Ave., Hillside; (908) 355-4425.

Dominick's Pizzaria, 486 S. Washington Ave., Piscataway; (732) 752-1440.

Dominick's Pizzeria, 19 E. Clinton St., Newton; (973) 383-9330.

Dominick's Pizzeria, 49 Reaville Ave., Flemington; (908) 782-6518.

Dominick's Pizzeria & Restaurant, 128 Route 94, Blairstown; (908) 362-6460.

Dominick's Pizzeria-Restaurant, 2595 Woodbridge Ave., Edison; (732) 248-1010.

Don's Pizza King, 811 Main St., Belmar; (732) 681-6373.

Donatos Pizza, 1174 Fischer Blvd., Toms River; (732) 270-9822.

Donatucci Pizza, 115 E.17th Ave,. North Wildwood; (609) 729-6110.

Donika Jonuzi Pizzaria, 5012 Wellington Ave., Ventnor City; (609) 823-5500.

Donna Bella, 115 Bowers St., Jersey City; (201) 653-1235.

Donna's Pizza, 404 Broad Ave., Palisades Park; (201) 944-2158.

Donnagio's Pizzeria, 61 New Road, Parsippany; (973) 882-9200.

Donnagio's Pizzeria, 487 Market St., Saddle Brook; (201) 712-9400.

Donte's Pizza, 440 Route 130, East Windsor; (609) 371-8900.

Doraldo Restaurant & Pizza, 21 S. Hope Chapel Road, Jackson; (732) 364-5191.

Doraldo Restaurant & Pizzeria, 2465 S. Broad St., Trenton; (609) 888-2090.

Doria Pizza Restaurant, 432 Springfield Ave., Summit; (908) 277-0909.

Dough Boy Pizza Unlimited, 22-06 Maple Ave., Fair Lawn; (201) 956-6727.

Dough Boys Pizzeria, 58 Carr Ave., Keansburg; (732) 769-5110.

Douglas Halal Pizza & Grill, 821 Somerset St., Somerset; (732) 846-9292.

Douglas Pizza & Grill, 298 George St., New Brunswick; (732) 514-0097.

Downtown Eddy's Mixed Grill, 516 Jersey Ave., Jersey City; (201) 451-8883.

Downtown Pizza, 10 N. Broad St., Trenton; (609) 393-2248.

Dragos Pizza, 2775 State Route 23, Newfoundland; (973) 208-6700.

Due Bambini Brick Oven Pizza, 879 Main Ave., Passaic; (973) 773-3773.

Due Bambini Brick Oven Pizza, 125 Market St., Passaic; (973) 777-5003.

Dusal's, 3300 Route 27, Kendall Park; (732) 821-9711.

Dusal's Italian Restaurant, 345 W. Main St., Freehold; (732) 431-0004.

Dusal's Italian Restaurant & Pizza, 100 Ryders Lane, Milltown; (732) 745-7311.

Dusal's Pizza, 340 Union Hill Road, Manalapan; (732) 536-4089.

E & V Pizza & Wraps, 286 Route 34, Matawan; (732) 566-5666.

E J's Place, 1448 Queen Anne Road, Teaneck; (201) 862-0611.

E Z Pizza, 155 State Rt 17, Hasbrouck Heights; (201) 257-8808.

Eagles Pizza, 2891 Route 73 S., Maple Shade; (856) 414-9334.

East Ridge Pizzeria Restaurant, 621 Beverly Rancocas Road, Willingboro; (609) 871-5151.

Eastside Pizzeria & Grill, 519 Market St., Paterson; (973) 881-9230.

Eddie's Pizzeria, 353 Totowa Ave., Paterson; (973) 942-1938.

Edison Pizza Restaurant, 2303 Woodbridge Ave., Edison; (732) 985-1733.

El Greco Pizza, 404 Irvington Ave., South Orange; (973) 763-2030.

El Mexicano Restaurant & Pizza, 3215 Atlantic Ave., Longport; (609) 572-0700.

El Pollo Y La Pizza, 100 Clifton Ave., Lakewood; (732) 905-1177.

El Tricolor Pizzeria & Mexican, 211 S. New Road, Absecon; (609) 641-0072.

Eli's Pizza Pasta, 602 E. Jersey St., Elizabeth; (908) 436-0436.

Elin's Pizza, 701 Elizabeth Ave., Elizabeth; (908) 355-3320.

Elis's Pizzeria, 116 White Horse Pike, Chesilhurst; (856) 809-1000.

Elizabeth Pizzeria, 871 Elizabeth Ave., Elizabeth; (908) 289-9412.

Ellison Pizza & Deli, 88 Ellison St., Paterson; (973) 742-8683.

Emilia Romagna Pizza, 247 Valley Blvd., Wood Ridge; (201) 935-8383.

Emilio's Restaurant & Pizza, 305 Whitesville Road, Jackson; (732) 901-0331.

Emilio's Restaurant & Pizza, 1889 Ridgeway Road, Toms River; (732) 244-5600.

Emilio's Restaurant & Pizzeria, 12 E. Maryland Ave., Somers Point; (609) 927-7343.

Emilio's Restaurant & Pizzeria, 700 Tennent Road, Manalapan; (732) 972-6162.

Emilios Restaurant, 4534 Route 9, Howell; (732) 370-2666.

Emma's Brick Oven Pizza & Cafe, 101 N. Union Ave., Cranford; (908) 497-1881.

Empire Pizza, 80 Centre St., Nutley; (973) 667-7922.

Enrico's Pizza & Pasta, 19 Old York Road, Bridgewater; (908) 541-1333.

Enrico's Restaurant & Pizzaria, 301 Avenue C, Bayonne; (201) 436-5504.

Enza's Restaurant & Pizzeria, 266 Warburton Ave., Hawthorne; (973) 423-4080.

Enzo Pizza, 237 W. Commodore Blvd., Jackson; (732) 928-8088.

Enzo Pizza, 268 New Road, Somers Point; (609) 927-9477.

Enzo Pizza & Restaurant, 382 Route 46, Budd Lake; (973) 691-1330.

Enzo Pizzeria & Pasta Grill, 328 W. Washington Ave., Washington; (908) 689-3652.

Enzo Pizzeria & Restaurant, 150 Valley Road, Montclair; (973) 509-0999.

Enzo's La Piccola Cucina, 1906 Princeton Ave., Lawrenceville; (609) 396-9868.

Enzo's Pizza, 39 Mill Road, Matawan; (732) 583-2777.

Enzo's Pizzeria, 585 Stelton Road, Piscataway; (732) 752-9552.

Enzo's Pizzeria & Pasta Grill, 1916 Route 57, Hackettstown; (908) 813-8535.

Enzo's Pizzeria & Restaurant, 903 High St., Hackettstown; (908) 850-0010.

Enzo's Pizzeria & Restaurant, 877 N. Stiles St., Linden; (908) 587-9100.

Enzos Pizzeria, 491 Manalapan Road, Spotswood; (732) 251-2951.

Enzzo's Trattoria-Restaurant, 514 Millburn Ave., Short Hills; (973) 379-7111.

Epiro's Pizza, 1785 Williamstown-Erial Road, Sicklerville; (856) 346-2700.

Erma Deli & Pizzeria, 635 Breakwater Road, Cape May; (609) 884-0958.

Ernie & Dom's Pizzeria, 433 Route 31 S., Washington; (908) 537-6454.

Esavel's Pizzeria, 124 Locust St., Roselle; (908) 259-1211.

Esperanto's Pizza, 500 Jersey Ave., Jersey City; (201) 451-9999.

Esposito's Pizza & Deli, 465 Pompton Ave., Cedar Grove; (973) 239-0807.

Esposito's Pizza & Restaurant, 425 Forest Road, Mahwah; (201) 848-7411.

Esposito's Pizza & Restaurant, 433 Old Hook Road, Emerson; (201) 262-2595.

Europa Pizza & Restaurant, 24369 W. Main St., Columbus; (609) 324-0902.

Exit 9 Pizzeria, 87 Remsen Ave., New Brunswick; (732) 545-9555.

Express Pizza & Steaks, 719 Battersea Road, Ocean City; (609) 398-3322.

Ez Pizza, 184 Essex St., Lodi; (201) 845-5080.

F & J Italian Specialties Deli, 563 Main St., Sayreville; (732) 238-5126.

Fabrizio Pizza, 4801 Westfield Ave., Pennsauken; (856) 663-2820.

Fairfield Pizzeria, 103 Route 46, Fairfield; (973) 227-5456.

Falcone & Son Italian Restaurant, 3 Nevius St., Raritan; (908) 575-0113.

Falcone & Son Italian Restaurant, 69 W. Somerset St., Raritan; (908) 575-0113.

Family Chicken & Pizza, 559 Chancellor Ave., Irvington; (973) 371-6100.

Family Pizza, 115 Franklin St., Hightstown; (609) 443-8246.

Family Pizza & Restaurant, 455 Route 23, Sussex; (973) 702-1436.

Family's Pizza & Restaurant, 390 Route 57 E., Washington; (908) 689-8669.

The Famous & Original King of Pizza, Route 70 & Cornell Ave., Cherry Hill; (856) 665-4824.

Famous City Pizza LLC, 89 Van Houten St., Paterson; (973) 742-9400.

The Famous King of Pizza, Route 130 and Market Street, Gloucester City; (856) 456-0922.

Famous Ray's Pizza, 10 Pompton Ave., Verona; (973) 857-3434.

Fat Daddy's Subs & Pizza, 334 Tilton Road, Northfield; (609) 641-3060.

Father & Son Pizzeria, 6810 Bergenline Ave., Guttenberg; (201) 869-3336.

Fedelos Family Pizzeria, 1241 Lawrenceville Road, Lawrenceville; (609) 406-1818.

Federici's Pizzeria, 14 E. Main St., Freehold; (732) 462-1312.

Federici's South, 6469 Route 9, Howell; (732) 364-8220.

Federico's Pizza Express, 620 Bay Ave., Point Pleasant Beach; (732) 899-8655.

Ferraro's Famous Tomato Pie, 400 Main St., Bradley Beach; (732) 775-1117.

Ferraro's Pizza, 600 Park Ave., Plainfield; (908) 756-0886.

Ferraro's Pizzeria, 1067 Inman Ave., Edison; (908) 561-7373.

Ferraro's Pizzeria, 1061 Amboy Ave., Edison; (732) 225-3113.

Ferraro's Restaurant, 14 Elm St., Westfield; (908) 232-1101.

Ferrulli Pizza, 80 Centre St., Nutley; (973) 667-7900.

Fevola's Pizza, 370 Atlantic City Blvd, Bayville; (732) 269-7500.

Fiesta Pizza, 4200 Ventnor Ave., Atlantic City; (609) 347-1222.

Fiesta Pizza II & Restaurant, 41 S. Bartram Ave., Atlantic City; (609) 344-6100.

Figaro Pizza, 396 Paterson Ave., East Rutherford; (201) 729-9056.

Filippo Famous Pizza, 336 George St., New Brunswick; (732) 846-9060.

Filippo's Pizza Cafe, 267 1st St., Hoboken; (201) 659-3333.

Filippo's Restaurant, 406 Washington St., Hoboken; (201) 798-8210.

Fior D'Italia Food Center, 1400 Burnet Ave., Union; (908) 686-8178.

Firehouse Pizza, 15 Central Ave., Madison; (973) 765-0565.

Fireplace, 718 N. Route 17, Paramus; (201) 444-2362.

Five Star Pizzeria, 101 W. Rio Grande Ave., Wildwood; (609) 522-1390.

Flanders General Store, 20 Hillside Ave., Flanders; (973) 584-2443.

Florham Park Pizza, 187 Columbia Turnpike, Florham Park; (973) 966-1062.

Floyd's, 1801 Route 37 E., Toms River; (732) 929-1300.

Fontana Restaurant & Pizzeria, 1011 Broadway, Bayonne; (201) 823-4946.

Fontanini Pizzeria & Rest, 3515 Kennedy Blvd., Jersey City; (201) 420-9777.

Fords Pizza Restaurant, 530 New Brunswick Ave., Fords; (732) 738-0299.

Forno Pizzeria & Grille, 28 Church Road, Maple Shade; (856) 608-7711.

Fort Lee Pizzeria & Italian, 2469 Lemoine Ave., Fort Lee; (201) 947-2420.

Forte Pizzeria, 182 Bloomfield Ave., Caldwell; (973) 403-9411.

Forte Pizzeria, 486 Route 10, Randolph; (973) 328-4300.

Fortissimo Osteria Pizzeria, 484 Pleasant Valley Way, West Orange; (973) 731-8095.

Fortunata's, 2940 Yorktowne Blvd., Brick; (732) 920-3999.

Foschini's Brick Oven Kitchen, 298 Ridge Road, Lyndhurst; (201) 460-7600.

Foschinis Brick Oven, 21 E. Madison Ave., Dumont; (201) 387-9998.

Four Boys Pizza, 42 Ramtown Greenville Road, Howell; (732) 785-2626.

Four Brothers Pizza, 106 Park Ave., Paterson; (973) 553-2280.

Four Brothers Pizzeria, 579 W. Side Ave., Jersey City; (201) 332-8056.

Four Musketeer's Pizza, 3181 Route 27, Franklin Park; (732) 297-1980.

Fraconi's Pizza, 3318 Boardwalk, Wildwood; (609) 522-2800.

Francello Pizzeria & Restaurant, 3909 Marlton Pike, Pennsauken; (856) 665-7045.

Francesca's Pizza Pasta-Grill, 127 Ark Road, Mount Laurel; (856) 802-2882.

Francesca's Pizzeria, 652 Westwood Ave., River Vale; (201) 497-6617.

Francesca's Pizzeria & Restaurant, 81 McWhorter St., Newark; (973) 344-9233.

Francesco's, 297 Route 72 W., Manahawkin; (609) 597-0040.

Francesco's Pizza Restaurant, 228 S. Pavilion Ave., Riverside; (856) 461-4880.

Francesco's Pizzeria, 279 Bay Ave., Highlands; (732) 291-4729.

Francesco's Pizzeria & Restaurant, 52 N. Beverwyck Road, Lake Hiawatha; (973) 335-0009.

Franco's Pizza, 170 Talmadge Road, Edison; (732) 248-2484.

Franco's Pizzeria, 157 N. Broadway, Pennsville; (856) 540-0777.

Franco's Place, 67 Ellis St., Haddonfield; (856) 857-9889.

Franco's Restaurant & Pizzeria, 1475 Bergen Blvd., Fort Lee; (201) 461-6651.

Francolli's Pizza & Restaurant, 888 Fischer Blvd., Toms River; (732) 270-5661.

Francos Pizzeria, 4 Mercer St., Hopewell; (609) 466-2991.

Francos Restaurant & Pizza, 65 E. Route 70, Marlton; (856) 983-4746.

Francesco Pizzeria-Ristorante, 351 High St., Burlington; (609) 747-1400.

Frank & Joe's Pizza, 519 Park Ave., Paterson; (973) 881-1525.

Frank & Son Pizzeria, 355 Parsippany Road, Parsippany; (973) 887-2181.

Frank's Famous Pizza, 3167 Route 9 S., Rio Grande; (609) 465-0101.

Frank's Famous Pizzeria, 415½ Monmouth St., Jersey City; (201) 798-1173.

Frank's II Pizzeria, 508 Hurffville-Crosskeys Road, Sewell; (856) 582-8911.

Frank's Pizza, 31 Marshall Hill Road, West Milford; (973) 728-2539.

Frank's Pizza, 14 Eisenhower Pkwy, Roseland; (973) 403-8070.

Frank's Pizza, 19 Wanaque Ave., Pompton Lakes; (973) 248-8333.

Frank's Pizza, 240 Route 206, Flanders; (973) 584-0379.

Frank's Pizza, 5762 Berkshire Valley Road, Oak Ridge; (973) 208-5700.

Frank's Pizza, 300 Enterprise Drive, Rockaway; (973) 328-3833.

Frank's Pizza, 181 Howard Blvd., Mount Arlington; (973) 398-7300.

Frank's Pizza, 7 Naughright Road, Hackettstown; (908) 979-3113.

Frank's Pizza, 50 Hopatchung Road, Hopatcong; (973) 398-4663.

Frank's Pizza, 725 Route 15 S., Lake Hopatcong; (973) 663-1337.

Frank's Pizza, 140 N. Main St., Manville; (908) 685-7717.

Frank's Pizza, 235 Ridgedale Ave., Cedar Knolls; (973) 889-0276.

Frank's Pizza & Italian Restaurant, 152 Route 94, Blairstown; (908) 362-1588.

Frank's Pizza & Pasta, 268 Route 202/31, Flemington; (908) 788-3739.

Frank's Pizza & Restaurant, 13 Belleville Ave., Bloomfield; (973) 429-9636.

Frank's Pizza & Restaurant, 67 Walmart Plz, Clinton; (908) 735-9293.

Frank's Pizza & Restaurant, 1900 Highway 70, Lakewood; (732) 477-4103.

Frank's Pizza & Restaurant, 205 Route 23, Sussex; (973) 875-1250.

Frank's Pizza & Restaurant, 189 Route 46, Saddle Brook; (201) 587-1979.

Frank's Pizza & Restaurant, 11 Theatre Ctr, Sparta; (973) 729-3354.

Frank's Pizza of Oakland, 350 Ramapo Valley Road, Oakland; (201) 651-0900.

Frank's Pizza Restaurant, 162 Orlando Drive, Raritan; (908) 218-8887.

Frank's Pizzeria, 1070 Delsea Drive, Westville; (856) 384-1790.

Frank's Pizzeria, 1107 Old York Road, Ringoes; (908) 782-0909.

Frank's Pizzeria, 329 Valley St., South Orange; (973) 763-4837.

Frank's Pizzeria, 161 Bloomfield Ave., Newark; (973) 482-8891.

Frank's Trattoria, 1250 Route 22, Phillipsburg; (908) 454-8790.

Frank's Trattoria, 80 Main St., Hackettstown; (908) 852-2405.

Frank's Trattoria, 802 Bloomfield Ave., West Caldwell; (973) 575-4594.

Frankie Fed's Pizza & Pasta House, 831 Route 33, Freehold; (732) 294-1333.

Frankie's Cafe Fine Dining, 304 Georges Road, Dayton; (732) 329-2603.

Frankie's Famous Pizzeria, 3001 Ocean Heights Ave., Egg Harbor Twp; (609) 926-5566.

Frankie's Pizza & Restaurant, 305 Atlantic City Blvd., Bayville; (732) 269-6500.

Frankie's Pizza II, 565 Route 50, Mays Landing; (609) 625-7566.

Franklin Lakes Pizzeria, 799 Franklin Ave., Franklin Lakes; (201) 891-3366.

Franklin Pizza, 3151 Route 27, Franklin Park; (732) 297-9798.

Franklin Pizza & Grill, 1991 Route 27, Somerset; (732) 422-0111.

Franks Pizza, 1885 Route 57, Hackettstown; (908) 684-8403.

Franks Pizza & Restaurant, 518 Old Post Road, Edison; (732) 287-0228.

Franks Pizzeria Inc, 4410 Bergen Turnpike, North Bergen; (201) 866-3267.

Fratelli's Pizza, 307 E. Evesham Road, Runnemede; (856) 939-9900.

Fratelli's Pizzeria & Cafe, 201 Stelton Road, Piscataway; (732) 752-5300.

Fratelli's Restaurant Pizzeria, 500 Route 35, Middletown; (732) 747-4737.

Freddie's Pizzeria, 563 Broadway, Long Branch; (732) 222-0931.

Frederico's Pizza Express, 700 Main St., Belmar; (732) 681-7066.

Fresco Pizza & Pasta, 1210 Raritan Road, Cranford; (908) 276-0407.

Fresh Hot Pizza Inc, PO Box 8, Cliffside Park; (201) 945-4500.

Fusaro Pizzeria, 31 N. Main St., Manahawkin; (609) 978-3888.

Gabby's Pizza & Pasta, 203 Main St., Flemington; (908) 237-9990.

Gabriellas Pizzeria, 733 Route 72 W., Manahawkin; (609) 978-7750.

Galasso's Pizzeria Inc, 48 Bridge St., Frenchtown; (908) 996-2511.

Galaxia International, 2801 John F Kennedy Blvd., Jersey City; (201) 239-4554.

Galaxy Pasta & Pizza, 7000 Kennedy Blvd., Guttenberg; (201) 854-4116.

Gallery Pizza, 2905 New Brooklyn-Erial Road, Sicklerville; (856) 346-0040.

Gallery Pizza & Restaurant III, 386 White Horse Pike, Atco; (856) 768-3016.

Gallo's Pizzeria, 211 W. Front St., Plainfield; (908) 222-9191.

Gambino Pizza Pallace, 1892 Marlton Pike E., Cherry Hill; (856) 751-3278.

Gandolfo Pizzeria & Restaurant, 7523 Bergenline Ave., North Bergen; (201) 662-8004.

Gara's Pizza, 200 Route 57, Phillipsburg; (908) 454-9272.

Garbo's Italian Deli & Liquors, 7 Sheridan Ave., Ho-Ho-Kus; (201) 652-4494.

Garden Pizza, 153 Bergen Blvd., Fairview; (201) 941-8510.

Garden Pizza Ice Cream & Cafe, 326 Garden St., Carlstadt; (201) 933-8887.

Gaspare's, 501 Zion Road, Egg Harbor Twp; (609) 653-2112.

Gasper Pizza, 4 N. Main St., Pennington; (609) 737-8520.

Gattinelli Pizza & Pasta, 117 Greentree Road # 5, Blackwood; (856) 228-5336.

Genaro's Old World Brick Oven, 66 Brick Blvd., Brick; (732) 255-1955.

Gencarelli Restaurant & Pizza, 25 W. Main St., Rockaway; (973) 625-7520.

Gencarelli's Pizzeria & Restaurant, 6 Lake Drive W., Wayne; (973) 633-0009.

Gencarelli's Pizzeria & Restaurant, 501 Bloomfield Ave., Newark; (973) 481-6900.

Gene O's Tavern, 100 S. White Horse Pike, Waterford Works; (856) 753-8810.

Generoso's Pizza Inc, 1357 Prince Rodgers Ave., Bridgewater; (908) 526-5260.

Gennaro's Il Pizzeria & Restaurant, 498 Inman Ave., Colonia; (732) 827-8554.

Gennaro's Italian Restaurant, 100 Summerhill Road, Spotswood; (732) 723-0753.

Gennaro's Pizza, 75 Route 27, Edison; (732) 549-8554.

Gennaro's Pizzeria, 4613 Nottingham Way, Hamilton; (609) 587-4992.

Gennaro's Pizzeria, 1100 South Ave. W., Westfield; (908) 654-7472.

Geno D's Pizzeria & Restaurant, 197 Route 70, Toms River; (732) 363-4246.

Genova Pizzeria, 132 Cuthbert Blvd., Audubon; (856) 546-8727.

Genteel's Trattoria, 1378 Route 206, Skillman; (609) 252-0880.

Genuardi's, 912 W. Bay Ave., Barnegat; (609) 607-9360.

George's Pizza of NJ, 1309 Boardwalk, Seaside Heights; (732) 793-7229.

George's Pizzeria, 654 Main St., Leesburg; (856) 785-0700.

Georgio's Pizzeria & Restaurant, 309 Main St., Sayreville; (732) 651-2333.

Geppetto's Pizza, 365 Ringwood Ave., Wanaque; (973) 835-7086.

Geppteeo's, 1967 Morris Ave., Union; (908) 687-4222.

Gerlanda's Pizza, 604 Bartholomew Road, Piscataway; (732) 463-1616.

Gerlanda's Pizza Cafe, 126 College Ave., New Brunswick; (732) 846-9375.

Gerry's Pizza, 200 Main St., Fort Lee; (201) 944-9482.

Gia Nina Pizza & Italian Restaurant, 312 S. Evergreen Ave., Woodbury; (856) 845-6500.

Giacomo Pizzeria, 1061 N. Pearl St., Bridgeton; (856) 451-8777.

Giampapa's Pizzeria, 1808 Route 37 E., Toms River; (732) 270-6460.

Gianangelos Pizzeria, 324 Route 24, Chester; (908) 879-0669.

Gianmarcos Pizza & Restaurant, 504 Monmouth St., Trenton; (609) 259-5300.

Gianni's Pizzarama, 1006 Stelton Road, Piscataway; (732) 981-9507.

Gianni's Pizzeria, 495 Prospect Ave., Little Silver; (732) 530-9277.

Gianni's Pizzeria, 1504 Roosevelt Ave., Carteret; (732) 541-5004.

Gina's Pizzeria, 503 Frank E. Rodgers Blvd N., Harrison; (973) 482-4883.

Gino's of Italy Pizza, 553 Grove St., Irvington; (973) 374-9015.

Gino's Pizza, 1200 Atlantic Ave., Atlantic City; (609) 347-4747.

Gino's Pizza, 585 Blackwood-Clementon Road, Lindenwold; (856) 783-4433.

Gino's Pizza & Luncheonette, 545 Washington Ave., Belleville; (973) 751-5848.

Gino's Pizzeria, 844 Delsea Drive N., Glassboro; (856) 307-9000.

Gino's Pizzeria, 380 Central Ave., Jersey City; (201) 659-6464.

Gino's Pizzeria, 130 Market St., Paterson; (973) 523-0002.

Gino's Pizzeria & Restaurant, 1576 Irving St., Rahway; (732) 382-9774.

Gio's Pizza, 435 Hope-Blairstown Road, Hope; (908) 459-0091.

Giovanna's Pizzeria, 741 Harrison Ave., Harrison; (973) 268-4848.

Giovanni Italian Style Pizza, 429 S. Evergreen Ave., Woodbury; (856) 845-0045.

Giovanni Italian Style Pizza, 1 N. Virginia Ave., Penns Grove; (856) 351-0700.

Giovanni Pizza & Restaurant, 603 Washington St., Hoboken; (201) 714-4232.

Giovanni's Best of Italy, 801 Tilton Road, Northfield; (609) 383-1155.

Giovanni's Italian Cuisine, 525 Cedar Hill Ave., Wyckoff; (201) 444-0944.

Giovanni's Pizza, 205 E. Collins Road, Galloway; (609) 748-0444.

Giovanni's Pizza, 118 1st St., Hackensack; (201) 487-5849.

Giovanni's Pizza, 1320 Englishtown Road, Old Bridge; (732) 251-8419.

Giovanni's Pizza, 570 Clifton Ave., Clifton; (973) 470-0500.

Giovanni's Pizza, 7709 Park Ave., Pennsauken; (856) 662-9467.

Giovanni's Pizza, 380 New Brunswick Ave., Perth Amboy; (732) 442-0100.

Giovanni's Pizza & Pasta, 431 Route 22 E., Whitehouse Sta; (908) 534-1958.

Giovanni's Pizza Restaurant, 105 Ellison St., Paterson; (973) 279-7174.

Giovanni's Pizzeria, 11 Grant Ave., Dumont; (201) 385-1944.

Giovanni's Pizzeria, 649 Broadway, Bayonne; (201) 339-1550.

Giovanni's Place, 1295 Route 23, Butler; (973) 838-5510.

Giovannis Pizza, 250 Sicklerville Road, Sicklerville; (856) 885-8675.

Giulietta e Romeo Pizzeria, 7 Ronald Drive, East Hanover; (973) 599-0550.

Giulios Pizzeria & Restaurant, 201 North Ave., Dunellen; (732) 424-7885.

Giuseppe Homestyle Pizzeria, 1576 Maple Ave., Hillside; (973) 351-5103.

Giuseppe Pizza, 175 Monmouth Road, West Long Branch; (732) 728-2225.

Giuseppe Pizza & Restaurant, 620 Beers St., Hazlet; (732) 888-2944.

Giuseppe Pizzeria & Restaurant, 24 Summerfield Blvd., Dayton; (732) 274-8803.

Giuseppe's Gourmet, 108 Route 50 # A, Ocean View; (609) 390-8797.

Giuseppe's Pizza & Pasta, 3316 Sunset Ave., Ocean; (732) 775-6633.

Giuseppe's Pizza & Restaurant, 557 Pompton Ave., Cedar Grove; (973) 857-1982.

Giuseppe's Pizza Restaurant, 5200 Route 42, Blackwood; (856) 232-4545.

Giuseppe's Pizza-Green Brook, 937 N. Washington Ave., Green Brook; (732) 968-8800.

Giuseppe's Pizzeria, 1200 Delsea Drive, Westville; (856) 848-8008.

Giuseppe's Restaurant, 960 Sherman Ave., Elizabeth; (908) 352-4183.

Giuseppe's Ristorante, 40 Bridge St., Lambertville; (609) 397-1500.

Giuseppe's Trattoria, 191 Route 206 S., Chester; (908) 879-6364.

Giussseppe's Pizza, 2581 Route 516, Old Bridge; (732) 607-2066.

Giustino's Pizzeria Restaurant, 821 Summer Ave., Newark; (973) 483-3900.

Glendale Pizza, 1367 Stuyvesant Ave., Union; (908) 964-6266.

Go Go Pizza, 204 Broad St., Elizabeth; (908) 354-2333.

Godfather's On the Boardwalk, 1523 Boardwalk, Atlantic City; (609) 347-4882.

Godfather's Pizza, 8 Bennetts Mills Road, Jackson; (732) 928-3529.

Godfather's Pizza, 661 New Road, Somers Point; (609) 653-4825.

Godfather's Pizza, 200 Route 10, East Hanover; (973) 887-4830.

Godfather's Pizza, 701 E. Edgar Road, Linden; (908) 862-3485.

Godfather's Pizza, 1021 Route 9 S., Woodbridge; (732) 593-0174.

Godfather's Pizza, 623 Spring St., Elizabeth; (908) 351-9284.

Godfather's Pizza, 1420 Admiral Wilson Blvd., Pennsauken; (856) 964-2357.

Godfather's Pizza, 2880 Route 1, North Brunswick; (732) 940-3725.

Golden Pizzeria, 377 S. Orange Ave., Newark; (973) 643-5003.

Good Fellows Pizza & Italian, 736 King George Road, Fords; (732) 738-7500.

Goodfellas, 27 Old Highway 22, Clinton; (908) 713-1236.

Goodfellas, 40 Route 31, Flemington; (908) 806-3341.

Goodfellas Pizzeria & Restaurant, 241 Bloomfield Ave., Bloomfield; (973) 748-4180.

Goodfellows, 229 Main St., Hackettstown; (908) 850-9301.

Goomba's Pizza, 1424 Morris Ave., Union; (908) 688-7500.

Gourmet Italian Cuisine & Pizzeria, 324 S. Pitney Road, Galloway; (609) 652-1398.

Gourmet Pizza, 1351 Route 38, Hainesport; (609) 261-8016.

Gourmet Pizza City, 150 1st St., Keyport; (732) 203-0048.

Grande Pizza, 400 Newark St., Hoboken; (201) 459-6070.

Grande Pizzarama, 293 Route 18, East Brunswick; (732) 238-9790.

Grandma's Pizza truck, along Hudson Street near Harborside Financial Center, Jersey City; (973) 941-2372.

Grant St Pizza, 661 Grant St., Camden; (856) 379-4866.

Graziano's Italian Restaurant, 3119 Route 88, Point Pleasant; (732) 899-6336.

Graziella Ristorante-Tomato, 3681 Nottingham Way, Trenton; (609) 890-0099.

Great American Pizza & Grill, 276 E. Main St., Denville; (973) 625-2223.

Greco Roma Pizza & Grill, 615 Boulevard, Kenilworth; (908) 272-1221.

Greg's Pizzeria La Union area, 2726 Morris Ave., Union; (908) 964-9550.

Grimaldi's, 133 Clinton St., Hoboken; (201) 792-0800.

Grossi Fat Pan Pizza, 301 Springfield Ave., Berkeley Heights; (908) 665-8555.

Grotto Restaurant, 454 River Styx Road, Hopatcong; (973) 398-2037.

Grove Pizzeria, 1279 Liberty Ave., Hillside; (973) 923-6677.

Guallpa's Famous Pizza, 624 Inman Ave., Colonia; (732) 815-9555.

Guido's Old World Pizza, 280 Young Ave., Moorestown; (856) 234-7080.

Guido's Pizza, 513 Market St., Camden; (856) 338-0444.

Guidos, 22 Lewis St., Eatontown; (732) 389-8989.

Guiducci & Margiottiello, 175 3rd St., Elizabeth; (908) 558-1959.

Guiseppe's, 365 Convery Blvd., Perth Amboy; (732) 324-8770.

Gulistan Pizza, 783 S. Orange Ave., Newark; (973) 375-2100.

Gus's Pizzeria, 4520 Park Blvd., Wildwood; (609) 729-2981.

Gus's Pizzeria & Texas Weiners, 54 S. Broadway, Pennsville; (856) 678-6699.

Gus's Pizzeria Woodstown Inc, 14 S. Main St., Woodstown; (856) 769-0888.

Haledon Pizza, 303 Belmont Ave., Haledon; (973) 595-6676.

Hanky's Pizzeria, 435 E. Brinkerhoff Ave., Palisades Park; (201) 944-6780.

Happy Days Pizzeria, 312 Smith St., Perth Amboy; (732) 442-4802.

Happy Pizza, 9 Hamilton St., Bound Brook; (732) 469-9515.

Harbors Bizaare Tomato Pie, 261 96th St., Stone Harbor; (609) 368-1175.

Hawthorne's Best Pizza, 191 Diamond Bridge Ave., Hawthorne; (973) 427-7555.

Helen's Pizza, 183 Newark Ave., Jersey City; (201) 435-1507.

Hickory Pizzeria & Restaurant, 641 Shunpike Road, Chatham; (973) 822-2124.

Highland Pizza, 601 Raritan Ave., Highland Park; (732) 572-6744.

Hillman's Luncheonette, 45 W. Pleasant Ave., Maywood; (201) 843-5088.

Hoboken Pizza, 55 Newark St., Hoboken; (201) 222-7500.

Holiday City Plaza Pizzeria, 730 Jamaica Blvd., Toms River; (732) 341-5070.

Hollywood Pizza Steaks & Subs, 434 Pine St., Mount Holly; (609) 267-8228.

Hollywood Pizzeria & Restaurant, 376 Fairfield Road, Fairfield; (973) 808-0123.

Hopewell Sub & Pizza, 608 Shiloh Pike, Bridgeton; (856) 451-0261.

Hot Grill, 669 Lexington Ave., Clifton; (973) 772-6000.

Hot Pizza, 1396 Oak Tree Road, Iselin; (732) 283-1097.

Hot Pizza Inc, 2104 Kennedy Blvd., Union City; (201) 617-7779.

House of Pizza, 210 Ocean Gate Drive, Bayville; (732) 269-1950.

House of Pizza, 7447 Maple Ave., Pennsauken; (856) 488-5588.

Iano's Rosticceria, 86 Nassau St., Princeton; (609) 924-5515.

III Brothers Pizza, 6690 Black Horse Pike, Egg Harbor Twp; (609) 484-1613.

Il Carrettino Pizza & Restaurant, 169 Union Blvd., Totowa; (973) 942-3313.

Il Forna Pizza, 349 Chestnut St., Union; (908) 686-3999.

Il Forno, 1536 Paterson Plank Road, Secaucus; (201) 864-6576.

Il Forno Restaurant, 1260 Route 28, Somerville; (908) 252-4500.

Il Giardino, 153 Paris Ave., Northvale; (201) 750-0060.

Il Giardino '86 Restaurant, 41 Ridgedale Ave., Cedar Knolls; (973) 984-9594.

Il Monacone, 843 Route 33, Freehold; (732) 409-6462.

Il Mondo Della Pizza, 4625 Park Ave., Union City; (201) 867-4011.

Il Palazzo, 600 Ringwood Ave., Wanaque; (973) 839-9696.

Il Pomodoro, 65 Route 36, Keyport; (732) 203-2222.

Il-Giardino Restaurant, 103 Miln St., Cranford; (908) 272-2500.

Illiano's, 705 12th St., Hammonton; (609) 561-3444.

Illiano's Cafe Over Eatontown, 1 Corbett Way, Eatontown; (732) 542-2520.

Illiano's Italian Restaurant, 933 W. Park Ave., Ocean; (732) 493-2003.

Imposto Restaurant & Pizza, 102 Washington St., Hoboken; (201) 963-3160.

Indian Mills Pizza, 43 Willow Grove Road, Shamong; (609) 268-0069.

Inzillo's Pizzeria & Restaurant, 2103 W. County Line Road, Jackson; (732) 370-0310.

Ippolito's Cucina Italina, 700 Highway 70, Lakewood; (732) 363-0103.

Irene's Delicious Pizza, 242 Plainfield Ave., Edison; (732) 572-2622.

Irene's Pizzeria, 103 Route 71, Spring Lake; (732) 974-9224.

Isabella's Pizzeria, 107 Route 46, Parsippany; (973) 808-7028.

Island Cafe, 1611 Route 37 E., Toms River; (732) 929-3030.

Italia Pizza, 48 Washington St., Bloomfield; (973) 429-2768.

Italian Affair, 3845 Bayshore Dr., North Cape May; (609) 884-0505.

Italian Affair Restaurant, 900 Delsea Drive N., Glassboro; (856) 881-2121.

Italian Brick Oven Pizzeria, 1901 Cinnaminson Ave., Cinnaminson; (856) 786-4800.

Italian Connection, 55 W. Shore Ave., Dumont; (201) 385-2226.

Italian Garden Pizza & Family, 9700 3rd Ave., Stone Harbor; (609) 368-0656.

Italian Kitchen Inc, 339 N. Hook Road, Pennsville; (856) 678-2098.

Italian Time Pizza, 29 N. Franklin Turnpike, Waldwick; (201) 444-3033.

Italian Touch Catering, 1522 Oak Tree Road, Iselin; (732) 321-4005.

Italian Villa, 173 Ridge Road, North Arlington; (201) 991-0025.

Italian Village, 467 River Drive, Garfield; (973) 767-2771.

Italian Village Pizza, 300 Main St., Madison; (973) 822-3344.

Italiano Pizza, 600 Park Blvd., Cape May; (609) 898-2200.

Italiano's Pizza, 400 S. New Prospect Road, Jackson; (732) 367-1144.

Italy Pizza, 6394 Harding Highway, Newtonville; (609) 625-0373.

Italy's Best III, 984 Route 166, Toms River; (732) 240-9449.

Ivy Tavern & Liquor Store, 3108 S. Broad St., Trenton; (609) 888-1435.

J & D Frank's Pizzeria Inc, 463 21st Ave., Paterson; (973) 278-7440.

J & J Pizzeria Inc, 266 Clove Road, Montague; (973) 293-3300.

J Porter's Restaurant & Pub, 110 Davidson Ave., Somerset; (732) 560-0500.

Jack's Bricktown Pizza, 405 Thomas St., Phillipsburg; (908) 859-1008.

Jack's Famous Pizza, 326 S. Main St., Pleasantville; (609) 641-5179.

Jack's Pizza JP & S. & Steaks, 307 Shore Road, Somers Point; (609) 926-5225.

Jack's Pizzeria, 55 Main St., Flemington; (908) 782-4266.

Jacks Pizza, 40 Bridge St., Lambertville; (609) 397-1500.

Jacquelines Pizza & Pasta, 108 S. Broadway, Gloucester City; (856) 742-5522.

Jake's Pizza Co & Resturante, 126 Sunset Blvd., Cape May; (609) 898-8300.

Jakes Grill & Pizzeria, 9 Spring St., New Brunswick; (732) 846-5330.

Jamesburg Pizza, 27 E. Railroad Ave., Jamesburg; (732) 521-1414.

Jay's Famous Pizza, 849 Green St., Iselin; (732) 750-4433.

Jenkinson's Ice Cream & Sweet, 300 Ocean Ave., Point Pleasant Beach; (732) 892-0272.

Jenkinson's Pavilion, 300 Ocean Ave., Pt Pleasant Bch; (732) 892-0600.

Jeppy's Pizzeria, 23 Anderson St., Trenton; (609) 989-1242.

Jerrey's 1 Pizza, 1203 Teaneck Road, Teaneck; (201) 837-8485.

Jerry's Pizza, 701 S. Broad St., Trenton; (609) 392-2944.

Jersey Boys Pizza & Subs, 130 State Route 17, Mahwah; (201) 529-3222.

Jerusalem Pizza, 150 Elmora Ave., Elizabeth; (908) 289-0291.

Jerusalem Pizza, 231 Raritan Ave., Highland Park; (732) 249-0070.

Jerusalem Pizza Falafel, 233 Main Ave., Passaic; (973) 778-0960.

Jerusalem Pizza of Deal, 106 Norwood Ave., Deal; (732) 531-7936.

Jezif Fried Chicken & Pizza, 119 1/2 Halsey St., Newark; (973) 643-1500.

Jim & Mike's Pizza & Steaks, 7 S. Broadway, Pitman; (856) 582-8044.

Jimmi's, 555 N. Evergreen Ave., Woodbury; (856) 848-6668.

Jimmy's Pizza, 493 Martin Luther King Jr Drive, Jersey City; (201) 433-4700.

Jimmy's Pizza, 900 Bergen Ave., Jersey City; (201) 659-9900.

Jimmys Pizzeria & Restaurant, 357 Union Blvd., Totowa; (973) 956-0031.

Jo Ann's Pizza & Restaurant II, 913 Route 50, Mays Landing; (609) 625-4114.

Jo Jo Mo's Belmar Pizza, 1508 Main St., Belmar; (732) 280-1133.

Jo Jo's Brick Oven Pizza, 1901 Ocean Ave., Point Pleasant Beach; (732) 295-0020.

Jo Jo's Italian Grille, 6106 Black Horse Pike, Egg Harbor Twp; (609) 641-8332.

Jo Jo's Pizza, 726 Ridge Road, Lyndhurst; (201) 933-0360.

Jo Jo's Pizzeria, 6397 Beacon Ave., Mays Landing; (609) 476-3000.

Jo Jo's Pizzeria & Restaurant, 6501 Ventnor Ave., Ventnor City; (609) 822-6475.

Jo-Jo's Italian Grille, 2 E. Black Horse Pike, Pleasantville; (609) 646-8332.

Jo-Jo's Pizza & Restaurant, 101 W. Jimmie Leeds Road, Galloway; (609) 652-6700.

Jo-Jo's Tavern & Restaurant, 2677 Nottingham Way, Mercerville; (609) 586-2678.

Joe & John's Pizza & Italian, 136 New Jersey Ave., Absecon; (609) 641-6612.

Joe Joes Pizza, 412 Route 71, Spring Lake; (732) 359-7184.

Joe Pops, 466 W. Holly Ave., Pitman; (856) 589-9589.

Joe's Pizza & Pasta, 2062 Springfield Ave., Vauxhall; (908) 964-3157.

Joe's Pizza, 1006 N. Pearl St., Bridgeton; (856) 455-3421.

Joe's Pizza, 1938 Washington Valley Road, Martinsville; (732) 469-3356.

Joe's Pizza, 943 Kings Hwy., West Deptford; (856) 848-4921.

Joe's Pizza, 108 Swedesboro Road, Mullica Hill; (856) 223-9921.

Joe's Pizza, 4717 Bergenline Ave., Union City; (201) 617-5755.

Joe's Pizza, 217 Wisteria Ave., Cherry Hill; (856) 488-2421.

Joe's Pizza & Restaurant Inc, 18 Commerce St., Flemington; (908) 788-2616.

Joe's Pizza Pasta & Subs, 501 Tansboro Road, Berlin; (856) 767-3434.

Joe's Pizzaria & Restaurant, 230 Wall St., West Long Branch; (732) 222-1027.

Joe's Pizzeria, 185 Changebridge Road, Montville; (973) 335-4120.

Joe's Pizzeria, 102 Broadway, Paterson; (973) 345-4707.

Joe's Pizzeria, 956 Broadway, Bayonne; (201) 437-6677.

Joe's Pizzeria, 586 Route 46, Kenvil; (973) 584-3335.

Joe's Pizzeria, 415 Delanco Road, Beverly; (609) 877-9500.

Joe's Pizzeria & Restaurant II, 1933 Route 35, Wall Township; (732) 974-4006.

Joe's Pizzeria & Vittoria, 101 Springfield Ave., Summit; (908) 522-0615.

Joe's Restaurant & Pizzeria, 853 Kearny Ave., Kearny; (201) 997-3887.

Joe's Restaurant & Pizzeria, 856 Route 206, Hillsborough; (908) 874-6661.

Joewi's Pizzeria, 691 Main St., Hackensack; (201) 489-6451.

Joey D's Pizzeria, 279 Central Ave., Metuchen; (732) 494-3900.

Joey Tomatoes, 311 Central Ave., Point Pleasant Beach; (732) 295-2624.

Joey's Italian Kitchen, 2704 Morris Ave., Union; (908) 964-7655.

Joey's Pizza, 2201 Long Beach Blvd., Ship Bottom; (609) 361-5000.

Joey's Pizza, 516 Route 9, Waretown; (609) 693-0005.

Joey's Pizza & Pasta, 1340 Route 72 W., Manahawkin; (609) 978-0006.

Joey's Pizza of Hamilton, 1201 Whitehorse Mercerville Road, Hamilton; (609) 585-3500.

Joey's Pizza of Hamilton, 1800 Highway 33, Hamilton; (609) 588-0811.

Joey's Pizzeria, 460 Joralemon St., Belleville; (973) 751-8839.

Joeys' Pizza & Pasta, 8106 Long Beach Blvd., Long Beach Twp; (609) 361-1122.

John's Boy Pizzeria, 206 1/2 Rock Road, Glen Rock; (201) 652-8188.

John's Pizza, 14-25 River Road, Fair Lawn; (201) 796-3442.

John's Pizza, 87 Sussex St., Jersey City; (201) 433-4411.

John's Pizza, 700 Crescent Blvd., Brooklawn; (856) 456-6644.

John's Pizza, 1971 N. Black Horse Pike, Williamstown; (856) 629-8688.

John's Pizza & Restaurant, 229 3rd Ave., Long Branch; (732) 222-2525.

Johnny D's Pizza, 46 N. Main St., Pleasantville; (609) 383-9393.

Johnny D's Restaurant & Ice, 46 N. Main St., Pleasantville; (609) 383-6969.

Johnny G's Pizza Factory, 200 Boardwalk, Seaside Heights; (732) 793-9200.

Johnny G's Pizzeria, 1812 Hooper Ave., Toms River; (732) 255-8900.

Johnny Jrs Pizza, 4 Main St., Netcong; (973) 527-4404.

Johnny's II, 257 Bergen Blvd., Fairview; (201) 943-2420.

Johnny's Pizza, 717 Kings Hwy N., Cherry Hill; (856) 667-3232.

Johnny's Pizzeria, 273 Egg Harbor Road, Sewell; (856) 256-9111.

Johnny's Pizzeria, 34 Main St., West Orange; (973) 731-9505.

Johnny's Pizzeria, 55 Parsippany Road, Whippany; (973) 515-5006.

Johnny's Pizzeria, 520 Bergen Blvd., Palisades Park; (201) 944-4476.

Jolly Time Pizzeria, 599 Central Ave., East Orange; (973) 678-6212.

Jolly's Restaurant & Pizzeria, 271 Morris Ave., Springfield; (973) 376-0392.

Jonni's Pizza & Grill, 705 Tilton Road, Northfield; (609) 407-1717.

Jonuzi Chelsea Pizza, 9404 Ventnor Ave., Margate City; (609) 822-1700.

Jonuzi's Pizza, 2309 Atlantic Ave., Atlantic City; (609) 347-6666.

Jorge Pizza Pasta Italian, 71 5th St., Elizabeth; (908) 353-2777.

Joseph Pizza Restaurant, 189 Hudson St., Hackensack; (201) 488-6200.

Joseph's Pizza, 165 S. New Prospect Road, Jackson; (732) 367-8903.

Josie's Pizzeria Catering, 228 Stuyvesant Ave., Lyndhurst; (201) 933-1966.

Joyce's Subs & Pizza, 655 Newman Springs Road, Lincroft; (732) 741-9660.

Jules Italian Restaurant, 1861 Hooper Ave., Toms River; (732) 255-5599.

Jumbos Pizza & Subs, 495 Main Ave., Wallington; (973) 778-1122.

Junior's Pizza, 1281 Main Ave., Clifton; (973) 340-3900.

Junior's Pizza & Subs II, 600 Myrtle Ave., Boonton; (973) 335-0086.

Juniors Pizza & Subs, 400 Ramapo Valley Road, Oakland; (201) 337-2228.

Junt Pizza, 370 Memorial Pkwy, Phillipsburg; (908) 213-3326.

Just Round the Corner, 1142 Ocean Ave., Sea Bright; (732) 741-7775.

Justin's Ristorante, 234 Layayette Ave., Hawthorne; (973) 423-4345.

K C's Pizzeria & Italian Restaurant, 151 Woodbridge Road, Rahway; (732) 381-7999.

K G 37 Llc, 357 7th St., Jersey City; (201) 798-9539.

Kalamata Cafe & Pizza, 424 Route 206, Hillsborough; (908) 359-7144.

Kate & Al's Pizza, 2919 Route 206, Columbus; (609) 267-1147.

Kay Cafe, 140 Route 10, Randolph; (973) 366-2996.

Kendall Park Pizza & Restaurant, 7 Allston Road, Kendall Park; (732) 297-4880.

Kennedy Fried Chicken & Pizza, 1400 Main St., Asbury Park; (732) 776-6010.

Keyport Pizzeria & Restaurant, 42 W. Front St., Keyport; (732) 264-2667.

Kinchley's Tavern, 586 N. Franklin Turnpike, Ramsey; (201) 934-7777.

King & Sons Pizzeria Inc, 718 Hamburg Turnpike, Pompton Lakes; (973) 839-6006.

King of Pizza, 3 S. White Horse Pike, Berlin; (856) 753-8797.

King of Pizza, 2300 Marlton Pike W., Cherry Hill; (856) 665-4824.

King of Pizza, 1690 Route 38, Mount Holly; (609) 261-5765.

King Pizza, 22 Church St., Ramsey; (201) 818-3318.

King Pizza, 63 E. Ridgewood Ave., Paramus; (201) 265-6370.

King's Italian Restaurant, 105 Easton Ave., New Brunswick; (732) 846-5855.

Kings Highway Pizza, 1400 Kings Hwy N., Cherry Hill; (856) 795-1220.

Kirk's Pizzeria, 44 Route US 9 S., Marmora; (609) 390-1845.

Knockout Pizza, 60 Chambersbridge Road, Lakewood; (732) 363-3000.

Koltuv Pizza, 325 7th St., Lakewood; (732) 367-3364.

Krispy Pizzeria, 2323 Highway 516, Old Bridge; (732) 679-9600.

La Bella Napoli Pizzeria, 205 Williams Ave., Hasbrouck Hts; (201) 288-0359.

La Bella Pizza, 300 Lanza Ave., Garfield; (973) 478-8877.

La Bella Pizza, 102 N. Maple Ave., Ridgewood; (201) 652-0444.

La Bella Pizza, 199 Medford-Mount Holly Road, Medford; (609) 953-9148.

La Bella Pizza, 904 Livingston Ave., North Brunswick; (732) 249-4040.

La Bella Roma Pizzeria, 35 N. Farview Ave., Paramus; (201) 843-8687.

La Bella Via, 41 3rd St., Phillipsburg; (908) 387-8070.

La Bella Vita Pizzeria, 600 Ridge Road, Lyndhurst; (201) 935-3355.

La Calpena, 2103 River Ave., Camden; (856) 963-1999.

La Casa Pizza & Restaurant, 1014 South Ave. W., Westfield; (908) 789-9119.

La Cucina Trattoria, 291 Essex St., Millburn; (973) 379-6700.

La Dulce Vita, 400 Ocean Ave., Belmar; (732) 749-3272.

La Famigilia Pizza & Restaurant, 2090 Oak Tree Road, Edison; (732) 767-9797.

La Famiglia, 751 Route 37 W., Toms River; (732) 240-7212.

La Famiglia Sorrento, 631 Central Ave., Westfield; (908) 232-2642.

La Fontana Restaurant-Pizzeria, 375 Drum Point Road, Brick; (732) 920-6200.

La Galleria, 310 Ward Ave., Bordentown; (609) 291-1980.

La Gondola, 1300 Route 17, Ramsey; (201) 825-8990.

La Gondola Pizzeria, 2193 Morris Ave., Union; (908) 687-2280.

La Gondola Restaurant-Pizzeria, 419 Route 70, Lakehurst; (732) 657-9874.

La Guardia's Salumeria, 511 Route 72 E., Manahawkin; (609) 978-6402.

La Guardiola Pizzeria, 819 Broadway, Bayonne; (201) 823-3399.

La Locanda Restaurant & Pizza, 1406 S. Main Road, Vineland; (856) 794-3332.

La Mezzaluna Restaurant, 791 Midland Ave., Garfield; (973) 772-2768.

La Mia Cucina, 1259 Paterson Plank Road, Secaucus; (201) 553-9711.

La Nonna's Pizza, 900 12th St., Hammonton; (609) 567-4992.

La Piazza, 150 7th St., Clifton; (973) 478-3050.

La Piazza Discotto, 29 Mill St., Mount Holly; (609) 265-1630.

La Piazza Enterprises Inc, 11 Church St., Allentown; (609) 208-0640.

La Piazza Trattoria Pizza, 101 Newark-Pompton Turnpike, Little Falls; (973) 256-0005.

La Pizza, Delsea Drive, Malaga; (856) 694-4474.

La Pizza, 178 Eagle Rock Ave., Roseland; (973) 226-6268.

La Pizza, 240 Harrison Ave., Harrison; (973) 350-1999.

La Pizzeria, 318 Routes 202/206, Pluckemin; (908) 781-5525.

La Riviera Gastronomia, 429 Piaget Ave., Clifton; (973) 772-9099.

La Roma Pizza, 1449 N. Black Horse Pike, Blackwood; (856) 227-5733.

La Rosa's Il Pizza, 104 Woodbridge Ave., Highland Park; (732) 572-0880.

La Rosa's Pizza Inc, 335 Lake Ave., Metuchen; (732) 549-6505.

La Rustique Cafe, 611 Jersey Ave., Jersey City; (201) 222-6886.

La Sicilia, 155 Washington Ave., Belleville; (973) 751-5726.

La Strada, 355 Millburn Ave., Millburn; (973) 467-3420.

La Strada Pizza, 1 Gaston St., Matawan; (732) 583-9600.

La Strada Pizzeria, 393 Somerset St., North Plainfield; (908) 561-7676.

La Strada Pizzeria, 118 Mountain Blvd Ext., Warren; (732) 469-2625.

La Tinatjita, 5517 Hudson Ave., West New York; (201) 867-4566.

La Tombora Restaurant, 106 3rd Ave., Paterson; (973) 684-1200.

La Toscana Pizza, 626 Kinderkamack Road, River Edge; (201) 483-8144.

La Vigna Pizzeria Restaurant, 47 Hopatchung Road, Hopatcong; (973) 398-7514.

La Villa Italian Restaurant, 355 Applegarth Road, Monroe Twp; (609) 655-3338.

La Villa Pizzeria & Cafe, 149 Midland Ave., Kearny; (201) 991-1100.

La Villa Restaurant & Pizza, 335 Atlantic City Blvd., Beachwood; (732) 240-4931.

La Vinga Pizzeria Restaurant, 406 Main St., Boonton; (973) 334-3400.

La Vita Pizzeria, 12 High St., Mount Holly; (609) 267-8957.

La Vita Pizzeria II, 1710 Route 38, Mount Holly; (609) 265-9645.

Lakewood J II Kosher Pizza, 1700 Madison Ave., Lakewood; (732) 364-9119.

Landicini's Family Restaurant, 3600 E. Landis Ave., Vineland; (856) 691-3099.

Larchmont Pizza, 2726 Morris Ave., Union; (908) 964-9550.

Larios Restaurant & Pizzeria, 261 Union Ave., Paterson; (973) 790-7272.

Larry & Joe's Pizzeria, 533 Newark Ave., Jersey City; (201) 656-0073.

Lasolas Market, 3462 Route 35 N., Lavallette; (732) 830-1660.

Laurel Station Pizza & Deli, 6719 Battle Lane, Millville; (856) 825-8595.

Lavalette Pizzeria & Restaurant, 1700 Grand Central Ave., Lavallette; (732) 830-4101.

Lavilla Pizzeria & Cafe, 15 Smallwood Ave., Belleville; (973) 759-0777.

Lavita Pizza, 121 W. Main St., Moorestown; (856) 235-0052.

Leandro's Pizzeria, 397 Piaget Ave., Clifton; (973) 253-6030.

Leftys Pizza & Pasta, 152 8th St., Passaic; (973) 928-3418.

Legends Gourmet Pizza & Salads, 318 High St., Burlington; (609) 386-3001.

Lenny's Brick Oven Pizzeria, 459 Route 31, Hampton; (908) 537-9595.

Lenny's Pizza & Family Restaurant, 88 Morristown Road, Bernardsville; (908) 766-0465.

Lenny's Pizza-Point Pleasant, 2708 Bridge Ave., Point Pleasant; (732) 892-6112.

Lenny's Pizzeria & Italian, 46 Chestnut St., Ridgewood; (201) 652-4111.

Lenny's Pizza, 8 Reading Road, Raritan Township; (908) 237-0002.

Leonardo Da Vinci Restaurant, 71 Smith St., Perth Amboy; (732) 442-1261.

Leonardo's Mediterranean Grill, 654 Marketplace Blvd., Trenton; (609) 585-8202.

Leone's Pizza City, 1815 Route 37 E., Toms River; (732) 929-0550.

Leone's Pizzeria & Restaurant, 368 Market St., Elmwood Park; (201) 791-5400.

Levy's Kosher Italian Cuisine, 335 Route 9, Englishtown; (732) 683-9978.

Lido Restaurant, 701 Main St., Hackensack; (201) 487-8721.

Lils Luncheonette Deli & Pizza, 52 W. Main St., Bogota; (201) 488-1477.

Lina's Pizza, 440 Chandler Road, Jackson; (732) 364-5760.

Lincoln Pizza, 3722 E. Landis Ave., Vineland; (856) 692-1116.

Linda's Pizza, 932 Fischer Blvd., Toms River; (732) 573-1906.

Linda's Pizza, 318 Ocean Gate Ave., Ocean Gate; (732) 269-8282.

Linda's Pizzeria & Italian, 136 S. Main St., Forked River; (609) 242-3474.

Lino Pizza, 139 Ridge Road, Lyndhurst; (201) 728-9055.

Lino's Pizzeria, 2969 Route 9, Howell; (732) 367-0535.

Linos Pizza, 721 Avenue A, Bayonne; (201) 455-3032.

Linwood Pizza, 140 Linwood Plaza, Fort Lee; (201) 944-6789.

Linwood Pizza, 465 Route 46, Totowa; (973) 256-9050.

Linwood Pizza, 444 Rochelle Ave., Rochelle Park; (201) 291-8500.

Liquid Assets, 118 New Market Ave., South Plainfield; (908) 753-0290.

Lisa Restaurant & Pizza, 864 Route 37 W., Toms River; (732) 505-4489.

Lisa's Pizza, 417 Broadway, Westwood; (201) 664-8676.

Liscio's Italian Bakery & Deli, 3321 Route 42, Sicklerville; (856) 629-3232.

Liscio's Italian Bakery & Deli, 373 Egg Harbor Road, Sewell; (856) 218-2400.

Little Anthony's Pizza, 530 Route 515, Vernon; (973) 764-9800.

Little Beefs Deli Grill, 4201 Church Road, Mount Laurel; (856) 722-1101.

Little Italy, 1016 Route 34, Matawan; (732) 765-1414.

Little Italy, 654 Amboy Ave., Woodbridge; (732) 636-1119.

Little Italy Pizza, 13 Lacey Road, Forked River; (609) 693-0002.

Little Italy Pizzeria-Linden, 1728 E. Saint Georges Ave., Linden; (908) 925-5111.

Little Italy Restaurant II, 3704 Bayshore Road, North Cape May; (609) 889-6610.

Little Italy's, 306 Roseberry St., Phillipsburg; (908) 454-1216.

Little Jim's Pizza, 312 S. Delsea Drive, Clayton; (856) 307-9300.

Little John's Pizza, 401 Water St., Belvidere; (908) 475-8556.

Little Nicky's Pizza, 1610 Boardwalk, North Wildwood; (609) 522-2237.

Little Sicily Pizza, 513 N. Warwick Road, Somerdale; (856) 783-3232.

Little Sicily Pizza, 46 N. Main St., Glassboro; (856) 881-7977.

Little Slice of NY, 120 N. 3rd St., Camden; (856) 964-0404.

Livingston Pizza, 73 W. Mount Pleasant Ave., Livingston; (973) 740-0066.

Lo Chiatto's Pizzeria, 501 Old Post Road, Edison; (732) 248-0233.

Lo Presti Pizza, 1701 Boardwalk, Atlantic City; (609) 344-0292.

Lo Presti's Pizza II, 2601 Boardwalk, Atlantic City; (609) 344-8646.

Lockwood Tavern, 77 Route 206, Byram; (973) 347-0077.

Lodi Pizza Restaurant, 19 Route 46 W., Lodi; (973) 478-3306.

Log Cabin Inn, 47 Route 46, Columbia; (908) 496-4291.

Long Valley Pizza, 59 E. Mill Road, Long Valley; (908) 876-3112.

Lorenzo's Pizza, 1735 Route 27, Somerset; (732) 545-8333.

Lorenzo's Pizzeria & Restaurant, 67 Main St., Sussex; (973) 875-5055.

Los Arcos Pizzeria Restaurant, 305 Monroe St., Passaic; (973) 773-0899.

Los Toritos Pizzeria, 50 Joyce Kilmer Ave., New Brunswick; (732) 247-6870.

Louie's Pizza, 711 Beach Ave., North Cape May; (609) 884-0305.

Louies Pizza, 411 Route 46, Great Meadows; (908) 637-4488.

Lovey's Pizza & Grill, 91 W. Hanover Ave., Morris Plains; (973) 455-0677.

Lovey's Pizzeria, 211 Boulevard, Hasbrouck Heights; (201) 288-1606.

Lubrano's Pizzeria & Restaurant, 1830 Easton Ave., Somerset; (732) 271-1144.

Luca's, 3849 S. Delsea Drive, Vineland; (856) 327-2200.

Luca's Pizza, 115 Harris Ave., Middlesex; (732) 560-1292.

Luca's Ristorante & Pizza, 2019 Route 27, Somerset; (732) 297-7676.

Luca's Ristorante & Pizza, 1 Walters Lane, Flemington; (908) 284-9777.

Lucia's Pizzeria, 729 Roosevelt Ave., Carteret; (732) 969-0200.

Luciano's, 406 Broadway, Bayonne; (201) 858-2448.

Luciano's Pizza, 29 Broadway, Denville; (973) 983-8833.

Luciano's Pizzeria, 394 Franklin Ave., Wyckoff; (201) 848-8808.

Lucisano's Pizza, 42 Church St., Keansburg; (732) 495-5020.

Lucky Bones, 1200 Route 109, Lower Township; (609) 884-2663.

Lui's Pizza & Liquors, 507 Route 46, Belvidere; (908) 475-1673.

Luigi & Tony's, 32 Bloomfield Ave., Bloomfield; (973) 429-2999.

Luigi's, 4864 Route 9, Howell; (732) 364-5008.

Luigi's Famous Pizza, 3329 Doris Ave., Ocean; (732) 531-7733.

Luigi's Famous Pizza, 477 Middle Road, Hazlet; (732) 787-4669.

Luigi's Famous Pizza, 1208 Route 34, Matawan; (732) 290-3030.

Luigi's Famous Pizza, 650 Newman Springs Road, Lincroft; (732) 842-2122.

Luigi's Famous Pizza, 500 Washington Ave., Point Pleasant Beach; (732) 899-4848.

Luigi's Famous Pizza, 86 Oceanport Ave., Little Silver; (732) 758-0222.

Luigi's Italian Restaurant, 300 E. 9th St., Ocean City; (609) 399-4937.

Luigi's Pizza, 475 Spotswood Englishtown Road, Jamesburg; (732) 656-1890.

Luigi's Pizza, 35 S. Main St., Neptune; (732) 502-0015.

Luigi's Pizza, 275 Route 10 E., Succasunna; (973) 584-0181.

Luigi's Pizza, 1192 Green St., Iselin; (732) 283-2175.

Luigi's Pizza, 93 Smith St., Perth Amboy; (732) 826-5900.

Luigi's Pizza & Restaurant, 3 Skyline Lake Drive, Ringwood; (973) 839-0268.

Luigi's Pizza Fresca, 1700 Columbus Road, Burlington; (609) 239-8888.

Luigi's Pizza Restaurant Inc, 1580 Route 9, Toms River; (732) 349-4511.

Luigi's Pizza-New York Style, 2239 S. Clinton Ave., South Plainfield; (908) 756-8293.

Luigi's Pizzeria, 73 Wilson Ave., Manalapan; (732) 792-0434.

Luigi's Pizzeria & Restaurant, 201 E. Main St., Millville; (856) 327-1500.

Luigi's Pizzeria Restaurant, 21 Union Ave., Lakehurst; (732) 657-7000.

Luigi's Restaurant & Pizzeria, 2984 Highway 516, Old Bridge; (732) 607-1099.

Luke's Pizza, 2601 E. Hurley Pond Road, Wall Township; (732) 280-9255.

Luna Pizza, 5404 Park Ave., West New York; (201) 864-0230.

Luna Restaurant, 429 Main St., Three Bridges; (908) 284-2321.

Luna Rossa By Biagio Lamberti, 3210 Route 42, Sicklerville; (856) 728-4505.

Lupitas, 2312 Federal St., Camden; (856) 963-7390.

Lyndhurst Restaurant & Pizza, 29 Ridge Road, Lyndhurst; (201) 964-1210.

M & M II Pizzeria, 1271 Liberty Ave., Hillside; (973) 923-0800.

M & S. Pizza, 333 Route 46, Dover; (973) 361-3756.

M & S. Pizza II, 456 Route 46, Dover; (973) 361-9137.

Ma Daddy's Pizzeria Cafe, 312 Clinton Pl, Newark; (973) 923-4700.

Mac's Amusements, 500 Boardwalk, Point Pleasant Beach; (732) 892-7499.

Mack & Manco Inc, 920 Boardwalk, Ocean City; (609) 399-2548.

Mack & Manco Pizza, 2 Ocean Heights Ave., Somers Point; (609) 927-9900.

Mack's Pizza, 4200 Boardwalk, Wildwood; (609) 729-0244.

Macopin Pizza, 707 Macopin Road, West Milford; (973) 697-0224.

Mad Hatter Pub & Pizzeria, 10 E. Ocean Ave., Sea Bright; (732) 530-7861.

Maestro Pizza & Grill, 199 Dayton Ave., Passaic; (973) 998-7744.

Mag Pizza Inc, 4 Forest Lane, Monroe Township; (732) 656-1654.

Maggio's Pizza & Pasta, 1450 Clements Bridge Road, Woodbury; (856) 251-1515.

Magma Pizza, 445 Nassau Park Blvd., West Windsor; (609) 452-8383.

Mahwah Pizza & Pasta, 1035 MacArthur Blvd., Mahwah; (201) 825-1776.

Mahwah Pizza Master, 115 Franklin Turnpike, Mahwah; (201) 529-5711.

Maietta's Ristorante, 11 Tennent Ave., Englishtown; (732) 446-7387.

Main Line Pizza, 8 E. Main St., Little Falls; (973) 256-3976.

Main Street Pizza, 288 Main St., Keansburg; (732) 495-1000.

Main Street Pizza & Subs, 104 N. Main St., Pleasantville; (609) 646-4141.

Mama Della's Pizza & Pasta, 20 Jackson St., , Freehold; (732) 409-2611.

Mama Francesa Pizzeria, 1241 Kings Hwy., Swedesboro; (856) 467-5020.

Mama Lena's Restaurant & Pizza, 22 W. Pond Road, Perth Amboy; (732) 442-3636.

Mama Leona Pizzeria & Italian, 249 Central Ave., Jersey City; (201) 659-0550.

Mama Mia, 15 Route 516, Old Bridge; (732) 257-0007.

Mama Mia Pizzeria, 415 1/2 Monmouth St., Jersey City; (201) 798-1173.

Mama Mia Pizzeria LLC, 745 Poole Ave., Hazlet; (732) 335-8000.

Mama Mia's, 2087 S. Shore Road, Seaville; (609) 624-9322.

Mama Nuccio's Pizzeria, 600 S. Warwick Road, Somerdale; (856) 627-4444.

Mama Rosa Cucina Pizzeria, 795 Broadway, Bayonne; (201) 823-0500.

Mama Rosa Pizzeria, 332 Union Ave., Rutherford; (201) 939-2342.

Mama's Gourmet Pizza, 576 Raritan Road, Roselle; (908) 259-1100.

Mama's Pizza, 106 White Horse Road E., Voorhees; (856) 346-0600.

Mama's Pizza, 347 South Ave., Garwood; (908) 789-3220.

Mama's Pizza, 150 Halsey St., Newark; (973) 642-6262.

Mama's Pizza & Cafe, 260 Mountain Ave., Hackettstown; (908) 852-2820.

Mamma Maria Pizzeria, 40 Washington St., West Orange; (973) 731-0632.

Mamma Mia Pizzeria, 174 Lanza Ave., Garfield; (973) 478-0055.

Mamma Rosa's Restaurant, 572 Klockner Road, Trenton; (609) 588-5454.

Manasquan Pizza, 179 Main St., Manasquan; (732) 223-3388.

Mancino's Pizza, 2442 Route 38, Cherry Hill; (856) 482-6400.

Mangia Brick Oven, 262 Dunns Mill Road, Bordentown; (609) 298-7499.

Mangia Mia Pizzeria, 2297 Route 57 W., Washington; (908) 835-8600.

Mangia Pizzeria, 328 Somerset St., North Plainfield; (908) 222-1076.

Mangiabella Pizza, 3568 Route 22, Branchburg; (908) 823-1873.

Mannino's 3, 2235 Highway 33, Trenton; (609) 890-3344.

Mannino's 4 Pizza & Restaurant, 124 Main St., Hightstown; (609) 443-6363.

Mannino's Pizza, 543 Hamilton Ave., Trenton; (609) 396-4660.

Manny & Vic's Pizzeria, 1687 N. Delsea Drive, Vineland; (856) 696-3100.

Manny's Pizzeria Inc, 426 N. High St., Millville; (856) 327-5081.

Manny's Sicilia Pizza, 17 W. Broad St., Palmyra; (856) 829-6363.

Manville Pizza Restaurant, 31 S. Main St., Manville; (908) 526-1194.

Maplewood Pizzeria & Family, 489 Valley St., Maplewood; (973) 378-8588.

Marc's Deli & Pizzeria, 14 Park Ave., Park Ridge; (201) 391-4333.

Marcella's Restaurant & Pizza, 207 Route 530, Southampton; (609) 894-4700.

Marcello Pizza & Italian, 3112 Mount Ephraim Ave., Haddon Township; (856) 962-0700.

Marcello's II Italian, 260 Main Ave., Stirling; (908) 604-6200.

Marcello's Pizza, 421 S. White Horse Pike, Lindenwold; (856) 309-9511.

Marcello's Pizza & Restaurant, 300 E. Greentree Road, Marlton; (856) 596-0984.

Marcello's Pizzeria, 268 Springfield Ave., Berkeley Heights; (908) 464-4222.

Marcello's Pizzeria & Restaurant, 572 21st Ave., Paterson; (973) 278-7676.

Marcello's Restaurant, 225 Bellevue Ave., Hammonton; (609) 704-1901.

Marcello's Restaurant, 206 Farnsworth Ave., Bordentown; (609) 298-8360.

Marchioni's Pizza & Pasta, 912 W. Bay Ave., Barnegat; (609) 660-2424.

Marciano's Restaurant, 947 N. Delsea Drive, Vineland; (856) 563-0030.

Marco Polo Pizza, 1200 Harbor Blvd, Weehawken; (201) 863-0057.

Marco's Pizza, 2580 Pennington Road, Pennington; (609) 737-0072.

Marco's Pizzeria, 180 Parsippany Road, Parsippany; (973) 503-1177.

Margherita's Pizza & Cafe, 740 Washington St., Hoboken; (201) 222-2400.

Marguerita Pizzeria & Restaurant, 1882 Route 130, North Brunswick; (732) 297-8150.

Maria Rosa Restaurant & Pizza, 541 Sergeantsville Road, Flemington; (908) 788-4945.

Maria's Pizza & Subs, 119 N. Main St., Milltown; (732) 214-0033.

Maria's Pizzeria, 1193 Turnerville Road, Pine Hill; (856) 767-7422.

Maria's Pizzeria & Restaurant, 671 Harris Ave., Middlesex; (732) 748-1122.

Maria's Pizzeria & Restaurant, 49 N. Main St., Wharton; (973) 366-4790.

Maria's Restaurant, 381 Park Ave., Scotch Plains; (908) 322-2322.

Marialinda Pizza & Italian, 1144 E. Veterans Highway, Jackson; (732) 363-9310.

Mariannas Pizza Cafe, 12 Claremont Road, Bernardsville; (908) 766-6535.

Maria's Three Corners Cafe, 671 Harris Ave., Middlesex; (732) 748-1122.

Marie's Pizza, 376 Dover Road, Toms River; (732) 240-1051.

Marina's Pizza & Restaurant, 435 Paterson Ave., Wallington; (201) 935-4476.

Marinelli's Pizza, 505 Route 12, Flemington; (908) 806-7562.

Marino Pizzeria, 1 S. Virginia Ave., Penns Grove; (856) 299-1670.

Marino's Pizza, 100 N. Black Horse Pike, Runnemede; (856) 939-5523.

Marino's Pizza, 720 Somerset St., Watchung; (908) 769-8388.

Mario & Frank's Pizza & Subs, 2083 Route 130 N., Burlington; (609) 499-0095.

Mario & Frank's Pizza & Subs, 50 Magnolia Road, Pemberton; (609) 894-8073.

Mario & Franks, 1580 Nottingham Way, Trenton; (609) 587-6958.

Mario & Franks II, 231 4th St., Fieldsboro; (609) 324-2737.

Mario & Joe's Pizzeria, 321 W. Branch Ave., Pine Hill; (856) 566-0003.

Mario Pizza, 426 Madison Ave., Paterson; (973) 278-9199.

Mario's 2 Pizzaria, 1541 Boardwalk, Atlantic City; (609) 344-1888.

Mario's Classic Pizza, 742 Garden St., Hoboken; (201) 659-0808.

Mario's Famous Pizza, 3 Stephenville Pkwy, Edison; (732) 516-9300.

Mario's Famous Pizza, 140 Route 10, Randolph; (973) 537-0444.

Mario's Famous Pizza, 1279 Broad St., Bloomfield; (973) 338-4477.

Mario's Famous Pizza, 211 W. Front St., Plainfield; (908) 756-9300.

Mario's Famous Pizza, 173 3rd St., Elizabeth; (908) 558-1959.

Mario's Famous Pizza, 141 Fayette St., Perth Amboy; (732) 324-7773.

Mario's Pizza, 1184 Haddon Ave., Camden; (856) 225-1500.

Mario's Pizza, 5531 Berkshire Valley Road , Oak Ridge; (973) 697-2127.

Mario's Pizza, 3291 E. State Street Ext., Trenton; (609) 587-4460.

Mario's Pizza, 330 Broadway, Bayonne; (201) 339-0191.

Mario's Pizza, 109 W. Pleasant Ave., Maywood; (201) 843-8700.

Mario's Pizza, 220 Broadway, Hammonton; (609) 567-5555.

Mario's Pizza & Italian Restaurant, 422 S. Main St., Forked River; (609) 693-4349.

Mario's Pizza & Restaurant, 184 Main St., Andover; (973) 786-5666.

Mario's Pizza & Subs, 7 Victorian Village Plaza, Cape May; (609) 884-0085.

Mario's Pizzeria, 1594a Union Valley Road, West Milford; (973) 728-9171.

Mario's Pizzeria, 1510 Bay Ave., Ocean City; (609) 398-0490.

Mario's Pizzeria, 308 S. Black Horse Pike, Blackwood; (856) 228-2232.

Mario's Pizzeria & Etc, 15 Broad St., Norwood; (201) 767-1366.

Mario's Pizzeria Inc, 186 W. Market St., Newark; (973) 693-4422.

Mario's Restaurant & Pizzeria, 710 Van Houten Ave., Clifton; (973) 777-1559.

Mario's Saddle Brook Pizza, 439 Market St., Saddle Brook; (201) 845-6556.

Mario's Trattoria, 495 Chestnut St., Union; (908) 687-3250.

Mario's Uptown Grill & Pizza, 126 Philadelphia Ave., Egg Harbor City; (609) 965-4476.

Mark's Pizza & Restaurant, 306 Main St., Hackensack; (201) 487-8778.

Marlboro Pizza & Dusals Restaurant, 460 Route 520, Marlboro; (732) 946-4650.

Marretta Pizzeria, 189 Passaic St., Garfield; (973) 773-3320.

Martinos Trattoria & Pizzeria, 2614 E. Chestnut Ave., Vineland; (856) 692-4448.

Marty's Pizzeria & Family Deli, 410 Ridgewood Road, Maplewood; (973) 762-6731.

Maruca Tomato Pies, 1927 Promenade, Seaside Park; (732) 793-0707.

Maruca's Tomato Pie, 1615 Kings Hwy N., Cherry Hill; (856) 857-0500.

Maryann's Pizza, 121 Route 537 E., Colts Neck; (732) 389-0561.

Massimo's Ristorante Caffe, 1633 Hamilton Ave., Trenton; (609) 586-3777.

Massimo's Trattoria, 1035 Washington Blvd., Trenton; (609) 448-2288.

Masso's Deli & Pizzeria, 11 Lakeview Drive N., Gibbsboro; (856) 783-1800.

Master Pizza, 1326 Main Ave., Clifton; (973) 772-4333.

Master Pizza, 379 E. Northfield Road, Livingston; (973) 992-4500.

Master Pizza Restaurant, 55 River Road, Bogota; (201) 343-9025.

Matta Donna, 304 Myrtle Ave., Boonton; (973) 334-7138.

Matteo's Pizza, 359 Pennington Ave., Trenton; (609) 392-0300.

Matteo's Pizza & Pasta, 305 Elizabeth Ave., Somerset; (732) 356-1677.

Mauceri's Pizza Pasta & Steaks, 945 Liberty St., Trenton; (609) 394-9698.

Maurizio's, 4215 Black Horse Pike, Hamilton (Atlantic County); (609) 645-0028.

Maurizio's Pizzeria, 81 Cassville Road, Jackson; (732) 928-0222.

Maurizios Pizzeria & Italian, 2200 Route 66, Neptune; (732) 502-9111.

Mazzone's Pizza, 486 Kinderkamack Road, River Edge; (201) 261-9550.

Mc Carthy's Bar & Grill, 600 E. Main St., Bridgewater; (908) 526-1420.

Me 'N You Pizzeria, 1391 Delsea Drive, Deptford; (856) 845-1460.

Mecca Pizza Restaurant, 52 4th Ave., East Orange; (973) 675-0700.

Mediterranean Bistro, 301 W. Washington Ave., Washington; (908) 689-5107.

Mega Pizza & Lunchonette, 596 Market St., Newark; (973) 344-0054.

Mengo's Pizzeria, 911 Swartswood Road, Newton; (973) 300-1066.

Menlo Pizza, 170 Lafayette Ave., Edison; (732) 548-0660.

Merendino Pizza & Restaurant, 901 W. Park Ave., Ocean; (732) 493-0202.

Mezza Luna Italian Restaurant, 357 Route 9, Englishtown; (732) 536-0207.

Mezza Luna Pizza, 633 Milford Warren Glen Road, Milford; (908) 995-4111.

Mia's Pizza, 1506 Grand Central Ave., Lavallette; (732) 793-1030.

Mia's Pizza & Cafe, 1907 Bay Blvd., Lavallette; (732) 830-5030.

Micchelli's Pizza, 3121 Fire Road, Egg Harbor Township; (609) 646-0042.

Micchelli's Pizza, 558 New Road, Somers Point; (609) 927-9753.

Michael Angelos, 2150 Route 35, Sea Girt; (732) 974-2100.

Michael Anthony's Pizzeria, 365 Palisade Ave., Jersey City; (201) 795-0019.

Michael's Pastaria, 143 Franklin Ave., Nutley; (973) 661-5252.

Michael's Pizza, 907 N. Main Road, Vineland; (856) 692-5073.

Michael's Pizzeria, 74 Erie St., Jersey City; (201) 798-3633.

Michael's Pizzeria & Restaurant, 669 Bloomfield Ave., West Caldwell; (973) 226-8862.

Michael's Pizzeria-Restaurant, 25 Main St., High Bridge; (908) 638-4410.

Michaelangelo's Pizza Restaurant, 1334 Brace Road, Cherry Hill; (856) 428-3231.

Michaelangelos, 72 Ocean Ave., Long Branch; (732) 222-8449.

Michelangelo's Pizza, 6 Edgeboro Road, East Brunswick; (732) 967-0111.

Michelino's Pizzeria, 1600 E. Saint Georges Ave., Linden; (908) 925-7020.

Michelino's Pizzeria, 79 E. Milton Ave., Rahway; (732) 396-9229.

Michelinos Pizzeria, 169 Washington Ave., Elizabeth; (908) 355-8393.

Middletown Pizza, 94 Leonardville Road, Belford; (732) 787-5400.

Middletown Pizza, 300 Bay Ave., Highlands; (732) 708-1111.

Midtown Pizza, 399 Dover Road, Toms River; (732) 281-0080.

Midtown Pizza Catering, 399 Dover Road, Toms River; (732) 281-0606.

Miele's Italian Restaurant, 125 Bloomfield Ave., Verona; (973) 239-3363.

Mijo Pizza, 427 Lake Ave., Colonia; (732) 382-2992.

Mike & Nonna's Pizza-Caffe, 4613 Nottingham Way, Trenton; (609) 587-4992.

Mike's Handy Pizza Inc, 314 Handy St., New Brunswick; (732) 545-2255.

Mike's Pizza & Sub Shop, 4004 Route 130, Delran; (856) 461-5552.

Mike's Pizza Bistro, 2001 SE Central Ave., Seaside Park; (201) 736-0397.

Mike's Pizzaria & Italian, 474 Avenue C, Bayonne; (201) 437-9550.

Mike's Pizzeria, 319 Drum Point Road, Brick; (732) 920-3388.

Mikes Coffee Shop & Pizzeria, 873 Broad St., Newark; (973) 624-0933.

Mikeys Famous Pizzaria, 1000 S. Elmora Ave., Elizabeth; (908) 352-4040.

Milan Pizza, 304 North Ave., Garwood; (908) 232-3036.

Milanese Pizza, 519 Howard St., Riverton; (856) 786-1414.

Milanese Pizza, 1 Saint Mihiel Drive, Delran; (856) 461-1212.

Milanese Pizza, 484 E. Evesham Road, Cherry Hill; (856) 346-2000.

Milano Gourmet Pizza, 61 South St., Morristown; (973) 285-9090.

Milano Pizza, 725 Corkery Lane, Williamstown; (856) 629-1093.

Milano Pizza, 527 E. Browning Road, Bellmawr; (856) 931-6411.

Milano's Pizza, 762 West Side Ave., Jersey City; (201) 413-1399.

Milano's Pizza Cafe, 45 S. New York Road, Galloway; (609) 652-6500.

Milano's Pizzeria, 687 Florida Grove Road, Perth Amboy; (732) 634-2610.

Miller's Tavern, 2 Beaver Ave., Annandale; (908) 735-4730.

Mimi's Pizzeria, 357 W. Clay Ave., Roselle Park; (908) 245-9696.

Mimmas Pizza, 233 Main St., Lebanon; (908) 236-0006.

Mina Brasil Pizerria, 47 3rd Ave., Long Branch; (732) 222-4567.

Mirabile's Brothers, 34 S. Livingston Ave., Livingston; (973) 535-3033.

Molfetta Pizzeria, 1122 Washington St., Hoboken; (201) 963-3236.

Molto Pizza, 2529 Boardwalk, Atlantic City; (609) 428-7280.

Mom's Bake at Home Pizza, 560 Stokes Road, Medford; (609) 654-8885.

Momento Pizza Restaurant, 493 S. Washington Ave., Bergenfield; (201) 439-0971.

Mona Lisa Pizza, 2387 Route 36, Atlantic Highlands; (732) 291-8500.

Mona Lisa's Pizzeria, 165 Broadway, Bayonne; (201) 858-1812.

Mona Lyssa Restaurant, 1635 Bay Ave., Point Pleasant; (732) 899-1999.

Monetti's Pizza, 201 Hackensack Ave., Weehawken; (201) 863-7474.

Monroe Pizzeria, 239 Monroe St., Passaic; (973) 773-7708.

Montagnaro's Pizza Express, 117 Merchants Way, Marlton; (856) 810-8181.

Montagnaro's Pizza Restaurant, 2999 E. Evesham Road, Voorhees; (856) 751-1166.

Montegrillo Pizza & Restaurant, 5825 Westfield Ave., Pennsauken; (856) 910-9000.

Montesini Pizza & Pasta Grmt, 33 E. Rudderow Ave., Maple Shade; (856) 482-2973.

Monti's Pizza Grille & Water, 320 Evesboro Medford Road, Marlton; (856) 797-9977.

Montville Pizzeria & Restaurant, 263 Changebridge Road, Pine Brook; (973) 227-7702.

Morgano's Pizza & Restaurant, 1207 Route 35, Middletown; (732) 671-1148.

Morris Pizzeria, 78 Morris St., Morristown; (973) 267-4375.

Mozzarella Grill, 415 Egg Harbor Road, Sewell; (856) 589-1000.

Mozzarella's Pizza, 381 Summit Ave., Jersey City; (201) 876-4100.

Mr. Assante Pizza, 201 Route 22, Green Brook; (732) 968-3515.

Mr. Bruno's Pizzeria, 472 Market St., Saddle Brook; (201) 845-0990.

Mr. Bruno's Pizzeria & Restaurant, 240 Route 10, East Hanover; (973) 884-9595.

Mr. Bruno's Pizzeria & Restaurant, 439 Valley Brook Ave., Lyndhurst; (201) 933-1588.

Mr. Bruno's Restaurant, 684 Main Ave., Passaic; (973) 470-0854.

Mr. D's Pizzeria Steaks & Subs, 4711 New Jersey Ave., Wildwood; (609) 522-2026.

Mr. Dino's Pizza Restaurant, 3 1st Ave., Bloomfield; (973) 748-7202.

Mr. Dino's Pizzeria & Restaurant, 119 Watchung Ave., Montclair; (973) 783-7110.

Mr. J's Pizza, 58 Harbor St., Newark; (973) 868-5467.

Mr. Nick's, 2641 Arctic Ave., Atlantic City; (609) 345-8464.

Mr. Nino's III Family Restaurant, 258 Kearny Ave., Kearny; (201) 991-2333.

Mr. Nino's Pizza & Restaurant, 1030 Stuyvesant Ave., Union; (908) 688-8443.

Mr. Pizza, 118 Carlton Ave., East Rutherford; (201) 935-6367.

Mr. Pizza, 1500 Springwood Ave., Asbury Park; (732) 869-4100.

Mr. Pizza & Pasta LLC, 233 Route 18, East Brunswick; (732) 846-5022.

Mr. Pizza Slice, 10 Monmouth St., Red Bank; (732) 747-9165.

Munchy Time, 701 N. 9th St., Camden; (856) 541-8108.

Murine Inc, 213 S. Virginia Ave., Penns Grove; (856) 299-1600.

Mystic Island Pizza-Restaurant, 841 Radio Road, Little Egg Harbor; (609) 296-0257.

N & A Pizza, 1661 Blackwood Clementon Road, Blackwood; (856) 228-1177.

Na's II Pizzeria, 572 Union Ave., Bridgewater; (732) 469-9200.

Nana's Pizza, 142 Cedarville Road, Bridgeton; (856) 455-5031.

Nancy's Towne House, 1453 Main St., Rahway; (732) 388-8100.

Naples Pizza & Restaurant, 600 Fischer Blvd., Toms River; (732) 270-2800.

Naples Pizza & Restaurant, 550 N. Main St., Barnegat; (609) 698-3830.

Naples Pizzeria, 115 E. 2nd Ave., Roselle; (908) 241-4440.

Naples Pizzeria, 191 Broadway, Bayonne; (201) 437-8879.

Naples Pizzeria, 2407 Route 71, Spring Lake; (732) 449-8620.

Naples Pizzeria, 872 Main St., Belford; (732) 787-9479.

Napoli Pizza, 2030 Route 88, Brick; (732) 785-0580.

Napoli Pizza, 25 Washington St., Lodi; (973) 473-5721.

Napoli Pizza, 408 Mount Arlington Blvd., Landing; (973) 398-5343.

Napoli Pizza & Grill, 157 Halsey Road, Parsippany; (973) 515-4800.

Napoli Pizza & Italian Restaurant, 5 Kingwood Ave., Frenchtown; (908) 996-6110.

Napoli Pizza Grill, 319 E. Jimmie Leeds Road, Galloway; (609) 748-8585.

Napoli Pizzeria & Restaurant, 74 Lyons Ave., Newark; (973) 923-2070.

Napoli's Pizza, 1118 Washington St., Hoboken; (201) 216-0900.

Napoli's Pizzeria, 2228 Route 130, North Brunswick; (732) 940-0200.

Nappoli Pizza, 275 Chestnut St., Newark; (973) 522-1950.

Natale's Italian Restaurant, 56 Payne Road, Clinton Township; (908) 735-4455.

Natale's Pizzeria & Catering, 14 W. Prospect St., Waldwick; (201) 445-2860.

Natales Pizza & Restaurant, 600 Valley Road, Gillette; (908) 647-1834.

Natalino's Pizza, 139 Ridge Road, Lyndhurst; (201) 728-9053.

Natoli's Deli, 300 Clarendon St., Secaucus; (201) 864-2243.

Nauna's Bella Casa, 148 Valley Road, Montclair; (973) 744-3232.

Neil's Pizzeria, 568 Valley Road, Wayne; (973) 305-0405.

Neil's Pizzeria, 46 Bergen Turnpike, Little Ferry; (201) 641-4212.

Neil's Pizzeria, 57 Harding Ave., Clifton; (973) 546-8889.

Nellie's Place, 9 Franklin Turnpike, Waldwick; (201) 652-8626.

Nelsons Corner Pizza, 601 Route 206, Hillsborough; (908) 359-2253.

Nemo's Pizza & Italian Cuisine, 2542 Dune Drive, Avalon; (609) 967-8084.

Nemo's Pizza & Italian Cuisine, 9817 3rd Ave., Stone Harbor; (609) 368-1414.

Ness Pizza House, 11-14 Saddle River Road, Fair Lawn; (201) 791-0040.

New Corner Restaurant, 22 E. Front St., Red Bank; (732) 530-1007.

New Famous Pizza, 1522 Oak Tree Road, Iselin; (732) 321-5005.

New Jersey Crispy Pizza Crust, 345 Florida Grove Road, Perth Amboy; (732) 826-1704.

New Pizza On the Block, 6415 Park Ave., West New York; (201) 861-0600.

New World Pizza & Cafe, 1147 Route 601, Skillman; (609) 333-1300.

New York Chicken & Pizza, 514 Clinton Ave., Newark; (973) 824-5158.

New York City Pizzeria, 121 Broadway, Newark; (973) 268-9888.

New York Pizza, 57 Main St., Chester; (908) 879-4424.

New York Pizza & Deli, 19 Interstate Shopping Center, Ramsey; (201) 327-0808.

New York Style Pizza, 10 S. King St., Gloucester City; (856) 742-8370.

New York Style Pizza & Restaurant, 230 N. High St., Millville; (856) 825-8010.

Newton Pizza, 47 Sparta Ave., Newton; (973) 383-6525.

Nick & Joe's Pizzeria, 668 W. Cuthbert Blvd., Haddon Township; (856) 858-0077.

Nick Terrigno's Pizza & Restaurant, 63 Cedarbrook Ave., Bridgeton; (856) 451-2525.

Nick's A Pizza & Restaurant, 1820 Lanes Mill Road, Brick; (732) 458-8523.

Nick's Pizza, 44 W. Main St., Bergenfield; (201) 385-9240.

Nick's Pizza, 7715 Kennedy Blvd., North Bergen; (201) 861-3588.

Nick's Pizzeria, 47 S. Main St., Williamstown; (856) 728-3322.

Nick's Pizzeria & Restaurant, 1413 Wickapecko Drive, Ocean; (732) 775-4646.

Nick's Pizzeria & Steak House, 644 Delsea Drive N., Glassboro; (856) 307-1100.

Nick's Pizzeria & Steak House, 3 N.E. Blvd., Newfield; (856) 697-4774.

Nick's Pizzeria & Steak House, 20 N. Main St., Elmer; (856) 358-3181.

Nick's Pizzeria & Steak House, 2553 Delsea Dr., Franklinville; (856) 694-3440.

Nick's Pizzeria & Steakhouse, 4 N. Delsea Drive, Clayton; (856) 881-3222.

Nick's Restaurant & Pizzeria, 34 W. Clinton St., Dover; (973) 442-7600.

Nicky B's Pizza, 2501 Church Road, Cherry Hill; (856) 667-1666.

Nicky-B's Pizza, 21 S. Haddon Ave., Haddonfield; (856) 354-7600.

Nicky's Best Pizza, 430 Greenwood Ave., Wyckoff; (201) 891-0404.

Nicola Pizza, 427 Route 513, Califon; (908) 832-0024.

Nicola's Pizza, 8 N. Franklin St., Lambertville; (609) 397-0212.

Nicola's Pizzeria, 627 Hamilton St., Somerset; (732) 246-4141.

Nicolosi's Pizza, 755 Memorial Parkway, Phillipsburg; (908) 859-0759.

Nicolo's Pizza of Old Bridge, 1120 Englishtown Road, Old Bridge; (732) 251-3010.

Nicos Pizzeria, 1038 S. Orange Ave., Newark; (973) 399-9494.

Nina's Pizzeria, 999 Amboy Ave., Edison; (732) 225-3267.

Ninja Pizzeria, 246 Park Ave., Orange; (973) 674-0094.

Nino's Festival Pizza, 3962 Black Horse Pike, Mays Landing; (609) 625-0701.

Nino's Italian Restaurant, 810 N.E. Central Ave., Seaside Park; (732) 793-2002.

Nino's Ninos Special Pizza Cty, 3620 Atlantic-Brigantine Blvd., Brigantine; (609) 266-1201.

Nino's Original Pizza & Subs, 6279 Old Harding Highway, Mays Landing; (609) 625-8989.

Nino's Pizza, 66 E. Madison Ave., Dumont; (201) 385-1999.

Nino's Pizza & Restaurant, 442 Bergen St., Harrison; (973) 484-5770.

Nino's Pizza & Subs, 1825 Route 130, North Brunswick; (732) 297-2235.

Nino's Pizzarama, 1937 Chambers St., Trenton; (609) 394-9523.

Nino's Pizzeria & Restaurant, 1115 Kennedy Blvd., Bayonne; (201) 436-0770.

Nino's Restaurant & Pizzeria, 300 Harrison Ave., Lodi; (973) 772-5056.

Nino's Tratorria & Pizzeria, 111 Lawrenceville Road, Trenton; (609) 695-0588.

Ninos Pizza & Pasta, 664 River St., Paterson; (973) 553-1404.

Ninos Pizzarama, 182 N. White Horse Pike, Hammonton; (609) 567-4653.

Nomad Pizza, 10 E. Broad St., Hopewell; (609) 466-6623.

Nonna Rosa's Pizzeria Cafe, 3294 Washington Road, Parlin; (732) 553-0050.

Nonna's Pizza & Italian Restaurant, 176 Columbia Turnpike, Florham Park; (973) 410-0030.

Nonna's Pizza & Restaurant, 11 Franklin St., Mahwah; (201) 529-1151.

Nonno Domenico's Pizza & Pasta, 525 Beckett Road, Swedesboro; (856) 467-9677.

Nonno Sal's Pizza, 1905 Highway 33, Hamilton; (609) 890-7474.

Nonnos Pizzeria, 4118 Route 9, Howell; (732) 367-3599.

North Haledon Pizza, 5 Sicomac Road, North Haledon; (973) 423-9066.

Not Just Pizza, 1715 Sicklerville Road, Sicklerville; (856) 374-1114.

Nottingham's Pizza & Deli, 2106 Nottingham Way, Trenton; (609) 631-7333.

Nucci Pizza, 58 Carr Ave., Keansburg; (732) 495-8800.

Nunzio's Pizzeria, 675 Route 1 S., Iselin; (732) 750-0990.

Nunzio's Pizzeria, 2387 Mountain Ave., Scotch Plains; (908) 889-4464.

Nunzio's Pizzeria, 230 Westwood Ave., Long Branch; (732) 222-9798.

Nunzio's Pizzeria & Restaurant, 426 Raritan St., Sayreville; (732) 727-1060.

Nunzios II, 568 W. Grand Ave., Rahway; (732) 882-1818.

O'Malleys Pizza & Grill, 302 N. Bay Ave., Beach Haven; (609) 207-0300.

Oakhurst Pizza & Restaurant, 2001 Bellmore St., Oakhurst; (732) 531-4478.

Oakland Pizzeria Restaurant, 347 Ramapo Valley Road, Oakland; (201) 337-3955.

Oakwood Pizza, 167 Wood Ave., Edison; (732) 494-0340.

Ocean Beach Shack, 3257 Route 35 N., Lavallette; (732) 793-6622.

Oceanport Pizza & Subs, 18 1/2 Wolfhill Ave., Oceanport; (732) 542-2211.

Odyssey Pizza & Restaurant, 6227 Westfield Ave., Pennsauken; (856) 486-3534.

Old Bridge Restaurant & Pizzeria, 3165 Route 9, Old Bridge; (732) 679-3322.

Old Lorenzo's Pizzeria, 301 Jackson St., Hoboken; (201) 714-9446.

Old Village Pizza, 897 Rancocas Road, Westampton; (609) 261-3737.

Old World Pizza, 242 1/2 Nassau St., Princeton; (609) 924-9321.

Old York Pizza, 85 Old York Road, Bridgewater; (908) 595-9590.

Olde Silver Tavern Bar, 149 Route 522, Manalapan; (732) 446-4010.

Olde World Bakery & Cafe, 1000 Smithville Road, Mt Holly; (609) 265-1270.

Original Amato's, 782 S. Brewster Road, Vineland; (856) 692-1377.

Original Dominicks Pizza, 206 Sanhican Drive, Trenton; (609) 656-4300.

Original Luigi's, 275 Route 10, Succasunna; (973) 584-0181.

Original Presto's Brick Oven, 440 Main St., Fort Lee; (201) 461-4400.

Original Presto's Brick Oven, 375 Route 46, South Hackensack; (201) 440-4235.

Original's Pizza & Subs, 2450 Kuser Road, Trenton; (609) 586-6484.

Orlando Italian Restaurant & Pizzeria, Routes 34 and 537, Colts Neck; (732) 577-8808.

Oscar's Pizza & Restaurant, 270 Chambersbridge Road, Brick; (732) 920-2233.

Oven Pizza & Restaurant, 1907 Grand Central Ave., Lavallette; (732) 793-0702.

Oxford Furnace Pizza, 35 Wall St., Oxford; (908) 453-4000.

P J's Grill & Pizza, 166 Easton Ave., New Brunswick; (732) 249-2919.

P J's Pizza & Subs, 816 Sheridan Ave., Elizabeth; (908) 355-4494.

P J's Pizza Restaurant, 151 Van Zile Road, Brick; (732) 840-3012.

Pacific Pizza, 303 Pacific Ave., Jersey City; (201) 369-0100.

Padrino's Pizza & Restaurante, 821 Route 57, Stewartsville; (908) 454-9090.

Paesano's Pizzeria, 108 Kennedy Blvd., Bayonne; (201) 437-3200.

Paisano's Pizza & Restaurants, 1511 Route 22, Watchung; (908) 755-1944.

Paisano's Trattoria, 701 S. Main St., Stewartsville; (908) 479-6200.

Palace Restaurant & Outfitters, 6924 Black Horse Pike, Mays Landing; (609) 625-8552.

Palermo Pizza & Italian, 7407 Broadway, North Bergen; (201) 861-8333.

Palermo's, 674 Route 206, Bordentown; (609) 298-6771.

Palermo's II, 49 Main St., Roebling; (609) 499-9195.

Palermo's III, 1292 Lower Ferry Road, Ewing; (609) 883-0700.

Palermo's Pizzeria & Restaurant, 1209 S. Black Horse Pike, Williamstown; (856) 629-6447.

Palermos Pizza Primo, 1876 Springfield Ave., Maplewood; (973) 763-0777.

Palumbo Restaurant & Lounge, 4057 Asbury Ave., Tinton Falls; (732) 922-6690.

Palumbo Restaurant & Pizza, 2101 Route 35, Holmdel; (732) 671-8820.

Palumbo's Restaurant & Pizza, 2243 Route 9, Old Bridge; (732) 727-0970.

Pan Pizza Bakery #3, 392 21st Ave., Paterson; (973) 247-0044.

Panatieri Pizza, 249 Talmadge Road, Edison; (732) 248-9650.

Panatieri Pizza & Pasta, 1910 Washington Valley Road, Martinsville; (732) 469-2996.

Panatieri's Pizza, 1010 Route 202 S., Branchburg; (908) 725-9455.

Panichelli's Pizza, 425 Hurffville-Cross Keys Road, Turnersville; (856) 218-1200.

Panico's Pizza, 94 Church St., New Brunswick; (732) 545-6161.

Panini, 1297 Centennial Ave., Piscataway; (732) 562-9696.

Panzarotti Pizza King, 349 Marlton Ave., Camden; (856) 966-5725.

Panzarotti Tarantini Pizza, 2060 Springdale Road, Cherry Hill; (856) 489-0026.

Panzone's Pizza, 22nd and Long Beach Blvd., Surf City (609) 494-1114.

Panzone's Pizza & Pasta, 1106 N. Bay Ave., Beach Haven; (609) 492-5103.

Paone Pizzeria Restaurant, 555 Amboy Ave., Perth Amboy; (732) 826-2700.

Papa Joes, 27 Snowhill St., Spotswood; (732) 251-9040.

Papa Joes Pizza Factory, 2849 Woodbridge Ave., Edison; (732) 548-2020.

Papa Lou's Pizza, 300 Bay Ave., Highlands; (732) 291-9300.

Papa Luigi, 600 W. Sherman Ave., Carmel; (856) 459-2100.

Papa Luigi, 382 E. Holly Ave., Pitman; (856) 256-1311.

Papa Luigi, 251 N. Broadway, Pennsville; (856) 678-3011.

Papa Luigi's, 572 Porchtown Road, Franklinville; (856) 694-1000.

Papa Luigi's, 119 N. Main St., Elmer; (856) 358-4700.

Papa Luigi's Pizzeria, 39 N. Main St., Woodstown; (856) 769-4455.

Papa Vito Restaurant & Pizza, 1008 Saint Georges Ave., Rahway; (732) 499-9119.

Papa-Roni's Restaurant, 514 Lafayette Road, Sparta; (973) 579-2002.

Papa'A Pizza, 7 Taylor Ave., Monroe Township; (732) 416-9599.

Papa's Pizzeria, 265 Queen Anne Road, Bogota; (201) 487-3515.

Papa's Tomato Pies, 804 Chambers St., Trenton; (609) 392-0359.

Papi's Pizza, 600 Summit Ave., Union City; (201) 330-9898.

Papi's Pizza, 402 Rutherford Ave., Trenton; (609) 656-1318.

Papi's Pizzeria, 558 Lakehurst Road, Browns Mills; (609) 893-5447.

Papouli's Pizza, 44 Manchester Ave., Forked River; (609) 693-4333.

Pappa Luigi's, 11 Village Center Drive, Swedesboro; (856) 467-0850.

Pappa Pizza, 6418 Ventnor Ave., Ventnor City; (609) 822-3800.

Paradise, 523 Hamilton Ave., Trenton; (609) 393-8479.

Paradise Pizza & Pasta, 132 W. Browning Road, Bellmawr; (856) 931-0999.

Paradiso Pizza, 179 Route 46, Rockaway; (973) 586-3313.

Park Pizza, 85 Park Ave., Park Ridge; (201) 391-9393.

Park Tavern & Restaurant, 250 Park Ave., East Rutherford; (201) 939-9445.

Parkside Pizzeria & Restaurant, 455 Broad St., Bloomfield; (973) 743-7441.

Parkway Pizza, 836 Parkway Ave., Ewing; (609) 883-0391.

Parkway Pizza, 12 Lanes Mill Road, Brick; (732) 458-9895.

Parma Johns, 49 Lakeside Blvd., Hopatcong; (973) 398-3400.

Pasquale Pizza Parlor, 85 Crescent Ave., Wyckoff; (201) 485-7555.

Pasquale's Cuisine & Pizzeria, 78 Maple Ave., New Egypt; (609) 758-8600.

Pasquale's Pizza, 2114 Route 9, Toms River; (732) 286-7880.

Pasquale's Pizza, 307 Main St., Boonton; (973) 335-8686.

Pasquale's Pizza, 179 Route 46, Rockaway; (973) 335-8686.

Pasquale's Pizza & Carry Out, 395 Brick Blvd., Brick; (732) 920-2224.

Pasquale's Pizza III, 147 Cherry Tree Farm Road, Middletown; (732) 615-9800.

Pasquale's Pizzeria & Ristorante, 46 Route 23, Little Falls; (973) 256-8246.

Passariellos Pizzaria Italian, 111 Laurel Oak Road, Voorhees; (856) 784-7272.

Passariello's, 13 W Main St., Moorestown; (856) 840-0998.

Pastabilitys, 202 Conklintown Road, Wanaque; (973) 831-8400.

Pat's Pizza, 3103 Route 88, Point Pleasant; (732) 892-1018.

Pat's Pizza, 539 Chews Landing Road, Lindenwold; (856) 566-6554.

Pat's Pizza & Pasta, 650 Shunpike Road, Chatham; (973) 377-3666.

Pat's Pizzeria, 104 N. Main St., Mullica Hill; (856) 223-9977.

Pat's Pizzeria, 2298 Chapel Ave. W., Cherry Hill; (856) 779-1111.

Pat's Pizzeria, 102 S. Broadway, Pennsville; (856) 678-5888.

Pat's Pizzeria, 1603 Route 38, Lumberton; (609) 265-7707.

Pat's Pizzeria, 325 N. Black Horse Pike, Runnemede; (856) 939-2600.

Pat's Pizzeria, 2700 Route 130 N., Cinnaminson; (856) 303-2323.

Pat's Pizzeria, 4 Colfax Ave., Pompton Lakes; (973) 616-8212.

Pat's Pizzeria, 532 Glassboro Road, Woodbury Heights; (856) 251-1111.

Pat's Pizzeria, 400 S. Broadway, Gloucester City; (856) 456-1111.

Pat's Pizzeria, 16 S. Broad St., Penns Grove; (856) 299-7272.

Pat's Pizzeria, 500 W. Broad St., Paulsboro; (856) 423-3838.

Pat's Pizzeria, 702 Hessian Ave, National Park; (856) 853-6060.

Pat's Pizzeria, 380 Egg Harbor Road, Sewell; (856) 582-9091.

Pat's Pizzeria, 1423 Kings Highway, Swedesboro; (856) 467-1188.

Pat's Pizzeria, 1056 S. Black Horse Pike, Williamstown; (856) 262-7755.

Pat's Pizzeria, 244 E. State St., Trenton; (609) 695-5155.

Pats Pizzeria of Marlton, 201 Route 73 S., Marlton; (856) 810-9999.

Patsy's Pizza, 133 Clinton St., Hoboken; (201) 792-0800.

Patsy's Tavern & Restaurant, 72 7th Ave., Paterson; (973) 742-9596.

Paul's Pizza Place, 550 White Horse Pike N., Magnolia; (856) 782-0055.

Paulie's Pizzeria, 11 Washington Ave., Tenafly; (201) 567-9099.

Paulies Pizzeria Cafe, 34 Easton Ave., New Brunswick; (732) 227-0900.

Paulis Pizza, 1314 Richmond Ave., Point Pleasant Beach; (732) 899-2900.

Paulus Hook Brick Oven, 84 1/2 Morris St., Jersey City; (201) 333-3939.

Pavilion Pizzeria, 211 S. Harding Highway, Landisville; (856) 697-0240.

Pavo Pub & Pizzeria, 600 Mule Road, Toms River; (732) 914-9550.

Pavolo Pizzeria, 123 E. Main St., Denville; (973) 627-2453.

Pazza Luna, 52 Chestnut St., Garfield; (973) 478-8070.

Peace A Pizza, 2010 Marlton Pike W., Cherry Hill; (856) 661-9300.

Peace A Pizza, 9709 3rd Ave., Stone Harbor; (609) 368-3990.

Penn Pizza Palace, 860 Route 168, Blackwood; (856) 228-6662.

Penn Pizza Palace, 1 S. Broadway, Camden; (856) 757-0055.

Penn Pizza Palace, 4525 Route 130 S., Burlington; (609) 387-4466.

Pennella's Restaurant/Pizzeria, 510 Van Houten Ave., Passaic; (973) 472-4065.

Pennington Pizza Grill, 15 Route 31 N., Pennington; (609) 737-9240.

Pennsville Pizza & Pasta, 709 S. Broadway, Pennsville; (856) 935-1570.

People's Pizza, 752 W. Route 70, Marlton; (856) 596-2626.

Peoples Pizza Inc, 1500 Route 38, Cherry Hill; (856) 665-6575.

Pepe's Deli & Pizza, 113 Throckmorton St., Freehold; (732) 780-6914.

Pepe's Italian Restaurant, 117 Watchung Ave., North Plainfield; (908) 753-5727.

Peppermill Cafe & Pizzeria, 147 Route 70 # 7, Toms River; (732) 905-9300.

Pepperoni Pizza, 71 Springside Road, Westampton; (609) 835-9800.

Pepperoni's Grill Inc, 6572 Mill Road, Egg Harbor Twp; (609) 601-9111.

Pepperoni's the Super Slice, Flying J Plaza, 329 Slapes Corner Road, Carneys Point; (856) 351-1804.

Pepporoni Pizza & Grill, 7501 River Road, Pennsauken; (856) 662-1766.

Perfect Pizza, 6229 Kennedy Blvd., North Bergen; (201) 869-3544.

Perfetto's Pizza, 410 Lalor St., Trenton; (609) 278-0699.

Perlins Pizza, 2442 Route 38, Cherry Hill; (856) 755-1116.

Perricone's Market, 371 Pittstown Road, Pittstown; (908) 730-8515.

Pete & Elda's/Carmen's Pizzeria, 96 Woodland Ave., Neptune City; (732) 774-6010.

Pete's Pizza, 2919 Route 206, Columbus; (609) 267-0166.

Pete's Pizza & Italian Grill, 604 W. Kings Highway, Mount Ephraim; (856) 931-3030.

Pete's Pizzeria & Pub, 119 Morris St., Morristown; (973) 539-5878.

Peter's Pizzeria, 449 Kearny Ave., Kearny; (201) 997-6606.

Pfeffer's Market, 297 Shell Road, Penns Grove; (856) 299-0358.

Phil's Pizza & Subs, 1173 Route 202 N., Branchburg; (908) 526-2388.

Phil's Pizzeria & Italian, 67 E. Mill Road, Long Valley; (908) 876-4415.

Phil's Pizzeria & Restaurant, 4 Chestnut Ridge Road, Montvale; (201) 391-1080.

Philadelphia Pizzeria, 1012 Pennington Road, Ewing; (609) 530-0909.

Philip's Grille, 561 Erial Road, Pine Hill; (856) 435-6122.

Philippo's Pizzeria, 1053 Raritan Road, Clark; (732) 381-4800.

Philly's Phatties, 215 W. Clinton Ave., Oaklyn; (856) 858-5500.

Piasano's Pizza, 530 S. Philadelphia Ave., Egg Harbor City; (609) 965-5611.

Piazella Pizzaria Restaurant, 754 Franklin Ave., Franklin Lakes; (201) 848-8220.

Piazza Di Roma, 1178 Route 34, Matawan; (732) 583-3565.

Piazza Orsillo, 120 Cedar Grove Lane, Somerset; (732) 805-9506.

Piazzella, 430 Greenwood Ave., Wyckoff; (201) 891-5800.

Picasso's II Pizza & Italian, 1311 Route 37 W., Toms River; (732) 341-1167.

Picasso's Pizzeria & Restaurant, 550 Bridgeton Pike, Mantua; (856) 468-8820.

Piccini Wood Fired Brick Oven, 1260 West Ave., Ocean City; (609) 525-0767.

Piccolissimo Pizza Restaurant, 25 Homestead Drive, Columbus; (609) 291-1033.

Piccolo's Pizza & Liquors, 913 Main St., Paterson; (973) 742-4608.

Pichirillos Pizza, 2301 Route 88, Point Pleasant; (732) 899-8757.

Pie-Zon Pizza Cafe, 539 Northfield Ave., West Orange; (973) 325-8008.

Pie-Zons Pizzeria, 1295 Roosevelt Ave., Carteret; (732) 969-3098.

Pies On, 1500 Route 37 E., Toms River; (732) 270-4444.

Pierre's Pizza, 7 N. Washington Ave., Margate City; (609) 822-4409.

Pietro, 95 Lincoln Ave. , Fair Lawn; (973) 427-3333.

Pietro's Coal Oven Pizzeria, 140 W. Route 70, Marlton; (856) 596-5500.

Pietro's Pizza, 46 W. Main St., Ramsey; (201) 327-0580.

Pietro's Pizzeria, 712 E. Bay Ave., Manahawkin; (609) 597-6708.

Piezon's Pizza, 539 Northfield Ave., West Orange; (973) 325-8008.

Pigray's Pizzeria & Resturaunt, 540 Route 10, Randolph; (973) 361-2000.

Pina's Pizza, 109 Harris Ave., Middlesex; (732) 469-5399.

Pine Brook Pizzeria Restaurant/Gencarelli's, Route 46, Pine Brook; (973) 575-6745.

Pine Hill Pizza & Grill, 561 Erial Road, Pine Hill; (856) 435-1200.

Pinehill Restaurant, 123 Paramus Road, Paramus; (201) 843-0170.

Pino's Pizza, 225 Newark Ave., Jersey City; (201) 435-2070.

Pino's Pizza & Restaurant, 10 Main St., Woodbridge; (732) 634-9304.

Pinocchio Pan & Pizza, 545 Bayway Ave., Elizabeth; (908) 355-7768.

Pioneer Pizza, 1260 Springfield Ave., New Providence; (908) 665-8100.

Pirates Pizza, 135 S. Orange Ave., South Orange; (973) 762-6286.

Pirone's Restaurant & Pizza, 798 Woodlane Road, Westampton; (609) 265-9530.

Pisa Pizza, 812 Boardwalk, Ocean City; (609) 399-7353.

Pittala's LLC, 48 Mud Pond Road, Blairstown; (908) 362-6687.

Pizza, 1636 Saint Georges Ave., Avenel; (732) 382-1100.

Pizza & Panini, 452 Route 37 E., Toms River; (732) 573-0099.

Pizza & Pasta, 25b Campus Drive, Edison; (732) 225-7800.

Pizza & Pasta, 600 William St., Piscataway; (732) 271-0010.

Pizza & Pasta, 930 S. Main St., Manville; (908) 725-5522.

Pizza & Sandwich Barn, 323 Bloomfield Ave., Caldwell; (973) 226-9020.

Pizza & Sandwich Express, 59 Main St., Little Falls; (973) 812-1199.

Pizza 1, 1185 Ringwood Ave., Haskell; (973) 835-1600.

Pizza 2000, 19 Court St., Newark; (973) 623-2300.

Pizza 46, 1200 Route 46, Little Falls; (973) 256-4646.

Pizza 46 Inc, 1664 East Drive, Point Pleasant; (732) 295-7038.

Pizza Alla Gargiulo, 101 Greene St., Jersey City; (201) 433-9000.

Pizza Amore, 77 Hartford Road, Delran; (856) 764-4143.

Pizza Barn, 2670 Route 206, Mount Holly; (609) 265-8801.

Pizza Box, 522 Atlantic Ave., Long Branch; (732) 728-0044.

Pizza Box, 460 Hurffville Cross Keys Road, Turnersville; (856) 589-5200.

Pizza Brothers, 462 Main St., Bedminster; (908) 470-4457.

Pizza Brothers, 440 Towne Centre Drive, North Brunswick; (732) 940-2272.

Pizza Brothers, 97 Godwin Ave., Midland Park; (201) 857-5021.

Pizza Brothers of Green Brook, 34 Route 22, Green Brook; (732) 968-6363.

Pizza Brothers of Martinsville, PO Box 567, Martinsville; (732) 469-6611.

Pizza Brothers of Raritan, 26 Thompson St., Raritan; (908) 526-7474.

Pizza Brothers-Scotch Plains, 1742 E. 2nd St., Scotch Plains; (908) 490-0007.

Pizza Cake LLC, 61 New Road, Parsippany; (973) 575-4224.

Pizza Cave, 439 Cedar Lane, Teaneck; (201) 836-1700.

Pizza Center, 319 Main St., Orange; (973) 678-6500.

Pizza Center & Restaurant, 580 Union Ave., Middlesex; (732) 356-7714.

Pizza City, 297 Somerset St., New Brunswick; (732) 214-1991.

Pizza City, 145 Easton Ave., New Brunswick; (732) 937-9597.

Pizza City, 218 Market St., Newark; (973) 242-0044.

Pizza City, 1051 McBride Ave., Woodland Park; (973) 890-0990.

Pizza City, 265 Main St., Paterson; (973) 881-8377.

Pizza Club, 725 River Road, Edgewater; (201) 945-1111.

Pizza Co, 4 Prospect Plz, Little Silver; (732) 842-4599.

Pizza Como, 5 Old Highway 22, Clinton; (908) 735-9250.

Pizza Corner, 589 Anderson Ave., Cliffside Park; (201) 945-9347.

Pizza Crib, 169 Main St., Orange; (973) 676-6200.

Pizza Di Palermo, 2212 Ocean Heights Ave., Egg Harbor Township; (609) 601-7797.

Pizza Di Roma, 954 N. Main St., Pleasantville; (609) 646-0909.

Pizza Enotica, 2 W. Mt. Pleasant Ave., Livingston; (973) 740- 2385.

Pizza Express, 6007 Mansion Blvd., Pennsauken; (856) 665-6740.

Pizza Express, 559 Livingston St., Norwood; (201) 767-3636.

Pizza Express, 2408 Route 88, Point Pleasant; (732) 295-1414.

Pizza Express, 130 Hardenburgh Ave., Demarest; (201) 768-8030.

Pizza Express, 101 S. Olden Ave., Trenton; (609) 396-9555.

Pizza Express, 187 Route 94, Blairstown; (908) 362-6099.

Pizza Express, 70 Main St., Netcong; (973) 691-0009.

Pizza Express & More, 537 Monmouth Road, Jackson; (732) 833-8090.

Pizza Factory, 7 Cross St., Madison; (973) 236-9999.

Pizza Factory Inc, 25 Dixon Pl., East Hanover; (973) 386-5859.

Pizza Fresca, 529 Old Marlton Pike W., Marlton; (856) 810-8888.

Pizza Fresca By Luigi, 1700 Columbus Road, Burlington; (609) 239-8888.

Pizza From Heaven, 120 N. 6th St., Camden; (856) 342-6800.

Pizza Fusion, 33 Godwin Ave., Ridgewood; (201) 445-9010.

Pizza Fusion, 95 Broad St., Red Bank; (732) 345-1600.

Pizza Gallery, 272 River Road, Edgewater; (201) 941-5060.

Pizza Galore, 804 White Horse Pike, Egg Harbor City; (609) 965-6910.

Pizza Garden, 303 N. Broadway, Pitman; (856) 589-4111.

Pizza Grill, 45 George Dye Road, Trenton; (609) 586-5770.

Pizza Heaven, 715 Sicklerville Road, Williamstown; (856) 740-0545.

Pizza Heaven, 777 Washington Road, Parlin; (732) 390-3311.

Pizza House, 123 N. Union Ave., Cranford; (908) 276-0939.

Pizza Joe's, 1370 N. Main Road, Vineland; (856) 691-0220.

Pizza King, 2316 Atlantic Ave., Atlantic City; (609) 340-8000.

Pizza King, 807 Abbott Blvd., Fort Lee; (201) 224-3070.

Pizza King, 313 Morris Ave., Elizabeth; (908) 352-9795.

Pizza King, 123 Creek Road, Mount Laurel; (856) 234-3500.

Pizza King, 2090 Oak Tree Road, Edison; (732) 372-7110.

Pizza King of Mercerville, 333 Highway 33, Trenton; (609) 631-0130.

Pizza Kitchen, 4351 S. Broad St., Yardville; (609) 581-5815.

Pizza Loolu, 2889 Route 35, Hazlet; (732) 769-2875.

Pizza Man, 574 Newark Pompton Turnpike, Pompton Plains; (973) 835-3383.

Pizza Mania, 390 Midland Ave., Garfield; (973) 859-0855.

Pizza Master, 300 Park Ave., Rutherford; (201) 933-7600.

Pizza Masters, 278 Central Ave., Jersey City; (201) 659-2232.

Pizza Masters, 532 Broadway, Bayonne; (201) 437-4802.

Pizza Mill, 1893 Long Hill Road, Millington; (908) 647-8383.

Pizza More, 62 Park Ave., Rutherford; (201) 460-9787.

Pizza Nova, 1605 Lemoine Ave., Fort Lee; (201) 346-0990.

Pizza Nova, 24 Washington Ave., Tenafly; (201) 894-9700.

Pizza On Main, 812 1/2 Main St., Bradley Beach; (732) 988-8500.

Pizza On the Edge, 19 Route 5, Edgewater; (201) 969-1919.

Pizza One, 1185 Ringwood Ave., Haskell; (973) 835-1600.

Pizza Palace, 1169 Sussex Turnpike, Mount Freedom; (973) 895-3344.

Pizza Palace Restaurant, 920 Hamilton St., Somerset; (732) 545-1776.

Pizza Party, 4309 Ventnor Ave., Atlantic City; (609) 344-3371.

Pizza Pasta, 1 S. Main St., Lodi; (973) 405-6666.

Pizza Pasta & Stuff, 3041 Route 35, Hazlet; (732) 335-8888.

Pizza Pino, 1553 Springfield Ave., Maplewood; (973) 762-5580.

Pizza Pizzazz, 484 S. Brewster Road, Vineland; (856) 692-7007.

Pizza Place, 18 Marshall Hill Road, West Milford; (973) 728-2228.

Pizza Place, 12 Woodport Road, Sparta; (973) 729-3355.

Pizza Place, 5010 Route 33, Wall Township; (732) 256-9191.

Pizza Place, 100 Hillside Blvd., Lakewood; (732) 730-1144.

Pizza Plus, 712 State Route 440, Jersey City; (201) 435-3777.

Pizza Plus, 241 4th St., Lakewood; (732) 367-0711.

Pizza Plus, 538 Georges Road, North Brunswick; (732) 418-1000.

Pizza Plus, 1897 Woodbridge Ave., Edison; (732) 572-6080.

Pizza Plus Inc, 900 Main St., Asbury Park; (732) 774-3338.

Pizza Point, 218 Somerdale Road, Blackwood; (856) 401-1420.

Pizza Pro's, 42 State Route 94, Vernon; (973) 209-8186.

Pizza Pronto Cafe, 701 N. White Horse Pike, Somerdale; (856) 784-0007.

Pizza Pros I Inc, 1448 Queen Anne Road, Teaneck; (201) 862-0815.

Pizza Pub, 395 Dover-Chester Road, Ironia; (973) 584-4141.

Pizza Putt, 10 42nd St., Sea Isle City; (609) 263-4663.

Pizza Rustica, 1047 Broad St., Bloomfield; (973) 338-1555.

Pizza Shoppe, 270 Route 23, Franklin; (973) 209-2299.

Pizza Shoppe LLC, 60 1/2 Main Ave., Ocean Grove; (732) 776-5466.

Pizza Star, 301 N. Harrison St., Princeton; (609) 921-7422.

Pizza Station, 294 Route 94, Vernon; (973) 209-2800.

Pizza Station, 3043 State Rt 23, Oak Ridge; (973) 697-2222.

Pizza Stop, 333 Meadowlands Pkwy., Secaucus; (201) 866-2669.

Pizza Stop, 290 S. Michigan Ave., Kenilworth; (908) 245-6262.

Pizza Stop, 1172 Stuyvesant Ave., Irvington; (973) 371-9191.

Pizza Stop, 422 Madison Ave., Paterson; (973) 278-4898.

Pizza Stop, 340 Hamilton Blvd., South Plainfield; (908) 755-0101.

Pizza Stop of Berkely Heights, 430 Springfield Ave., Berkeley Heights; (908) 665-7867.

Pizza Store, 7936 River Road, Pennsauken; (856) 486-1111.

Pizza Subwich LLC, 108 S. Essex Ave., Orange; (973) 672-7220.

Pizza Time, 599 Broad Ave., Ridgefield; (201) 943-2071.

Pizza Time Restaurant, 1076 Saint Georges Ave., Avenel; (732) 636-5195.

Pizza Town Pizzeria, 883 Mount Prospect Ave., Newark; (973) 483-5179.

Pizza Town USA, 302 White Horse Pike, Atco; (856) 767-8811.

Pizza Town USA, 366 Upper Mountain Ave., Montclair; (973) 744-1164.

Pizza Town USA, 89 Route 46, Elmwood Park; (201) 797-6172.

Pizza Tree, 2673 Haddonfield Road, Pennsauken; (856) 665-8733.

Pizza Villa, 700 2nd St., Swedesboro; (856) 467-5000.

Pizza Villa, 550 North Ave., Union; (908) 289-3684.

Pizza Villa, 3502 Park Ave., Weehawken; (201) 223-0400.

Pizza Village, 1817 Mount Holly Road., Burlington; (609) 387-9344.

Pizza Villagio Cafe, 311 Ferry St., Newark; (973) 344-0707.

Pizza Villagio Cafe II, 229 Main St., Belleville; (973) 450-1818.

Pizza Wings Steaks Things, 541 Highway 33, Trenton; (609) 631-7172.

Pizza World, 200 Haddonfield Berlin Road, Voorhees; (856) 616-9300.

Pizzaland, 260 Belleville Turnpike, North Arlington; (201) 998-9095.

Pizzalicious, 1483 Route 23, Wayne; (973) 305-0565.

Pizzamia Pizzeria, 168 Union Ave., East Rutherford; (201) 460-1460.

Pizzapella, 15 Cotters Lane, East Brunswick; (732) 238-1800.

Pizzatella, 755 Route 18, East Brunswick; (732) 238-1800.

Pizzeria Di Amici, 255 Hackensack St., Wood-Ridge; (201) 438-7451.

Pizzeria Monterviero, 531 Bayway Ave., Elizabeth; (908) 355-2305.

Pizzeta, 44 Main St., Millburn; (973) 376-3773.

Pizzeta Livingston, 62 W. Mount Pleasant Ave., Livingston; (973) 740-2264.

Pizzette, 31 W. Main St., Ramsey; (201) 934-6000.

Pizzicato, 500 Route 73 S., Marlton; (856) 396-0880.

Pizzutillo's Pizza Restaurant, 720 S. Church St., Mt Laurel; (856) 234-3120.

Planet Pizza, 618 Broadway, Bayonne; (201) 339-5600.

Plaza Luna, 52 Chestnut St., Garfield; (973) 272-8123.

Plaza Pizza, 100 Dorigo Lane, Secaucus; (201) 864-0858.

Plaza Pizza Palace, 845 Cooper Landing Road, Cherry Hill; (856) 779-9797.

PMN Pizza, 484 E. Evesham Road, Cherry Hill; (856) 428-0202.

Pomodoro Pizza, 310 Howard Blvd., Mount Arlington; (973) 601-7270.

Pomodoro Pizza, 125 Morris St., Morristown; (973) 538-1002.

Pomodoro Pizza & Restaurant, 795 Abbott Blvd., Fort Lee; (201) 224-0800.

Pompei Pizza, 480 Broadway, Bayonne; (201) 858-9026.

Pompei Pizza, 722 W. Side Ave., Jersey City; (201) 433-3941.

Pompeii Pizzeria, 72 Westfield Ave., Clark; (732) 381-6240.

Pompilio's Pizza, 223 Westwood Ave., Westwood; (201) 664-9292.

Pop Pop's Eatery, 200 White Horse Road E., Voorhees; (856) 770-8282.

Pop's Pizza Cafe, 122 N. Haddon Ave., Haddonfield; (856) 857-1772.

Pop's Pizzeria, 430 Oak St., Passaic; (973) 779-4488.

Poppa Pizza, 297 Main St., Keansburg; (732) 787-9761.

Poppy's Pizza, 1617 Main St., Belmar; (732) 280-6990.

Porta Bella Pizzia, 37 E. Broadway, Hackensack; (201) 820-3414.

Portifino Pizzeria, 396 Central Ave., Jersey City; (201) 420-0795.

Portobello Pizzeria & Restaurant, 315 Route 206; Hillsborough; (908) 904-4111.

Positano Pizzeria & Restaurant, 107 Washington Ave., Little Ferry; (201) 440-5556.

Positano Restaurant, 1500 State Rt 23, Butler; (973) 838-1700.

Positano Restaurant & Pizzeria, 245 Berdan Ave., Wayne; (973) 628-6863.

Preakness Pizza, 15 Preakness Shopping Ctr, Wayne; (973) 696-0375.

Preps Pizzeria & Dairy Bar, 1004 Boardwalk, Ocean City; (609) 398-0636.

Presto Brick Oven Pizza, 6001 Park Ave., West New York; (201) 861-2000.

Presto's Pizza, 90 Laroche Ave., Harrington Park; (201) 750-1077.

Prestos Pizza, 772 Main St., Hackensack; (201) 968-0090.

224

Prilins Pizza, 2428 Route 38, Cherry Hill; (856) 755-1116.

Prima Pizza, 224 Brook Ave., Passaic; (973) 471-9866.

Prima Pizza, 328 Avenue B, Bayonne; (201) 339-3100.

Prima Pizza, 719 Mountain Ave., Springfield; (973) 379-9660.

Prima's Gourmet Pizza & Subs, 5 Bowling Green Pkwy., Lake Hopatcong; (973) 663-4400.

Primavera Pizza & Pasta, 1102 Boardwalk, Ocean City; (609) 814-0187.

Primavera Pizzaria, 754 Clifton Ave., Clifton; (973) 685-7387.

Primavera's Pizza, 401 Speedwell Ave., Morris Plains; (973) 539-0041.

Primo Pizza, 3009 Atlantic Brigantine Blvd., Brigantine; (609) 266-4288.

Primo Pizza, 2230 Hamburg Turnpike, Wayne; (973) 839-8777.

Primo Pizza, 832 Boardwalk, Ocean City; (609) 525-0022.

Primo Pizza, 190 Elmora Ave., Elizabeth; (908) 352-5111.

Primo Pizza, 183 S. New York Road, Galloway; (609) 748-4200.

Primo Pizza, 1400 White Horse Pike, Egg Harbor City; (609) 965-2200.

Primo Pizza Cafe, 500 N. Black Horse Pike, Runnemede; (856) 939-2800.

Primo's Pizza, 396 Lake Shore Drive, Hewitt; (973) 853-0400.

Prince of Pizza, 763 Bergen Ave., Jersey City; (201) 434-9453.

Princess Pizza, 420 Grand St., Jersey City; (201) 209-0091.

Pronto Pizza, 441 Lewandowski St., Lyndhurst; (201) 939-2210.

Pronto Pizza, 206 Broadway, Westville; (856) 742-8778.

Pronto Pizza, 6 E. Park Ave., Merchantville; (856) 488-1805.

Prontos Pizzeria & Restaurant, 1965 Route 57, Hackettstown; (908) 813-0624.

Provesi of Morristown Inc, 50 South St., Morristown; (973) 993-1944.

Pudgy's Restaurant & Pizzeria, 55 Brick Blvd., Brick; (732) 255-3770.

Pugliese's Deli & Pizzeria, 147 Malvern St., Newark; (973) 344-0121.

Pulcinella Inc, 3067 Bordentown Ave., Parlin; (732) 316-9292.

Pullella's Pizza Parlor, 2 Berlin Road N., Lindenwold; (856) 783-4664.

Puzo's Family Restaurant, 16 W. Ridgewood Ave., Ridgewood; (201) 445-3332.

Pyro Pizza, 515 Brick Blvd., Brick; (732) 262-7976.

Pyro's Pizza, 4023 New Jersey Ave., Wildwood; (609) 729-3235.

Quakerbridge Plaza Eatery, 6 Quakerbridge Plaza, Trenton; (609) 587-7274.

Quattro Stajione, 353 Route 22, Green Brook; (732) 563-0707.

Queen Margherita, 246 Washington Ave., Nutley; (973) 662-0007.

Queen Pizza, 114 Halsey St., Newark; (973) 624-7322.

Queen Pizza & Deli, 938 Broad St., Newark; (973) 802-1661.

Queen Pizza II, 48 Commerce St., Newark; (973) 242-1829.

Queen's Pizza, 74 Broad St., Elizabeth; (908) 289-6790.

R Square Pizza, 408 Renaissance Blvd., North Brunswick; (732) 297-8805.

R-U Grill & Pizza Inc, 142 Easton Ave., New Brunswick; (732) 828-1128.

Race Zone Bar & Grill, 1194 Englishtown Road, Old Bridge; (732) 251-2332.

Ragazzi Pizza & Restaurant, 44 W. Route 70, Marlton; (856) 810-8810.

Rahway Pizza, 978 Saint Georges Ave., Rahway; (732) 574-3222.

Ralph Piccolo's Pizza, 312 Union Ave., Paterson; (973) 942-0282.

Ralph's Italian Restaurant-Pizza, 230 Paterson Ave., East Rutherford; (201) 935-2228.

Ralpho's Pizza, 794 Broad Ave., Ridgefield; (201) 945-3031.

Ralph's Pizzeria, 564 Franklin Ave., Nutley; (973) 235-1130.

Rana's Pizzeria, 674 Avenue A, Bayonne; (201) 823-2222.

Randazzo Italian Cuisine, 1299 Route 38, Hainesport; (609) 267-8333.

Randazzo Pizza & Pasta, 288 Egg Harbor Road, Sewell; (856) 582-3555.

Randazzo Pizza & Restaurant, 10 Bank St., Summit; (908) 273-1713.

Randazzo's Family Restaurant, 401 34th St., Ocean City; (609) 814-1600.

Randy's Pizza, 2906 S. Black Horse Pike, Williamstown; (856) 629-7575.

Rani Pizzeria, 6310 Park Ave., West New York; (201) 430-9706.

Raphael's Pizza, 67 N. Laurel St., Bridgeton; (856) 459-0500.

Ray's Famous Pizza Inc, 10 Pompton Ave., Verona; (973) 857-3434.

Ray's New York Pizza & Restaurant, 545 Mill Creek Road, Manahawkin; (609) 597-5050.

Ray's Pizza, 4000 Route 130, Delran; (856) 824-0001.

Ray's Pizza, 284 Closter Dock Road, Closter; (201) 768-5390.

Ray's Pizza, 663 Ocean Ave., Jersey City; (201) 434-0404.

Ray's Pizza, 95 Woodstown Road, Swedesboro; (856) 467-9911.

Ray's Pizzeria, 110 Main St., Paterson; (973) 278-0043.

Ray's Real Pizza, 3429 Route 35, Hazlet; (732) 203-1600.

Ray's Traditional Pizza, 321 Broadway, Hillsdale; (201) 722-0700.

Ray's Traditional Pizza, 28 Union Ave., Cresskill; (201) 266-6660.

Ray's Traditional Pizza, 60 Essex St., Rochelle Park; (201) 226-1030.

Ray's Waldwick Pizza & Restaurant, 21 Wyckoff Ave., Waldwick; (201) 445-4286.

Ray's New York Pizza, 545 Mill Creek Road, Manahawkin; (609) 597-5050.

Real Pizza LLC, 831 Conifer St., Toms River; (732) 244-2033.

Red Bank Pizza, 9 Westwood Drive, Lincroft; (732) 741-9868.

Red Moon Pizza, 3371 Route 1, Lawrenceville; (609) 452-1510.

Red Moon Pizzeria & Restaurant, 66 E. Kennedy Blvd., Lakewood; (732) 363-0292.

Red Moon Restaurant & Pizzeria, 4027 Route 9, Howell; (732) 364-6668.

Red Star Pizza, 1805 Route 206, Southampton; (609) 859-1773.

Red Star Pizza 3, 608 Bear Tavern Road, Ewing; (609) 406-1600.

Reggio Pizzeria, 895 Magie Ave., Union; (908) 354-9466.

Renato's Pizza, 36 S. Maple Ave., Ridgewood; (201) 652-3554.

Renna's Pizza & Restaurant LLC, 106 Bordentown Hedding Road, Bordentown; (609) 298-0123.

Renna's Pizza Restaurant, 1032 Route 206, Bordentown; (609) 291-0303.

Reservoir Restaurant, 106 W. South Orange Ave., South Orange; (973) 762-9795.

Reservoir Tavern, 90 Parsippany Blvd., Parsippany; (973) 334-0421.

Rexy's Bar & Restaurant, 700 Black Horse Pike, Mount Ephraim; (856) 456-7911.

Ricardos Pizza, 522 Saddle River Road, Saddle Brook; (201) 843-1396.

Riccardo's Pizza, 2510 River Ave., Camden; (856) 541-4914.

Riccardo's Pizza & Restaurant, 240 John F Kennedy Way, Willingboro; (609) 871-3330.

Riccardo's Pizza Restaurant, 567 Lakehurst Road, Browns Mills; (609) 735-0162.

Ricky's Pizza & Pasta, 1400 Parkway Ave., Ewing; (609) 530-1888.

Riders Pizzeria & Subs, 236 Frelinghuysen Ave., Newark; (973) 242-0771.

Ridge Restaurant & Pizza, 25 S. Finley Ave., Basking Ridge; (908) 766-5701.

Ridgedale Pizza, 86 Ridgedale Ave, Cedar Knolls; (973) 267-6262.

Ridgewood Pizza, 37 Godwin Ave., Ridgewood; (201) 444-1055.

Rifici's Ristorante, 308 W. Absecon Blvd., Absecon; (609) 272-9260.

Rigatony's, 3 Church St., Vernon; (973) 764-3700.

Right Pizza, 1554 Teaneck Road, Teaneck; (201) 833-4005.

Rigoletto Trattoria, 418 Route 35, Red Bank; (732) 842-2277.

Ringwood Pizza, 55 Skyline Drive, Ringwood; (973) 962-4722.

Rino's Pizza, 1201 Bayshore Road, Villas; (609) 889-1147.

Rio Steaks & Pizza, 3159 Route 9 S., Rio Grande; (609) 465-7888.

Rita's Steak House & Pizzeria, 185 Broadway, Westville; (856) 456-7472.

Ritacco Brothers Brick Oven, 18 Washington Ave., Nutley; (973) 667-9662.

Riunite Pizzeria & Restaurant, 835 Roosevelt Ave., Carteret; (732) 969-2442.

Riverbank Tavern & Pizzeria, 554 Market St., Newark; (973) 344-8683.

Riverside Pizza, 591 River St., Paterson; (973) 569-3440.

Riviera Pizza, 61 Main St., Southampton; (609) 859-1221.

Riviera Pizza, 212 Taunton Blvd., Medford; (856) 983-2111.

Riviera Pizza, 6 Stokes Road, Medford Lakes; (609) 654-4300.

Rizzo's Pizza, 1594 Route 35, Ocean; (732) 493-2727.

Robert's Pizzeria, 63 New St., Newark; (973) 642-0082.

Roberto Pizza, 521 Main St., East Orange; (973) 674-5211.

Roberto's Pizza, 1 Lackawanna Plaza, Montclair; (973) 509-7055.

Roberto's Pizza, 125 Avon Ave., Newark; (973) 645-1941.

Roberto's Pizza & Restaurant, 399 Main St., Metuchen; (732) 548-5440.

Roberto's Pizza Cafe, 165 Ferry St., Newark; (973) 491-0003.

Roberto's Pizza Cafe, 179 Franklin St., Belleville; (973) 844-1900.

Rocco's Bella Vita, 1594 Route 9, Toms River; (732) 286-0733.

Rocco's Pizza, 661 Bridgeton Pike, Mantua; (856) 464-9300.

Rocco's Pizza, 360 S. Main St., Phillipsburg; (908) 454-1555.

Rocco's Pizza, 25 S. Main St., Manahawkin; (609) 978-1234.

Rocco's Pizza & Restaurant, 466 Route 202 206, Bedminster; (908) 781-2300.

Rocco's Pizza & Subs, 82 Taylor Ave., Manasquan; (732) 223-4884.

Rocco's Pizzeria, 57 Avenel St., Avenel; (732) 750-5800.

Rocco's Restaurant, 30 Cook Plz, Madison; (973) 377-7161.

Rock-It Pizza, 560 Valley Road, West Orange; (973) 325-6352.

Rockafellers Pizza, 421 Prospect St., Long Branch; (732) 923-1700.

Rocky's Restaurant & Pizzeria, 420 Franklin Ave., Nutley; (973) 667-2234.

Rodolfo Pizza, 1325 Route 206, Skillman; (609) 924-1813.

Rodolfo Pizza, 124 Sampton Ave., South Plainfield; (908) 561-0878.

Rodolfo's Pizza & Restaurant, 6 Elizabeth St., New Brunswick; (732) 247-2622.

Rojan Plaza, 25 Elizabeth St., New Brunswick; (732) 246-0841.

Roma Pizza, 656 Boardwalk, Ocean City; (609) 399-6597.

Roma Pizza, 840 S. Route 73, West Berlin; (856) 753-5252.

Roma Pizza, 245 Adams St., Newark; (973) 465-9555.

Roma Pizza, 88 Godwin Ave., Ridgewood; (201) 389-6810.

Roma Pizza, 140 Franklin Turnpike, Waldwick; (201) 857-3381.

Roma Pizza, 438 Boulevard, Hasbrouck Heights; (201) 288-5454.

Roma Pizza, 214 Main St., Keansburg; (732) 787-2929.

Roma Pizza, 708 Old Bridge Turnpike, South River; (732) 254-3334.

Roma Pizza & Chicken, 26 1st St., Elizabeth; (908) 393-7269.

Roma Pizzeria, 100 Pemberton Browns Mill Road, Browns Mills; (609) 893-7760.

Roma Pizzeria, 8620 Kennedy Blvd., North Bergen; (201) 869-4090.

Roma Pizzeria, 709 Main St., Boonton; (973) 335-1614.

Roma Pizzeria, 98 North Ave., Garwood; (908) 789-1170.

Roma Pizzeria & Restaurant, 895 Ringwood Ave., Haskell; (973) 835-3355.

Roman Delight, 180 Route 35, Eatontown; (732) 544-1692.

Roman Delight Pizza, 250 Woodbridge Center, Woodbridge; (732) 636-3600.

Roman Gourmet, 153 Maplewood Ave., Maplewood; (973) 762-4288.

Roman Inn, 19 W. Hudson Ave., Englewood; (201) 567-2654.

Roman Pizza, 81 W. Main St., Chester; (908) 879-9228.

Roman Pizza, 858 River Road, New Milford; (201) 265-9371.

Roman Pizza, 1200 Route 22, Phillipsburg; (908) 859-4114.

Roman's Pizza, 3618 Marlton Pike, Pennsauken; (856) 486-9605.

Roman's Pizzeria & Restaurant, 4437 Route 27, Princeton; (609) 683-7770.

Roman's Pizzeria Restaurant, 31 Broadway, Passaic; (973) 777-1676.

Romanelli's Italian Eatery, 42 Lincoln Pl, Madison; (973) 377-9515.

Romano Pizza Steaks & Subs, 9 Plainfield Ave., Piscataway; (732) 981-9353.

Romano's Pizza & Chicken, 571 Bound Brook Road, Middlesex; (732) 424-0466.

Romanza's, 1900 Springdale Road, Cherry Hill; (856) 424-1255.

Rome Pizza, 334 North Ave., Dunellen; (732) 968-1394.

Rome Pizzaria & Cafe, 20 Hudson Pl, Hoboken; (201) 683-9600.

Romeo Pizzeria, 408 Central Ave., Orange; (973) 674-8907.

Romeo's Express, 3352 Route 9, Freehold; (732) 431-2002.

Romeo's Pizza, 130 Route 33, Manalapan; (732) 308-9100.

Romeo's Pizza, 199 Main Ave., Passaic; (973) 777-1450.

Romeo's Pizza, 843 Route 33, Freehold; (732) 845-5454.

Romeo's Pizza, 3205 Route 88, Point Pleasant; (732) 892-3334.

Romeo's Pizza & Pasta Factory, 10 S. New Prospect Road, Jackson; (732) 905-8999.

Romeo's Pizza & Restaurant, 1721 Union Ave., Hazlet; (732) 264-8182.

Romeo's Pizza & Restaurant, 300 Route 35, Keyport; (732) 290-7119.

Romeo's Pizza & Restaurant, 325 Route 36, Middletown; (732) 787-1110.

Romeo's Pizzeria, 3421 Pacific Ave., Wildwood; (609) 523-0230.

Romeo's Pizzeria, 3707 Pacific Ave., Wildwood; (609) 523-1515.

Romeo's Restaurant & Pizza, 300 Gordons Corner Road, Manalapan; (732) 972-1180.

Romeo's Restaurant & Pizza, 20 Jernee Mill Road, Sayreville; (732) 254-6252.

Romeo's Restaurant & Pizza, 2602 Route 516, Old Bridge; (732) 679-4900.

Romeo's Restaurant & Pizza, 8 S. Main St., Marlboro; (732) 431-2424.

Romeo's Restaurant & Pizzeria, 49 Village Center Drive, Freehold; (732) 308-0933.

Romona's Italian Pizzeria, 901 White Horse Pike, Haddon Twp; (856) 833-0001.

Rondo's Pizzeria, 380 Drum Point Road, Osbornville; (732) 477-8665.

Rosa's Pizzeria, 207 Kinderkamack Road, Emerson; (201) 265-8111.

Rosa's Pizza, 142 Passaic St., Passaic; (973) 473-3511.

Rosa's Restaurante & Pizziera, 3442 S. Broad St., Trenton; (609) 581-9053.

Rosario's at Willow, 1132 Willow Ave., Hoboken; (201) 418-8717.

Rosario's Pizza, 248 Route 130, Bordentown; (609) 298-1335.

Rosas Pizza & Restaurant, 567 Mantoloking Road, Brick; (732) 920-1717.

Rose Pizza, 73 River Drive, Garfield; (973) 773-9205.

Rose's Pizza & Ice Cream, 4 Brunswick Ave., Edison; (732) 416-6560.

Rosie's Pizzeria, 8404 Kennedy Blvd., North Bergen; (201) 868-3468.

Rossano's Pizzeria, 1509 Route 38, Hainesport; (609) 261-4626.

Roy's Bar & Grill, 207 Mallory Ave., Jersey City; (201) 435-3800.

Royal Pizzeria, 921 Main Ave., Passaic; (973) 365-0777.

Rudy's Spaghetti House & Pizza, 71 Vervalen St., Closter; (201) 768-8444.

Ruffino's Restaurant, 178 Route 35, Eatontown; (732) 542-0110.

Russillo Pizzeria & Ristorante, 675 Bloomfield Ave., West Caldwell; (973) 228-4100.

Russo, 320 Beverly Rancocas Road, Willingboro; (609) 880-1811.

Russo Brothers Pizza, 20 W. Park Ave., Vineland; (856) 205-9998.

Russo's Pizza Shop, 713 E. Main St., Bridgewater; (732) 469-0625.

Russo's Pub, 1302 Monmouth Road E., Mt Holly; (609) 261-3277.

Ruthie's Bar-B-Q/Thin Crust Pizza, 64 1/2 Chestnut St., Montclair; (973) 509-1134.

S & J Pizzeria, 226 E. Broad St., Millville; (856) 825-1070.

Sal & Gino's Pizza, 216 Broad St., Keyport; (732) 739-1411.

Sal & Pat's Deli, 103 Nicholson Road, Gloucester City; (856) 742-0514.

Sal & Tommy's Pizzeria & Subs, 457 Main St., Orange; (973) 672-0005.

Sal Vito Pizza, 910 Haddonfield Berlin Road, Voorhees; (856) 566-8486.

Sal's Gourmet Pizzeria & Restaurant, 220 Triangle Road, Hillsborough; (908) 369-6944.

Sal's Pizza, 1 W. Washington Ave., Washington; (908) 689-6336.

Sal's Pizza, 8500 New Jersey Ave., Wildwood Crest; (609) 729-7606.

Sal's Pizza & Italian Restaurant, 404 Egg Harbor Road, Sewell; (856) 589-5115.

Sal's Pizza & Restaurant, 222 Bridgeton Pike, Mantua; (856) 468-2226.

Sal's Pizza & Restaurant, 175 Lakeside Blvd., Landing; (973) 770-1183.

Sal's Pizza & Restaurant, 416 Route 40, Elmer; (856) 358-2929.

Sal's Pizza Corner, 71 W. Main St., Ramsey; (201) 327-8929.

Sal's Pizza Works, 10 W. Main St., Marlton; (856) 985-5111.

Sal's Pizzeria, 6127 Bergenline Ave., West New York; (201) 868-1999.

Sal's Pizzeria, 1005 Market St., Palmyra; (856) 786-1150.

Sal's Pizzeria, 1085 Broad St., Shrewsbury; (732) 460-0222.

Sal's Pizzeria Restaurant, 510 Route 130, East Windsor; (609) 448-7786.

Salerno Pizza Ristorante, 1597 Park Ave., South Plainfield; (908) 754-8204.

Salerno's Pizza Sub, 301 Union Ave., Brielle; (732) 528-5566.

Salerno's Restaurant & Pizzeria, Route 24 and Old Farmers Road, Long Valley; (908) 876-1283.

Sally's Starr's Pizza, 439 Jackson Road, Atco; (856) 768-1114.

Sam's Cafe & Pizzeria, 489 Fairlawn Pkwy, Saddle Brook; (201) 797-1114.

Sam's Pizza, 2120 Kennedy Blvd., Union City; (201) 223-4449.

Sam's Pizza, 847 Main St., Paterson; (973) 684-5929.

Sam's Pizza Palace, 2600 Boardwalk, North Wildwood; (609) 522-6017.

San Remo Pizza, 101 New Brunswick Ave., Perth Amboy; (732) 442-9190.

San Remo Pizza, 87 Main St., Woodbridge; (732) 634-7151.

San Remo Pizza & Restaurant, 579 Route 22, North Plainfield; (908) 756-1661.

San Remo Pizzeria, 1102 Main Ave., Clifton; (973) 779-5885.

San Remo Restaurant & Pizza, 479 Route 79, Morganville; (732) 591-1386.

Sandy's Luncheonette, 322 Rues Lane, East Brunswick; (732) 254-1313.

Sansone Brothers Pizzeria, 3191 Route 27, Franklin Park; (732) 297-9666.

Santillo's Brick Oven Pizza, 639 S. Broad St., Elizabeth; (908) 354-1887.

Santini Brothers Pizzeria, 355 Franklin Ave., Nutley; (973) 661-5205.

Santini Pizzeria, 408 E. Church St., Blackwood; (856) 228-8008.

Santini's II Pizzeria & Restaurant, 660 Woodbury Glassboro Road, Sewell; (856) 468-0444.

Santino's Italian Restaurant & Pizzeria, 567 Main St., Sayreville; (732) 721-3163.

Santino's Pizza, 1240 Route 130, Trenton; (609) 443-5600.

Santino's Pizza Etc, 35 Sylvania Ave., Neptune City; (732) 775-1800.

Santino's Pizzeria, 2802 Boardwalk, Wildwood; (609) 846-0021.

Santo's Italian Deli & Pizza, 83 Main St., Edison; (732) 906-8886.

Santoni's Ristorante-Pizzeria, 42 Outwater Lane, Garfield; (973) 546-3411.

Santoro's, 1609 Ocean Ave., Belmar; (732) 681-1162.

Santucci Square Pizza, 115 E. 17th Ave., North Wildwood; (609) 729-6110.

Sanvinos Pizzeria, 3204 Kennedy Blvd., Jersey City; (201) 795-1700.

Saporito Pizza, 100 Route 22, Springfield; (973) 379-7191.

Saporito Pizza, 3130 Route 10, Denville; (973) 989-0022.

Sarge's Boulevard Pizza, 678 Shaler Blvd., Ridgefield; (201) 941-5040.

Savino's Pizza, 285 Oradell Ave., Paramus; (201) 265-3888.

Scala's Pizza, 88 Brighton Ave., Long Branch; (732) 222-8728.

Scalici's Pizza & Restaurant, 138 Center Grove Road, Randolph; (973) 361-3616.

Scardino's Pizzeria & Restaurant, 63 S. Main St., Lodi; (973) 473-3409.

Schiano Restaurant & Pizza, 2649 Route 516, Old Bridge; (732) 679-6061.

Schiano's Pizza, 580 N. Main St., Barnegat; (609) 698-3394.

Schiano's Pizzeria, 215 Route 37 W., Toms River; (732) 240-0110.

Schiano's Pizzeria & Restaurant, 451 Atlantic City Blvd., Bayville; (732) 269-4476.

Sciortino's Harbor Lights, 132 S. Broadway; South Amboy; (732) 721-8788.

Scolaro New Roma Pizzeria, 1442 Queen Anne Road, Teaneck; (201) 837-9798.

Scotti Pizza & Restaurant, 159 Main St., East Brunswick; (732) 613-9613.

Scotto & Crimani Restaurant, 15 Sunnybrae Blvd., Trenton; (609) 585-9800.

Scotto Pizza, 233 S. White Horse Pike, Berlin; (856) 767-0029.

Scotto Pizza, 200 Haddonfield Road, Cherry Hill; (856) 662-3773.

Scotto Pizza, 58 Main Ave., Clifton; (973) 667-5697.

Scotto Pizza, 230 N. Maple Ave., Marlton; (856) 985-9554.

Scotto Pizza, 62 Freneau Ave., Matawan; (732) 583-7031.

Scotto Pizza Cafe, 3111 Route 38, Mt Laurel; (856) 778-4800.

Scotto's Pizza, 16 Berlin Road, Clementon; (856) 784-9200.

Scully's Asbury Cafe, 955 Asbury Ave., Ocean City; (609) 391-1111.

Sea Bright Pizzeria & Restaurant, 1066 Ocean Ave., Sea Bright; (732) 219-8770.

Seasons Pizza, 1014 N. White Horse Pike, Stratford; (856) 783-9333.

Secaucus Pizza, 161 Front St., Secaucus; (201) 863-0037.

Sejal's Famous Pizza, 3391 Route 27, Franklin Park; (732) 422-0007.

Semolina, 343 Millburn Ave., Millburn; (973) 379-9101.

Serafinas Ristorante & Pizzeria, 1712 E. Main St., Millville; (856) 327-2928.

Serpico's Pizzeria & Restaurant, 307 Main St., Allenhurst; (732) 531-4774.

Short Hills Pizza, 38 Chatham Road, Short Hills; (973) 912-8899.

Sicilia Pizza, 558 S. Delsea Drive, Clayton; (856) 881-9566.

Sicilian Pizza & Deli, 1162 Broad St., Clifton; (973) 779-7228.

Sicilian Sun Restaurant, 604 N. Maple Ave., Ho Ho Kus; (201) 444-3494.

Sicillian Pizza, 1471 Haddon Ave., Camden; (856) 964-0400.

Siino's Pizzeria, 17 Broad St., Eatontown; (732) 544-1333.

Sila Belli Pizzeria, 1341 Route 9, Toms River; (732) 286-9222.

Silvana's Restaurant-Pizzeria, 153 Washington Ave., Little Ferry; (201) 440-4776.

Singa's Pizza, 319 Route 130, East Windsor; (609) 371-1700.

Singas Famous Pizza, 840 Newark Ave., Jersey City; (201) 222-5141.

Singas Famous Pizza, 95 Broadway, Elmwood Park; (201) 796-1200.

Singas Famous Pizza Corp, 1655 Oak Tree Road, Edison; (732) 549-8665.

Skelly's Hi-Point Pub, 5 N. Shore Road, Absecon; (609) 641-3172.

Skinny Vinnie's Italian Food, 60 Sicard St., New Brunswick; (732) 545-6671.

Skyline Pizzeria & Restaurant, 130 Skyline Drive, Ringwood; (973) 962-4848.

Slice of Heaven, 610 N. Bay Ave., Beach Haven; (609) 492-7437.

Slices Inc, 250 Norwood Ave., Oakhurst; (732) 531-6811.

So Mang Restaurant, 260 Bergen Turnpike, Little Ferry; (201) 440-8260.

Sofia's Pizzeria & Restaurant, 140 Newark Pompton Turnpike, Little Falls; (973) 890-7090.

Soho Pizza, 540 Valley Road, Montclair; (973) 744-8708.

Sollena's Pizza, 291 Delsea Drive, Sewell; (856) 589-7100.

Sonny & Tony's Pizza & Italian, 400 Ridge Road, Mahwah; (201) 529-4001.

Sonny's Pizza II, 915 Route 517, Hackettstown; (908) 852-1116.

Sonny's Restaurant & Pizzeria, 512 Grand Ave., Englewood; (201) 569-9808.

Soprano's III, 1116 S. Main St., West Creek; (609) 597-2777.

Soprano's Pizzeria, 152 Adamsville Road, Bridgewater; (908) 722-4088.

Soprano's Restaurant, 228 2nd St., Elizabeth; (908) 353-8000.

Sopranos Pizza, 400 Minnisink Road, Totowa; (973) 200-0885.

Sopranos Pizza, 900 Barnegat Blvd N., Barnegat; (609) 735-9900.

Sopranos Pizza & Sandwiches, 1100 Dehirsch Ave., Woodbine; (609) 861-1100.

Sopranos Pizza Haven & Deli, 916 Bayshore Road, Del Haven; (609) 889-0641.

Sorrento II Pizzeria & Restaurant, 2424 Boardwalk, North Wildwood; (609) 522-6401.

Sorrento Pizza, 5 E. Main St., Mendham; (973) 543-2777.

Sorrento's Pizza, 602 Collings Ave., Oaklyn; (856) 854-2920.

South Amboy Pizza Palace, 346 Bordentown Ave., South Amboy; (732) 525-2474.

South End Pizza, 9702 Ventnor Ave., Margate City; (609) 822-5402.

South End Pizza II, 4006 Ventnor Ave., Atlantic City; (609) 348-3315.

South Street Cafe Pizza, 217 South Ave., Fanwood; (908) 322-0200.

Spano's Tomato Pies, 2505 Bridge Ave., Point Pleasant; (732) 295-8878.

Special Pizza City, 1597 N. Olden Avenue Ext., Ewing; (609) 393-0330.

Special Pizza City & Adriano's, 3003 English Creek Ave., Egg Harbor Township; (609) 641-5500.

Spinners Pizzeria, 946 S. Elmora Ave., Elizabeth; (908) 527-0800.

Spirito's, 700 N. Broad St., Elizabeth; (908) 289-3666.

Splash Seafood & Pasta, 1 Fairmount Road, Long Valley; (908) 876-9307.

Spot Pizza, 100 Memorial Drive, Asbury Park; (732) 776-6266.

Spot Pizza Grill, 1426 Route 9, Toms River; (732) 240-2215.

Spring Lake Gourmet Pizzeria, 1110 3rd Ave., Spring Lake; (732) 449-9595.

Spyros Pizzeria Carneys Point, 328 Shell Road, Penns Grove; (856) 299-5778.

Stadium Plaza Pizzeria, 725 Route 440, Jersey City; (201) 434-0100.

Stan's Chitch's Cafe, 14 Columbus Place, Bound Brook; (732) 356-0899.

Stanley's Deli & Pizza, 972 Teaneck Road, Teaneck; (201) 833-0855.

Star Tavern, 400 High St., Orange; (973) 675-3336.

Starlite Pizzeria, 993 Pleasant Valley Way, West Orange; (973) 736-9440.

Starting Point, 2 Avenue A, Bayonne; (201) 243-0092.

Stefano's Pizza & Restaurant, 71 Broadway, Elmwood Park; (201) 797-0068.

Stefano's Pizzeria, 569 Route 23, Pompton Plains; (973) 616-6620.

Stefano's Ristorante & Pizza, 3815 Church Road, Mount Laurel; (856) 778-3663.

Stefano's Woodburning Pizza & Ristorante, 1297 Centennial Ave., Piscataway; (732) 562-9696.

Stefanos Italian Restaurant, 3 Lexington Ave., East Brunswick; (732) 257-7778.

Stefanos Pizza & Restaurant, 35 E. Main St., Freehold; (732) 462-5656.

Stella Pizza, 2431 Church Road, Cherry Hill; (856) 482-0055.

Stella Pizza, 232 New Brunswick Ave., Perth Amboy; (732) 442-1040.

Stella Pizza & Restaurant, 498 Haddon Ave., Collingswood; (856) 869-3232.

Stella Pizzeria, 266 Hall Ave., Perth Amboy; (732) 442-0700.

Stella's Pizza, 202 Scotch Road, Ewing; (609) 883-3880.

Stella's Pizza, 315 Grove St., Jersey City; (201) 435-4650.

Stelton Pizza & Restaurant, 1315 Stelton Road, Piscataway; (732) 985-2626.

Steve's Pizza, 900 Easton Ave., Somerset; (732) 247-0400.

Steverino's Pizzeria, 1889 Hooper Ave., Toms River; (732) 255-4320.

Stone Harbor Pizza, 315 96th St., Stone Harbor; (609) 368-5454.

Strawberry's Pub & Pizza, 110 Amboy Ave., Woodbridge; (732) 634-3131.

Struga Pizza, 662 River St., Paterson; (973) 742-2700.

Sub-King Pizzeria, 181 N. Washington Ave., Bergenfield; (201) 384-3405.

Subworks Pizza & Subs, 1683 Saint Georges Ave., Rahway; (732) 388-6220.

Summit Brick Oven Pizza, 21 Union Place, Summit; (908) 598-0045.

Summit Pizza, 1013 Summit Ave., Union City; (201) 863-0707.

Sun Tavern, 600 W. Westfield Ave., Roselle Park; (908) 241-0190.

Sun Tavern, 15 South Ave., Fanwood; (908) 490-0278.

Sun-Ray Pizzeria, 440 Main St., Little Falls; (973) 256-0304.

Sunrise Grill & Pizza, 1235 McBride Ave., Woodland Park; (973) 785-8540.

Sunrise Pizzeria, 1606 Route 37 E., Toms River; (732) 929-0777.

Sunrise Pizzeria, 329 Valley St., South Orange; (973) 763-9618.

Supreme Pizza, 520 Central Ave., East Orange; (973) 673-0711.

Supreme Pizza, 977 S. Orange Ave., East Orange; (973) 673-0311.

Surf City Pizza, 1017 Long Beach Blvd., Surf City; (609) 361-8150.

Suvio Pizzeria & Restaurant, 83 Washington St., Morristown; (973) 538-1660.

Suzy's Tomato Pizzeria, 355 Warwick Turnpike, Hewitt; (973) 853-8100.

T & J Pizzeria, 120 Kipp Ave., Lodi; (973) 777-2549.

T J's Family Pizza, 209 S. Burnt Mill Road, Voorhees; (856) 354-0444.

T J's Pizza, 709 Main St., Asbury Park; (732) 988-1657.

T J's Pizza, 39 Loomis Ave., Sussex; (973) 875-0700.

T J's Pizza & Subs, 3107 Bordentown Ave., Parlin; (732) 721-2381.

T J's Pizzaria, 25 Route 31 S., Pennington; (609) 737-7166.

T J's Pizzeria & Pasta, 2661 Main St., Lawrenceville; (609) 896-0440.

Tabor Pizzeria & Restaurant, 976 Tabor Road, Morris Plains; (973) 540-0898.

Tacconelli's Pizzeria, 450 S. Lenola Road, Maple Shade; (856) 638-0338.

Tanolla's Pizza, 713 Riverview Drive, Brielle; (732) 528-5544.

Taormina Pizza, 1117 S. Black Horse Pike, Blackwood; (856) 232-5335.

Taormini Pizzeria & Italian, 301 Madison Ave., Paterson; (973) 742-9650.

Taste of Italy Pizzeria, 4059 S. Main Road, Vineland; (856) 765-0666.

Taste of Tuscany, 1051 Bloomfield Ave., Clifton; (973) 916-0700.

Taste of Tuscany Restaurant, 500 S. River St., Hackensack; (201) 641-7500.

Tastee Pizza, 717 Lafayette Ave., Hawthorne; (973) 427-9655.

Tata's Pizza, 208 Hamilton St., New Brunswick; (732) 846-6232.

Taxi Pizza, 286 Route 46, Rockaway; (973) 627-3655.

Teaneck Pizza & Kebab House, 251 Degraw Ave., Teaneck; (201) 836-8555.

Ted's Pizzeria, 1752 Whittier St., Rahway; (732) 381-6665.

Telemark Pizza, 533 Green Pond Road, Rockaway; (973) 627-6342.

Temple II Pizza, 1580 Mount Ephraim Ave., Camden; (856) 365-0448.

Tenares Restaurant, 1068 Kaighns Ave., Camden; (856) 225-9700.

Termini Pizzeria Inc, 4107 Bergenline Ave., Union City; (201) 866-7336.

Terrace Inn Pizza Parlor, 270 Pointville Road, Pemberton; (609) 894-9820.

That's Amore, 99 Bloomfield Ave., Denville; (973) 586-8856.

Theos Pizza, 375 Route 46, South Hackensack; (201) 440-5455.

Three Boys From Italy, 238 Livingston St., Northvale; (201) 767-7790.

Three Brothers, 749 Delsea Drive N., Glassboro; (856) 863-5999.

Three Brothers From Italy Pizza, 1020 Ocean Terrace, Seaside Heights; (732) 830-3327.

Three Brothers From Italy, 1921 Promenade, Seaside Park; (732) 830-4188.

Three Brothers From Italy, 646 Kennedy Blvd., Bayonne; (201) 823-1055.

Three Brothers From Italy, 609 Boardwalk, Seaside Heights; (732) 793-5052.

Three Brothers From Italy, 1715 Clifton Ave., Lakewood; (732) 364-3790.

Three Brothers Pizza, 944 Boardwalk, Ocean City; (609) 398-6767.

Three Guys From Italy, 19 N. 20th St., Kenilworth; (908) 272-2553.

Three Guys Pizzeria, 366 Franklin Ave., Belleville; (973) 751-4602.

Three J's Pizzeria & Restaurant, 3715 Bergenline Ave., Union City; (201) 865-8624.

Tim Kerwin's Tavern, 353 Bound Brook Road, Middlesex; (732) 968-9855.

Tina Marie's Pizza & Subs, 500 Locust Island Road, Hancocks Bridge; (856) 935-8283.

Tina's Pizza & Italian, 1470 S. Olden Ave., Trenton; (609) 890-1446.

Tino's Pizza, 1716 New York Ave., Union City; (201) 865-1010.

Tino's Pizzeria, 1317 Highway 77, Bridgeton; (856) 455-2016.

Tirreno Pizza, 8 E. Ramapo Ave., Mahwah; (201) 529-4373.

Todaro Pizza, 3010 Route 35, Hazlet; (732) 739-2244.

Tom's Pizza Pasta & Subs, 250 Mountain Ave., Springfield; (973) 258-9144.

Tomato Pie Co., 524 Delsea Drive N., Glassboro; (856) 881-8871.

Tommy D's Pizza & Pasta, 547 Route 22 E., Whitehouse Sta; (908) 534-5976.

Tommy G's Pizza, 711 E. 1st Ave., Roselle; (908) 298-7772.

Tommy's Original Pizza Cafe, 20 Plauderville Ave., Garfield; (973) 478-2313.

Tommy's Pizzeria & Restaurant, 1063 Fairmount Ave., Elizabeth; (908) 289-2277.

Tonio's Pizza, 2475 Ocean Drive, Avalon; (609) 368-5558.

Tony Boloney's Pizza, 300 Oriental Ave., Atlantic City; (609) 344-8669.

Tony D's Pizza, 271 Center Ave., Westwood; (201) 358-0888.

Tony May's Pizza & Grill, 53 Kennedy Blvd., Bayonne; (201) 471-7351

Tony Soprano's Pizza, 11 Shoppers Lane, Blackwood; (856) 401-8131.

Tony Soprano's Pizza, 908 Kings Highway, Haddon Heights; (856) 546-0888.

Tony Soprano's Pizza, 1227 Haddonfield Berlin Road, Voorhees; (856) 719-1010.

Tony Soprano's Pizza, 3747 Church Road, Mount Laurel; (856) 231-0505.

Tony Soprano's Pizzeria, 4202 Route 130, Willingboro; (609) 877-0014.

Tony's, 228 Morris Ave., Long Branch; (732) 222-3535.

Tony's Baltimore Grill, 2800 Atlantic Ave., Atlantic City; (609) 345-5766.

Tony's Brothers Pizza & Restaurant, 20 W. Oakland Ave., Oakland; (201) 337-3100.

Tony's Cafe of Cranford, 21 N. Union Ave., Cranford; (908) 272-2874.

Tony's Family Restaurant Pizza, 2771 Route 23, Stockholm; (973) 697-5680.

Tony's Italian Kitchen, 648 Godwin Ave., Midland Park; (201) 444-1612.

Tony's Morris Plains, 668 Speedwell Ave., Morris Plains; (973) 267-8825.

Tony's Pizza, 264 Wanaque Ave., Pompton Lakes; (973) 835-3353.

Tony's Pizza, 218 S. Center St., Orange; (973) 674-4440.

Tony's Pizza & Cafe, 160 Frederick St., Garfield; (973) 340-1155.

Tony's Pizza & Cafe, 1085 Broadway, Rahway; (732) 388-9667.

Tony's Pizza & Luncheonette, 769 River St., Paterson; (973) 345-9547.

Tony's Pizza & Restaurant, 716 Oak Tree Ave., South Plainfield; (908) 754-1181.

Tony's Pizza Gallery, 6718 Black Horse Pike, Egg Harbor Township; (609) 646-2929.

Tony's Pizza Palace, 300 Route 18, East Brunswick; (732) 238-6917.

Tony's Pizzaria, 419 N. Haddon Ave., Haddonfield; (856) 795-4200.

Tony's Pizzeria, 731 Main Ave., Passaic; (973) 472-0444.

Tony's Pizzeria, 78 Main St., Farmingdale; (732) 938-7707.

Tony's Pizzeria, 1199 Amboy Ave., Edison; (732) 548-2770.

Tony's Pizzeria, 59 Pacific St., Newark; (973) 732-1030.

Tony's Pizzeria & Restaurant, 1208 Route 109, Cape May; (609) 884-2020.

Tony's Pizzeria & Restaurant, 2040 Route 33, Neptune City; (732) 988-1325.

Tony's Pizzeria II, 138 Fries Mill Road, Blackwood; (856) 740-1884.

Tony's Place, 18 Forest Hill Drive, Wayne; (973) 838-7892.

Tony's Restaurant & Pizzeria, 104 Main St., Little Falls; (973) 785-3548.

Tony's the Original Pasta House, 1334 Route 9, Toms River; (732) 286-6117.

Tony's Touch of Italy, 315 Valley Road, Wayne; (973) 694-7787.

Top Road Tavern & Pizza, 1042 Brunswick Ave., Trenton; (609) 393-5911.

Topo Gigio Pizza, 984 Creek Road, Bellmawr; (856) 931-6766.

Torellia's Pizzeria I, 1427 S. 9th St., Camden; (856) 225-1133.

Torna's Pizzeria, 254 9th St., Hoboken; (201) 798-8873.

Toscana Pizza Restaurant, 271 Route 46, Mine Hill; (973) 659-0044.

Toscana Pizzeria & Grill, 127 S. Bridgeton Pike, Mullica Hill; (856) 478-2288.

Toscana Pizzeria & Restaurant, 51 E. Kings Highway, Audubon; (856) 310-0940.

Toscana Restaurante & Pizzeria, 309 Main St., Sayreville; (732) 651-2330.

Toscanas Pizzeria & Restaurant, 474 Route 28, Bridgewater; (908) 595-2000.

Tosko Fried Chicken & Pizza, 890 Springfield Ave., Irvington; (973) 371-2929.

Town Pizzeria, 462 Joralemon St., Belleville; (973) 751-8839.

Tpr Restaurant Pizzeria Inc, 38 W. Railroad Ave., Tenafly; (201) 871-0444.

Track Side Grille, 14-26 Plaza Road, Fair Lawn; (201) 796-3113.

Trattoria Bella Gente, 642 Bloomfield Ave., Verona; (973) 239-4416.

Trattoria la Sorrentina, 7831 Bergenline Ave., North Bergen; (201) 869-8100.

Trattoria Ravello, 14 Wilson Ave., Manalapan; (732) 792-9696.

Trattoria Rustica, 259 Main St., Matawan; (732) 566-9991.

Trattoria Rustica, 517 Bloomfield Ave., Montclair; (973) 783-3436.

Trattoria Uno, 1067 Route 202 N., Branchburg; (908) 203-8666.

Trevi Pizza & Restaurant, 570 Park Ave., Freehold; (732) 780-2440.

Triboro Pizzeria, 105 Essex St., Maywood; (201) 845-6820.

Trio Pizzeria Restaurant, 931 Fischer Blvd., Toms River; (732) 270-1117.

Trio's Pizza & Pasta, 386 Kinderkamack Road, Oradell; (201) 261-0122.

Triponi Pizza & Grill, 1 Raymond Plaza, Newark; (973) 424-0094.

Tu Sei Bella Pizza & Pasta Hse, 130 Black Horse Pike, Audubon; (856) 547-3773.

Turano's Pizza Pasta Grill, 609 Stuyvesant Ave., Lyndhurst; (201) 939-8055.

Turvino's Pizzeria, 932 Prospect St., Glen Rock; (201) 447-6969.

Tuscan Pizza Kitchen, 200 Young Ave., Moorestown; (856) 234-7080.

Tuscany Bistro, Routes 202/206 and Washington Valley Road, Pluckemin; (908) 658-3388.

Tusei Bella Restaurant, 1164 Chews Landing Road, Laurel Springs; (856) 346-6701.

Two Brother's Pizza, 50 E. State St., Trenton; (609) 394-2004.

Two Brothers Pizza, 1608 Pennington Road, Ewing; (609) 882-8844.

Two Brothers Pizza, 101 Route 46, Pine Brook; (973) 882-8111.

Two Brothers Pizza-Restaurant, 2275 W. County Line Road, Jackson; (732) 905-3003.

Two Guys Pizza & Grille, 21-16 Morlot Ave., Fair Lawn; (201) 794-1001.

Two Tony's Pizza Cafe, 628 N. Stiles St., Linden; (908) 925-1977.

Ultimate Pizza, 8 Riverside Plz, Hackettstown; (908) 850-0900.

Umberto Restaurant, 583 River Road, Fair Haven; (732) 747-6522.

Uncle Dante's Pizza & Steak, 6208 Black Horse Pike, Egg Harbor Twp; (609) 641-8055.

Uncle Gino's Pizza, 7306 Ventnor Ave., Ventnor City; (609) 822-2556.

Uncle Lou Pizza, 41 Mill St., Paterson; (973) 333-5074.

Uncle Ralphy, 9 Route 27, Edison; (732) 452-9110.

Uncle Tony's Pizzeria, 200 Hackensack St., Wood Ridge; (201) 939-7788.

Union Beach Pizza, 900 Union Ave., Union Beach; (732) 217-1536.

Union Landing Restaurant, 622 Green Ave., Brielle; (732) 528-6665.

Up Town Pizzeria, 54 14th St., Hoboken; (201) 610-9955.

Upper Crust/Dimaio's, 468 Springfield Ave., Berkeley Heights; (908) 464-8585.

Upper Crust Pizza & Italian, 113 Winchester Way, Shamong; (609) 268-8100.

Upper Crust Pizza & Italian, 1576 Route 206, Tabernacle; (609) 268-8100.

Uruguay Pizzeria, 815 3rd Ave., Elizabeth; (908) 355-2208.

US Fried Chicken & Pizza, 1200 E. Saint Georges Ave., Linden; (908) 486-4300.

V & J Pizza, 500 State Rt 23, Pompton Plains; (973) 839-9757.

Val's Tavern, 123 E. River Road, Rumson; (732) 842-3452.

Valaggio Pizza, 211 E. Westfield Ave., Roselle Park; (908) 298-0028.

Valentino's, 103 Spring Valley Road, Park Ridge; (201) 391-2230.

Valentino's, 7 N. Beverwyck Road, Lake Hiawatha; (973) 263-2022.

Valentino's, 293 Route 206, Flanders; (973) 584-2828.

Valentino's Pizza, 137 Main St., Bloomingdale; (973) 838-3300.

Valentino's Pizzeria, 110 Rockingham Row, Princeton; (609) 520-1191.

Valentino's Restaurant, 89 Leonardville Road, Belford; (732) 495-4599.

Valentinos, 201 E. Westfield Ave., Roselle Park; (908) 245-7555.

Valentinos Pizza, 498 N. Beverwyck Road, Lake Hiawatha; (973) 794-4812.

Valle Pizza, 41 Freeman St., West Orange; (973) 243-2400.

Varriales Pizza, 400 Lacey Road, Whiting; (732) 849-1400.

Varsity Pizza & Subs, 1296 Lawrenceville Road, Lawrenceville; (609) 882-4100.

Vena Brothers, 300 Ewan Road, Mullica Hill; (856) 417-3625.

Veneto Gourmet Pizza & Deli, 554 Allen Road, Basking Ridge; (908) 901-0111.

Venice Pizza, 104 N. Wood Ave., Linden; (908) 925-5858.

Venice Pizza, 881 Main St., Sayreville; (732) 727-0077.

Venice Pizza, 5400 Hudson Ave., West New York; (201) 867-7222.

Venice Pizza & Restaurant, 68 S. Broadway, Pitman; (856) 582-0770.

Ventura's Offshore Cafe, 2015 Shore Road, Northfield; (609) 641-5158.

Venuto's Old World Pizza, 901 White Horse Pike, Haddon Township; (856) 858-1810.

Venuto's Old World Pizza, 1486 Blackwood Clementon Road, Clementon; (856) 939-8697.

Venuto's Old World Pizza, 497 Cross Keys Road, Sicklerville; (856) 629-6007.

Veras Trattoria, 840 Franklin Ave., Franklin Lakes; (201) 560-0023.

Verona Italian Pizzaria, 59 N. Beverwyck Road, Lake Hiawatha; (973) 331-9910.

Verona Pizzeria, 557 Bloomfield Ave., Verona; (973) 239-4645.

Vesuvio Pizza, 1305 Beaver Dam Road, Point Pleasant; (732) 899-4495.

Vesuvio Pizzeria, 1223 Westbrook Road, West Milford; (973) 697-1090.

Vesuvio Pizzeria & Restaurant, 916 Radio Road, Little Egg Harbor; (609) 294-3400.

Vesuvio Pizzeria Ristorante, 550 Kings Highway, Swedesboro; (856) 467-6262.

Vesuvio Restaurant of Belmar, 705 10th Ave., Belmar; (732) 681-5556.

Vesuvio Ristorante & Pizzeria, 725 S. Main St., Forked River; (609) 693-3333.

Via Mare Restaurant, 2319 Ocean Drive, Avalon; (609) 368-4494.

Via Roma, 4118 Route 9, Howell; (732) 370-8908.

Via Roma, 761 Route 33, East Windsor; (609) 371-6200.

Via Roma, 1280 Yardville Allentown Road, Allentown; (609) 259-2229.

Via Roma, 2360 Route 9, Toms River; (732) 364-1980.

Via Roma III, 1743 Route 88, Brick; (732) 458-0298.

Via Rustica, 271 Livingston St., Northvale; (201) 750-1001.

Vic's Italian Restaurant & Bar, 60 Main St., Bradley Beach; (732) 774-8225.

Victor's Pizzeria & Italian, 540 Cedar Lane, Teaneck; (201) 836-0306.

Victorio's Restaurant, 69 Belleville Ave., Bloomfield; (973) 748-4646.

Victors Pizzeria & Restaurant, 450 Amwell Road, Hillsborough; (908) 359-6364.

Villa Barone, 753 Haddon Ave., Collingswood; (856) 858-2999.

Villa Bate Pizzeria Restaurant, 314 Morristown Road, Matawan; (732) 566-2122.

Villa Borghese Li, 66 Main St., Helmetta; (732) 521-3599.

Villa Capri Pizza, 270 Sparta Ave., Sparta; (973) 729-6654.

Villa Fazzolari/Terrazza Pizzeria, 821 Harding Highway (Route 440), Buena Vista; (856) 697-7107.

Villa Gennaro, 75 Route 27, Edison; (732) 549-8554.

Villa Italia, 746 Riverside Ave., Lyndhurst; (201) 460-1777.

Villa Laura Restaurant, 365 Spotswood Englishtown Road, Monroe Twp; (732) 723-9091.

Villa Mannino Ristorante, 73 Route 130, Trenton; (609) 298-9000.

Villa Maria Restaurant, 3800 Quakerbridge Road, Trenton; (609) 587-4445.

Villa Nuova Ristorante & Pizza, 1447 Good Intent Road, Deptford; (856) 227-4222.

Villa Pizza, 578 Newark Ave., Jersey City; (201) 795-5001.

Villa Pizza, 2200 Mount Holly Road, Burlington; (609) 386-6622.

Villa Pizza, 301 Mount Hope Ave., Rockaway; (973) 989-4266.

Villa Pizza, 4953 Stelton Road, South Plainfield; (908) 769-9395.

Villa Pizza, 1425 Frontier Road, Bridgewater; (732) 356-9716.

Villa Pizza & Restaurant, 2145 Route 35, Holmdel; (732) 888-1666.

Villa Pizzeria, 290 Lakeview Ave., Clifton; (973) 546-5707.

Villa Restaurant, 794 Route 35, Middletown; (732) 615-0770.

Villa Roma Pizzeria & Deli, 849 Clifton Ave., Clifton; (973) 472-4833.

Villa Rosa Italian Restaurant, 1 Kings Hwy E., Haddonfield; (856) 428-9240.

Villa Rosa Pizza & Restaurant, 41 Scotch Road, Ewing; (609) 882-6841.

Villa Rosa Restaurant, 34 W. Route 130 S., Burlington; (609) 386-6717.

Villa Rosa Restaurant, 472 Lafayette Ave., Hawthorne; (973) 427-3689.

Villa Stefano Pizzeria/Restaurant, 1129 Raritan Road, Clark; (732) 382-0220.

Villa Victoria Pizzeria, 11 Park St., Montclair; (973) 746-4426.

Village Gourmet Deli, 527 High Mountain Road, North Haledon; (973) 423-2269.

Village Pizza, 1075 Easton Ave., Somerset; (732) 246-0660.

Village Pizza, 789 Springfield Ave., Summit; (908) 522-1461.

Village Pizza & Pasta, 35 W. Allendale Ave., Allendale; (201) 818-9959.

Village Pizza Cafe, 911 E. County Line Road, Lakewood; (732) 905-0955.

Village Pizzeria, 319 S. Orange Ave., South Orange; (973) 762-8241.

Village Square Inn, 2887 Route 23, Newfoundland; (973) 697-7770.

Village Trattoria, 2 Inwood Place, Maplewood; (973) 761-7711.

Village Trattoria, 21 South Orange Ave., South Orange; (973) 762-2015.

Village Trattoria, 103 Summit Ave., Summit; (908) 608-1441.

Villaggio's Food Emporium, 67 Main St., South River; (732) 390-8390.

Villagio Iccara Trattoria, 104 Yardville-Allentown Road, Yardville; (609) 585-6668.

Villas Diner & Pizzeria, 2100 Bayshore Road, Villas; (609) 886-7699.

Vincent's Pizza, 480 Route 46, Fairfield; (973) 808-8337.

Vincent's Pizza, 2617 Nottingham Way, Mercerville; (609) 587-9256.

Vincent's Pizza, 1710 Kennedy Blvd., Jersey City; (201) 433-3330.

Vincent's Pizza, 17 W. Park Ave., Merchantville; (856) 663-8879.

Vincent's Pizzeria, 535 Anderson Ave., Cliffside Park; (201) 945-8625.

Vincenzo Pizzeria, 3 Netcong Road, Budd Lake; (973) 691-8282.

Vincenzo's Pizza, 45 S. New York Road, Galloway; (609) 652-2299.

Vincenzo's Pizza & Grill, 23 Charleston Road, Willingboro; (609) 835-9111.

Vincenzo's Pizza & Subs, 938 Inman Ave., Edison; (908) 822-1120.

Vinni's Pizzarama Inc, 1025 Hamburg Turnpike, Wayne; (973) 628-1510.

Vinnie & Son Pizza Restaurant, 1000 Aaron Road, North Brunswick; (732) 951-1600.

Vinnie's II Pizzeria & Restaurant, 86 N. Gaston Ave., Somerville; (908) 704-8822.

Vinnie's III, 431 Danforth Ave., Jersey City; (201) 433-5599.

Vinnie's Parkview Pizzeria, 414 Broad St., Bloomfield; (973) 748-0889.

Vinnie's Pizza, 334 Herbertsville Road, Brick; (732) 840-9144.

Vinnie's Pizza, 1817 Route 35, Wall Township; (732) 449-1330.

Vinnie's Pizza & Pasta, 990 Route 202 S., Branchburg; (908) 231-0034.

Vinnie's Pizza & Subs, 429 Ryders Lane, East Brunswick; (732) 257-1111.

Vinnie's Pizzeria, 3249 Route 9, Freehold; (732) 431-3888.

Vinnie's Pizzeria, 3417 Kennedy Blvd., Jersey City; (201) 420-0418.

Vinnies, 2825 Kennedy Blvd., Jersey City; (201) 332-2773.

Vinnies Pizza & Italian Restaurant, 275 Amboy Ave., Metuchen; (732) 321-1191.

Vinnies Pizzeria I, 637 Broadway, Bayonne; (201) 339-2111.

Vinny's Pizza, 801 Burlington Ave., Delanco; (856) 461-5556.

Vinny's Pizza, 312 Atlantic City Blvd., Toms River; (732) 244-9766.

Vinos Pizzeria, 701 Frank E. Rodgers Blvd N., Harrison; (973) 482-1800.

Virami's Pizza, 38 Mine St., Flemington; (908) 788-8644.

Vita Bella Italian Gourmet, 3016 N. Route 9, Ocean View; (609) 624-8300.

Vitarelli's Pizza & Restaurant, 1250 Kings Hwy N., Cherry Hill; (856) 429-9088.

Vito & Michael's Gourmet Pizzeria, 2019 Greenwood Lake Turnpike, Hewitt; (973) 728-2222.

Vito Pizza & Pasta, 120 Carr Ave., Keansburg; (732) 787-5115.

Vito's Pizza, 1249 Highway 33, Trenton; (609) 586-2888.

Vito's Pizza, 233 Ogden Station Road, Wenonah; (856) 468-1061.

Vito's Pizza, 2321 S. Delsea Drive, Vineland; (856) 691-9000.

Vito's Pizza & Restaurant, 429 Market St., Elmwood Park; (201) 797-3544.

Vito's Pizza & Sub Shop, 113 Clements Bridge Road, Barrington; (856) 546-7433.

Vittorio's Pizzeria, 59 Nathaniel Pl, Englewood; (201) 503-0177.

Viva La Pizza, 1005 McBride Ave., Woodland Park; (973) 785-7550.

Vivaldis Pizza Cafe, 900 Union Ave., Union Beach; (732) 264-6800.

Voltaco's Italian Foods, 957 West Ave., Ocean City; (609) 399-0743.

Waldorf Tavern, 4100 Federal St., Camden; (856) 541-7043.

Walt's Original Primo Pizza, 5107 English Creek Ave., Egg Harbor Township; (609) 601-9990.

Walt's Original Primo Pizza, 35 Shore Road, Somers Point; (609) 927-4464.

Wayne Brick Oven Pizza, 179 Hamburg Turnpike, Wayne; (973) 653-9700.

Weezys Pizza, 338 W. Railway Ave., Paterson; (973) 530-4402.

West End Pizzaria & Grill, 152 Easton Ave., New Brunswick; (732) 828-8030.

Wharton Pizza, 312 S. Main St., Wharton; (973) 989-8363.

Wheat Pizza & Sub, 837 Elizabeth Ave., Elizabeth; (908) 469-1213.

Wilmott's, 12 S. 7th St., Vineland; (856) 696-1525.

Wise Guys Pizza, 831 Route 10, Whippany; (973) 887-0693.

Wize Guyz Pizzeria & Restaurant, 380 W. Pleasantview Ave., Hackensack; (201) 343-1000.

Wonder Pizza, 433 Sip Ave., Jersey City; (201) 721-6864.

Woodbury Pizzeria, 830 N. Broad St., Woodbury; (856) 848-4340.

World Away Pizza & Party Hall, 520 Princeton Ave., Brick; (732) 899-2225.

Wyckoff Pizza & Restaurant, 525 Cedar Hill Ave., Wyckoff; (201) 493-0099.

Yellow Sub Pizza, 710 N. Forklanding Road, Maple Shade; (856) 667-8989.

Yordana's Ristorante, 67 Church St., Flemington; (908) 782-2276.

Yum Yum Pizza & Italian Food, 1253 Springfield Ave., Irvington; (973) 373-3733.

Zuchettes Pizzeria, 71 Walnut St., Montclair; (973) 744-4333.

ALPHABETICAL INDEX